N E P A L
NAMASTE

Published by:

Sahayogi Press
Tripureshwar, Kathmandu, Nepal
Phone 11489

Price : Nep. Rs 75 in Nepal   Indian. Rs 60 in India
US $ 7 without postage
US $ 10.00 (Airmail postage paid)
2000 Copies

Printed in Nepal
at Sahayogi Press, Tripureshwar, Kathmandu

ROBERT RIEFFEL

NEPAL

NAMASTE

Revised and Updated New Edition

SAHAYOGI PRESS
Tripureshwar, Kathmandu, Nepal

ROBERT RIEFFEL

FOREWORD

NAMASTE, done with palm joined together, is a traditional Hindu greeting. The posture has both religious (prayer) and secular (greeting) connotation. NEPAL, once a secluded Kingdom, is now modernizing in every sphere including tourism, welcoming and greeting foreigners. But there must be a good guide for new places, whether religious or secular. Robert Rieffel provides this through his book NEPAL NAMASTE.

The author's rich experience in travel trade and long residence in Nepal is well reflected in the book. The cultural activity of Kathmandu Valley is described vividly. He reveals a good anticipation when he explains the various sights and sounds that would invariably attract the visitor. The local festivals are described as to their timing, locale and legendary context. There is much historical and cultural informaton whether he is introducing a temple or an artisan at work.

Mr. Rieffel, being himself an inveterate trekker, has given a good description of most trekking routes. This includes an account of the Manang trek which he made when the area was first opened. The book has much useful information for visitors. I commend the book NEPAL NAMASTE as a useful compendium for learning a great deal about Nepal.

Dr. Harkha Gurung
Former Minister of State for Tourism
(NEPAL)

INTRODUCTION

Neither the biased publicity, the sensation-films and books, nor – still less – the now prohibited sale of drugs, can explain the spectacular increase (from *one* to *twenty* in sixteen years) of the number of tourists having visited Nepal (6,179 in 1962–124753, Indian citizens excluded, in 1979)*

These foreign visitors were attracted by something else : the manifold characteristics of an extraordinary and beautiful country: here some of its outstanding features:

- the fact that it opened its doors to foreigners as late as 1950 !
- its perfect climate, never too warm nor too rainy in summer, sunshine and blue skies in witner.
- the highest mountains in the world, deep green jungles in the plains and in between, terrace-covered hills and picturesque villages.
- the possibility for almost anybody, irrespective of training, equipment and age, to undertake those famous *treks* along the valleys, across barren passes and up to yak-pastures, glaciers and snow-covered peaks.
- a friendly population – always smiling and hospitable.
- a nation which is a mosaic of many ethnic groups who have remained attached to their traditions, customs, and festivals.
- unique expressions of superb art and finest handicraft : pagodas of original style, temples with golden roofs, wood-and stone sculptures of designs unknown elsewhere.
- a rich flora and fauna protected in National Parks, where tigers and rhinos, monkeys, crocodiles and hundred varieties of birds live freely in their natural surroundings.
- a rare example of most liberal co-existence of two creeds, Hinduism and Buddhism.
- last but not least, a nation wholly dedicated to make up for centuries of isolation by concentrating its efforts on development and progress in all fields.

To enjoy a visit, a stay longer than the usual 3 or 4 days is a "must" to appreciate the charm of the cities, the beauty of the landscape and to learn something about the people.

---

* See break up nationality-wise, page 351.

Neither the biased publicity, the sensation –
nor – still less – the now prohibited sale of drugs, ca.
spectacular increase (from one to twenty in sixteen years) c.
number of tourists having visited Nepal (6,179 in 1962–124753,
Indian citizens excluded, in 1979)*

These foreign visitors were attracted by something else : the
manifold characteristics of an extraordinary and beautiful country :
here some of its outstanding features :

– the fact that it opened its doors to foreigners as late as 1950 !

– its perfect climate, never too warm nor too rainy in summer,
  sunshine and blue skies in winter.

– the highest mountains in the world, deep green jungles in
  the plains and in between, terrace-covered hills and picturesque villages.

– the possibility for almost anybody, irrespective of training,
  equipment and age, to undertake those famous treks along
  the valleys, across barren passes and up to yak-pastures,
  glaciers and snow-covered peaks.

– a friendly population – always smiling and hospitable.

– a nation which is a mosaic of many ethnic groups who have
  remained attached to their traditions, customs, and festivals.

– unique expressions of superb art and finest handicraft :
  pagodas of original style, temples with golden roofs, wood-
  and stone sculptures of designs unknown elsewhere.

– a rich flora and fauna protected in National Parks, where
  tigers and rhinos, monkeys, crocodiles and hundred varieties of birds live freely in their natural surroundings.

– a rare example of most liberal co-existence of two creeds,
  Hinduism and Buddhism.

– last but not least, a nation wholly dedicated to make up
  for centuries of isolation by concentrating its efforts on
  development and progress in all fields.

To enjoy a visit, a stay longer than the usual 3 or 4 days is
a "must", to appreciate the charm of the cities, the beauty of
the landscape and to learn something about the people.

---

* See break up nationality-wise, page 351.

TABLE OF CONTENTS

6

A BRIEF BIOGRAPHICAL NOTE ON
HIS MAJESTY THE KING OF NEPAL

The present Sovereign, His Majesty BIRENDRA BIR BIKRAM SHAH DEV was born at the Narayanhity Royal Palace in Kathmandu on 28th December 1945. He became King of Nepal on the death of his father, the late King MAHENDRA BIR BIKRAM SHAH, on 31st January 1972.

The Crown Prince received school and college education first at Darjeeling then at Eton, England. He then toured many countries, including USSR, Iran and Indonesia where he led the official delegation of Nepal to the Bandoeng Conference. In 1956/66, he extensively travelled and trekked in Nepal, sometimes "incognito" to collect first-hand knowledge of the needs of his people as well as the progress of development projects.

In 1966, he paid an official visit to the people's Republic of China and was received by Chairman Mao. In 1976, he toured Asia, Europe and the two Americas to acquaint himself with some of the problems of both developing and advanced countries.

While in Japan, he studied at Tokyo University political science, concentrating on the spectacular transformation of Japan into a modern industrial power. The same year, the Crown Prince went to the U.S.A. to attend the fall semester at Harvard University studying public administration, economy, social science and the feature of the US presidency. After completing this academic year, the Crown Prince made another tour of Latin America, Canada, Europe and countries in Africa and Asia.

On 14th February 1970, Crown Prince BIRENDRA married AISHWARYA RAJYA LAXMI DEVI, the present Queen of Nepal. The Coronation of Their Majesties took place on 24th February 1975.

The young Sovereign made state visits to India and China in 1973 to strengthen the traditional links of friendship between Nepal and its neighbours.

On 27th June 1971, the Royal couple was blessed with a son, the present Crown Prince DIPENDRA BIR BIKRAM SHAH DEV. A daughter, Princess SHRUTI RAJYA LAXMI DEVI SHAH was born on 16th October 1976.

In June 1976. H. M. the King paid an official visit to LHASSA, thus being the first foreign Head of State to be invited to the ancient capital of Tibet.

A BRIEF BIOGRAPHICAL NOTE
ON HER MAJESTY QUEEN AISHWARYA OF NEPAL

Her Majesty QUEEN AISHWARYA RAJYA LAXMI DEVI SHAH was born on 7th November 1949 at Lazimpat, a residential part of Kathmandu. She is the eldest daughter of Lieutenant-General Kendra Shumshere J. B. Rana. Her two younger sisters are married to H.M. King BIRENDRA's younger brothers H.R.H. Prince GYANENDRA and H.R.H. Prince DHIRENDRA respectively.

Queen AISHWARYA had had her early education at St. Helen's Convent at Kurseong (India) and at St. Mary's School-Jawalakhel (Kathmandu). In 1963, after passing the School Leaving Certificate examination, she continued her studies at Padma Kanya College (Kathmandu), from where she passed the Intermediate Arts Examination in 1965, and was placed in second division. She then pursued her studies independently and, as a private candidate, obtained the degree of Bachelor of Arts from Tribhuvan University.

Her Majesty the Queen accompanies H. M. the KING in most of his journeys throughout the kingdom in order to get better acquainted with the problems and needs of the population. Queen AISHWARYA is the Chairman of the "Social Services National Coordination Council."

In this capacity, Her Majesty the Queen contributes actively in the many fields of development in the social sectors.

8

* Domestic cats
* Drugs and drug addicts
* The "Yeti".

Section II

PRACTICAL HINTS TO JOURNEY AND STAY

CHAPTER THREE : THE JOURNEY

* Visas
* Authorized entry points
* Vaccinations
* Foreign currencies
* What to wear

* By Air
    Regular international flights
    Coming from the West
            From Delhi
    Coming from the South
            From Calcutta
            From Colombo
            From Patna
            From Varanasi (Benares)
    Coming from the East
            From Bangkok
            From Dacca
            From Rangoon
    Charter flights

* By Land
    Important remarks
    By train
    By road
        By private car
            Customs and Immigration entry-points
            Documents required and formalities
            How long it takes
        By public bus services

CHAPTER FIVE : USEFUL ADDRESSES AND INFORMATION

14

"NAMASTE"

WELCOME TO NEPAL

NAMASTE

This is how you will be greeted by everybody in Nepal.

It embraces all the following meanings:

> *You are welcome*
>
> *How do you do ?*
>
> *Good morning*
>
> *Good evening*
>
> *I am pleased to make your acquaintance*
>
> *I hope to meet you again soon.*

The literal translation however is something much more refined:

> *"I salute all divine qualities in you"*.

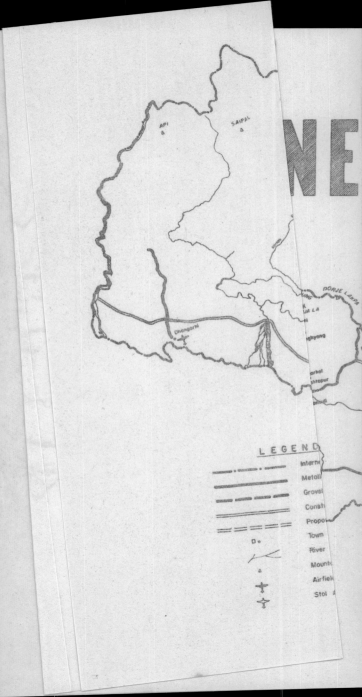

NE

API
△

SAIPAL
△

DORJE LAKPA

A LA

ghyang

arkot

htapur

Dhangarhi

PAL

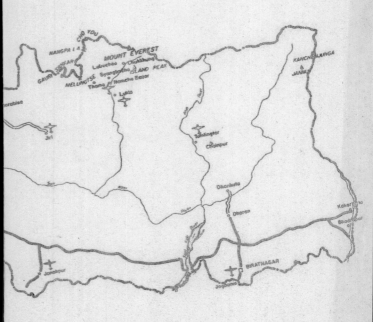

SECTION I

THE COUNTRY

CHAPTER ONE

THE SETTING

GEOGRAPHY

Situated between India and China, approximately at the latitude of Central Florida, the Canary Islands or the southern most tip of Morocco, the Kingdom of Nepal covers an area of 55,463 sq.m. (143.650 km²) which corresponds roughly to either Switzerland and Austria combined, England and Wales or an area half-way between the size of Arkansas and Michigan states in the U. S. A.

On the map Nepal looks like a humped rectangle of about 500 m. (800 km.) from West to East and between 56 m. (90 km.) and 143 m. (230 km.) from North to South. The country is oriented from North–West to South–East, which entails among other peculiarities. that Kathmandu lies slightly more to the south than New Delhi, a favorite geographical quiz in this part of the world.

The general configuration of the country is like a succession of strips running, roughly, from West to East.

The "terraced" profile of Nepal is best illustrated by the following, very rough outline :

35% of the whole area lies, below 3000 ft (1000m.)

25% ”   ”   ”   ”   ” between 3.000 and 6000 ft (1000 and 2000m.)

30% ”   ”   ”   ”   ”   ” 6.000 and 15.000 ft (2000– 5000 m.)

10% ”   ”   ”   ”   ” above the snow-line.

Terai

Starting from the southern border, the first of these tracts is the tropical band of the Terai which, from a purely geographical angle, may be considered as a part of the Gangetic plains. The Terai occupies the whole length of the southern part of Nepal, but its width does not exceed 30 km. anywhere. Its total area is just about 8,800 sq.m. (22.850 km²), which corresponds to less than 15.9% of the total area of Nepal.

SIWALIK AND MAHABHARAT LEKH

North of the Terai, there are two mountain ranges: first, the SIWALIK range, which rises abruptly from the jungle plains to an average altitude of 5,000 ft. (1.525 m). Then slightly further to the North, the MAHABHARAT LEKH, certain summits of which reach 10,000 ft. (3.050 m.). Between these two ranges, there are the valleys, called "duns" which are not more than 30 miles (54 km.) long and 9 m. (14.5 km.) wide.

The best known duns are those of the Rapti, Chitwan, Nawalpur and Dang.

CENTRAL HILLS

Still more to the North, begins the area commonly referred to as the "Central Hills", or "Pahar". This is a very broken, undulating part of the country. Its northern border leans against the first Himalayan slopes. The altitude of these Central Hills varies between 2,000 ft. and 6,500 ft. (600 m. and 2.000 m.). Many rivers and streams flow across this region, most of them in a north–south direction with some west–east segments.

The Pahar "plateau" constitutes the largest part of the whole country, since it covers an area of roughly, 30,500 sq. m. (80.000 km².), i. e. 55% of Nepal.

HIMALAYAS

In the extreme North of the country, the Himalayan range. It includes 10 of the existing 18 summits that exceed an altitude of 26,247 ft. (8.000 m.).

These 10 summits are :

NAME OF PEAK	Location	Altitude in Feet	Meters
EVEREST	North-East	29,028	8.848
KANCHENJUNGA	East	28,166	8.584
LHOTSE	North-East	27,890	8.501
MAKALU	East	27,805	8.475
YALUNG KANG	North-East	27,626	8.420
LHOTSE SHAR	North-East	27,430	8.363
DHAULAGIRI	Central-West	26,795	8.167
MANASLU	Central	26,760	8.156
CHO-OYU	North-East	26,742	8.153
ANNAPURNA I	Central West	26,565	8.090

Approximately 125 miles (200km.) north–east of Kathmandu stands Mount Everest ("Sagarmatha" in Nepali, "Chomolungma" in Tibetan,) which Gunther–Oskar Dyhrenfurth, the famous Swiss mountaineer, so aptly called "The Worlds' Third Pole", dominating the globe from the top of its 29,028 ft. (8.848 m.). It is closely followed by Kanchenjunga (28.166 ft. 8.584m.), Lhotse, Makalu, Dhaulagiri, Annapurna and many others the names of which are less familiar.

GEOLOGY

Compared to other mountain-chains, the Himalayas are relatively "young".

They are estimated to have been building up towards the end of the mesozoic ara, i. e. between 70 and 80 millions years ago The theory generally admitted nowadays is that the "layer" on which rested the vast ocean (called "Tethys") that covered the northern part of the Indian sub-continent, knocked against the continental masses that have later become China. This movement is supposed to have led, on the one hand, to the disappearance of the original ocean and on the other, to the lifting of the huge masses of earth up to the present size and shape of the Himalayas, covering 195,000 square miles !

However that may be, and going back to the present day Himalayas, it may be noteworthy to mention that they extend over 1,850 miles (3.000 km.) out of which 500 miles (800 km.) are part of Nepal. Nevertheless, it does not really stand as a barrier which could not be crossed, though this is often believed.

RIVERS

Indeed, first of all, there are the rivers. At least eight of them have their source in Tibet and manage to get across the Himalayan chain through deep gorges and valleys. After having travelled all through Nepal, they find their way into the Ganges or one of its tributaries.

The most spectacular of these rivers is undoubtedly the KALI GANDAKI that runs at an altitude of approx. 8,500 ft. (2.500 m.). Its beautiful gorges are flanked by such giants as Dhaulagiri on its right bank and Annapurna on its left, both mountains exceeding 26,500 ft. (8.080 m.). Thus, on each side of the Kali Gandaki the mountain slopes rise more than 18,000 ft. (5.580 m.)!

Here a short list of the main streams without which Nepal could hardly survive !

Starting from the Western border of Nepal to its Eastern, the country's main rivers, are called:

MAHAKALI, which marks the Western border between Nepal and India.

HUMLA KARNALI, which, in its lower course is simply called KARNALI. This river enters NEPAL, from Tibet at an altitude of 14,760 ft. (4.499 m.)

MUSTANG KHOLA which later changes its name into KALI GANDAKI. This river also, has its source in the Tibetan plateau.

BURI GANDAKI which has its source in the region of Larkya, far to the north of the Annapurna and the Manaslu ranges.

BHOTE KOSI which penetrates into Nepal at the well-known frontier point of Rasua Garhi and which receives, a little later, the waters of LANGTANG KHOLA, at Syabrubensi. A few miles further south, the Bhote Kosi joins up with the TRISULI, one of the most important river of the country. It has its source in the Gosainkund lakes, inside the territory of Nepal and receives successively the following tributaries : First, the MARSYANGDI which comes from way up north of the Annapurna range, then the BURI GANDAKI. Ultimately, the Trisuli added to the Kali Gandaki becomes the NARAYANI river, as this stream is called when it reaches the lowlands of the Terai.

There is a second BHOTE KOSI , also coming from the Tibetan Plateau, which penetrates into Nepal at Kodari, the frontier-point on the "Chinese Road" leading to Kathmandu, at an altitude of 5,400 ft. (1.646m.) This Bhote Kosi joins up with the SUN KOSI river near the small, picturesque village of Barabise. Then Sun Kosi the pursues its course through the rest of Nepal in a North-West to South-East direction before reaching in its turn the Terai, where it takes the name of SAPT KOSI.

Finally, in the eastern part of Nepal, there are two important rivers too: the ARUN that comes from Tibet and which, after crossing the whole country from North to South, mixes its waters with the Sapt Kosi. Still further East, the second important river is the TAMUR which springs from the Kanchenjunga Massif and joins the Sapt Kosi, in the Terai.

The valleys these rivers follow constitute natural "gate-ways", linking Tibet with Nepal.

PASSES

In addition to rivers and valleys, there are other routes, namely the mountain-passes. Since the first inhabitants settled in these areas, not less than 12 passes have been traditionally used by yak and mule caravans loaded with goods. These passes

are located beween 16,000 and 19,500 ft. (4.875 m.–5.945 m..).
  The most important are:
   In the West: THAKU (16,076 ft. 4.900.m.)
                NAMSA (16,200 ft. 4.938 m.)
                KHUNG (19,500 ft. 5.945 m.)
   In Central Nepal: LARKYA (18,370 ft.   5.600 m.)
                     THAPLE (17,230 ft.   5.252 m.)
   In the Eeast: NANGPA (18,745 ft.   5.715 m.)
                 RAKHLA (16,230 ft. 4.947 m.)
  Among these passes. NANGPA-LA ("La" means "pass" in
the Sherpa and Tibetan languages) is the best known, It lies north
of Namche Bazar and, for centuries, has been the normal road
connecting the two countries.
  Even nowadays, the high valleys as well as the passes are used
by caravans carrying salt and raw wool from Tibet to Nepal in
exchange for surplus barley and manufactured goods, Of course
the volume of this barter trade has been reduced lately. Instead
of the Nepalese caravans being allowed to penetrate into Tibet
and proceed with their transactions in the main towns such as
Shigatse, Gyantse and Lhassa, where traders had their regular
correspondents and coustomers, the exchange of goods now takes
place at the first commercial counter or village near the border.
  Another consequence of Nepal's geographical situation,
namely the fact that the Himalayas lie approximately 900 miles
(1. 500 km.) more to the South than the Alps is that the snow-line
on the southern slopes is situated as high as 16,000 ft. to 16,500 ft.
(4.880 m.–5.030 m.) in the months of October and November,
i.e. the dry season. It also explains the unexpected peculiarity
that barley ripens at an altitude of 14,270 ft. (4.350 m.) and that
potatoes grow in the Sherpa land at an altitude of 14,250 ft.
(4.344 m.) !

INNER HIMALAYAS

  In the North–Western part of the country, there is another
"plateau" usually called the "Inner Himalayas" which constitutes,
at least in part, the water–shed line between the Ganges in the
South and the Tsang–po, i. e. the Brahmaputra in the North.
  It is here that some of well--known settlements with their
romantic names are located: MUSTANG, TARAP, MUGU, LANG-
TANG etc. Farmers and cattle breeders live all year round on this
plateau, although it lies at an average altitude of 14,750 ft
(4.500 m.) the land is barren and dry most part of the year.

KATHMANDU VALLEY AND OTHER NOTEWORTHY FEATURES

The capital, Kathmandu, lies in a sort of basin or circular valley at an average altitude of 4,360 ft. (1.330 m.).

In the same tract, which has some of the richest farm-land, there are two other capital–cities, namely PATAN and BHADGAON. The whole valley measures approximately 18.6 miles (30 km.) from east to west and 2, 4 m. (20km.) miles from north to south.

A "crown of forest–covered hills" surrounds the Valley. It is one of the most picturesque features of the whole area. The highest point of this range of hills reaches 9,188 ft. (2.800 m): It is called *Pulchowki* and lies in the south–esastern part of the Valley. Towards the north, there is another famous summit: *Shivpuri,* culminating at 8,900 ft., (2.713 m.) followed, towards south–west, by *Champa Devi* 7,380 ft. (2.250 m.) Nearer to the city itself just between Swayambhu hill and Shivpuri, there lies *Nagarjun* 6.526 ft. (1.989m.) a holy place topped by a stupa, a favourite hiking and picnic place which can be reached through the Balaju Gardens or branching off the Trisuli, road.

Once this "crown of hills" is crossed, the lower regions are very rapidly reached, in particular the Indrawati valley which lies at only 1,600 ft. (488 m.). There, the scenery is clearly sub-tropical: banana and mango–trees abound. The roads are lined with bamboo groves and various kinds of cacti.

It may be interesting to mention here another striking geographical feature about Kathmandu Valley: It is roughly equidistant (125 miles as the crow flies) from Mount Everest and Mount Annapurna, the former in the East, the latter in the West.

A second "round basin" in many respects similar to that of Kathmandu is the Pokhara "Valley", except that the latter is only located at an altitude of 2,959 ft. (970 m). instead of 4,360 ft. (1.330 m.)

All other main cities are to be found further south, in the Terai, which is the richest part of Nepal. A few industrial establishments have been set up and others may be installed there in the future.

One word about NEPAL'S borders: Since the incorporation of the former Kingdom of Sikkim into the Indian Union, Nepal has been left with two neighbours only: in the North, the People's Republic of China and India on all three other sides.

CLIMATE

Unerringly the best season to visit Nepal is between the beginning of October and the beginning of May. During all these months, the sky remains clear, mornings and evenings are pleasantly cool but never really cold, even in the three winter months, December, January and February. (It never snows in Kathmandu) In winter, temperature rises quickly from 50° F to 77° F (17° C-25°C.) in the course of the morning. At noon you can sunbathe in the open air. Late afternoon is cool again.

Pre-monsoon begins in April or May. Heavy clouds gather about midday or in the early afternoon. Sometimes showers or thunderstorms occur towards evening. The sky is overcast and the mountains remain usually hidden from view except in the first morning hours. At Pokhara, which is much lower than Kathmandu, temperature, even in winter, often reaches 85° F. (30° C) during the day. May and June are the warmest months of the year: maximum temperature: 95° F. (35°C.).

Here are the minimum and maximum temperatures registered in Kathmaddu, as given by the official statistics of the Meteorological Department:

Month	Temperature In Fahrenheit		in Centigrades	
	Mini (x)	Maxi.	Mini (x)	Maxi.
January	32.8	64.4..	1.0	18.0
February	38.3	68.0	3.5	20.1
March	44.4	75.4	6.9	24.1
April	51.8	81.3	11.0	27.4
May	58.3	84.6	14.6	29.2
June	66.4	84.4	19.1	29.1
July	68.2	82.2	20.1	27.9
August	67.6	82.0	19.8	27.8
September	65.1	81.7	18.4	27.6
October	55.9	83.5	13.3	26.4
November	44.1	72.5	6.6	22.5
December	35.0	67.1	1.7	19.5

(x) Note: Whereas most visitors are able to enjoy the maximum temperatures, for they occur in the middle of the day, they will very seldom suffer form the above indicated "minimum" for these are registered at 2 or 3 a.m.; This has to be kept in mind, and shows that the climate of Kathmandu Valley is milder than the above statistics seem to indicate:

FLORA

Seen from more than one point of view, Nepal is really a country of many blessings. The variety and exuberance of its flora is one of them.

Although Nepal's area is not a very large one, all climatic and ecological conditions are present, thanks to its peculair geographical structure :

A little arbitrarily perhaps, Nepal may be divided into three geographical and, hence, botanical and floral regions :

(1) The Southern plains, which stretch along the border with India, called the "Terai" and its surrounding areas are of a definite sub-tropical character. They are the only real low-lands of the country. The altitude of the Terai varies between 300 and 1,000 feet. (90m – 305m.)

(2) The Central hill region, called "Pahar", has a sub-tropical and temperate climate. Two main hill ranges separate this central region from the Terai : In the South, the Siwalik range, and further to the North, the Mahabharat. as already mentioned.

In the "Pahar" regions are located the two most fertile and flat basins, namely the Kathmandu and the Pokhara "valleys." The altitude of this region extends from 1,000 to 9,000 feet (305 m.– 2750 m.)

(3) The Himalayan Mountainous region, of temperate, alpine and even arctic climate, ranging from 9,000 to 29,000 ft. (2590m – 8840m.)

Trees and flowers

Two excellent books deal with Nepal's flora :

– "Himalayan Fowers and Trees", by Dorothy Mierow and Tirtha Bahadur Shrestha– published by Sahayogi Press, Tripureshwar, Kathmandu 1978.

– "Forests of Nepal", by N.D.A. Stainton–published by John Murray – London 1972

Last but not least, the French Centre of Scientific Research undertook in 1965, 1970 and 1971 extensive cooperative research in the fields of geology and ecology covering various regions, in particular the Annapurna—Dhaulagiri, Kathmandu—Everest and Central Himalaya—Manaslu areas. Ecological maps, articles and books were published after the completion of these scientific works.

FLORA FOUND IN THE LOWLAND

Trees : The Terai abound in many varieties of industrially useful trees. In the first place, the "sal" tree (Shorea robusta), a very high and straight tree. It produces an extremely resistant kind of timber which has been traditionally used not only by carpenters but also by those wood-carvers who produced all these magnificent doors and windows for palaces and temples, which resisted victoriously many hundreds of monsoons !

In the second place, the two "cousin-trees", the banyan and, the pipal : both belong to the "ficus" family. The **banyan** is called "ficus bengalensis". It is easy to identify thanks to its strange hanging roots which sprout from the branches and once they touch the ground, develop into supporting pillars.

The **pipal** is called "ficus religiosa". Its heart-shaped leaves tapering to a fine, needle-like tip, hang loosely from the twigs, allowing the slightest breeze to stir them, giving the whole tree a beautiful silver glittering.

An interesting feature is the fact that both the banyan and the pipal are solitary trees. They never grow together to form a forest. Furthermore, they are to be found at the entrance of almost every village, usually growing on a stone platform called a "chautara", where the villagers like to gather in the evening and enjoy sitting in the cool shade.

The shade is guaranteed by the fact that one of these trees looses its leaves three months after its "cousin" does, and by that time, the latter will have already grown a new set of leaves! This may testify at least partially, to the popular belief that banyan and pipal are to be considered as "husband and wife". However that may be, the pipal is a most sacred tree since it was while sitting under one of them, in the gardens of Sarnath, that Buddha reached Englightenment.

Among other spectacular trees of the Terai, the "**silk cotton tree**" ('bombax malabaricum") popularly known as the "kapok-tree" must also be mentioned. It is covered in the beginning of spring with thousands of large red blossoms even before the tree grows its leaves. In autumn, its bulky pods are full of white kapok cotton.

The "flame-of-the-forest" which blossoms in March is followed, in May, by the gorgeous blue-flowered "jacaranda" tree.

Fruit trees and fruits

There are not many varieties in the Terai. Bananas and mangoes are plenty, of course (mangoes ripen at the beginning of the monsoon season, i. e. in May-June.) There is also the "bel"-tree, a sacred one which produces a hard fruit of the shape of a big apple. Also grow in the Terai various kinds of oranges, tangarines, grape-fruit, lime and lemons etc.

Flowers

Orchids: There are but a few species in the lowlands. Most of them grow in the hills or the mountaineous areas. Prof. R. FLEMING mentions only the "bamboo-orchid" and another species called "fox-tail".

Another peculiarity of the Terai forests are the numerous climbing and twining plants and creepers which, sometimes, destory - as if by asphyxia – the trees on which they grow.

Finally, the Terai counts numbers of jasmin, mimosa, acacia weeds and bamboo, as well as an infinite variety of herbs (elephant-grass among others, which reach over 5 feet).

FLORA FOUND IN THE CENTRAL HILL REGIONS

Trees: "Honour to whom honour is due": the rhododendron, the national flower of Nepal, Rhododendrons grow between altitudes of 5,000 and 14,000 ft. (1.525 m. 4.270 m. The Nepalese name of the rhododendron is a very pretty one: "laliguras".

The flowers come in all shades, from dark red to snow-white. The higher the altitude, the paler the red and the pink, The peculiarity of the Nepalese rhododendrons is their tremendous height which reaches up to sixty feet, the size of a huge oak treek or asp, whereas in America or Europe, rhododendrons are commonly known only as small bushes or even as mere flower-pot plants.

—*Magnolia:* This beautiful tree which blossoms in April is not very common, at least not in the Kathmandu Valley. Professor Fleming found more in the eastern part of the country.

—*Chinaberry:* It grows abundantly in the Valley, unfolding pale purple blossoms in the spring. When autumn takes the leaves away from this tree, it will be covered with clusters of yellow round fruit which stay on throughout the winter.

—*Oaks:* All over Central and Eastern Nepal, four different species of oak are to be found, some of them having larger leaves than the European ones and very large cones.

—*Conifers:* In the Himalayan zone, various sorts of pines are dominant; they are the last trees to grow in the high altitude -up to 13,000 feet (4.000 m.) and sometimes even higher–before bushes, than grass, and finally lichens take over. One of the most beautiful pines which is found in the 7,000 to 12,000 feet (2150 m.- 3.650 m.) range is the "blue pine" so called because of the peculiar colour of its cones.

Around Kathmandu, there are many small patches of real pine forests, (mostly the red bark species similar to the one found near the Mediterranean), especially on the road to Bhadgaon and half-way up the slope of Shivpuri beyond Budanilkantha towards the convent. There are the "Chirtree": Pinus roxburghii, a subtropical pine tree.

—*Bottle-brush trees: silky oak, eucalyptus, and orchids.*

These four species, each with its particular beauty are very well adapted to the climatic conditions of Nepal. Originally, they were imported from Australia.

Another typically Nepalese tree is the "koiralo" a rather tall tree which in spring produces large pink flowers that remind of an orchid but is an edible flower. It is prepared like any vegetable and served with various spices. Its scientific name is "bauhinia variegata".

—*Jacaranda*

These elegant trees covered in May with bushy fair blue flowers are to be seen along various streets in Kathmandu.

Flowers: Most gardens, in and around the cities have beads of many indigenous and imported flowers. The following varieties may be spotted : begonia, bougainvillea, dahlias, daisies, daturas delphinias, gardenia, geranium, hibiscus, honeysuckle, hydrangea, jasmins, khannas, lupin, marigold, nasturtium, pansies, petuniae, phlox, poinsettias, sage, snapdragons, sunflowers, sweet peas blooming in January-February), violets, wisteria, zinnias and others.

November to February are the best months for some of these flowers, including orchids, a great variety of which grow wild, at an altitude of approx. 9,000 ft., (2.750 m.) for instance around Kakani, near Kathmandu, or Chomrong, in the Annapurna region.

In the Park of GODAVARI, near the School of St. Xavier, south
of Patan, the Royal Botanical Garden includes a very rich collection of orchids and other flowers of Nepal. No flower–lover
should miss visiting this garden.

FLORA FOUND IN THE HIMALAYAN ZONE

Trees: All varieties of conifers, pines, birches, junipers,
Norwegian pines, firs, yews, cedars and, in the barren regions the
typically Tibetan weeping willows! Of course, not to be forgotten,
the famous rhododendrons which reach here the height of oaks
and which are in full bloom in March–April at an altitude of
8,000 ft. to 13,000 ft. (2.440 m.–4.000m.) Their flowers are dark
red in the lower regions, then turn pink higher up and white still
higher up.

On the slopes of all high altitude mountains, berberis bushes
are to be found. Their small leaves give a warm touch of red
colour in October and November, and more particularly in the
Khumbu and Langtang areas.

Flowers: There are many alpine flowers between 10,000 and
15,000 ft., (3.000 m.–4.600 m.) mainly various species of delicate
primulas, yellow, blue and white ones, anemones, hawthorns
eg'antines, angeri (which are thin twigs holding series of tiny white
bells, blooming in autumn), and, in the higher areas: dwarf
rhododendrons, junipers and other scented bushes, some of which
are used by the local population to make various kinds of tea.

Finally, there are plenty of the two species of typically alpine
flowers: the white velvety "edelweiss", which abound in the
Langtang Valley and the delicate gentians which have usually
two different shades of blue petals alternating on the same flower.

FRUITS

AVAILABLE ON THE MARKET IN KATHMANDU VALLEY

(Whether grown locally or imported from India).

All year round:
Bananas, oranges, tangerines–best in October to Janaury
lemons and lime.

Seasonal fruits:
In spring-time (mid–February to May): peaches, apricots
    litchi, mangoes, "alla", a kind of pistachio wrapped in
    a whitish hard shell.

In summer and during monsoon (June to September): mangoes, *"naspatis"* (a kind of hard granular and brownish,
pear), guavas, pineapples, kakis, papayas and sometimes
melons.

In autumn and winter (October to February): apples, oranges
tangerines, grape–fruits of various kinds and sizes, pome-
granates.

Not available in any season, are cherries, strawberries,
pears, raspberries, mulberries, currants, gooseberries and
other soft fruits.

FOUND IN THE HILLS: There are relatively few fruits to
gleen in the hills: sometimes one may find very small yellow
raspberry–like berries (called *"ainselu"*) in thorny bushes in the
woods, some under developed wild strawberries, never any worth-
leberries or blueberries. Oranges and tangerines (called *"suntala"*)
grow up to an altitude of 6,000 to 6,500 ft. (1.800–2.000 m.) There
are also usually high trees, which are covered, in October-November with small pink flowers that look like cherry–blossoms. In
fact, these are wild cherry-trees. They never bear any edible
fruit. It is seldom to see more than one of these trees on passes
or at the village entrance.

FAUNA

INTRODUCTION

With its 30 different kinds of large wild animals, its 800 species
of birds, 80 kinds of mammals and countless varieties of butterflies, insects etc. undoubtedly, Nepal must be considered as one
of the richest natural animal reserves in the world, taking into
account its relatively modest geographical area.

Among the animals which contribute most ot Nepal's reputation as an animal's paradise, are:

— The *Tiger*, of which around 30 to 40 still roam around in the
Terai

— The *One-horned Rhinoceros*, of which there are still over 300
in existence, in the same region as the tigers

— The *Himalayan Yak* and its many cross-breed cousins and

— ......Of course, the *Yeti*.

Whereas tigers and rhinos are easy to spot when travelling
through the Wild-life Park of Chitwan (where tourists are welcome at various hotels and camps) and whereas the yak lives
only above 13,000 (4.000 m.) feet in the mountains, the Yeti

still remains to be discovered and..photographed or captured.

Tigers and rhinos are very strictly protected. In the past, they were seriously reduced by hunters and poachers, the tiger for of its skin and the rhino for its crushed horn that reaches a high price in certain Asian countries where it is considered to be a powerful aphrosidiac.

Yaks are the only livestock which lives at high altitudes. They are both pack and draught animals. They yield many valuable sub–products, besides their meat: the milk from the female yak (called "*nak*") feeds Sherpa–babies, and is also used for the production of "*curd*" and of a very hard kind of cheese which Tibetans and Sherpas alike usually carry in their "*chubas*" (robes) and munch for hours on end. This cheese remains edible for years. Furthermore, the nak milk, once churned and transformed into butter is traditionally added to the salted Tibetan tea. However, this butter does not *have to* go rancid in order to be mixed with the tea, as it is commonly believed. It just so happens that it often *gets* rancid ! Yak butter and yak grease are used in oil–lamps at temples and for manufacturing candles. Yak–wool gives the raw material for weaving quilts, blankets and clothing. The hide provides leather for boots, the hoofs is the basic element for manufacturing glue, their crushed horns are mixed with other substances to be used as gun-powder. Last but not least, yak dung is in many regions the only and best fuel easily available.

The zoological garden of Kathmandu is located at Jawalakhel, in Patan. It is not a very large one, but has a collection of some species of mammals and birds commonly found in the country.

NATIONAL WILD LIFE SANCTUARIES

There may still exist, in very remote regions, a kind of wild yak, but it may also be extinct by now. The same can be said about wild elephants and wild buffaloes whose presence in the Terai was still recorded a few decades ago.

In order to prevent further extinction and deterioration of race species, the government of Nepal decided to create four "National Wild–Life Preservation Parks" covering a total area 1,210 sq. m. (3.107 km.²) where hunting and poaching is strictly prohibited and where various steps are being taken for the preservation of animals and plants in their natural surroundings.

These National Parks are located in the following areas:
— CHITWAN: In the Terai 210 sq. m., (540 km.²) Animals to

be particularly protected: tigers, rhinos, Gangetic dolphins, leopards, sloth bears, sambars, chital, hog–deer, barking deer, wild boars and all kind of birds.

— SAGARMATHA: In the Everest region 480 sq. m. (1.230 km.²). Animals to be particularly protected are: Himalayan thar, musk deer, ibex, wild goat, nayan, makhar and other species of the antelope and deer families. Also the national bird of Nepal, called the 'lophophorus impejanus', or "impejan pheasant", or in Nepali: "daphe". This is a pheasant and peacock–like bird which lives exclusively above 12,000 feet. (3.650 m.) When the wandering tourist comes across this magnificent bird, he will recognize it immediately. A precise and colourful description as contained in a book by Salim Ali dedicated to all hill birds of the Indian subcontinent, says:

"It is a large , dumpy bird with a short, broad and square–cut tail. The brilliant metallic green head and crest (of wire–like spatula-tipped feathers), the glistening purple upper parts, white patch on back, cinnamon–coloured tail and velvety black breast, render the cock unmistakable. The hen is a plain looking brown bird, mottled and streaked dark and pale, with a white throat short crest of normal feathers." The impejan pheasant is a very shy bird, difficult to photograph, It is good sport to try. They wander around Thyangboche monastery and in the surrounding area and may be found in field and near houses.

—LANGTANG: 480 sq. m. (1.240 km.²) the beautiful high-mountain valley just north of Kathmandu, where bears, snow-leopards, many birds and alpine flowers (edelweiss, among others !) are to be found abundantly.

The Langtang airstrip is covered with these rare white flowers. Probably the only one in the whole world !

– LAKE RARA: 40 sq. m (103 km²). One of the most picturesque lakes of Nepal, three days walk north-west of Jumla.

It is the home of many migratory waterfowl, as well as of some rare mammal species, such as the Himalayan bear, the Himalayan thar, serow, ghoral, musk deer and red panda.

An entrance fee of Rs. 60.– is levied at each of these National Parks (Sherpas, guides and porters are exempted). Inside the national parks, it is prohibited to collect or to buy firewood for campfires or cooking.

In addition to these four national parks, the government has also decided to create five "Wildlife reserves", totalling another 472 sq. miles (1.222 km²) namely:

— Sukla Phanta in the western Terai
— Karnali in the Bardia district (also in the Terai)
— Shey in the barren Dolpa district, not far from the Chinese border
— Koshi Tappu on the banks of the Kosi river in the eastern Terai
— Narayani an extension of the Royal Chitwan wild Life Preservation Park, in the central Terai.

FISHES

Whereas Nepal is extremely rich in birds, butterflies and mammals, the varieties of fishes in rivers and lakes are not very large.

In the Kathmandu Valley the main rivers and rivulets yield only very tiny fishes which are caught by hand or nets, then dried and eaten.

In the larger rivers and the glacial lakes, the "asla", or river trout (*Shizothoraz*) is found in small numbers. These trouts rarely weigh over two lbs.

The only big size fish is the "masheer" (*Sahar* or *Barbus tor*) which travels from the open sea through India and the Terai to spawn in the headwaters of the mountain streams. The northward journey takes place in October-November and the southward one in March–April 20 to 50 pounders (9-23 kg.) are not unfrequent.

Measures are being contemplated to stem the gradual decrease of the masheer which, at present, is sometimes prevents from undertaking its seasonal spawning journey because of the existence of closed barrages, in particular in the Narayani river, at Tribeni.

(Information about fishing is given in Chapter 5 under "*Sports*"

BIRDS

Nepal is really a bird's paradise. The number of varieties is stupendous. It approaches 900, and covers almost all families from the tiniest flycatchers and flower-peckers to eagles, herons, falcons and peacocks; partridges and parakeets, snow-pheasants and quails, cuckoos, maynahs, minivets and bulbuls, storks, egrets, kites, hawks, crows and vultures in the low lands and the valleys, whereas in the upper hills and the Himalayas live lammergeiers, eagles, raven, choughs, snow-pheasants, and last but not least, the most beautiful of all, the national bird of Nepal, the "*Daphe*", a description of which has been included in the chapter dealing with the National Wild-Life Preservation Parks.

To be remembered : In March-April, there are three different birds, in addition to the familiar cuckoo, that announce the approach of the yearly monsoon.

Those readers who are particularly interested in birds are advised to get the very comprehensive and scientific, richly illustrated book "Birds of Nepal" written and edited by the two best experts in the field : Pr. T. L. Fleming Sr. and his son, Robert L. Fleming Jr., in close cooperation with Mr. Lain Singh Bangdel, the outstanding Nepalese painter, Art historian as well as Chancellor of the Royal Nepal Academy. This book describes no less than 900 individuals in colour, i. e. 741 species classified in 212 families or groups. It took Prof. Fleming around 20 years to produce this remarkable work.

BUTTERFLIES AND INSECTS

Butterflies are another specialty of Nepal, for there are several hundred varieties. Since the present book is intended for the average tourist, and not the specialist, this may not be the right place to deal in detail with all these Latin-named little jewels of the animal world. There is little literature on the subject with the exception of "Commoner Butterflies of Nepal" by C. Smith and of a chart or map, published under the suspices of the Department for Wild-Life Protection and UNICEF, which may be obtained from either sources.

As far as insects are concerned, following few facts about them may be mentioned:

—mosquitoes appear in large numbers just before and during the whole monsoon period (June to October). In the Terai, they are present throughout the year.

—fleas and bugs are not to be met in the hills.

—in the Valley and the hills, neither scorpions nor dangerous spiders have ever been spotted. In the Terai they may appear here and there, as well as centipedes and irritating kinds of ants and caterpillars. Also in the Terai, interesting insects to watch are the termites of which there are plenty.

To end this paragraph of unpleasant animals, two more points have to be noted:

—snakes, whether poisonous or not, do not constitute a hazard, neither for tourists nor for trekkers, except in the jungles of the Terai.

—the only creatures which are somewhat unpleasant to meet and to deal with are leeches. During the rainy season, in forests and on grassy land, in particular where cattle graze leeches are very abundant. However, they disappear above 9,000 ft. (2.745 m.).

(The question of how to deal with them is to be found in the chapter dedicated to trekking).

MAMMALS

This guide book has no ambition to present a complete picture of Nepal's mammals.

The average tourist–and even the trekker–does not usually spot bears, antelopes, civets and rodents, either because they are not present in great quantities or becasue of the difficulties of the terrain and the living habits of some of these animals.

The reader is kindly requested to overlook with indulgence, any error he may detect in this paragraph. Should he be especially interested in zoology, the best book available is "The book of Indian Animals " by S. H. PRATER, Bombay 1971–Bombay Natural History Society.

There exists also a comprehensive map published by the National Parks and Wildlife Conservation of H.M.G's "Department of Forests", in cooperation with UNICEF. This map is called "Animals found in and around Nepal".

As for the information concerning hunting, see Chapter 15 under "Sports".

Coming back to the animals, it may be well to mention that the best seasons to spot the rarer species are:

In the lowlands: March and April

In the midlands: throughout the year, except in the rainy season from June to October.

In the highlands: October and May-June.

We shall maintain this division of the country into these three areas, although many mammals may be found in more than one of them.

(1) *Lowlands* (Terai).

This part of the country abounds in antelopes and deers, such as the Swamp Deer ("*Barasingha*"), the Black Buck, the Spotted Deer ("*Chital*") the Four–horned Antelope, a very rare one, the Hog-Deer and the Nilgai.

It is here also that one of the three species of bears may be found, namely the Sloth Bear, a sturdy, white muzzled dangerous animal.

Among the bovines, the buffalo is the most common domestic animal, together with the zebu and "western" cattle, as well as their crossbreeds. The "*Gaur*" or Indian bison are in the process of extinction and so are the wild buffaloes.

Wild and Jungle cats are not rare, while the various leopards, (the clouded one among others) are not often seen.   Tigers still roam in the various Wild Life Reserves; a reasonable estimate is 30–40 individuals.   Great efforts are made to protect them against poachers and to promote their growth.   Civets and mangoose are many, but not so domestic cats, an item on which we shall come back later.

Dogs however, whether domestic ones, stray-dogs and even wild ones are to be found everywhere. So are jackals, foxes and hyaena.

Monkeys are numerous, The two most common ones are: –The Langur which is a tall one with a black face framed in white and grey hair. It has a long tail which he uses as a fifth prehensile limb so to speak.   They are shy and live in large families. –The Rhesus which is small and brownish, has a short tail and is very aggressive. They are to be found in large flocks around Swayambhu and Pashupatinath, as well as in some parts of the city of Kathmandu itself. Monkeys are considered sacred animals.

One family of mammals that every tourists will probably see everywhere are some of the rodents, such as mice, rats and shrews while hares, rabbits, squirrels and hamsters etc. are very few.

To end this list of the lowland mammals, let us mention the presence, on the river banks of otters, badgers, martens and ratels.

(2) *Midlands* (Hill region of Central Nepal).

Only two species of deer may be found here, but not often: the tiny Barking Deer and the magnificent and proud Sambar.

An encounter with one of the two representatives of the bear family is certainly less pleasant. Fortunately they are not frequent:

In the midlands as well as the highlands roam, indeed, the black or Collar Bear (the *Selenarctos tibetanus*) the most dangerous animal the whole country and the Brown Bear (*Ursus arctos*).

In the hills, local inhabitants mention various wild cats (one of which is called the fishing cat, another the golden one but both are very elusive indeed.) as well as leopards.

(3) *Highlands*.

Official documents enumerate not less than 10 different species of mountain antelopes. But they are extremely rare, with the exception, perhaps of the Blue Sheep which is called *Naur* in Nepali, and the Musk–Deer which is looked for by poachers to extract the gland containing the precious musk from the male animal. As for all the other, whether the *Goral,* the *Thar*, the Ibex, the *Serow*–a sort of wild goat–or the Himalayan *Takin* and the *Nayan* not many Himalayists have ever seen one in the course of their treks.

On the other hand, the Himalayan bear, often called Red Bear (*Ursus arctos isabellinus*) appears sometimes to show his huge "V–shaped" white spot on his impressive chest.

A very curious but extremely elusive animal too, is the Red Panda which lives in the hemlock fir forests provided the finds plenty of bamboo shoots and leaves to munch nearby.

Every trekker would like to see one, but must be satisfied with the most typical of all Himalayan animals, the yak, about which much has been said in the introduction to this chapter.

The are the most precious companions of all Tibetan ethnic groups, such as the Sherpas, who have acquired, among other talents, a great skill in cross–breeding yaks with other bovines, each of them having its particular name "*dzos*", "*zhum*". "*zopkio*", "*urang*", "*tolmo*", etc and its peculiar qualities.

In very high altitude, above the snow-line, trekkers have sometimes seen Snow Leopards or, at least, their droppings and characteristic foot–prints. Wolves and marmots are very seldom spotted.

Before ending this chapter, let us just mention three strange mammals that live in Nepal:.

Flying mammals,: A variety of bats, the fruit–bat, also called "flying foxes" (*Pteropus gigantus*) which can be seen in great numbers in the tall trees close to Kaiser's Library where they are hanging at the branches, opening and closing their wide wings. Kaiser's Library is located in front of the western wing of the new Royal Palace.

Scaled mammals: The pangolin (*Manis carssicaudata*) which lives in the Terai and the hills, feeding exclusively on ants.

Swimming mammals: The dolphin (*Playtanista gangetica*) with lives only in a few rives in the South of the country, the Narayani and the Rapti, in the southern part of the contry, where two species of crocodiles, the long–nosed gharial and the blunt-nosed mugger may also be found.

CHAPTER TWO

PAST AND PRESENT

HISTORY

EARLY HISTORY

The origins of Nepal are lost in the mist of time and the twi-light of glorious legends. Here some of them.

—The legend of the wise BISPATI, who sowed a lotus in the middle of the lake which, in those times, covered the whole Valley, this seed brought forth a lotus holding within its petals the image of God Swayambhu (=the "self-born"),

—The legend of the God of wisdom, MANJUSHRI, who, when seeing the valley flooded, clove the rock at Chobhar with his magic sword and caused the water to flow out through the gorge, thus saving the whole population of the "Smiling Valley of the Gods". To this day, the Chobhar gorge is a magnificent spot for tourists and a place of worship for pilgrims. There is a small temple dedicated to the elephant–god Ganesh on the bank of the river. A little further along near the slope of the hill, there is the first cement factory of the Valley. It was built in 1973 to the dismay of all those who loved that spot of quiet beauty.

—The legend of Lord KRISHNA who enjoyed visiting the "gopis" (milk–maids and shepherdesses) herding their cattle on the banks of the Bagmati river. Here Lord Shiva turned into a gazelle. In 1672, the temple of Pashupatinath, one of the most sacred places of pilgrimage for Hindus was built neary–by. It is dedicated to *Pashupati*, the God known as the "*Lord-protector of cattle*".

But let's go back to Nepal's history. The ancient chapters are mainly the history of its rulers.

As to the word "NEPAL", its origin is very obscure and many different interpretations are given.

Most frequently the forwarded etymology refers to a certain "*Rishi*" (a wise man) whose name was "*NE*" and who came to

Kathmandu Valley. To his name was added another word of the local Newari language, namely "*PAL*", which means "protected". Thus, in this interpretation, the word NEPAL would mean "the land protected by the wise man NE".

According to another explanation, the world NEPAL is said to to be a distorition of the name of the NEWAR, the first inhabitants of the Valley. But others say just the opposite, namely that the name NEWAR derives from NEPAL, since the Newari language does not make any difference beteeen the sound (and therefore the written letter) "R" and "L". Thus, NEWAR may have become NEWAL and later NEPAL. But let us not pursue this digression any further and let us come back to facts.

The first time the name "NEPAL" appeared on any historical document was in the middle of the 4th century A. D. on a stone pillar erected at Allahabad (400 miles-640 km.) east of Delhi in an inscription believed to have been ordered by King Samudra Gupta, one of the great monarchs who reigned over the whole of northern India and part of what is now southern Nepal.

The first semi–historical rulers of Nepal proper–where the term "Nepal" has to be understood as covering only the present Kathmandu Valley– were the Kirats or Kiratis who had immigrated from the eastern part of the country. Little is known about the Kirats, except that one of their kings is mentioned in the Hindu epic "Mahabharata" for having taken part in the famous battle siding with the five Pandava brothers against their cousins, the hundred brothers called the Kauravas. The Kirats are believed to have ruled between the 7th century B. C. till the 2nd A. C.

One important event took place during the Kirat period, namely the introduction in Nepal of GAUTAM SIDDHARTHA'S teachings which developed gradually into the Buddhist faith and religion. These teachings were spread by those missionaries that the Indian Emperor ASHOKA (272–232 B. C.) the greatest promoter of Buddhism of all times, sent over Asia, to the Middle East and even to Europe.

The Kirat dynasty was replaced by that of the Licchavis who had immigrated to Nepal from the region of Benares and Patna. Few historical facts have remained from this reign which is said to have lasted from the middle of the 2nd century A. D. to the beginning of the 8th. However, one inscription from the Licchavis which dates back to the fifth century still exists on a stone slab erected in the courtyard of the Changu Narayan temple located on top of a hill between Bhadgaon and Sankhu. This inscription is one of the oldest discovered so far in Nepal.

The most outstanding Sovereign of this dynasty was, for certain, King AMSHUVARMA who gave his daughter BHRIKUTI in marriage to the King of Tibet, s Rong-bTsam-sGam-Po in the year 640 A.D. This Nepalese princess, a fervent Buddhist, converted her royal husband to her own creed and, thus, may be considered as having very actively contributed to the introduction of GAUTAM'S philosophy, ethics and religon into Tibet.

Later, BHRIKUTI was "deified" and became known in Lamaist–Tibetan iconography, as the "Green Tara" (the "white" one being the second wife of the same Tibetan monarch, a Chinese princess named WENCH'ENG, also a Buddhist.) Both "TARAS'" are always represented as very beautiful, sweet smiling young ladies, usually holding a large lotus flower in their left hand.

It is from the LICHAVIS' dyanasty onwards that the history of Nepal is substantiated with many inscriptions, monuments and records of various kinds such as the extremely detailed "travelogue" of the three Chinese pilgrims Hiuen Tsiang, Wang Hiuent'se and Li I–Piao who visited Nepal, where they were received in audience by King Narendra Deva–somewhere between 637 and 642 A. D.

Towards the middle of the 8th. century, another important dynasty, the THAKURIS took over from the Licchavis. This dynasty and still more, the Gupta kings who came to power a little later, succeeded in consolidating the independance of the country by setting up political and trade relations on the basis of bilateral agreements on an equal status, not only with India but also with Tibet and China.

Somewhere around the 12th century, during the reign of King GUNAKAMA DEVA (1184–1196), began the construction of the city of Kathmandu as the capital of the Valley kingdom.

Towards the beginning of the 13th century, a very important event, or a succession of events took place in neighbouring India, that brought major consequences to Nepal's future history: The conquest of Northern India by Muslim invaders, the Moghuls and the establishment of the Moghul Sultans and Kings in

DELHI, later in AGRA, as well as in other cities.

Many Indian princes and chieftains, in particular those from Rajasthan were determined to remain loyal to their Hindu faith and therefore refused to yield to the yoke of foreign occupants who lived according to completely different codes of ethics, customs and religious beliefs. Thus, many of these Indian princes left their country and went north to settle in the hilly areas which are today part of Nepal.

THE MALLA DYNASTY

From the 13th to the 18th century, the descendants of these refugees or immigrants (the MALLA dynasty) took over the leadership in the Valley and became the Kings of Kathmandu as well as of the other surrounding cities.

During this long period of time which was full of complex episodes, many of the Malla Kings stood out among their peers. One such is JAYA STHITI MALLA (1382–1395) who, among many other innovations, introduced or better said, codified the caste system laying emphasis, on the predominance of the priests, or Brahmins, as the highest social strata.

His son, JYOTIR MALLA (1396–1427) renovated the Buddhist shrine and stupa of SWAYAMBHU Hill and restored complete freedom to all ġuddhists to practice and follow their cults and rites, thus establishing, at this very early stage (at a time when incessant religious wars raged in Europe!) one of the most outstanding features of spiritual life in NEPAL, namely total freedom of thought, creed and peaceful coexistence. Therefore Nepal is one of the very few countries in the world which may be proud, and rightly so, not to have ever waged a war or even had internal tensions due to religious motives, from as far back as the 15th century up to today !

Another *MALLA* king was the son of Jyotir, YAKSHA MALLA (1428 to 1482) who left his mark in the history of the Valley, which at that time and for many centuries thereafter was the only part of the country to be called *NEPAL*. Just before passing away, he had the rather unfortunate inspiration, to divide his kingdom among his four children: His elder son, RAYA MALLA was made king of *BHADGAON;* another son, RANA MALLA, King of *BANEPA;* the second son, RATNA MALLA became King of *KATHMANDU.* while his daughter RAMA inherited *PATAN.* As might have been expected, this marked the beginning of a long series of feuds between the brothers and sisters as well as between their respective offspring and successors.

(Banepa remained only for a short period of time an independant kingdom. Soon, it was integrated into the Kingdom of Bhadgaon) Thus, "NEPAL", at that time consisted of three different kingdoms: KATHMANDU, PATAN and BHADGOAN or, as they were called then (and still are sometimes): KANTIPUR, LALITPUR and BHAKTAPUR.

PRATAP MALLA (1640–1674) and more so BHUPATINDRA MALLA (1696–1722) was among those who not only extended considerably the territory and the political importance of their respective kingdoms but also embellished its main cities with innumerable temples, pagodas, palaces, fountains and public baths. They also promoted the development of specifically Nepalese (Newari, to be more precise) handicraft in wood, stone and ivory carvings etc. . . . not to mention the beauty of the architectural masterworks themselves.

UNIFICATION OF NEPAL

Nepal's history took a dramatic turn with the appearance, in the small principality of GURKHA, of an extraordinary statesman, warrior and administrator, PRITHVI NARAYAN SHAH the Great. He was the direct descendant of nine successive kings who, since the founder of the dynasty, DRAVYA SHAH (1559–1570) had reigned over this small kingdom situated half-way between KATHMANDU and POKHARA, at a distance of approximately 60 miles from both cities.

DRAVYA SHAH was himself a descendant of a princely family originating from the town of Chittor in Rajasthan (India), a member of which, after a family quarrel, left his homeland and established himself in what is to–day Nepalese territory, in the vicinity of Palpa.

PRITHVI NARAYAN SHAH the Great was born in 1723. Before he was twenty years old, his dreams and the ambitions were to unify the whole of the country, and in particular, to dominate first the twenty–odd small principalities around his own of Gorkha, and then fight his way and conquer the "Valley of the three kingdoms". It took him almost 25 years to achieve this goal, 25 years of almost uninterrupted wars and delicate political manoeuvres. Ultimately he succeeded, although he had to fight simultaneously against an army sent to Nepal by the British East India Company (in 1767) which he forced into retreat. PRITHVI NARAYAN SHAH'S moment of glory was when, in the midst of the INDRA JATRA festival, on the 25th September 1876, he ascended the throne of KATHMANDU. Thus the territory under his control extended the Mahakali river in the West to the Sikkimese border in the East, which are more or less the borders of present–day NEPAL: PRITIHVI NARAYAN SHAH was then 45 years old.

Unfortunately for him, once he had reached his goal and materialized his childhood dream, he could enjoy it for 7 years only for he died on 10th of January 1775.

The present King of NEPAL is his direct descendant.

PRITHVI NARAYAN SHAH'S eldest son, PRATAP SINGH SHAH (1775–1777) succeeded his father to the throne but he lived as King of Nepal only for three years, during which he consolidated the Kingdom. When he died, at the age of 26, his son RANA BAHADUR SHAH (1777–1805) was only a two–year–old child. Nevertheless he became the nominal King of Nepal, while the real authority was entrusted to a Regent whose name was BAHADUR SHAH (similar to the King's own name, by coincidence). The Regent resisted valiantly an incursion of an army that penetrated NEPAL from TIBET, counter–attacked later and repelled the invaders across the border into their own territory. By force, he took the important town of SHIGATSE and the famous monastery of TASHI–LHUNPO, an action which triggered off a violent reaction on the part of the Emperor of China.

The latter sent an army to repel the Nepalese and this war ended only as late as 1792 by a treaty signed at BETRAWATI. There had been neither victor nor vanquished.

The years 1814–1816 were marked by fresh hostilities, this time between the Nepalese armed forces which numbered not more than 10,000 men and those of the British East India Company numbering more than 3 times their opponents. The motive for this war concerned the sovereignty over about 30 villages scattered in the Terai which both claimed as being part of their sphere of influence. This "war" ended in a compromise settlement that fixed the frontiers of Nepal again along the Mahakali river not far from Kashmir in the West and along the Mechi river in the

East, where they still are today.

One of the important clauses included in this peace treaty signed at Segauly in 1816 was the acceptance by the Nepalese authorities of a British "Resident" to be posted to Kathmandu. He was, so to speak, the first permanent Foreign Representative of any western power. The distrust of everything coming from "outside" led the authorities to restrict within narrow limits the freedom of movement of the British Resident.

THE "RANA" ERA

1846: One of the most important dates in the history of Nepal: The advent of the "RANA" regime which lasted until 1950: 104 years during which the King of Nepal, although still on his throne with all the external decorum and regalia was, in fact, relegated to a purely nominal and honorific role, deprived of all authority and power.

Here, briefly, how this came about:

Taking advantage of the intrigues which accompanied the struggle for power of those living in the entourage of the Palace, a young man of the clan of the RANAS, JUNG BAHADUR RANA by name, emerged as a powerful and intelligent, albeit a ruthless, leader. JUNG BAHADUR RANA (whose real name was Bira Nara SIMHA) was a direct descendant of the RAM SIMHA family which, like the SHAH dynasty, had ruled in the region of CHITTOR (Rajasthan) and had later moved out of India into NEPAL when their princedom fell into the hands of the Muslim-invaders.

JUNG BAHADUR was to be the first of the long line of RANA rulers. His first important appearance on the political scene took place during the historical hight of the 15th September 1846. In the courtyard called "Kot", he played a decisive role in the notorious massacre of noblemen, officers and courtiers which happened there. Then, with the assistance of the Queen he forced the legitimate King Rajendra Bikram Shah into exile to Benares and put on the throne young Crown Prince SURENDRA BIKRAM SHAH. At the same time, he appointed his brothers and other close and reliable relatives to all key posts in the government, army and administration. Another original idea JUNG BAHADIR put into practice was to appoint himself "Prime Minister" with absolute and unlimited powers in all fields. Simultaneously, he took the title of "*Maharaja*" which, etymologically means "*Great*

King" although he had decided to keep the legitimate Sovereign on the throne. This step may be explained by the belief, among the population, that the King was Vishnu's reincarnation. Jung Bahadur may have thought that it would be better not to hurt the people's feelings towards their King and the Dynasty.

A somewhat unexpected innovation was JUNG BAHADUR's decision to make the title and functions of the "Prime Minister" hereditary. But, wise as he was, the line of succession was not to be automatically from father to son, but to the Prime Minister's younger brother or, in any case, to a but adult member of the departing ruler. This was to avoid the complicatons which usually result from having a child formally in power, a situation which entails the necessity of appointing a regent; this, in the past, had always proved a dangerous procedure, whenever it had to be put in practice when the succession of a Sovereign was due.

At the time he took in his hands the destiny of the country and the nation, Jung Bahadur was but 27 years old !

In the eyes of many Nepalese, more revolutionary still than the institutions of hereditary prime-ministership must have appeared JUNG BAHADUR RANA's incredibly audacious initiative to accept an invitation extended to him by no less than the Queen and Empress Victoria of Great Britain and of the Prince President Napoleon of France. This meant, in particular for the priests and other cast Hindus, an acceptance of being "polluted" by "crossing the black waters of the ocean" and being in contact with the "untouchable" inhabitants of these foreign lands.

However, JUNG BAHADUR RANA went. His suite included not less than 32 dignitaries, cooks and servants. He arrived in England in April 1850.

He was brilliantly received at the court of the mightiest ruler of the time, Queen Victoria and, during his stay and visits to harbours, arsenals, mines, industries etc.. he was able to convince himself that the impressive and somewhat frightening power of the British had nothing to do with magic or other supernatural gifts or procedures, but was simply the result of rational planning, untiring effort and work, as well as the pursuit of efficiency in all fields of industrial and other means of production.

After having left England, he arrived in Paris of August 22nd,

1850 as the official guest of the French government in his capacity as Special Envoy of H. M. the King of Nepal. Prince–President Napoleon received Jung Bahadur Rana with honours usually reserved for kings. His stay in France lasted for 6 weeks, and he embarked in Marseilles on 4th. October 1850.

During the 104 years of the Rana regime, Nepal remained a closed coutry, into which no external influence was allowed to penetrate. The main rason for this policy of complete isolation may very well be found in the fact that this period corresponded to the rise of the ever more powerful British "*Raj*" in India, and the fear that the small and weak Kingdom of Nepal might meet with the same fate as so many other principalities and hitherto sovereign states of the Indian subcontinent, i. e. to fall sooner or later under foreign domination.

THE AWAKENING

This state of affairs lasted until November 1950, when King TRIBHUVAN, the present Sovereign's grand–father, went into voluntary exile in New Delhi. From there he inspired, master-minded and directed a popular revolt which had uprisen in the whole country against the Rana regime. This forced *Mohan Shumshere Rana,* the last of the "Rana Prime Ministers". to resign as absolute ruler.

On February 15th., 1951, King Tribhuvan returned to Kath-mandu, took the reins of government into his own hands with the whole-hearted support of the people, appointed a cabinet of minis-ters and, at the same time, laid the foundations of a non-autocratic regime. However, King Tribhuvan died in 1955, at the age of 48, in Zurich. His eldest son MAHENDRA BIR BIKRAM SHAH, succeeded him to the throne. During the first five yeas of his reign, he instituted a multi–party parliamentary democracy–the first Parliament was elected in February 1957–but it proved unsuccess-ful. So the King decided on fundamental reforms. He dismissed Parliament and took over the government himself. At the same time, he initiated the "*Panchayat*", (etymologically the "*council of five*)" a traditional institution which had existed all over the Indian subcontinent since time immemorial, in particular in the villages and the small towns.

Thus, King Tribhuvan put an end to the Rana regime and de-cided that it was time to abandon the policy of total isolation which had been maintained for over a century. For the first time, from 1751 onwards, foreign visitors, even tourists, were welcomed as honoured guests, irrespective of their nationality.

Now, the main preoccupation was–and still is–to develop the country in all fields. This entailed the necessity of accepting certain assistance in particular in the technical spheres from neighbouring or other friendly countries. From the foreign, political angle the principle of absolute "non–alignment", in particular the maintaining of good relations, on the basis of equality, with its two powerful neighbours, India and China, became the cornerstone of Nepalese policy. Nepal considers it to be the only way of preserving its complete independence–the independence of which Nepal is so rightly proud to have kept intact all through its history without ever having to submit to any foreign occupation or colonial domination.

CONSTITUTIONAL PRINCIPLES AND POLITICAL ORGANIZATION

The present Constitution promulgated in 1962 by the late King Mahendra, states clearly: *"The sovereignty of Nepal is vested in His Majesty"*.

The constitution adds.: *"All powers, excecutive, legislative and judicial emanante from Him. These powers are exercised by His Majesty through the organs established by or under this Constitution and other laws for the time being in force keeping in view the interest and wishes of His Majesty's subjects according to the highest traditions of the Shah dynasty"*.

Thus, the King is the Head of the Government and all important decisions are taken or inspired by Him.

Dr. Prachandra Pradhan, in *"Political Institutions of Nepal since 1961"*, adds: "It is also the Constitution which provides for a primary and paramount role of the Crown, supported by the subordinate roles of the Council of Ministers, the National Panchayat (National Assembly), the Supreme Court, the Public Service Commission and the Auditor–General"

After the student unrest in May 1979, H. M. the King appointed Mr. Surya Bahadur THAPA as the new Prime Minister, now (1980) heading a cabinet of 13 ministers, 3 state-ministers and 7 assistant ministers.

The King's policy is dominated by his firm determination to intensify, in all possible fields, the development of his country and he knows that in this endeavour he can count on the whole-hearted support of all. (See details of these development programmes in the following chapter.)

In the sphere of foreign policy, the directing and basic principles remain that of strict non-alignment, of maintaining friendly relations with all countries irrespective of their political ideologies and also of having NEPAL recognized as a "zone of peace". Another constant preoccupation is to obtain, through bilateral or multilateral agreements. all facilities needed by Nepal as a "land–locked" country. In this respect, cooperation with similarly placed countries such as Afghanistan, Austria, Switzerland etc. is particularly sought and promoted.

One of the most important events which marked the more recent years of Nepal's internal political life was H.M.'s the King's decision to invite the nation to express its views and wishes as to the future political structure of their country, by means of a national referendum – the first ever to take place in Nepal.

This decision was the objective of the Royal Proclamation made on 24th May 1979, a few days after some violent student agitation had taken place in Kathmandu and other cities.

According to the King's proclamation, all Nepalese citizens, men and women, who had attained the age of 21 years on or before the above mentioned date may vote, by secret ballot, in favour of:

—either the maintenance of the "partyless Panchayat system" that has been the basic political structure from 1961 onwards.

—or the introduction of a "multi-party system" as it exists in most democratic countries.

The characteristics of the "Panchayat system" are the following

At the bottom: 4000 village and 16 town "panchayats" (councils) whose members are elected by the population of the respective localities.

The second tier of the structure consists in 75 "district panchayats", whose members are elected by the village and town assemblies.

Higher up, the members of the 75 district panchayats and the assembly members elected 112 out of the 135 members of the

"National Panchayat", i. e. the Legislative Parliament that plays the same role as the "Lower House" in any democratic-parliamentary system.

(The remaining 23 members are nominated directly by H. M. the King.)

Major innovations in the above outlined system have already been introduced by decision of the King in December 1979, namely:

—The King shall nominate the Prime Minister on the recommendation of the Legislative Assembly

—The members of the government (Cabinet ministers) will henceforth be responsible to the Legislative Assembly – and not only to H. M. the King as hitherto.

—The members of the Legislative Assembly will henceforth be elected directly by those Nepali nationals having "adult franchise", i. e. voting rights.

These measures came into force irrespective of the result of the referendum. It took place on May 2nd. 1979. The long delay between the King's proclamation and the actual voting is to be explained, among other factors, by the King's wish to allow all political views to be expressed and also by the necessity of drawing an up-to-date voters list, on which all Nepalis having reached 21 years of age on May 24th., 1979, would duly be included. The number of voters amounted to 7.192.451. out of which 66.92% (i.e. 4.813.486) took part. The number of valid ballots was 4.441.417, corresponding to 61.75% of total electorate and the result was the following: 2.433.452 (i.e. 54.78% voted in favour of the maintainance of the Panchayat system, with appropriate reforms, and 2.007.965 (i.e. 45.21%) voted in favour of a multiparty system. The urban voters (Kathmandu, Bhadgaon, Patan, Biratnagar and some others,) were more in favour of the multiparty system, by a margin varying between 2 and 13% of the votes.

THE NATIONAL FLAG

Another peculiarity of Nepal is its national flag.

In fact, it is the only one in the world that is neither rectangular nor even square in shape but is composed of two superimposed triangles.

This geometric figure, the triangle, has more than one symbolic meaning. For Hindus, the most current one is that the triangle represents "dharma", i. e. moral law, religious virtue and sacred duties. The Royal Crest includes in its design a double triangle which looks like a six-pointed "David" star. There is no other connexion than this geometrical identity !

To come back to the flag, both triangles are red for it is the country's national colour, with a border in dark blue.

Whereas the upper triangle bears a white crescent moon emitting eight rays, the lower one has in its centre the sun, also white, radiating twelve beams.

Scholars have also given two extra meanings to this sun and moon composition:

—A reminder of the legendary "solar" and "lunar" dynasties which are believed to have succeeded each other as Nepal's rulers at the dawn of time.

—Since the Hindu and even more so, in the Buddhist tradition, flags are considered as "prayer carriers," the presence of the sun and the moon symbolizes the formula very often used in many prayers:

"May the nation live and prosper as long as the sun and the moon are present in the firmament".

ECONOMY

AGRICULTURE

Nepal has been and still is bound to remain an essentially agricultural country for a very long period of time. It is estimated that, at present, almost 90% of the population are working as farmers and/or cattle breeders.

Nevertheless, only around 14% of the total area of the country are under cultivation, since 32% are forests and the remaining parts are either mountains or jungle and marshes, unsuitable for agriculture. More than 55% of the cultivated area produces rice while one quarter gives corn and between 10 and 12% wheat, barley, millet, and various kinds of pulses. Even less is dedicated to potatoes.

The Kathmandu Valley is one of the richest parts of the country, albeit very small in area: 230 sq. m. (approx. 600 km2) i. e. 0.41% of the total country.) It produces a great variety of

crops: rice is planted before the monsoon and harvested in October-November, at the same time as soya beans which usually grow
on the edge of rice fields. Winter is the season for vegetables:
beans, peas, potatoes, giant radishes, cauliflower and cabbage,
onions and carrots. In spring the main crop is wheat which is sown
in automn In late summer the land yields an abundant crop
of maize, millet and mustard seeds.

One important fact which should be kept in mind is that, in
spite of all its difficulties, Nepal has succeeded in ensuring the
subsistence of its 13 million inhabitants. They are not threatened
by starvation as those of some other countries.

There are two main reasons for this:

On the one hand, the exceptional fertility of the Terai, the
area along the Indian border.

On the other hand, the untiring labour which is put in,
every year afresh, when the monsoon is over, in order to keep
up, rebuild and maintain the thousands of terraced fields which
cover practically all hill slopes. Some of these terraces are barely
six feet wide and all require back-breaking endless toil if they
are to be saved from being swept away by the rains.

In spite of all this, when compared with the majority of other
developing countries of Asia, Nepal's Gross National Product
is still relatively low: Approx. US $ 120 per capita and per annum,
according to the figures published in worlds Bank's "Development
Report".

INDUSTRY

In Nepal it is still at an early stage of development.
However the following industrial units already exist:
—Jute mills and processing factories, textile plants and manu-
facturing units for stainless steel articles, as well as a match
factory in the Biratnagar region (Terai).
—Sugar refineries at Biratnagar, Bhairawa and Birganj
(Terai).
—A cement factory at Hetauda.
—A factory producing agricultual implements and machinery
at Birganj (Terai).
—A cigarette factory at Janakpur (Terai).
—Tea processing factories in the Ilam region (in the extreme
east of Nepal).

—Fruit and fruit–juice canning industries at Biratnagar, Jhapa and Kathmandu.

—Fish rearing installations a cement factory, a cotton mill, Leather tannery and a brewery at Hetauda (Terai).

—A cement plant, a shoe factory, laboratories for pharmaceutical products and a marble quarry in Kathmandu.

—Brick and tile-kilns almost everywhere in the country.

MINERAL RESOURCES

The main ores are iron, copper, nickel, cobalt, lead and zinc; but so far, these ores have been detected in too small quantities and/or in areas difficult to reach, making their systematic exploitation very expensive, in particular because of the lack of adequate means of transport and roads.

Another potential wealth of Nepal consists in the semi–precious stones among which the most common ones are; garnet, tourmaline (green, pink, yellow and black varieties) aquamarine (the light–blue shade) quartz in its many colours, rock–crystal etc.

But turquoise, which is so popular among Sherpas and Tibetans is not found in Nepal. It originates from China and Iran, while coral and amber which are used as ornaments, necklaces etc., are usually imported from Japan, Italy or the Fuji Islands.

As Nepal remained closed to any foreign (western) contacts until 1951, its resources in hard currencies through export its products were minimal. Until a few years ago, the main source of foreign exchange had been the savings by the Gorkha soldiers out of their pay from the British and Indian armies. Now, for five or six years, may be a little more, tourism has became the most important "hard currency earning industry" of the country.

EXPORTS

The only products exported on a regular scale, for the time being, are:

—Jute (processed or not): it constitues 50.3% of the total exports !

—Hides and skins: 16.5%

—Handicraft (garments, hand–woven carpets, objects made of carved wood, etc.,: 14.7%

—Spices: 6.4%

Of course, most of these products are being exported to India, and, consequently they do not bring in the much–needed hard currencies. Some are exported to the People's Republic of China. (shoes, among other items).

The government is ever ready to welcome foreign investments, in particular those which will stimulate industrial development. It offers substantial financial and fiscal advantages to investors, provided the latter invite Nepalese partners as associates and offer Nepalese not only the lesser positions in their enterprises.

MAJOR FIELDS OF DEVELOPMENT

When staying in Nepal today, even the casual visitor should always keep in mind the very salient fact that Nepal "opened its windows to the outer world" only some 30 years ago. It is therefore not surprising that many problems, each more important than the next one, have to be solved and solutions to be fully implemented. Under these circumstances, it is extremely difficult to establish a fixed order of priorities and planning which would provide a panacea, although priorities and planning are both essential.

Thus, it is very praiseworthy indeed that Nepal was in a position to launch its first Five Year Plan as early as 1956. Now, it is starting its, which covers 1980 to 1985. One of the most important and valuable contribution to the history of Nepal's planning problem is Ludwig. STILLER S. J. and Ram P. YADAV's book "Planning for People" published by Sahayogi Press, 1979, Kathmandu.

Although it would exceed the framework of the present guidebook to go into the details of Nepal's economic development plans, it might prove interesting for the visitor to have some idea of the major fields on which emphasis was laid during the past years and which still heads the priority list today.

The most important factor is that no less than 70% of the state's total expenditure budget is allotted to the various "development" programmes, while only 30% is spent on "current" items.

For the budget year 1980/81, the priorities were the following, expressed in percentages of the total "Development expenditure" that amounted to 3.413,9 Millions Rupees, i. e. approx. 285 million US Dollars:

ITEM	Percentage of total development budget	In Millions of	
		Nep. Rs.	U.S. Dollars
1. Electricity	19.1%	653,8	54,5
2. Roads and bridges	16.0	549,4	45,8
3. Irrigation	12.1	412,3	34,3
4. Education	9.4	322,6	26,9
5. Agriculture	9.2	314,9	26,2
6. Health and drink-water	8.4	284,9	23,7
7. Mining and Industry	6.8	233,1	19,4
8. Panchayats	4.5	152,2	12,7
9. Forestry	4.2	144,6	12,0
10. Aviation	2.8	95,8	7,9
11. Communication	1.7	58,2	4,8
12. Misc. Social Services	1.2	42,3	3,5
13. Miscellaneous	4.6	149,8	12,4
	100.0%	3.413,9	284,1

LAND REFORM

—Another important move was to introduce and implement a land–reform programme in order to give the tillers of the soil the incentive to increase and improve food production. This is of course of primary importance in an agricultural country such as Nepal.

Nowadays, the vast majority of the land, in particular in the hills, belongs to the farmers themselves. The maximum area that can be the property of one family is fixed as follows: In the Terai: 16,7 ha – In the hills : 4 ha. and in Kathmandu Valley, 2,5 ha.

Although there are practically never acute and long–lasting food–shortages, with some exceptions due to excessive weather conditions, the food production leaves a very narrow margin of surplus.

According to the official statistics the agricultural production yielded the following quantities (expressed in thousands of metric tons, in the year 1978/79) :

Rice	:	2339	Millet	:	133
Corn	:	743	Oil seeds	:	92
Wheat	:	454	Jute	:	65
Sugarcane	:	379	Barley	:	22
Potato	:	268	Tobacco	:	5

At the same time as the land–reform, emphasis has been laid and still continues to be laid, on more irrigation and the use of better varieties of seeds, be they of rice, corn, wheat or barley, the main staple food of the population. And of course, the government is taking all possible steps to facilitate the use of the most suitable types of fertilizers.

TOURISM:

Tourist industry has become the most important foreign currency earning industry of the country: it yielded in 1962 not more than 78,000 US $, and over 30 million in 1980, i. e. over 380 times more, in merely 18 years.

FAMILY PLANNING

A delicate and complex problem if ever there was one ! In particular in a country where the problems are multifarious; communications are poor, the population is widely disseminated, there are few towns and farms are scattered over all hills and slopes. Illiteracy is still far too widespread for the written message to be circulated wih efficiency, broadcasting is relatively undeveloped and television non–existent. All these factors render the usual media impracticable.

But inspite of all these obstacles, the "message" is slowly getting through, mainly by means of posters and oral propaganda.

According to the latest official statistical data available (1976), the population's growth rate is approximately 2.46% per annum, which means that there are almost 320.000 more inhabitants in Nepal than twelve months before, i. e. 4/5th of the population of Kathmandu !

The same source indicates that the "crude birth rate" reaches 4.68% (i. e. almost five children are born, every year, to 100 inhabitants) while the death rate is about 2.22% , hence the net surplus mentioned above. (2.46%) Infant mortality (Live children not reaching one year of age)is estimated at 13.3%. Life expectancy is 43.4 for men and 41.1 for women.

To summarize, every year there are around 615,000 babies to feed and out of these, 530,000 reach more than one year.

This creates a vast problem, not only to find means and ways to cover the immediate needs of food, hygiene and medical care, but, to provide, for the years to come, more and more cultivable land, since up to 90% of the "added-on" population will be farming. At the same time, to fight erosion, a very serious reforestation programme has also become a major necessity.

TRANSPORT

In view of the peculiar geographic features of the country, the building of railways would be too costly for a volume of traffic which is likely to remain too low to make such a plan realistic.

Consequently efforts have been concentrated on the construction of ropeways, roads and bridges.

ROPEWAYS

This rather unusual means of transport links Kathmandu Valley to the Terai, passing over and above the hill ranges lying in between. They are used exclusively for carrying goods of the bulky and heavy type such as bags of cement, fertilizers etc.. The first ropeway was installed in 1922–25 under Prime Minister Chandra Shumsher Rana. It had a capacity of eight tons per hour each way. In 1958–60 it was replaced by a more powerful (25 tons per hour) aerial cable way financed by the U. S. Building such ropeways is, of course, much cheaper than roads, but their capacity is limited and :heir need good maintainance and management.

Some more are being planned, among others one between Dharan and Dhankuta, in the eastern part of the country.

ROADS

In the beginning of 1980 the network of highways totalled 1,550 miles (see details under "How to get around".)

In the near future, this mileage will be increased by another 621 m. (1000 km.) once the East–West Highway is completed. This is being built with the multinational assistance of Great Britain, India, the U. S. A. and the U. S. S. R., a noteworthy example of the kind of contribution big powers ought to give developing ones.

This highway is of so great importance because it is the first time in history that Nepal will have a border-to-border link, across the whole country in its southern and richest part. This link will undoubtedly entail not only a stronger cohesion between the

the nations various widespread ethnic groups but also between the farmers living in remote areas and the seat of the government and administration. Due to the fact that most of the
natural communication lines follow the valleys which, in their
majority, flow north to south, the "natural" trend for the
population was to move either to the Indian or to the Tibetan
border to find a market for buying, selling or bartering goods
but rarely did they proceed east–west or v.v. towards the capital
of the kingdom.

Another important road is planned to link Pokhara with Surkhet in the Western part of the country. It will be 238 miles
(400 km) long. Its construction is a part of the assistance programme set up by the Peoples' Republic of China.

The same programme included the building of a wide ring-
road encircling the urban area of Kathmandu. This road and the
four necessary bridges were completed in 1976.

The British Government Aid is concerning itself with the construction of a "branch–road" leading from Dharan to Birtanagar,
a stretch of around 40 miles.

Last but not least, the Swiss Association for Technical Assistance built a 60 mile long road which links the model–farm
site of JIRI halfway between Kathmandu and the Solu-Khumbu·
region, with the Chinese Road, thus creating the first road–link
between the capital and the northeastern part of the Kingdom.

COMMUNICATION FACILITIES

This programme includes telephone, telegraph, etc., whether
by cable, radio, micro–wave or satellite communications which
are an absolute necessity.

HYDRO – ELECTRIC PRODUCTION

This also constitutes one of the most needed pre–conditions
for the nation's development, both for its industry and as a sub-
stitute for the consumption of timber as heating material. Nepal
possesses an impressive number of river and mountain streams
containing a tremendous potential wealth of exploitable energy.

The need for electric power will be increasing for many decades
to come both in Nepal and in neighbouring countries. This must
surely be a most important if not *the* most important potential

export of Nepal.

So far, three major hydro–electric power plants have been completed, two with the financial and technical assistance of INDIA (namely the TRISULI "run-off" station with a maximum capacity of 21,000 kw, and the GANDAK station with a capacity of 15,000 kw) and the third built with the People's Republic of China's assistance, on the SUN KOSI between Lamosangu and Barabise, with a capacity of 10,400 kw.

Besides these major projects, many small-scale hydro-electric generators, turbines etc. . are planned to be installed in those areas that are most severely threatened by deforestation (one of the gravest problems facing many hill areas of the country.)

It must be underlined that the hydro-electric potential of Nepal is the most important source of wealth of the country. Indeed, this potential is estimated to amount approx. 83 million kw. i. e. more than that of India (41) and Japan (37) combined. Even if, by 1980, the total production of electric power will have reached 180.000 kw, this would only represent approx. 0.2% !

EDUCATION

There are still to few schools and teachers for all those who · wish – and need – to learn, inspite of the great efforts made in this field.

According to the latest available statistics (1976), the most important figures were the following :

    —Primary schools : 8314 (against 7537 in 1971)
    —Secundary   ”   : 2373   (”   1728 ”   ”)
Number of enrolled students:
    —In primary schools :   644.000
    —In secundary   ”   :   263.000

These represent only about 34% of the total of the primary school age-group and 18% of the secundary.

Thus, it is not surprising that the literacy rat is still relatively low : Official figures indicate 20% of the total population above 6 years of age, can read and write.   But this percentage is the "average" between 32% of men and boys on the one side, and 8% of women and girls. This imbalance tends however to diminish as and when the older generations disappear, who, in their youth, had not been offered any opportunity of going to school.

In addition to the above figures, colleges and the various faculties of Nepal University (presently consisting only of non-technical units) there are 23,500 students., as against only 17,250 in 1971. Approximately 4000 of them are girls, a proportion slightly higher than in primary and secundary schools.

Of course, the emphasis is laid on the formation and the training of more school–teachers and professors, as well as on the publication and distribution of sufficient school books in the national language, Nepali.

HEALTH AND WELFARE

All problems related to Health and Welfare, also rate very high in the priority list, not only in terms of campaigns aiming at the eradication of endemic diseases such as malaria, smallpox or tuberculosis but also in terms of the number and the better equipment of hospitals, dispensaries, health centres and aid–posts etc. The number of hospital beds (3,000 in 1979), doctors (400), nurses and midwives (2,000) is still far from sufficient.

OTHERS

Some other fields towards which the efforts of government branches, international specialized agencies as well as private initiative are directed, include:

* Forestry preservation.
* Research of mineral deposits and their exploitation.
* Development of small–scale and "cottage" industries.
* Improvement and extension of runways, radio installations and other facilities for air traffic.
* Last but not least, hotel building and provisions to suit the needs of the ever–increasing flow of tourists.

FOREIGN ASSISTANCE

It is obvious that the implementation of such vast programmes exceeds the present financial and technical possibilities of the Government and the nation. Thus, many countries offered Nepal their unselfish assistance, either financial or technical or both.

Foreign assistance manifests itself in two sectors of equal importance ; bilateral assistance, i. e. through agreements between a given "donor" country and Nepal, and multi-lateral agreements, i. e. through international bodies, such as the World Bank, the International Development Agency, the Asian Development Bank, and the various United Nation's agencies.

The 1980/1981 budget includes the following breakdown of the foreign assistance to Nepal:

| | | In millions of | |
		Nep. Rs.	U.S. Dollars
Bilateral assistance	Grants	825,3	68,8
	Loans	179,1	14,9
	T O T A L 1.004,4		83,7
Multilateral assistance	Grants	224,0	18,7
	Loans	819,8	68,3
	T O T A L 1.043,8		87,0
Total assistance		2.048,2	170,7

Of course this amount will be used exclusively to finance part of the "development expenditure". of which the foreign assistance represents thus exactly 60%. (It also represents approx. 59% of the estimated total revenue for 1980/81., in which the foreign assistance is always included.)

The remaining 41% are produced by the collection of taxes, custom and other duties etc...

It may also be of interest to set up the priority list of the "donor countries" which offered Nepal, during the last four fiscal years (1975 – 1978 incl.), their financial assistance :

Name of the Donor Country	Percent of the Total Bilateral Assistance (four years average)
INDIA	24.8%
CHINA	15.6%
U.S.A.	15.0%
GREAT BRITAIN	14.5%
FED. REP. OF GERMANY	7.3%
JAPAN	6.2%
KUWEIT	6.1%
SWITZERLAND	3.7%
DENMARK	1.6%
CANADA	1.3%
U.R.S.S.	0.9%
SAUDI ARABIA	0.5%
Miscellaneous	2.5%
TOTAL :	100.0%

POPULATION

INTRODUCTION

Nepal has a little over 13,500.000 inhabitants, with 700 million Indian neighbours in the South and 1 billion Chinese neighbours in the North.

Kathmandu Valley's population is estimated at around 700,000 approx. 400,000 of them live in Kathmandu itself, 173,000 in Patan and 122,600 in Bhadgaon.

Although the vast majority of the inhabitants of these three cities are pure Nepali or Newars, representative of many of the other ethnic groups such as Tamang, Gurung, Magar, Rai as well as Limbu, Sherpa, and Tibetan, each of them having their distinctive features and costumes, are to be found in the Valley.

One of the characteristics of the peoples of Nepal is their variety as well as the perfect harmony in which they live, irrespective of their ethnic regions or their religion.

Various books have been written on the subject of their customs and peculiarities and this is not the place for great details. However, three main sources are worth to be remembered.

—Those populations of *Gangetic* origin, living mostly in the Terai. They are dark with definite Caucasoid features. Their language, with some rare exceptions, is related to Hindu.

—Those of *Newar* stock, the oldest population of the Valley, have a tendency to Mongoloid features and use a language of their own which belongs to the Tibetan–Burmese branch.

—Those, more directly of *Tibetan* origin and who live mostly in the north–eastern and the northern part of Nepal (Sherpas and Thakalis for instance). These have strongly Mongoloid features and their language is Tibetan or a dialect close to it.

They have been living in the mountain areas for many centuries. They must not be looked upon the same way as the Tibetan refugees who settled in Nepal only after the exodus of the Dalai Lama from Lhassa to India in March 1959. and the number of which may be estimated at approximately 6,000.

SOCIAL STRUCTURE

As mentioned in the chapter on the history of Nepal, it was under the region of King Jaya Sthiti MALLA (1382–1422), that the caste–system was codified in the country.

In fact, this typically Hinduist concept was brought into the country at a much earlier stage as and when more and more people migrated from Muslim occupied areas of Northern and North-Western India into Nepal. Several remarks may however be made:

1. The basic principles around which the caste system is structured are the same in Nepal as in India, that is to say, the society is divided in four main social orders, namely, beginning with the highest one:

—The Brahmins, originally the caste of the priests, who are called "Bahun" in Nepali.

—The Kshatriyas, originally the caste of princes, rulers, warriors etc. to whom belong both the reigning Shah dynasty as well as the Rana families. In Nepali they are called "Chetris".

—The Vaishyas, originally the merchants and peasants.

—The Sudras, originally the servants and menial workers.

2. The Constitution of Nepal, as well as the civil and penal codes, abolished radically and definititvely the caste system and makes any action in court automatically illegal, when the litigation emanates from the concept of caste.

3. Nevertheless, caste-consciousness is still strong in Nepalese society and appears in particular on the occasion of important family events such as selecting a marriage partner, funeral and other rites, etc. Of course, the higher the caste one belongs to, the more caste-conscious one is tempted to be.

4. Among the Newars the caste system is slightly different from the one adopted by other Nepalis. Distinctive names are used and some of the occupational groups are classified in a somewhat different way.

5. Perhaps one of the most important factor about which foreigners might not be aware of : never any "new castes" are being created. This means that anybody, provided he has the schooling, training and professional capacities, may find employment in *any* "modern" profession, be it in accountancy, engineering, aviation, electronics, and practically all industrial enterprises. These professions are not and will not be "castified". Thus, the development and modernization of the country is in no way hampered by the "caste-system" as it is frequently believed in the western world.

ETHNIC GROUPS

The variety of ethnic and other groups living in Nepal is so vast that it is difficult to deal with this subject in too condensed a manner.

The following few indications should therefore only serve as a superficial guide-line to make the visitor a little more familiar with the various names and whom they represent as well as to give some of the most striking characteristics of the main communities which constitute the nation of Nepal.

Some of the information given below was extracted from the two most comprehensive books written on the subject, books which are highly recommended should more details be looked for. They are:

Dor Bahadur BISTA: *"People of Nepal"* –Kathmandu, 1972
D. B. SHRESTHA, C. B. SINGH and B. M. PRADHAN: *"Ethnic Groups of Nepal and their ways of living"* Kathmandu 1972.
Marc GABORIEAU: "Népal et ses populations" (in French)

In this chapter, we shall follow a somewhat artificial geographical classification, starting from the Lowlands of the Terai, through the Midlands of the Pahar up to the Highlands of the Himalayas. The numbers given for each ethnic groups are approximate: they were taken from the last official census (1971) and are slightly increased to take into account the yearly average 2.46% population increase, though this percentage has been applied in a uniform way to all the groups, which may not reflect the true situation regarding some of them.

1) Groups living mostly in the Lowlands

—DHANGARS:
Area	: South–Eastern Terai: Janakpur and Biratnagar districts
Population	: 14.000
Language	: A Dravidian (!) language close to those used in some parts of Central India,
Creed	: Hinduism
Race	: Dravidian mixed with Indo-Aryans,
Literature	: B. P. UPRETY : *"Dhangar tribe of Janakpur"*– Kathmandu 1966.

—DANWARS, DARAI and MAJHI
Area	: Central and Eastern Terai and Eastern hills

Population	: Danwars : around 16,000 Darai : 2,000 Majhi : 8,000
Language	: Their own language of Sanskrit origin
Creed	: Hinduism and home-deities; ancestor worship
Race	: Related to the Tharus, the indigenous inhabitants of the Terai.

—RAJBANSI, KOCHE and TAJPURI

Area	: Extreme Eastern Terai
Population	: 75,000
Language	: Related to Assamese but influenced by Maithili (the main dialect spoken in the Terai),
Creed	: Hinduism and a few Muslims.
Literature	: B. H. HODGSON : *On the Kooch Bodo and Dhiwal tribes"* London 1880.

—SATARS

Area	: South-Eastern Terai,
Population	: 28,000
Language	: Their own language linked with the ones spoken in Bihar,
Creed	: Polytheist but worship of a "Super-God", the World-Creator,

—THARUS

Area	: All over the Terai,
Population	: 600,000, i. e. one of the largest ethnic groups of the whole country.
Language	: A language which has affinities with Maithili Urdu, Nepali, Hindi, Prakriti, Bhojpur and Maghadi, depending on the location of th various sub-groups.
Creed	: Mainly animists, but Hindu festivals are also celebrated. Each family has its home-deity represented by a lump of earth mixed with cotton-threads, crude sugar-cane, and a gold coin in the centre.
Race	: Aboriginal inhabitants of the Terai. Tharus believe they have originally links, with the royal clan of the Sakya, the family of Lord Buddha, a belief strengthened by the worship of goddess Sahodhara, whose name sounds close to Yasodhara, Buddha's wife !

Literature   : D. N. MAJUMDAR, ROY CHAUDHAURY, L. R.
                 SINGH, S. K. SRIWASTAWA, and J. C. NESFIELD
                 have, all written studies on the Tharus, Some
                 may still be a available in Public Libraries.

2) Groups living mainly in the Midlands

—CHEPANGS

Area   : Central Nepal, Dhading, Makwanpur and
                 Gorkha regions
Population   : 15,000
Language   : Their own language of Tibeto–Burman family
Creed   : Animism, ancester–worship, belief in spirits,
                 etc. but nowadays influenced by Hinduism.
Race   : Chepangs believe they are descendants of
                 Sita, the princely wife of Rama, the hero of
                 the famous Hindu epic, Ramayana. Others
                 contend that Chepangs are an off–shoot of
                 the eastern Nepal's Kirantis, for they have
                 often Mongolian features and were formerly
                 nomads.

—GURUNGS

Area   : The whole western hill regions, Gorkha,
                 Annapurna, Ghandrung, Landrung, Kaski,
                 Lamjung districts.
Population   : 265,000
Language   : A Tibeto–Burman language
Creed   : Lamaist Buddhism
Race   : Mongoloid (related to Thakalis and Magars)

—KIRATS—RAIS and LIMBUS

Note   : The name "Kirat" is a collective name for a
                 historically famous indigenous tribe who
                 took part in the battles described in the Hindu
                 epic "Mahabharata"
                 Nowadays, they subdivide themselves into
                 two separate but still inter–related ethnic
                 groups, the Rais and the Limbus.
Area   : North-eastern and extreme eastern part of the
                 Terai and the hills of the eastern part of Nepal
Population   : 400,000 Rais and 250,000 Limbus.
Language   : Their own idioms derived from the Kirat
                 language

Creed	: A mixture of animism, Buddhism and Shaivism
Race	: Mongoloid–Tibetan with accentuated features: pale pigmentation of the skin, almond–shaped eyes, sometimes almost "flat" faces.
Literature	: Iman Singh CHEMJONG "*History and Culture of the Kirat people*"– Kathmandu 1967.

—MAGARS

Area	: Central and Western Nepal–Regions of Palpa and Gorkha
Population	: 430,000
Language	: A Tibetan–rooted dialect
Creed	: In majority Buddhists, but some Hindu Gods are venerated and Hindu festivals celebrated.
Race	: Tibetan origin, markedly Mongolian features.

—PANCHGAUNS

Area	: The "five villages" (which is, actually, the translation of the name Panchagauns), namely Jomosom, Syang, Marpha, Chivang and Chherok, in the upper Kali Gandaki Valley
Population	: A few hundred
Language	: A Tibetan dialect, similar to the one used by the Thak
Creed	: Mainly Buddhist with surviving rites of the pre–Buddhist, Tibetan "Bon" religion
Race	: Mongoloid–Tibetan

—SUNWARS and JIRELS

Area	: Eastern part of Mid–Nepal (The Jirels mainly around the village of Jiri, whence their name comes from)
Population	: 27,500 Sunwars and 3,600 Jirels
Language	: Sunwars use a dialect related to the Magar language whereas the Jirels language comes closer to the Sherpa dialect
Creed	: Sunwars are mostly Hindus, while Jirels Buddhists
Race	: Tibetan–Mongoloid

—TAMANGS

| Area | : Central and Eastern Hill regions, almost all over Nepal. |
| Population | : 780,000, a very important ethnical group |

Language	: Of Tibetan–Burman origin, related to Newari
Creed	: Mainly Buddhists (with surviving "Bon" influences). But several important Hindu festivals are also observed and Hindu deities venerated (Durga among others)
Race	: Tibetan–Mongoloid
Literature	: *Chr. v.* FURER--HAIMENDORF : "*Ethnographic notes on the Tamangs of Nepal.*"

—THAKALIS

Area	: All along the Kali Gandaki and in particular in and between the two villages of Ghasa and Tukuche
Population	: 6,500
Language	: An idiom of Tibeto–Burman family
Creed	: Buddhism with Jhankri and Shamanist rites. Some Thakalis have adopted Hinduism
Race	: Tibetan–Mongoloid
Literature	: Corneille JEST : "*Les Thakali*" Librairie Orientaliste Paul Geuthner–Paris 1965

3) Groups living mainly in the Highaland

—DOLPOS

Area	: The four barren valleys of Tarap, Barbung, Nangkhong and Panzang in the "Dolpo" district, north–west and beyond the Dhaulagiri range
Population	: 5000
Language	: A Tibetan dialect
Creed	: Lamaist Buddhism (of the Nyingma–pa sect) but influenced by animism, totemism and certain rites dating from the old "Bon" religion.
Race	: Tibetan
Literature	: Corneille JEST : "*Tarap, une vallée dans l' Himalaya*". Ed. du Seuil – PARIS 1974 Corneille JEST : DOLPO : *Communautés de langue tibétaine du Népal* – PARIS (CNRS) 1975

—LO–PAS

Area	: Exclusively the Mustang valley north of Jomosom and Kagbeni
Population	: A few hundred

Language   : A Tibetan dialect
Creed   : Lamaist Buddhism
Race   : Tibetan
Literature : Michel PEISSEL : *"Mustang"*, "the forbidden kingdom" New–York 1967.

—MANANG--PAS or NYESHANG

Area   : Upper Marsyangdi–Valley, north-east of the Annapurna range; in particular Nyeshang, Nar and Gyasundo, and, of course, the main village of Manang.
Population : Several hundreds.
Language   : Not a Tibetan dialect, but an idiom which is believed to be linked with the language of the Gurungs.
Creed   : Lamaist Buddhism, but not particularly religious mined people
Race   : Tibetan or Gurung; the question remains open

—SHERPAS

Area   : The Solu–Khumbu district, in particular the northern part of it. Also settlements in the Central hills (Malenchi and Tharkegyang, north of Kathmandu)
Population : 20,000
Language   : The Sherpa dialect, close to Tibetan
Creed   : Buddhist exclusively, mostly of the Nyingma-pa sect, commonly called the "Red-hat sect"
Race   : Tibetan. Literally, the word "sherpa" means, in fact : "People" ("pa") from the East ("sher" or "shar") The cradle of the Sherpas is believed to have been th "Selmagang" district in the "Kham" province situated in in eastern Tibet, some 1,300 miles away from their present area ! Their emigration is said to have taken plac some 6 centuries ago, via the Tibetan plateau and the "Nang–pa" pass (18,750 ft.)
Literature : *Chr. v.* Furer – HAIMENDORF : *"The Sherpas of Nepal"* University of California Press–Berkeley and Los Angeles, 1964. and *"Himalayan Traders"* 1977.

M. M. OPPITZ : "The *history and Social Structure of the Sherpas*" (Munich 1968–Published in German)
S. JEEVES : "*Land of the Sherpas*" London 1962
A. MAILLART : "*The Land of the Sherpas*"–London 1955.

4. Groups which are not geographically located

—*BRAHMINS* (Mostly called, "Bahun", in Nepali).

Brahmins are not, of course, an ethnic group as all those mentioned in the previous paragraphs although, originally, most of them, like the Kshatriyas must have migrated in the course of the centuries from various parts of India and therefore belong to the Indo-Aryan stock. But Brahmins, being the members of the highest social caste, have very distinctive features which deserve to be briefly expounded.

Among the Brahmins, there are however some groups who have different names according to the places where they originally came from (like the *"Kumaon Brahmins"*, Kumaon being the mountain region of Northern India closest to *Western* Nepal), or the *"Purbiya Brahmins"* who have settled some centuries ago, in the *East* of Nepal.

Traditionally Brahmins were concentrated in the mid–western parts of Nepal, but later, they spread throughout the country. In the Kathmandu Valley, together with the Chetris, they often occupy very high positions either in government service or in the business community, not to omit the fact of their being originally Hindu priests. This is still their exclusive prerogative as they belong to the highest caste in the Hindu social system.

Their number has not been recorded in the census of 1971, as they do not constitute in the strict sense of the expression, an "ethnic" group, although, in some parts of the country, Brahmins tend to live together in one homogeneous village.

Brahmins mostly speak Nepali as well as the language of the locality in which they live. They are, of course, all of Indo–Aryan stock.

A few lines about Brahmin traditions and customs:

Very caste-conscious, Brahmins observe very strictly all orthodox rites and traditions, religious as well as secular. They are very similar if not identical, to those observed in Northern

India, (Utter Pradesh and Rajasthan, in particular.)

Of course, marriage can only take place within the caste. Usually, the parents on both sides, select brides and bridegrooms. Girls are married when they are 11 or 12 years old. However, earlier child marriages tend to disappear among the upper class and well–educated Brahmin families. Law now restricts early marriages. It is still common tradition to consult astrologers before the choice of the bride and the bridegroom is made final. Astrologers will first compare the names of the betrothed, study their respective horoscopes in order to determine whether they are "in harmony" and lastly, will decide on the auspicious date and hour of the main ceremony. Normally, marriage can only take place in one of the following five months : *Magh* (mid--January to mid–February), *Falgun* (mid–February to mid–March), *Baisakh* (mid–May to mid–June), *Jyestha* (mid–June to mid–July, *Mangsir* (mid–November to mid–December). In addition to these limitations, planet Venus must be visible in the sky during the night of the wedding ceremony. Wedding rites are extremely complex and elaborate. They last at least 24 if not 36 hours. The rites involve, among others: fast, by parents as well as by the betrothed, foot–washing of the bride and bride–groom by the girls' parents, exchange of gifts mainly clothing (sarees) and ornaments to the bride, circumambulation around a central sacrificial fire, which also contains symbols of sky, wind, earth and water; finally the groom places a line of vermilion powder made of sandal wood paste along the parting of the bride's hair. In principle, she is required to apply it afresh every day with powder mixed with the orginal one, as long as her husband lives.

In the eyes of Brahmins–as well as Chetris–the two betrothed have been destined to live together from their previous lives. Therefore there is no provision–at least in theory–for a divorce.

Once the newly–wed bride joins her husband's home, she falls under the command of her mother–in–law more than that of her husband. But this custom also tends to become more relaxed, particularly when the husband is in a position to move in a house of his own, which is often the case in towns, albeit not among the lower social groups or among farmers.

Throughout their life, a Brahmin wears a sacred thread (called *janai*) resting on his left shoulder, tied underneath the right armpit. Once a year, on "Janai Purnima" festival, this sacred thread is replaced by a new one. The same rite applies to Chetris.

Some Brahmins or Chetris, when frustrated or tired of their worldly life, may choose to become mendicants and dedicate themselves to meditation and prayer, renouncing all their caste privileges. Thus they may become "*sadhus*" a special status which not only men but also women may join.

The deceased are always cremated on river banks and their ashes thrown in a river which will ultimately join up with the "mother River Ganges". This is the case for all streams flowing through Nepal.

The body of the deceased is placed on a green bamboo bier or tied to a green bamboo pole and taken to the cremation ground (Pashupatinath preferably, when the death occurs near or in the Kathmandu Valley.) To be remembered: Women are never present at cremations, and, of course, the ancient tradition of "suttee" which, in former times compelled widows to throw themselves on their husbands' pyre is once and for all abolished.

There is no definite Brahmin dress or costume, However, when acting as priests, Brahmins wear a long, wide and white robe. In the book "Ethnic groups of Nepal and their way of living", the following description may be found: "A typical Brahmin wears a "*labeda*", a kind of tight shirt, a "*cummerband*", a kind of suspender, an "*uparna*" or "*uttariya*", a garment made of ordindary white cloth folded four, on left shoulder, and a Nepali cap, called a "*topi*". A Brahmin lady wars a "*cholo*", a kind of blouse, and a "*fariya*", a kind of saree."

Literature : *Ch.* BERREMAN *: Hindus of the Himalayas*" Los Angeles. 1963.

CHETRIS

This is the name given, in Nepal, to the members of the second highest caste, those who, in India, are called "Kshatriyas", the caste of rulers and warriors.

Chetris are found all over Nepal with the sole exception, perhaps, of the highest valleys in the northern parts of the country.

All Chetris are of Indo-Aryan stock and, like Brahmins, are, of couse, strict orthodox Hindus.

Most of the present-day Nepali Chetris originated in Northern India, particularly in Rajasthan, from where they emigrated to Nepal during the 12th and 13th centuries, as the Brahmins did. Those of the Brahmins who settled in the hilly districts of Garhwal and Kumaon, in the Western parts of today's Nepal were in touch with a very powerful people called the Khas who had established a vast kingdom that spread up to the Tibetan border.   The progeny of a Brahman and a local Khas woman was given the name of Khatri, a corruption of the Sanskrit name of Kshatriya. They were also given the status of the warrior caste of the Chetris and popularly became known as *"Khatri Chetri"* (abbr. K. C.). The aristocrats among the Chetri caste are commonly called Thakuris, who can only be distinguished from other Chetris by their family names (see below.)

In modern Nepal, Chetris are among the most influential and wealthy social classes. They are mostly in government service, high-ranking officers in the army and police, or landlords, intellectuals or businessmen. Some have remained farmers.

Like Brahmins, Chetris wear the sacred thread. Whereas Brahmins and Chetris do not practice crosscousin marriage, the Thakuris accept such marriages within certain limits.

Chetris always cremate their dead by the riverbanks. While the bulk of the remains is thrown into the water, a small bone is usually preserved to be either buried in the middle of the stream or brought to Benares and cast into the holy river Ganges.

There is no special Chetri-dress, they adopt the dress of the social strata to which they belong.

Literature : B. H. HODGSON *I "Origin and classification of the warrior tribes of Nepal".* Calcutta 1857.

—MUSLIMS

The Muslim community of Nepal is a comparatively small one.   Their number may be estimated between 360,000 and 375,000.   There has been an increase of Muslims in Nepal during the years 1972 and 1973 due to the arrival of many refugees from Bangla Desh, after the Indo-Pakistan war.

Most of the older Muslim communiees that settled in Nepal are to be found in the Western Terai.

Their language is Urdu but, particularly those who live in the Kathmandu Valley, also speak Nepali.

The majority of them belong to the Hanfi school of the "Sunni" sect. There are two mosques in Kathmandu, the larger one is close to the clock-tower on Durbar Marg.

Ethnically speaking, they belong to the Indo–Aryan stock, and are not of Arab descent.

The first Muslims came to Nepal as traders in the late 15th. century when they were travelling to and fro between their native Kashmir and Lhasa. The local name given to those who much later settled down in the western hills is *"churante"*, which means bangle–sellers. In the Terai, most Muslims are farmers, leading the same kind of life as the other populations of the same areas. Elsewhere, however, they are mostly traders, shop–keepers and cobblers, washermen (*"dhobi"*), weavers, tailors or cotton teasers.

Marriage is mostly arranged by both parents. Polygamy is permitted but seldom put in practice. The deceased are always buried in grave yards.

Many Nepali Muslims have remained faithful to their traditional and typical dress as one sees in Kashmir, Afghanistan or Pakistan, i. e. wide and loose trousers, a waistcoat and a small, usually embroidered round cap or a turban.

Most of them let their beards grow and dye their hair with reddish henna. Women are in purdah, covering their heads and concealing their eyes. Marc GABORIEAU published two exhausitve studies concerning Nepali Muslims, in 1966, under the titles: *"Les Musulmans du Népal"* and *"Les Curautes du Népal"*.

—NEWARS

As mentioned before, the Newars are the ancient if not the first ethnic group that settled in the Kathmandu Valley, where many thousands of them have remained until today. Most of the surrounding villagers are also inhabited almost exclusively by Newars. This is the case, among others, in the typical and picturesque towns of Kirtipur and Sankhu.

The total number of Newars living in Nepal is estimated at 600,000, out of which approx. 350,000 are residing in the Valley. Thus, they represent not even 5% of Nepal's total population. Nevertheless, they play a far more important role not only in the history of the country but also in the life of present-day Nepal than their relatively small percentage may lead to think.

Newars speak their own language, called "newari" which has its own script and no linguistic connection with nepali, hindi or sanskrit. It belongs to the family of Tibeto–Burmese languages. Newari literature is extremely rich and diversified.

Of course, educated Newars speak Nepali and English as well. Nowadays, most Newars are Hindus though originally they were in majority, Buddhists. A large minority still professes Buddhism today. To add to the complexity, Newars have their own deities, rites, customs and festivals, as well as their own priests and even their proper caste system which is almost exclusively based on professions and trades.

A certain number of Newars show definite Tibetan or Mongoloid physical features. Some may have immigrated from Tibet but nothing is known for certain in this respect.

In spite of all these peculiarities which include even distinct clan and family names, the Newars nowadays constitute an integral part of the Nepali nation where they play a very important part in all fields of activity. They are rightly proud of their old traditions and skills in many branches of art and handicraft. In Kathmandu and Patan in particular, there are still woodcarvers, jewellers, gold, silver and copper-smiths who continue the traditions of their forefathers. If Nepal counts so many exquisite works of art, it is, to a very large extent, due to Newar craftsmen.

Whereas Patan is often referred to as the "city of arts", Bhadgaon which is also a *"Newar"* town, has remained to a greater extent a peasant and handicraft town which lives almost on its own. The inhabitants of Bhadgaon spin their own cotton and wool, weave their saris and other textiles and manufacture their jars and pots, importing from Kathmandu, as the saying goes: *"only the kerosene to cook the rice and the salt to flavour it"*.

The number of traditions, customs and beliefs, some of them really strange ones, are manifold. Here are a few examples, extracted from the remarkable book written about the Newars by Gopal Singh Nepali.:

—Women never take part in any kind of artistic activity such as playing a musical instrument, dancing or acting in a play.

—The rainbow is considered the "hookah" (a tobacco pipe in which smoke is drawn through water belonging to *INDRA*, the King of the Gods and with which he draws the water from the Ocean and sheds it, as rain, over the fields and the forests.

—When twins are born, if the first baby is a boy and the second a girl, this indicates that both had been husband and wife in a previous life, or that the wife had committed *"suttee"* on her husband's pyre, i.e. had immolated herself.

—Most of the Newars have remained faithful to their ancient profession : farming. Newari peasants are called *"jyapus"*. However, nowadays, many Newars are to be found in public services, trade and in the professions.

—Usually, marriages are still pre–arranged by the parents to avoid unwitting breaking of the rules and traditions of caste.

—An ancient tradition requires a young girl, when only 7 or 8 years old, to be married to a certain sacred tree called *"bel-tree"*, this marriage being performed in the presence of the family and the priest who directs all prescribed rites.

There are two reasons why this symbolic wedding is advantageous for the girl: since this marriage is considered the only "real" one, it is deemed to last her lifetime, whatever may happen. Thus: —Any subsequent marriage will be considered less important and may therefore be easily dissolved by divorce, —In former times, the widow was automatically exempted from committing "suttee", since her "true" tree–husband was still alive.

Newars celebrate many festivals of religious, traditional or other inspirations. Thus, Indra Jatra, Gai Jatra, Machhendra Nath as well as some of the aspects of the *"living Goddess"* ceremonies, are of Newar origin. (See chapter dedicated to Festivals in Napal).

Another interesting peculiarity of the Newar tradition is the complex institution of *"guthis"* a sort of association of people having some common link between them. This is at the same time a sort of fund which is constituted in order to finance certain festivals, rites and other ceremonies, The "guthi" administers this fund by buying land or other property which, then, belongs to the guthi members.

One last word about the Newars: their costumes have several peculiarities too: the *"jyapu"* (peasant) women always wear black sarees with red border; it is said that these sarees are usually a little longer in front than in the back, to enable men to admire the tatooing with which women adorn their ankles. Jyapu men usually wear the cotton coat called a *"labeda"*, generally in beige or grey. Their pants are also made of cotton and are very large at the top and very narrow along the legs. Around the waist, they wear a long piece of cotton wrapped around, like a belt.

Jyapus never stick the *"kukhri"*, the crescent–shaped cutlass of the Nepali, into this cotton belt.

One book dealing with all questions related to Newar history, culture and traditions is Dr. GOPAL SINGH NEPALI'S : *"The Newars"*, published in Bombay in 1965.

—TIBETANS

We are referring here to those estimated 6,000 Tibetans who settled in Nepal after the taking over of Tibet by the Chinese and after the Dalai Lama's exile into India (where he still resides, at Dharamsala, in North–West India). Therefore they do not constitute a part of the historical Nepali nation, in the true sense of the word. Only a few have acquired Nepali citizenship so far.

They are very faithful to their traditions, languagae and costumes and are therefore easy to identify by the visiting tourist who will find Tibetan communities not only in Bodnath and Patan but also in Pokhara.

Tibetan men wear long hair, usually plaited and worn around the head, braided with red wool. Their costume is brown or dark–red; they wear the "chuba" a kind of long robe which leaves the right shoulder and arm bare. Sometimes they also wear their typical brocade caps trimmed with fur and their multi-coloured felt boots.

Tibetan women always wear long gowns widely folded in the back and, on top of it, striped aprons divided in three parts, where the stripes never coincide! This apron is held by a silver or gilded buckle. They wear the same hats and boots as men do.

Trekkers will meet many Tibetans, of course in the Solu-Khumbu area where the latter feel much "at home", not only because of the altitude and familiar landscape and climate, but also because the are ethnically related to the Sherpas. This is true also for other regions, such as Mustang, the Jomosom and Thakali areas, as well as around Malemchi and Tharkegyang. Refugee camps, first set up and sponsored by the Swiss Association for Technical Assistance (S.A.T.A.) are to be found in Jawalakhel, near Patan, and Bodnath, where there are flourishing carpet weaving enterprises and souvenir shops. Two other Tibetan former refugee camps, which in the meantime have developed into real, permanent villages with schools, temples etc., are located near POKHARA. The most important is situated between Pokhara-town proper and Hyangcha. Today, all these settlements are mana-ged by the Tibetans themselves.

Family Names

In the previous chapter the designation *"Brahmin" "Chetri"* or *"Kshatriya", "Newar"* etc. have appeared in various paragraphs.

It might be of interest to mention now, briefly, some of the patronymic or family names which are to be found most frequent-

ly in some of these groups. Of course, the following list is far
from exhaustive. It has been established on the basis of *D. B.*
BISTA'S book : *"People of Nepal".*

1. Non Newars
— Some Brahmin names:

Kumain Brahmin (from Western Nepal)	: Bhatta, Bista, Dotel, Joshi, Kadariya, Khatiwada, Lohini, Paitola, Pandey, Paneru, Pant, Regmi, Soti, Upreti.
Purbiya Brahmin (form Eastern (Nepal)	: Acharya, Adhikari, Aryal, Baral, Baskota, Bastola, Basyal, Bhandari, Bhatta, Bhattarai, Chamlagain, Chapagain, Dahal, Devkota, Dhungel, Ghimire, Gotame, Khanal, Lamichhane, Nepal, Paudel, Pokhrel, Regmi, Rijal, Rimal, Sharma, Subedi, Upadhya.

— Chhetri names :

Thakuri	: Bam, Chand, Kalyal, Khand, Malla, Pal, Pande, Shahi, Shah (the Royal Family), Singh.
Other Chhetris	: Basnet, Bista, Karki, Khadka, Rana (The Rana families) Rawal, Thapa.

2. Newars
— Some Brahmin names : Raj Upadhyaya, Bhatta, Jha, Juju, Bajrachayra, Shakya, Vajracarya.
— Some merchant names: Amatya, Joshi, Malla, Maskey, Pradhan, Raj Bhandari, Raj Lawat, Raj Vamsi, Singh, Shrestha, Tuladhar.
— Some typical "occupational names" : These are family names which have become synonymous with certain professions, and vice-versa :
Bare : goldsmiths and jewellers
Chhipas : house-painters and dyers
Chitrakar : artists (mainly painters)
Dakarmi : masons and bricklayers
Jyapu : farmers
Kami : blacksmiths
Kulu : drum makers
Kumala : potters
Mali : gardeners

> Manandhar : oilpressers
> Napit : barbers
> Sikarmi : carpenters
> Suchikar : tailors
> Tamrakar : copper and bronze workers and... hundred of others.

3. Sherpas

Among the Sherpas there is another tradition : the boy is given the name of the day of the week of his birth as first name :

> Thus, *Nyima* on a *Sunday*
> *Dawa* on a *Monday*
> *Mingma* on a *Tuesday*
> *Lakpa* on a *Wednesday*
> *Phurbu* on a *Thursday*
> *Pasang* on a *Friday*
> and *Pemba* on a *Saturday*.

It goes without saying that this rule is not strictly adhered to. Besides, there are many other typically Sherpa and Tibetan names which do not indicate anything about the day of their birth.

Most Sherpas and Tibetans are given two names, the first one being usually one of the names of the lama whom the parents have consulted for selecting an auspicious name to be given to the child, and the second name being such a luck-bringing name.

Among the latter, which are common to both sexes, the following are the most frequent ones : Lobsang ("good mind"). Sangye ("Buddha"), Sonam ("the lucky one"), Tashi ("good women"), Tsering ("long life")

Typical boys given names are: Ang, Aula, Chak, Gyaltsen, Jigme, Khalden, Kami, Kunzang, Ngawang, Norkay, Tendsing, Tsewang, Urgyen etc.

Typical girls names are : Choden, Chodron, Deki, Dolkar, Dolma or Doma, Dronma, Kandro, Padma or Pema, Palmo. Rinchen or Rindzin, Tara, Wangmo etc.

LANGUAGES

The official language of the country is called "nepali" (or "parbatiya" as the Newars called the language of "the hill people"). This language, "parbatiya" or "nepali" is closely related to "hindi", the language of Northern India. Both have their roots in sanskrit, and both use the same script, called "devanagari".

"Nepali is currently spoken by approx. 55% of the population of Nepal, this being due to the many ethnic and linguistic groups spread all over the country, Only nepali is taught in all primary schools, English is part of the curriculum of secondary education.

Out of the 45% non-Nepali speaking people, half of them use one of the many dialects related to sanskrit of the Terai. "Newari" (a language connected with Tibetan) is spoken by approx. 4% of the population, and 1% use other Tibetan languages and dialects.

RELIGIONS

NEPAL is the only country in the whole world where state religion is Hinduism. The King is venerated as an incarnation of Lord Vishnu, also called Narayan, the god preserver of life and the world.

However, although the country has a state religion, a perfect spirit of absolute liberalism has always prevailed between followers of Hinduism and those of other creeds, particularly Buddhism, who, according to the latest statistics count for about 10 to 15%, whereas Hindus number approx. 90% and Muslims 1 to 2%. The followers of both the two main creeds have intermingled to the extent of influencing each other not only in the past but also still today. It is a well-known fact that Hindus and Buddhists, in Nepal, often worship the same deities, sometimes under different names, and celebrate the same festivals even though these may have a different meaning to the ones and the others.

Nepal may be justly proud of the fact that, in the course of its long history, there has never occurred even the slightest conflict, and certainly not a war, caused by religious considerations or motivations.

It may not be devoid of interest to recall briefly the basic principles on which the two religions, Hinduism and Buddhism, are founded, as well as to dedicate a short paragraph to Tantrism, which has had a strong influence in Nepal.

—**HINDUISM** appeared first between the 4th and the 1st millenium before Jesus Christ, when the Aryan immigrants from Anatolia and Persia who settled in the Indus and the Ganges plains of the Indian sub-continent brought with them the precepts and sacred books of the *"Vedas"*. In this northern part they met with the indigenous population that had remained mostly attached to primitive animist beliefs and rites.

Hinduism is something else and is more than a mere religion. Indeed, it is an ethical concept of thought, of action and of life at the same time as a rigid social structure based on the caste system, created and directed by those who had placed themselves on the highest level of the hierarchy, namely the priests, the *"Brahmins"*.

This is not the place either for an exhaustive or even a superficial analysis of Hinduism as a social system, a religion and a philosophy. Let us simply enumerate its basic principles. They are:

—*"dharma"*, meaning both the religious law i.e. the forces which maintain the world in harmony with the eternal laws and the moral law, which all human beings should abide by in order to stay on the right path.

—*"karma"*, which is the law of cause and effect, establishing the inescapable re-action to each action, cause which produces an effect which, in turn becomes a cause for some other effect etc. This process is symbolized by the wheel which turns endlessly and always comes back to its starting point.

—*"samsara"* which is one of the many illustrations of the preceding law of karma, namely the cycle of transmigrations and reincarnations.

—*"moksha"* finally, i. e. the possibility of escaping the cycle of re-birth by allowing the individual ego (or may it be called soul ?) to unite itself with the universal timelessness, opening the door to eternal and supreme serenity.

The road to moksha is followed when strictly observing all codes of laws of conduct, religious rites, from the daily ablutions and the precepts concerning food and drinks, including the fasts, prayers, offerings, sacrifices, active participation in festivals and pilgrimages, to strict obedience of the caste rules and finally, penance, retreats, ascetic exercises, etc.

Seen from outside, Hinduism presents itself as the pantheon of countless deities of strange aspects, to which we shall come back in the chapter dedicated to Art and Handicraft.

—BUDDHISM was, at the beginning, also much closer to an ethic and a philosophy than to a religion. Its doctrine or basic principles have been formulated and spread through teaching, first by GAUTAMA SIDDHARTHA himself, later by his disciples. GAUTAMA SIDDHARTHA, also called SAKYAMUNI, was born in a territory belonging nowadays to Nepal. It is called Lumbini or Rummindei. His birth took place around the year 560 B. C. He spent most of his life in northern India. The various episodes of Buddhas life are well known.

From more than one point of view, Buddhism appears to be

homogeneous to Hinduism for Buddhism has inherited and kept the principles of "moksha" which is often referred to as *"nirvana"* (or *"nibbana"*.)

The basic elements of Buddhist doctrine are contained in the "four noble truths", which are the following:

— the truth of suffering : In man's life everything is suffering, *("Existence is* his birth, the separation from the *unhappiness")* beloved ones, the effort which has to be made to respond to all human needs, getting old, getting sick and, finally, death.

— the truth of the origin of suffering : The origin lies in needs and *(Unhappiness is caused* man's desires, being attached to mate- *by selfish craving")* rial values, the main illusions of the senses and all passions.

— the truth of the end of sufferings : It lies in the renunciation of *("Selfish craving can* any form of need and desire; at once, *be destroyed")* suffering will vanish.

— the truth of the road leading to this renunciation : It is the *("It can be destroyed* road of the eight principles of ethical *by following* conduct which are : *the eightfold path")*

    1. – Right understanding, or right views
    2. – Right purpose or aspiration of intention
    3. – Right speech
    4. – Right conduct or action
    5. – Right vocation or livelihood
    6. – Right effort
    7. – Right alertness or mindfulness
    8. – Right concentration

This eightfold path is often expressed in the following simpler formula :

    "Avoid evil" and "keep good morals"
    "Do good actions" and "mental concentration
    "Keep your heart pure". and "wisdom"

Buddhism's "moral" rules are very close to the Christian one's. They have been formulated in the following "ten pro- ibitions":

    — Don't take life
    — Don't steal
    — Avoid unchastity

— Dont' lie
— Don't slander
— Don't insult
— Don't chatter
— Don't covet
— Don't give way to anger
— Don't let doubt command your mind.

Here we may recall in short the historical development of the Buddhist doctrine : After Gautama's death (around 480 B. C.), Buddhist principles of conduct were spread by his first disciples in particular by ANANDA and promoted strongly by the powerful ASHOKA, the Emperor of India who lived in the 3rd century B.C.

But towards the first century A.D., tendencies to transform Buddhist philosophy and ethical doctrines into a religion, appeared at various places and in various communities of Gautama's devotees. This was to make Buddhism more "competitive"- to use a modern expression– with the then prevailing other beliefs and creeds. For this, it became necessary to introduce also, into Buddhism, such external manifestations as rites, beliefs in supranatural powers, images, shrines, statues etc......

—An important schism occurred in the 3rd century A.D., which gave birth to the two great Buddhist schools of thought or churches, as one could almost say, the MAHAYANA, or Great Vehicle and the HINAYANA or Small Vehicle. The latter should be called THERAVADA, to avoid the prejudicial term of "small".

Whereas the first, the MAHAYANA developed mainly in the Indo-Chinese peninsula from where it spread to China, Korea and ultimately Japan, the second, HINAYANA flourished in Sri Lanka (Ceylon), Burma and Thailand.

A definition of these two schools is formulated in the following way by Mrs. M.M. THIOLLIER in her *"Dictionary of Religions"*

"MAHAYANA has no uniform doctrine, but the common denominator is the dominant cult to certain, if not all Bodhisatvas, those saints who desist from entering nirvana in order to assist other human beings atteigning enlightenment too. It has brought about many rites, adapted to the regional or local preferences and populations, stressing sometimes the popular aspect, sometimes the metaphysical one. It promoted the foundation of a large number of monasteries."

HINAYANA is essentially based on the *"formula of the three jewels"* i.e. BUDDHA as the teacher whose precepts have to be adhered to, DHARMA, the law, rules and rites, and SANGHA, the community, Its credo is formulated in the following sentence : *"I place my fullest trust in Buddha and his law and I join the Sangha as one takes shelter in the midst of a storm."*

BUDDHISM, as it appears in NEPAL belongs to a third "school" which has often been called the third vehicle, VAJRAYANA, or LAMAISM, i.e. a school strongly influenced by Tantrism. This school still exists to-day in BHUTAN, LADAKH, MONGOLIA and SIKKIM. Its roots are to be found in India from where it spread and developed primarily in Tibet.

TANTRISM

It is difficult to give a concrete and short definition of Tantrism. First, it may be stressed that *"Tantrism"* is *not* a religion as such. It is better described as a form of looking at and practising a religion. It has its source in Hinduism as well as in Buddhism.

Philip S. RAWSON, in his book on Tantra, gives even a broader definition ; *"Tantra is a special manifestation of Indian feeling, art and religion"* and he adds : (In Tantra), *"there are so many variations of practice and belief...with one thread on which all manifestations of Tantra can be strung on, namely, the idea that Tantra is a cult of ecstasy, focused on a vision of cosmic sexuality"*.

Seen from still another angle, Tantrism is based., essentially, on a certain number of works which were written around the 6th century A.D. such as the *RUDRAMALAYA, KALIKA, MAHA-NIRVANA,* etc. These books deal with such topics as the:
- creation of the universe
- destruction of the universe
- worship of the Gods
- means to attain supra-human powers
- the four ways to "unite oneself" with the Supreme Spirit

In practice, the most striking characteristics of Tantrism are the importance attached to symbolism, occultism, magic, image-worshipping, yoga, etc. in one word, to "rules of action" in opposition perhaps to rules of thought, since Tantric doctrine proclaims that "outside action, there can be no salvation". This action principally takes the shape of extremely complex and esoteric rites which progressively developed in what is now called lamaism, where greatest importance is attached to.

—certain designs, such as *"mandalas"*, *"yantras"* considered as symbolic representations of the universe and at the same time used as instruments of concentration and meditation.

—magic formulas, called among other names "mantras", addressed to the countless benevolent deities or malevolent demons and repeated thousands of times, where the sound of these mantras or spells more than their actual meaning, create their magic power.

—tools such as prayer–wheels, prayer–flags, incense–burners, sounds produced by strange musical instuments, *"dorje"* or *"vajra"* (i.e. the thunderbolt); bells, magic daggers, etc.

—ritual gestures, such as "mudras" which are prescribed movements of the hands.

Tantrism, when it spread from India to Tibet, Nepal and other neighbouring countries, made another striking innovation, i.e. the importance which was attributed to the *"shakti"* which is often, but wrongly, called the "spouse" of a given God, whereas it simply symbolizes the divine *energy,* (mostly referred to as 'wisdom') which is always represented in a *feminine* form. To emphasize the fact that the God and its (own) energy or power, are indissolubly linked together, they are often represented, in Tantra art, in an intimate embrace.

Now to come back to the religious customs in Nepal, even in a very short visit to the "Valley of the Gods", it becomes apparent that religious actions, such as offerings, prayers, songs, sacrifices, are intertwined with daily life of the common man and woman. Every morning, at dawn, men, women and children gather at temples, sanctuaries and river banks, to perform rites, take their ablutions, offer their first "puja" to their tutelary gods, whether they are Hindus or Buddhists. These daily "pujas" consist essentially in spreading over the statues and images of the deities, rice grains, flower–petals, coins, sweets, incense, fruits, etc. which the devotees carry on special plates mostly made of brass or copper.

A very rich bibliography exists, of course, on the subject of religion and rites. Among the best books, we may strongly recommend :

David Snellgrove : *"Buddhist Himalaya"*–Oxford 1957

L. A. Waddell : *"Buddhist Lamaism",* reprinted at W. Heffer & Sons, London, in 1975.

CALENDAR

The calendar question is somewhat complex :

In addition to the so-called western (better said Christian-Gregorian) calendar, which is accepted in Nepal, albeit unofficially. three traditional time computation eras are in use :

1) First and most important, the official *"Vikram Sambat"* era which is mandatory in all public administrations as well as in daily life, newspapers etc... *"Year One"* of this era coincides with 57 B.C. (to be precise, the era started on 23rd Febr. that year) Thus, our year 1980 corresponds to Vikram Sambat years part of 2036 and part of 2037, since the Vikram New Year does not start on 1st of January but in mid-April, between the 13rd and the 16th.

The origin of this era is not very clearly established.

Since this calendar is–still today–in use in North India too it is generally believed that its initiator was a legendary king who ruled there as well as in Nepal.   His full name was Vikramaditya.

During his reign, he defeated and chased away the former rulers called the *"Saka* – clan" who are said to have come from Turkey, Southern Russia and Persia and invaded India, establishing themselves in the region called Mala, which include greater part of the Punjab and present north-eastern part of Pakistan. When they took over, these Saka rulers established their own era to commemorate their victory. "Year One" was in or around 66 B. C.

Nine years later, Vikramaditya not only liberated his country but thanks to the blessings and the assistance of elephant god Ganesh, was able to pay off the debts of all his subjects. This was indeed, an excellent reason to turn the page and start a new era in 57 B. C.

2) 135 years later, the grand–grand son of the founder (Amsuvarma) of the new Licchavi dynasty, a certain Raja Nanda Deva wanted to introduce a new era in honour of his dynasty. This era is called *"Saka Salivahana Sambat"*. It remained in force for a great number of years and is still referred to in the astrological calendars which are worked. out and published every year in Nepal. *"Year One"* of this "new Saka–or "Sakya-era" coincides with 77–78 A.D.

3) The third calendar in use in called *"Nepal Sambat"*. Its "Year One" coincides with Christian era year 879–880 A. D.

The origin of this year is based on a legend very similar to the one which Vikramaditya is connected with :

According to the legend, one night a Newar Jyapu (farmer)

dreamed that the sand on a certain river–bank in Bhadgaon had through magic been turned into pure gold. He awoke, and, at once ordered his servants to fill as many baskets as they could with the precious "sand" and bring their loads back to his house. This was done. So he decided to settle the debts of all the people in the Valley, as Vikramaditya had done before.

Nowadays, this calendar, which makes 1780 become Nepal Sambat Year 1100, is exclusively used by the Newar community, who celebrate its New Year on the 4th day after the new moon of Kartik (mid–October–mid–November.)

In spite of these various eras, the official Nepalese year, like the western one, counts 365 days, but the internal division are somewhat different : the twelve Nepalese months vary from 29 to 32 days and they do not alternate in the same way as the ones of the Gregorian calendar. There is no simple formula to make the two coincide. It is an exercise in higher mathematics which at the same time, necessitates a good knowledge of astronomy. For who knows, by heart, the exact course of the moon around the earth ?

In addition to the ordinary calendar, a team of astrologers calculates and publishes every year an "almanac" which contains, among a great deal of other information, the auspicious and un auspicious days, weeks and months, the precise hours for the beginning of certain festivals etc.

As far as the tourist is concerned it may be sufficient, but necessary to list below the twelve Vikram calendar–months with their corresponding western calendar equivalents. This table concerns the Nepalese year 2037, i.e. 1980–1981.

Nepalese month		Corresponding to the period	
		from	to
Baisakh	(30 days)	13 April 80	12 May 80
Jesth	(32 ")	13 May	13 June
Ashad	(32 ")	14 June	15 July
Shrawan	(32 ")	16 July	16 August
Bhadra	(31 ")	17 August	16 September
Ashwin	(30 ")	17 September	16 October
Kartik	(30 ")	17 October	15 November
Mangsir	(27 ")	16 November	14 December
Poush	(30 ")	15 December	13 January 81
Magh	(29 ")	14 January	11 February
Phalgun	(30 ")	12 February	13 March

Chaitra   (30   ''   14 March   12 April

The names of the days of the week, curiously enough, are very close to the Greek-Latin ones :

Sunday	: Adityabar (or Ravibar) meaning: Day of the Sun
Monday	: Sombar : Day of the moon
Tuesday	: Mangalbar : Day of Mars
Wednesday	: Budhabar : Day of Mercury
Thrusday	: Brihaspatibar, Bihibar or Gurubar: Day of Jupiter or the "Teacher"
Friday	: Shukrabar : Day of Venus
Saturday	: Shanisharbar or Shanibar : Day of Saturn.

NOTE :

Of course, the Tibetan, and Sherpa communities residing in Nepal maintain and follow their own calendar, which does not begin with any given "Year One" of any "era", but which is simply constituted of cycles of 60 years that result from the succession of the five elements (wood, fire, earth, iron and water) combined with the 12 animals of the months, i. e. mouse, ox, tiger, hare, dragon, snake, horse, sheep, monkey, bird, dog and boar, which follow each other in the above indicated order.

This calendar, which may be of Chinese orgin, is supposed to have been introduced into Tibet by Princess Wench'eng, one of the two wives of king Song Tsan Gampo, in 642 A. D. However, the first of these 60–year cycles is said not to have started before the year 1026.

MEASURES AND WEIGHTS

The decimal system is in use in Nepal. But there are some exceptions, due to traditions and customs:

DECIMAL UNITS :

Two decimal units, unknown in Western countries, are currently used in Nepal, as in India. They are :

(a) the quantity or number 1,00,000 (one hundred thousand) which is called "one lakh". Thus the population of Kathmandu, which includes two hundred and fifty thousand inhabitants, will be counted as "two and a half lakhs" a number which will be written 2,50,000.

(b) the quantity or number 10,000,000 (ten million,) which is called 'one crore". Thus, the population of Nepal which include thirteen million inhabitants will be counted as "One crore and thirty lakhs," a number which will be written : 1,30,00,000

MONEY :

On rupee contains one hundred "paisa". However half a rupee is currently called "one mohar"and a quarter rupee, "one suka".

DISTANCES :

Kilometers have officially replaced miles, in particular on the 'mile–stone' along highways and roads.

WEIGHTS AND VOLUMES :

The official units are litres and kilograms. (One pound being roughly equal to half a kilogram, i.e.500 gr.). However, for certain items and wares, the traditional weights are still very currently used. The most frequent are :

For cereals. rice, sugar, milk etc. :

  1 *"Mana"* is approx. half a liter
  8 *"Manas"*=1 *Paathi"*, i. e. approx. 4 $1/2$ litres
 20 *"Paathis"*=1 *"Muri"*, i.e. approx. 91 litres

For fruits and vegetables :

  1 *"Pau"* equals approx. half a pound
  4 *"Paus"*=1 *"Ser"*, i.e. approx. 4/5 of a kilogram
  3 *"Sers"*=1 *"Dharni"*=i. e. approx. 2.5 kilograms.

A *"handful"* of certain vegetables is simply called "one Mutthaa".

LENGTHS :

For measuring length of material, the most common units are meters and yards, centimeters and inches.

The altitude of mountains are alos indiscriminately expressed cuments.

Let us remind briefly the most common equivalences :

1 metre—1.0936 yards–Thus : 1 yard—0.9144 metre
1 centimetre—0.3937 inches – Thus : 1 inch—2.54 centimetres
1 metre—3.2808 feet – Thus 1 foot—0.3048 metre.

WEIGHTS FOR PRECIOUS METALS AND STONES :

In this respect, only two traditional measures are in use :

Precious metals are weighed in *"tolas"*, where one tola is equivalent to approx. 11.5 grams.

Precious stones are weighed in *"carats"*, where one carat is equivalent to approx. 0.2 grams.

MAIN FESTIVALS

Nepal is rightly renowned for its numerous and always colourful festivals. There are certainly over 50 of them in a year and, although this book does not have the ambition to be a treatise of all religious and secular festivities, it may nevertheless interest the visitor to know something more about the ones he may witness while staying in the Valley.

The complexity of most of the festivals originates from the fact that they have, without scarcely any exception, four different roots and motivations, namely :

—*religious*:   the festival is dedicated to a specific deity

—*historical*:   it has been instituted by a certain King for a given reason or on the occasion of a given event

—*legendary*:   its origin is deeply rooted in one or several old, popular legends, beliefs or sometimes superstitions, the explanation of which may not always be easy to determine.

—*seasonal*:   in the eyes of the farmers, its objectives is to warrant a propitious monsoon, a rich harvest, etc.

On top of all this, it must also be rememberd that, as Nepalis are essentialy a liberal–minded people, festivals of Hindu origin may have changed under Buddhist influence, or vice–versa ! Thus, it is sometimes difficult to find out whether a given festival is essentially Hindu or Buddhist ! Any festival may be celebrated by followers of both creeds.

One more factor : Since most Nepalese festivals are linked not only with the lunar calendar but also with calculations by specialized astrologers, it is often difficult to ascertain the exact "western" date on which a festival will take place, Therefore, a booklet, issued every year by the Department of Tourism is very useful in this respect, as it gives the equivalent dates for the most important festivals.

Last but not least: Certain festivals take place in a given locality only, others are celebrated in the whole Valley, while some are of a national character and therefore held throughout the whole country.

Various books have been written on the subject of Nepalese festivals. The most comprehensive one is by Mary M. ANDERSON: *"The Festivals of Nepal"* in which some of the information and explanations given below were found.

To make things easier, the chronological order has been adopted.

APRIL–MAY
BISKET   To celebrate the beginning of the New Year

DATE: May–April
PLACE: All over the Valley, in particular at Bhadgaon
LEGEND: Once upon a time, there was a king of Bhadgaon
who had a somewhat....insatiable daughter. Every night
a different young man had to spend the night with her,
but, invariably, on the following morning, her lover was
found dead. Now it so happened that a young prince arrived
from a faraway country who said he was ready to accept the
challenge. He forced himself to keep awake. Towards midnight,
he noticed two thin threads moving out of the princess's nostrils.
These two "threads" swelled rapidly and became dangerous
snakes. With one stroke of his sword, the valiant prince killed
them both. The following morning, the princess' servants were
very surprised to find both the girl and the young man in eager
conversation and apparently satisfied with their respective
achievements.

Of course, the story ends by their being married. To
commemorate this "happy end", the King ordered the construction of a beautiful chariot topped by a huge pole. At the
highest tip of this mast, two long pieces of cloth had to be
attached : they were to symbolize the remains of the two slain
snakes. On New Year's day, the chariot is drawn through the
streets of the city, carrying also the image of goddess Bhadra
Kali, the spouse of Kala Bhairav, the tutelary patron of
Kathmandu Valley.

WHAT HAPPENS: 4 days before the New Year, the image of
goddess Bhadra Kali is taken out of its temple located in the old
part of Bhadgaon city. It is a small statuette, hardly 8 inches high.
Temple servants carry it to the Bhairav temple, the huge
building erected on the right side of the five-tiered Nyatapola
pagoda on the main square. Here, two chariots are ready to carry
Bhadra on the main square. The end-piece of the chariot's pole is
shaped as a serpent's head to commemorate the origin of
this festival.

Now the crowd grabs the thick rope sand drags the two chariots
in opposite directions. The team that succeeds in moving
his chariot first has won. It is therefore considered that the year
will be auspicious if placed under the protection of its particular
god (Bhadra Kali or Bhairav) to which the winning chariot was
dedicated and the image of which it was carrying.

The image will be worshiped, offerings will be made throughout the night. It will also be presented to all deities who, according to the general belief are always gathering in Bhadgaon on New Year's Eve. For that purpose, the procession proceeds from one one temple to the next. Usually this takes 48 hours.

Two days before New Year: In every home a real or a symbolic sacrifice of a goat is performed. Its blood is offered to the divinity. The sacrifice rite is accompanied by free distribution of "chang"– the popular local beer made of fermented rice or millet. Meals are served in large dried leaves sewn together with the ribs of other leaves.

On New Year's Eve : the chariots are dragged to a square located on the lower part of Bhadgaon.

In the morning, a huge pole, about 60 feet (18-20 m.) high lies on the ground, its thick end resting in a sort of hole which is walled with concrete and stones. People will erect this pole by pulling on two or three very thick ropes tied to it. The ropes are made of creeper fibre. Sometimes the ropes break, the pole falls down on the onlookers, killing or injuring some. This is considerd a very bad omen for the coming year. But most of the time, after much pulling and shouting, erecting the pole succeeds. At the top of it two *"snake--skins"* can be seen hanging. The crowd will manifest its joy very loudly. Some people sprinkle blood on the pole and decorate it with flowers, leaves and fruits.

Young men climb on to the top of the pole to take away some of the twigs, ribbons or flowers which are attached to it, They will keep these trophies throughout the year as luck-bringing tokens.

In the afternoon on New Year's day, there is again a new demonstration of skill : the pole has to be pulled down. The teams tear and pull from opposite sides and, again there will be a winning team. The moment the pole crashes on the ground is considered to mark really the beginning of the New Year.

BALKUMARI JATRA : To ensure the whole year through the protection of Goddess Balkumari, another of Bhairav's spouses or consorts.

DATE: On New Year's day, i.e. the first day of the month of Baisakh (mid–April   to mid-May and the day after.

PLACE: At Thimi the potters village located between Kathmandu air-port and Bhadgaon.

WHAT HAPPENS:A long procession of men carrying torches. Should these get extinguished, it would be considered as a bad omen.

During the night, the devotees remain lying on their backs, in front of the temple. On their chest, forehead and legs, they will have placed a series of small burning oil lamps. On the following day processions take place through the village and its immediate surroundings. Groups of 32 men carry, each a different portable sanctuary protected by a large hand–painted umbrella. While this procession is gonig on, the participants throw handfulls of yellow ochre powder on each other's faces and clothes. This is considered as an homage paid to the divinity and a good omen for a prosperous year.

The procession reaches its climax when it stops in front of the temple dedicated to the elephant–headed god Gansh, the son of Shiva and Parvati, who is able to decide whether any human enterprise should be successful or not. This power applies even to the fulfilment of prayers and offerings made to other gods !

At Pashupatinath, as well as in front of the Mahalakshmi temple, at Thimi, a devotee volunteers to spend the whole day with an iron spike thrust through his tongue. This penance will bring him many merits in particular if this spike, when pulled out, leaves the tongue non bleeding.

ASTAMI (also called Sano Dasain, which means Small Dasain.) This festival is performed to ensure an auspicious summer and autumn.

DATE: On the eighth day of the clear fortnight (*), of Baisak. (mid–April to mid–May)

PLACE: At many places of Kathmandu, in particular at Naxal, near the Police Headquarters.

WHAT HAPPENS: He–goats are sacrificed to various gods and goddesses with the request that the rains should start and in good time to bring about aboundant

(*) The "clear" fortnight is the time that elapses between new moon and full moon whereas the "dark" fortnight is the one spanning the full moon to the new one.

crops of rice and other cereals.

BHOTO MATSYENDRANATH (also called "Rato Mastsyendranath", meaning "Red Matsyendranath",
for there is another festival, later in the year,
called "White Matsyendranath").This festival
is especially held to ensure the beginning of the
monsoon at the most favourable time.

DATE: The whole dark fortnight of the month of Baisak
PLACE: Principally in and around PATAN
LEGEND: There are two legends to be told in relation to
the origins of this feasting :

1) The first one is to explain where the wold "matsya" (which
means "fish", in Sanskrit, Hindi and Nepali) comes into the picture : Once upon a time, Shiva decided to call upon AVALOKI-
TESHVARA, the spiritual son of Lord Buddha and to take him as
his "guru" (teacher, master).

PARVATI, Shiva's spouse asked him after each lesson, to
repeat it for her, which Shiva did with greatest zeal. But one evening, when they had been dallying near the sea–shore, Parvati
fell asleep while Shiva was still talking. The guru, who was present,
took, as a fancy, the shape of a fish and played the part of the one
who listens attentively. Imitating Parvati's sweet voice, he gave
answers and made appropriate remarks from time to time to
Shiva. When the latter realized that his wife was deeply slumbering,
he turned very angry and was about to slay the fish. Then, the
latter revealed himself as being Lokeshvar (another name of
Avalokiteshvara). Since then, this God received the nickname
of Matsyendranath.

The literal translation of this name is now "LORD (nath)
INDRA (king of gods) OF THE FISH (Mastsya). How INDRA became
to be considered as Lokeshwar remains somewhat mysterious.

2) The second legend explains why Matsyendranath had
become the divine provider of rain, hence, the protector of harvest.

The story goes back to a Nepalese king called NARENDRA
DEVA, who reigned during the 11th century A. D. At that time,
there was a wise man, a well-respected mystic called GORAKNATH,
who in reality, was an incarnation of Vishnu. He had succeeded
in keeping, as prisoners, the nine "nagas" (God–serpents) responsible for releasing the monsoon rains. Gorakhanath simply
sat down on the basket containing the nagas and did not budge.
Thus, the Valley remained dry and the crops were seriously

thereatend.   King Narendra Deva went to India and brought back the holy image of "Mastsyendranath', deliberately parading it in front of Goraknath who had to get up from his basket in order to prostrate himself before the image of the God. By this ruse, the nine snakes succeeded in escaping from their prison and in starting the rains all over the Valley.

There is a third legend, which will be dealt with under the "Naga Panchami" festival ("The Karkotak legend")

WHAT HAPPENS : A great many things: for this festival is one of the most spectacular and lasts two months in all ! There are three main stages :

a) the "bathing ceremony" of Matsyendranath's image; it takes place on the first day of the dark fortnight. A statue is carried in procession from TAHA BAHAL (also called Patan's Matsyendranath temple, a few hundred yards from the Durbar Square), up to the foot of the sacred tree standing in LAGANKHEL, where it is cleaned, washed and anointed. The same evening, the statue is carried back the same way.

b) the chariot procession through the streets of PATAN. This processon lasts from the 2nd to the 7th day of the clear fortnight of Baisakh and follows five different itineraries, starting from Pulchowk, not far from the western Ashoka stupa at the entrance of Patan. The statue of Matsyendranath, all dressed in red and white, coverd with a multitude of different ornaments, rides high on the chariot, visible to all.   This part of the festival takes place only in Patan.

3) The offering and homage rites. They last three days beginning after the chariot has gone back to Jawalakhel, near the Patan zoo. There finally it will be dismantled and hept until the following year.

NOTE : Every twelve years, the chariot is not erected in Pulchowk, as usual, but in Bungamati itslf, the place where the main temple dedicated to Matsyendranath was built, centuries ago. It will then have to be dragged a very long way before reaching Jawalakhel and its route includes a bridgeless stream which has to be forded. There next time, this is due in 1991.

RATO MATSYENDRANATH is undoubtedly one of the more complex festivals; thus, it is not surprising that a scholar, John K. Locke S. J. spent several years in research on this ceremony; he succeeded in retracing fully and explaining every deatail of the various stages of the festival, the people who take part in

it the minute description of the chariot itself, the places where it is
dragged by the devotees and all the rites which accompany its
display. The book Rev. John K. Locke wrote : *"Rato Matsyendranath of Patan and Bungamati"* has no less than 112 pages, all
about this one festival! On the whole cult of Avalokiteshvara–
Matsyendranath, the same author published in 1980, at Sahayogi Press, another book (of 500 pages) called: "KARUNAMAYA".

For a clear understanding of the aspects of Rato Mastsyendranath, these books are highly recommended.

BUDDHA JAYANTI: To celebrate Lord Buddha's birthday
(560 B. C.)

DATE : On full moon day in May

PLACE : Of course at Lumbini, Buddhas birthplace as well as
at all Buddhist sancturies and temples of the Valley, in
particular on Swayambhu hill,

WHAT HAPPENS : All stupas, "gompas" (monasteries) and other
sanctuaries are repainted and richly decorated. Thousands of
oil lamps illuminate Swayambhu Stupa. During the night
and early morning, thousands of pilgrims proceed to these
sanctuaries to make offerings and recite prayers. Some of
these pilgrims circumambulate around the stupas by first
prostrating themselves, then stretching out, lying full length
on the ground, finally straightening up again until they have
in this way completed the crircle several times.

The courtyard of Swayambhu is also decorated not only with
flags and flowers, but with a rare collection of old *"thang-kas"*
(painted scrolls) displayed along the walls. This is the only day
of the year when they are shown to the public. Of course, they are
not for sale !

Towards noon, a religious ceremony takes place at which foreign visitors and residents are most welcome. The lamas of the
Swayambhu *"Nyingma-pa"* gompa (the monastery)of the unre-
formed Lamaist, or *"red-hat"* order) wear their gorgeous silk
robes and perform their rituals around the main stupa. These
rituals are accompanied by music and "hand-dances" (*"mudras"*)
while the lamas hold the *"dorje"* (or *"vajra"* =thunderbolt)
in their right and the bell (*"dril-bu"*) in their left hand.

Similar ceremonies, but less colourful ones take place simultaneously in Bodnath.

MANI--RIMDU : The typical Sherpa religious festival which
takes place exclusively in Lamaist monasteries in the

Mount Everest region.

DATE : In the month of May, mostly on Full moon day, but it may vary if the Heard-Lama of the monastery so decides.

PLACE : At Thame monastery, in the Khumbu region, a few hours walk from Namche Bazar, at an altitude of 13,123 feet. (4,000 m.).

WHAT HAPPENS : All the lamas of the monastery take part in this very elaborate and complex "masked–dance drama" which lasts three full days, the first been dedicated to a general rehearsal. The monks dress up in very colourful costumes and wear masks representing either historical or legendary figures, or else deities and sprities.

The origins of these dances are very remote and probably have to be found in the "*red-tiger devil's dances*" a rite followed in pre–Buddhist "*Bon*" religion.

Nowadays, the main reasons for the faithful to attend the Mani–Rimdu festival, gathering at Thame from all the surrounding village and hamlets, are, on the one hand, to gain merits and on the other hand to ensure long life by taking the "long–life pills", called in Tibetan "*rhil-bu*",

It should be remembered that this Mani–Rimdu, which ought really to be called mani-rhilbu, is a typically Sherpa celebration, unknown in other Lamaist region.

A similar festival, also called Mani Rimdu takes place in the month of November at the Thyangboche monastery, one day walk from Namche Bazar.

MAY JUNE

SITHINAKHA : To commemorate the birthday of Kumar, the "divine warrior" For the farmers : the beginning of the rainy season.

DATE : The sixth day of the clear fortnight of the month of Jeysth (May–June)

PLACE : In all cities and villages of the Valley.

LEGEND : The demons having imposed on themselves very severe penances, succeeded one day in defeating the gods. after a series of heavy battles. The king of demons placed himself on the throne of INDRA, the "king of gods".

The gods met in a secret session to try to find a way out of the predicament in which they found themselves. VISHNU expressed his conviction that without the assistance of a son of Shiva, they could not win back their former posi-

tions of power. AGNI, the God of Fire was sent to the
abode of Lord Shiva on top of Mount Kailash. This
mountain, the most sacred one for Buddhists as well as
for Hindus, is situated in Tibet. A drop of Shiva's semen
fell in the Ganges. From this contact, Kumar, the Lord–
warrior was to be born. He saved the Gods and all was
well again. (Under the name of KARTIKEYA, Kumar is
worshipped as the brother of Ganesh, who is also a son
of Shiva.)

WHAT HAPPENS: In town, i. e. on squares and in the streets, images of Ganesh and Kumar-Kartikeya are everywhere on
display. Young boys roam around waving paper–wheels
and throwing pebbles at each other.

On the threshold of the houses, Kumar is symbolized by a red
circle drawn with chalk or powder. Inside the houses (each
Nepali house contains a special "puja–room", for offerings and
religious rituals), a red circle, usually decorated with a six-petalled
lotus–flower, reminds the members of the household that Kumar
is supposed to have six "powers" or "faces, namely:

— to throw light on the world
— to eliminate ignorance
— to fulfil devotees prayers
— to protect the fires of the sacrifies
— to reveal supreme knowledge
— to destroy demons and evil spirits.

Offerings, in the shape of flowers, sweets, eatable cereals, seeds,
etc. are placed inside the circle for Kumar to take away.

In the villages, the Kumar festival has a prosaic aspect:
it announces or starts the rainy season. Corn is planted in the
fields and paddy seeds are sown in wooden boxes, to be transplan-
ted in the fields later. A curious small detail : all farmers, on
Kumar–day, clean their musical instruments and put them away
in cupboards; this means that the idle winter months, when they
could indulge in music-playing, are over. The instruments are
put in Shiva's safekeeping until next autumn.

Before the rains come, a curious tradition has to be observed:
On Sithinakha day, the wells have to be cleaned in order to
"purify" the water. This is followed by a few scraps of mica being
thrown into the well. (Mica is found everywhere in the Valley.)

On the seventh day of the "growing moon" a procession takes
place in the old part of Kathmandu. It starts at the Jaisidewal

temple near Hanuman Dhoka. A chariot carries the image of
Kumar seated on a peacock, a symbol of royality and warrior
virtues. The procession is accompanied by musicians playing
cymbals and drums. The god's image is "protected" by an umbrella which, in the whole of Asia is always regarded as a royal
if not divine symbol. It is even believed, though it is difficult
to prove, that the typical Nepalese temple style with their three
four or even five superimposed roofs, represent the "royal umbrella" and bear the same significance.

JULY–AUGUST

GHANTAKARNA: The festival directed against evil spirits
    Also the end of paddy transplanting.

DATE : On the 14th day of the month of Srawan (July–August)
PLACE : In PATAN and all other Newar towns and villages.
WHAT HAPPENS : At every street crossing, boys and girls erect and
    guard a curious tripod structure made of reed or sugar
    cane sticks on which fruit, corn, coloured paper stripe
    or flowers are fastened.

    These structures are supposed to stop evil spirits (in particular
those that may threaten the rice harvest). The boys also stop
passers–by and even cars, sometimes blocking streets with a
symbolic rope, in an attempt to jokingly ransom them. In the
evening, dolls made of straw representing those evil-spritits are
thrown triumphantly into one of the Valley's rivers.

NAGA PANCHAMI : The festival dedicated to the "nagas"
    (deified snakes).

DATE : On the 5th day of the clear fortnight of Srawan. (mid
    July to mid-August).
PLACE : All over the Valley, in particular in Kathmandu City and
    at Pashupatinath.

LEGENDS :
    Generalities: Since time immemorial, the cult of snakes has
taken an important place in all creeds, not only in Nepal and India
but in Persia and other countries as well. (Men seem to have
always had a tendency of propitiating by worship and rites all
natural forces which makes them feel helpless, be it lightning, storm
floods, wind .. or snakes.) Peculiarities concerning Nepal: Here
snakes are regarded as being a shape, an appearance chosen by
certain deities. They are also considered–and hence, venerated
for being responsible for the monsoon rains, and thus, indirectly
for the harvest, that is, ultimately, for the prosperity if not the

urvival of the whole people.

Besides that, it should always be remembered that Kathmandu Valley was once (some 200.000 years ago) a large lake which, according to the strong belief of all, was full of serpents and for this reason, called "Nagarhida", i.e. the abode of snakes. These snakes were finally chased away by MANJUSRI when he left the Chhobar mountain in two with his magic sword. The King of Snakes was the only one allowed to remain he Valley. Its dwelling place is said to be–still today–the small ake of TAUDAHA, very close to Chhobar. This is a very pictures-que lake, with a tiny island in its centre, No Nepali would ever dare to take a dip or swim in this lake's water, for fear of KARKOTAK, the king of the nagas.

Mrs. Mary ANDERSON, in her remarkable book "Festivals of Nepal" tells a certain number of specifically Nepalese legends where Nagas play a prominent part.

–The legend of Karkotak

King of the "nagas", he lived in a glittering palace on the bottom of lake Taudaha. His wife suffered from an eye–ailment. KARKOTAK swam to the shore of the lake, took the shape of a Brahmin and went to see a famous "eye–specialist" who consented to examine the eyes of this "priest's wife". When they arrived at he shore of the lake, Karkotak asked the doctor to close his eyes. The doctor obeyed. One second later he found himself at the gate of the King's Palace. He cured the queen, and the king, over-whelmed with gratitude offered him many precious presents, among which the famous stone–studded velvet vest called the 'bhoto" which, once a year, is shown to the population, on the occasion of the Bhoto or Rato Mastyendranath festival.

–The legnd of Takshaka Naga

This snake was carried away by the water, after Manjusri had cleaved the Chhobar–rock. Takshaha was so furious for having been chased away from his original dwelling–place that he could not help biting every living being he met. The gods punished him by cursing him with leprosy. Takshaka decided to try to liberate himself from this terrible disease by devoting himself to Lord Shiva. One day, GARUDA, the mythical bird (half-man, half-bird) who is Vishnu's traditional mount and the fiercest enemy of all nagas, met Takshaka. A terrific battle ensued, which forced the intervention of both Shiva and Vishnu. The two enemies were reconciled and Tahshaka coiled himself in a friendly way

around Garuda's neck. Vishnu mounted on Garuda's back an
both flew off in a north-eastern direction. They ultimately lande
on the hill of Changu Narayan where a beautiful temple is dedica
ted to Vishnu and his mount Garuda, in memory of their commo
adventure.

—*The legend of Siddhi Pokhari*

The pond located near the entrance of the village o
Thimi not far from Bhadgaon which is well known for its potter
and paper-maché masks, was the abode of a terrible snake
Once upon a time, there was a farmer who possessed supernatura
powers, took up the challenge and promised he would kil
this naga.

He decided to take the shape of a snake before plunging int
the lake. But before that, he gave very clear and precise instruc
tions to his servant :Should the water turn a milky colour, he tol
his servant, it would mean that his master had failed and had bee
killed by the snake. But if the colour of the water turned red, i
meant, on the contrary, that his master had overpowered and kil
ed the naga. His master would then emerge from the lake, still i
the shape of a snake, when the servant had only to throw hir
some grains of magic rice which would make him recover hi
original shape as a man. A little while after the farmer ha
immersed himself in the lake, the water started to turn red. A snak
appeared shortly after that at the shore. The servant, seized wit
panic, ran away as fast as he could, completely forgetting the in
structions his master had given him. The latter tried to pursue an
catch up with him but in vain. The magic grains of rice remaine
for ever in the servant's pockets. Thus, there was no alternative fo
the farmer but to return to the lake, where he still lives. The in
habitants of Thimi, fearing that the serpent might emerge at an
time, are in the habit of making a wide detour around the lake.

—*The legend of the three small snakes.*

Once upon a time , a farmer was ploughing his field and, quit
inadvertently, killed three small snakes with his ploughshare
The mother of these snakes went after the farmer, reached hi
house and killed him, as well as his wife and two young sons
There remained only their young daughter who, on seeing th
snake, had the presence of mind to offer it a cup of creamy
milk. The naga, moved by this gesture, promised to grant th
girl any wish she might express. So she asked the snake for th
revival of her beloved parents and brothres. Her wish wa

immediately granted.

WHAT HAPPENS: On every square in the town and in the open
fields, where a snake is suspected of living, a small cupful of milk
is placed as well as rice or barley cakes, flowers and "simrik".
This is the vermilion powder used for the "tika" on the forehead.
The purpose of all these offerings is to appease the snake. All
houses are decorated with a "naga" portrait, usually a simple
sheet of paper with one or several snakes drawn or painted in
vivid colours. This paper is affixed to the upper beam of the
main door which has previously been washed and thoroughly
cleaned. A priest then places a "tika" on the forehead of the
snake image.

At Pashupatinath, many pilgrims make offerings to the hundreds of snake symbols and images that are displayed in and
around this sacred place of worship of Hindus.

It may be as well to recall here that many Nepalis refuse
to kill a snake that they may find in or around their house or
garden, for fear of the snake's mate to appear the next day and
take revenge on the killer.

JANAI PURNIMA : A festival of special homage to MAHADEV-
SHIVA, celebrated by both Hindus and Buddhists.

DATE : On the last day of the month of Srawan (mid-July to
mid-August).

PLACE : At the temple of Kumbheshwar, in PATAN, ten minutes
from the Durbar Square.

LEGEND : Six day's walk from Kathmandu, in a north-western
direction the lakes of GOSAINKUND are to be found. In
the centre of the lowest of these lakes which lies at an
altitude of 13,123 ft., (4.000 m.) a big rock protrudes
from under the surface of the water. This rock is looked
upon–and worshiped accordingly–as a manifestation of
or, at least, a symbol of Shiva. It is generally believed that
secret channels bring the water of this lake to the square
pool close to the Kumbheshwar temple.

WHAT HAPPENS : At the Gosainkund lake itself : large numbers of
pilgrims gather along the shore after having walked for
days and weeks to reach this place in time, Throwing
coins into the water towards the "Shiva–rock" is one of
the peculiar features of this pilgrimage.

At Patan, in the courtyard of Kumbheshwar temple, the
crowd presses on to a narrow gangway which links the square pool

with the small platform built in its centre. It is on this platform
that the Shiva–Mahadev sanctuary stands. The devotees throw
rice grains and flowers on and around the statue. They circumambulate the small image, sometimes by diving into the water and
swimming around. it They pay special homage to the silver
"*lingam*" erected on the sanctuary. On this particular day, all
devotes are supposed to fast and to take only one evening meal
consisting of "kwati", a special dish prepared from nine different
kinds of peas, beans, lentils and cereals.

Two other ceremonies take place on the occastion of Janai
Purnima :

1) The renewal of the "sacred thread" (called "*janai*") worn
by Brahmins and Chetris throughout their live from boyhood
onwards. It goes over the left shoulder, across the chest and under
the right armpit.

2) Priests tie a yellow sacred thread around the wrists of all
those who, whether Hindus, Buddhists or Christians, ask for
it. This thread is tied on the right wrist of men and on the left
wrist of girls and women. It is deemed to protect the bearer from
all evil influences and sickenss. It should never be cut or torn
away violently. This thread is called "rakshya bandhan".

On Janai Purnima, at various places and in the streets of Patan.
"*jhankris*" appear. They are, musicians, doctors and sorcerers
who visit one temple after another and who put themselves in
a state of trance to perform their role. In his right hand, the
jhankri holds a long and curved stick (called a "*dhyanre*") with
which he beats his drum in an increasingly rapid rythm.

AUGUST – SEPTEMBER

GAI JATRA : The "cow–festival" – Also a celebration in homage
to those who have passed away during the year.

DATE : The day following the Full–moon of Srawan. One day-
after the Janai Purnima festival.

PLACE : Around Hanuman Dhoka in Kathmandu as well as in
all the other towns of the Valley.

LENGENDS : 1) To render homage simultaneously to the dead and
the cows finds its explanation in the belief that the day
following Srawan's Full moon is the only day of the year when one
finds open the gates of the underworld, the kingdom of YAMA, the
King of the dead, who presides over the self–judgement of all
deceased.

Now, it is believed that the road leading to YAMA is full of obs-tacles. Therefore, those deceased who, at the moment of their death, had the good fortune to be holding the tail of a cow, would be led by the sacred animal straight to the Court of justice of the deceased. (This is why, even to-day, holding a cow's tail at the moment of death is a strongly recommended practice, at least among the very orthodox Hindus).

2) The reason why this festival of the dead and the cows seems to degenerate in a sort of wild and merry carnival throughout the day (see below, under "What happens") is explained by a histori-cal legend : PRATAP MALLA, King of Kathmandu from 1639 to 1689 was a learned and very religious monarch. He built not only Hanuman Dhoka gate and had the famous red paint cove-red image of the monkey–god Hanuman erected on the left side of this gate, but also Budanilkantha, originating the tradition accor-ding to which any king who would look at the Vishnu figure lying on the bed of snakes would instantly die. After having followed one of his counsellor's advice to let his four sons rule in turn each for one full year, his youngest son, *Chakravartindra,* the favourite son of his second official wife, died mysteriously the day he ascended the throne. His mother (Queen *Ruppamati Lakshmi Narayana,*) remained inconsolable, First, the king ordered all women of Kathmandu who had lost a child in the course of the year to march past the Royal Palace where the Queen would watch the procession from her balcony. This parade took place and it convinced the Queen that others had suffered the same ordeal as herself. But this did not bring any relief to her own grief.

Then Pratap Malla let it be known all over the city that he would give honours, rewards and wealth to any-one who would succeed in bringing back a smile to the lips of the distressed queen.

Thus, men, boys and girl disguised themselves as all sorts of animals, fairies or clowns and paraded in front of the Royal Palace, dancing and merry–making. This is the historical back-ground to the carnivalesque character of Gai Jatra.

WHAT HAPPENS : From early morning onwards, children and youngsters roam around in the streets, wearing painted paper masks on their heads. These masks look–very remotely–it must be added–like cow's heads; the horns, which are in fact small flags, are stuck on the masks, Others wear cow's heads made of cane or wicker, bearing the "face" of the cow on one side and the head of the elephant–god Ganesh on the other. Later in the

day, the festival turns more and more into a sort of carnival with
music, dances and all sorts of merry–making.

KRISHNA ASTAMI : To celebrate Lord KRISHNA's birthday.
Lord Krishna is considered to be the eighth reincarnation
of Vishnu. He is also the deified hero of the Hindu epic "*Mahabharata*".

DATE : On the 7th and 8th day of the dark fortnight of Srawan

PLACE : In any temple and around any sanctuary dedicated to
Krishna, in particular, of course, at the "Krishna Mandir"
on the Durbar Square of PATAN.

LEGENDS : KRISHNA, being one of the most popular dieties in the
whole Hindu world, venerated as the personification of
manhood, strength, gallantry and righteousness, the legends
around his birth are many.

These stories as well as all the episodes of his adventours
life would fill a book bigger than this one. Let us simply mention
some of the most striking characteristics of this outstanding
personality :

KRISHNA was brought up by a family of cattle herdsmen, so
that he might remain hidden and therefore protected from his
parent's enemies who had conspired to kill him. When he was
still a baby, a demon called KAMSA put him in the arms of a wet-
nurse whose milk contained a deadly posion. Krishna not only
remained unaffected but also "sucked" all the milk and poison
out of the nurse's breasts and thus caused her death.

According to a popular story, the fact that Krishna is mostly,
if not always, represented with a dark blue, sometimes even a
black face, recalls the fact that he absorbed the poisoned milk of
the wicked nurse.

While a young man, Krishna loved to roam around and play
among the "*gopi*", i. e. the cow–herd girls. His adventures and
feats as a "*Don Juan*" are as numerous as the accounts of his
gallantry as a warrior, notably the prominent part he played during
the famous battle of the Mahabharata, where, on the side of
the Pandava brothers, he was the conductor of Arjuna's chariot.

WHAT HAPPENS : During the night preceding the 7th day of the
dark fortnight of Srawan, thousands of men and women
gather around and near Krishna Mandir in PATAN as well
as other sanctuaries dedicated to the same god; they exhibit
images of Lord Krishna representing him either as a young baby
full of life, as the young hero of the gopi, or as the warrior–prince.

These images are also displayed in all shops and on the front of private houses.

On certain squares in the city, old sages tell some of the stories and legends from Lord Krishna's life. Dozens of people sit there, cross–legged on the ground and listen to the story–teller. In the evening, the women, all dressed up in their most gorgeous red-and-gold saris congregate on the narrow balconies of Krishna Mandir and sing hymns in homage to the god, beating the rhythm with their hands. (Non–Hindus are not admitted to the upper storeys of this temple.) The Mandir is illuminated with thousands of small oil–lamps which should never be allowed to go out during the night. At day-break, the devotees will eat some biscuits and may drink a glass of warm tea. This will be their first food since 24 hours.

MATI-YA FESTIVAL : A Buddhist festival to honour the dead

DATE : The day following Gai-Jatra

PLACE : All over Patan-city, and in Patan only.

WHAT HAPPENS : Gaily dressed groups, young men and women parade through the lanes of Patan, some holding long burning candles, others brandishing sticks, others again carrying tins full of red sindur power.

They have to visit and pay homage to all major 31 temples and over a hundred chaityas located in Patan's viharas and courtyards. Paying homage consists mainly in throwing red powder over the conical sanctuaries. Girls and women usually carry precious silver boxes containing "tika" paste, rice grains, flower petals which are being offered to the Buddhist deities.

Most of these groups are hurrying as if they were chasing something. In fact they are anxious not to lose track of the head of the procession which would mean that they may miss to "visit" one or the other of the sanctuaries and thus, render their participation worthless.

The dominating impression is one of carnavalesque gaiety which, at first glance, is somewhat difficult to conciliate with the object of this festival : to honour the deceased.

But the masquerade, the frolicking, the songs and dances are meant to mock Yama, the "god" of the realm of the dead. !

TEEJ : The festival of women in honour of their husbands.

DATE : From the 2nd to the 5th of the clear fortnight of Bhadra (mid–August to mid–September).

PLACE : In all cities of the Valley, in particular around and at the

Pashupatinath sanctuary.

LEGEND : This festival commemorates the circumstances of the wedding of SHIVA and PARVATI. The latter's father, although he knew of his daughter's love for Lord Shiva, had decided to give her in marriage to VISHNU.

On the eve of the main ceremony, PARVATI implored her friends and maid-servants to help her escaping from her father's palace. They succeeded in abducting her and taking her to a faraway forest, where she hoped she could meet her beloved Shiva.

From his abode in heaven, Shiva followed her evasion and watched her while she prayed to him and imposed many penances on herself. Shiva's heart was moved by her sincere devotion but he wanted to submit her to a final test. Thus, he took the shape of Vishnu himself. Then, he approached Parvati in her forest hide-out, flattering her with compliments while, at the same time, telling her many revolting lies about Shiva. In spite of this, Parvati reffirmed again and again her determination to marry Shiva and no one else. Shiva then abandoned the disguise of Vishnu, reappeared as himself and agreed to marry Parvati. Thus, the festival of TEEJ commemorates the assistance given to Parvati by her friends and maid-servants when she ran away from her father's palace: in a broader sense, TEEJ celebrates friendship and solidarity among all women.

WHAT HAPPENS : The festivities start with a convivial meal, usually a rich mutton and chicken curry which is meant to enable the women to endure more easily the ensuing complusory fast which lasts not less than 24 hours. On this occasion, the husband has no right to grumble against his wife for the cost of this elaborate meal ! In the afternoon, there is a lively exchange of visits.

Then, the women stay together, chatting and feasting until midnight. This is when Teej is deemed to start and, with it, the fast. Not the tiniest crumb of food or drop of drink should be absorbed during the whole of this period. It is customary for women to stay together the rest of the night, dress up in the early morning and then proceed towards Pashupatinath at sunrise. Very often, girls and women hold hands, walking two by two or three by three. During the whole day, the women either stay away from home, or when inside their houses, obstinately abstain from any menial domestic work. When proceeding towards the temple, they are all dressed in red-and-gold saris, similar to those that girls wear when they get married.

It should not be forgotten that TEEJ is celebrated because
PARVATI finally succeeded in marrying Lord Shiva. Once
in Pashupatinath, they bathe in the sacred Bagmati river, but
will change their saris before stepping into the water. Throughout
this day, the temple and its immediate surroundings will be
crammed with women. Of course, all statues and images of Shiva
and Parvati are the object of a special homage and lavish offerings,
INDRA JATRA : This is the festival in homage to INDRA, the
"King of the abode of the gods". or sometimes called
"the King of the gods." It is also a festival in memory of the
deceased, an homage to Bhairav, the patron–god protecting the
Valley, as well as the date when the "living goddess', the Royal
Kumari would officially be consecrated for anotheer year. In
addition to all these different aspects, INDRA JATRA commemorates
the victory of the campaigns fought for 25 years by Prithvi Narayan Shah the Great to create a united Nepal, as it is today. It
was, indeed, on the very day of the Indra Jatra festival that the
founder of the present dynasty ascended the throne of Nepal, in
the year 1768. A very complex festival, indeed !

DATE : From the 12th day of the clear fortnight of Bhadra to the
         4th day of the dark fortnight of Ashwin (mid–September
to mid–October).

PLACE : Everywnere in Kathmandu, in particular around Hanu-
         man Dhoka and the Royal Palace,as well as at the Kuma-
ri's Palace, nearby.

LEGENDS : 1) Referring to INDRA :

         Once upon a time, DAGINI, the mother of Indra, "King of
the gods", and himself "God of lightning and thunderstorms",
was unable to find, in the Kingdom of the Gods, a certain white
flower called "parijat" which she needed to perform a given
'puja'. So she requested her son to fetch some flowers from below
on the Earth, where they were plentiful. INDRA took the disguise on an ordinary human being, wrapped himself in a cloud and
landed on Earth, on a morning when the silvery mist was covering
the Valley of Kathmandu. He found the flowers on the first meadow he reached. But he was caught red–handed by the owner
of this pasture. They put him in fetters and kept him prisoner in
a certain house in Kathmandu. DAGINI, anxious not to see her
beloved son come back to Heaven, also went down to the Earth
and made herself known to the local inhabitants. Discovering
the identity of their prisoner, the people of Kathmandu released

INDRA immediately. As a token of her gratitude, DAGINI promised to spread enough dew over the Valley during the winter-months to ensure very rich crops during the year. The other promise she made was to take to the "abode of the gods" all those who had died during the year.

This legend explains, at least in part, the various stages of the festival : exuberant rejoicing for having succeeded in capturing none less than the "King of the Gods", homage paid to Dagini, representing the "Mother" as such, and finally, homage paid to the deceased.

2) Referring to the "Kumari", the "living Goddess". JAYA PRAKASH MALLA, the last King of Kathmandu (1736 – 1768) liked to play dice with Goddess TALEJU. One day, fascinated by the Goddess' beauty, the King almost forgot that she was not a simple human being. Taleju immediately fled, vowing and telling the King that she would never again appear in a human shape when the king could see her. During the same night, she appeared in a dream and warned the King that his dynasty was nearing its end. However, she added, she would forgive the King's insult and avert the threat to his throne if he would find a Newar girl in whom she, TALEJU, would be reincarnated. Furthermore, the King should commit himself to the building of a splendid Palace where this girl would live henceforth. Finally, the King should personally pay homage to her, once a year. JAYA PRAKASH MALLA immediately made all these promises. Nevertheless, TALEJU'S prediction proved true since it was during the very festival of INDRA JATRA in 1768 that Prithvi Narayan Shah, the "Father of Modern Nepal" took over Kathmandu and forced Jaya Prakash Malla to go into exile to save his own life. The surrender of Kathmandu put an end to the dynasty of the Mallas who had ruled over the Kingdom for more than five centuries !

WHAT HAPPENS : On the eighth day of the clear fortnight of BHADRA, the inhabitants of Kathmandu carry the trunk of a huge tree form THUNDIKHEL, the parade-ground of Kathmandu, down to HANUMAN DHOKA, where the old Royal Palace stands.

This is no random choice of a tree. It has to be made a year before, by letting a sacred goat loose until it rubs its flanks against one of the trees in a specific forest, miles away from the city. This goat is sacrificed to INDRA immediately. When the tree reaches Hanuman Dhoka, another goat, sometimes a cock is sacrificed over the hole which has to receive the thick end of the stake. While it is still lying on the pavement, the devotees prostrate themselves in front of the pole by bending down and touching it with their forehead. This ceremony takes place at dawn on the first day at a precise moment calculated by the official astrologers.

From this moment onward, images of INDRA carved in wood, copper or brass and even painted on pieces of paper are displayed everywhere. The *"King of the God's abode"* is always represented with outstretched arms–a sign of submission–his body covered with many threads and strings, to symbolise that he was once a prisoner. At the foot of the pole, a priest places a box containing a small gold statue of an elephant, the traditional mount of God Indra.

At another pre–determined moment, the people start erecting the pole. Of course, its main significance is Shiva's "lingam" Again, roosters and goats are sacrificed once the post is set up.

A huge crowd greet this occasion with loud cries of "INDRA with us" which ensures a prosperous and peaceful year.

Simultaneously, BHAIRAV, the patron–deity of the Valley, is venerated in a specia lway : the huge image of this fierce-looking god which is placed behind a wooden screen on Hanuman Dhoka all year round is now shown to the devotees. The screen is taken away and from early morning, children climb up to his golden face while men and women throw rice grains and flower petals at him. A wooden kind of duct sticks out of his half-open mouth, held between his protruding canine teeth. Later in the day, when the procession of the Living Goddess will pass in front of Bhairav, it will start sputtering gallons of beer, through this duct ! it goes without saying that this *"miracle"* is greeted by enthusiastic cheers from the crowd.

The day before the whole show starts, three golden chariots stand ready along the northern side of Basantpur square, very near to the Living Goddess' house.

On INDRA JATRA's first day, at around 11 A.M. many women and children, start taking place on the steps of all surrounding temples and buildings. The sight of this extraordinary colourful gathering that makes the temples look as if draped in bright red, golden and blue skirts is really unforgettable.

The festival starts in the early afternoon. Teams of especially designated men and boys are still busy giving the three chariots the finishing touch by decorating them inside and outside. The larger one will be carrying the Living Goddess, the two smaller ones Bhairav and Ganesh.

Very soon–around 1 p. m.–the whole district of Hanuman Dhoka will be crammed with people so that is it difficult to get nearer to the Living Goddess' House or the old Royal Palace's neo–Greek façade where the main ceremonies will take place. Police will prevent on-lookers from proceeding further. However, foreign visitors, in particular when in groups and carrying cameras, will be able to reach the special area usually reserved for them, facing the balcony where His Majesty the King and prominent Nepalese and Foreign dignitaries will soon appear. To get through the cordoned off access points, it needs sometimes a little persistence and jovial smiles.

At the auspicious moment ascertained by astrologers (usually between 2 and 4 p.m.) the first act takes place : two men will be seen coming out of the Living Goddess' house, not out of the façade's door but a small one in a nearby narrow lane.

In their arms, thery carry two young boys dressed in girls clothes, their faces showing exactly the same make-up as the Living Goddess herself. For they represent her "servants", Ganesh and Bhairav who will be lifted on to their respective small chariots.

A little later, the "Kumari" herself appears through the same door. She is not carried. Assisted by her attendants, she will walk to her chariot. Now, since she is not supposed to get soiled by the dirt of the street, a servant spreads in front of her a long piece of immaculate white cotton serving as a "carpet" on which she steps forward.

Meantime, Foreign diplomats will have taken place on the regal balcony. His Majesty the King, Her Majesty the Queen and their children arrive soon, cheered by the crowd.

The chariot starts moving and stops in front of the balcony or one of the Palace's windows. H. M. the King greets the Kumari and throws coins among the gathered onlookers. So do also members of the Royal Family and high dignitaries.

During the whole afternoon, the chariot will be dragged through the streets and the lanes of the old city before returning to the place where it started from earlier.

While this is going on, a dancer wearing a fierce-looking mask is gesticulating and jumping around. He is a "Lakhe" the name given to the representation of DAKINI, INDRA's mother. Her popping in and out of the square facing the balcony may remind how frantically she was looking for her son Indra, whom she had sent

down to earth and whom the people of Kathmandu took prisoner.
Later, "Lakhe" will join up with other groups of masked dancers
who will perform their acrobatics throughout the night.

Slowly, the crowd disperses, but many spectators stay on for
in the evening other spectacular ceremonies take place.

Around 8 p. m., there will be the procession of DAGINI, now
dressed up as an old woman wearing a white mask and staggering
along the narrow streets as if drugged. This procession starts at
Kastamandhap and ends there one hour later.

Since DAGINI solemnly promised to take all souls of deceased
persons to "Heaven", the symbolism of this procession is that
its participants (men and women) are on the look-out for any
departed persons' soul in order to prevent it from following an
ancient tradition: i.e to throw itself in "Indira's lake" located out
of the boundaries of the city, near Thankot, on the road to India.

As soon as DAGINI returns to Kathmandhap, in front of
which stands a structure of bamboo poles carrying
a dummy that represents Indra with outstretched arms, another
procession is preparing to move : this one is exclusively
led by young men. They carry a *"snake"*, a sacred *"naga"*, made
of four bamboo poles tied together to give it the shape of a long
flexible plank on which are placed dozens of small oil lamps
containing burning wicks.

A third procession takes place, this time composed of women
holding hands or the panel of each others skirts forming also
long "snake" . It also proceeds through the old part of the city,

Four days later, on the last day of INDRA JATRA, it was customary that H. M. the King should call on the Kumari in her
own house and receive the "tika" mark, made of santalwood
paste, from her hands. But this is not a compulsory rite.

The last act of Indra Jatra's festival consists in the lowering
of the famous pole set up in front of Kalo Bhairav's image, on
Hanuman Dhoka. Once on the ground, it is dragged down to
Bagmati river and left there to float away or to be sawn in pieces
and used as firewood.

SEPTEMBER – OCTOBER

DASAIN : This is the most important and most popular festival
in Nepal. It may be said to correspond to "Christmas"
not because it commemorates the birth of any divinity, but as a
festival of "peace to all men of good will" and of the victory of
Good over Evil. In the eyes of the Hindus, DASAIN essentially

commemorates the victory of the hero RAMA over the evil demon–king RAVANA, who , according to the epic poem RAMAYANA, kidnapped Rama's wife SITA and kept her imprisoned for many years on the island of Ceylon (now Sri Lanka).

At the same time, DASAIN is the festival of fertility, for it coincides with the time when barley seeds must be sown. The name "DASAIN" indicated that the festival takes ten days ("das", in Nepali, means ten) There are many other names for this festival : Dusserah, Durga Puja, Nava Ratri (the nine nights) etc.

DATE : DASAIN begins on the first day of the clear fortnight of the month of Ashwin (mid–September to mid–October) and ends ten days later.

PLACE : In every town, village and hamlet of the country.

WHAT HAPPENS : At the entrance of each locality and often also on its main square, the villagers build a strange-looking scaffolding which consists of four huge bamboo poles strongly tied together two by two on top, their "legs" widespread and fixed in the ground. A horizontal bar links the four pole–tops together. A swing made of bamboo and other fibres twinted together is attached to this bar with thick ropes.

In some places, these swings are replaced by huge rotating wheels called "roti ping". Both are the delight of the younger generation.

On the banks of each river : The devotees make their ritual ablutions and offer fruits and flowers to DURGA, for she assisted RAMA in his fight against the demon-king RAVANA.

— In front of every village house : a few grains of barley are planted with great care in a square box. This box is full of sand which should be collected from the banks of sacred river, preferably Bagmati. Every day, somebody will pour water over the seeds and the small sprouts. On the tenth or the last day of DASAIN, it is important that they should have grown to about four inches otherwise it would be a bad omen.

Then they are extracted from the box, bound into small bundles which men and women will wear as an ornament above their left ears. The way these seeds have sprouted will give the farmer an indication of what the barley crop will be like that year.

During the nights of DASAIN, masked dances take place in PATAN, Usually these dances are accompanied with and interrupted by "chang" drinking, which has the effect of making them even more frantic.

The 7th day is particularly important : it marks the real
egining of the DASAIN festivities : In the morning, the children
pend their time in kite flying and kite fights.

(In fact, kite flying starts much earlier, for it is closely linked
ith the monsoon. According to the general belief, kites are
onsidered as a kind of prayer–letter that is sent to the skies,
e. to the abode of the gods to implore them to start the rains.).

As far as the kite battles are concerned, this is a typical "sport"
f Nepal, very likely introduced either from China or from Tibet
r both.

The children rub their kite-strings with a mixture of glue and
lass powder. The fight consists in trying to cut the opponents
ite's string with one's own.

One author, Pierre DELATTRE, in his book "Tales of a Dalai
ama" gives the following, somewhat unexpected and strange
oteric explanation of this sport : "The game, he writes, sym-
olizes the cutting of the cord that keeps a child bound to his
other and the human spirit bound to the earth. Though kites
ll when the string is cut, the spirit soars ever upward. The aim
 the game, as of all life, is to assist one another's release to
gher levels of consciousness."

But let us come back to the Dasain festival :

On that same morning of the 7th day, on HANUMAN DHOKA
uare, a strange procession starts : It proceeds through many of
e small streets to end, finally, at the place which nowadays is
ccupied by the yellow building called "Trichandra College"
 front of the "Clock Tower", The main personality to take
rt in the procession is a young girl, but not the "living Goddess"
ough she too is magnificently dressed and covered with jewel-
ry. On arriving at the final station of the procession, she is offer-
 "phulpati", meaning a basket full of flowers and fruits which
e collected at the royal sanctuary of GURKHA, the ancient
pital of the present Kings' ancestors.

At the same time, on the vast parade ground of Tundikhel, an
pressive military parade takes place in the presence of H. M.
e KING, members of the Royal family, the dignitaries of the
ingdom, members of the Diplomatic Corps etc.

The 8th day, called ASTAMI, is the day of sacrifices. Every
ar approximately 10,000 goats are imported from Tibet. These
ge flocks cross the 18,000 feet. (5,500 m.) high pass of NANG-
 LA, and are brought down to the Kathmandu Valley, where

they graze wherever they find grass or bushes. Sacrifices take place
during the night, around the TALEJU temple–on Hanuman Dhoka.
At midnight, there are 8 buffaloes which will have their heads
chopped off with one stroke of a special long sword called a
"khora", and 108 goats which will be decapitated with a khuhri.

On the 9th day, the series of sacrifices continue, from dawn
onwards, in the ill–famed Kot courtyard, close to the Police Head
Quarters. This ceremonial is a very complex one; it is open to the
public, including to foreigners. The blood of the sacrificed
animals is sprinkled over any vehicle, cars, trucks and even
airplanes to ward-off any accident during the year.

The 10th day is the climax of the whole festival : it is known
as the "*tika - day*", for it is then that the "*tika*", the vermilion
mark is solemnly affixed to the forehead of all members of
the families. Besides being made of sandal wood paste as in
India, this mark is made, in Nepal, with an addition of other
powders and curd. The King and the Queen participate actively
in this ceremony, by putting tikas on the foreheads of many
dignitaries of the government, the army, administrative bodies
corporations etc.

OCTOBER – NOVEMBER

TIHAR (Also called Dipawali, Yama Panchak, Swanti or
Laxmi Puja) It is mainly a festival of lights, but it is also a
festival to celebrate Laxmi, the Goddess of Wealth. Besides that
it marks the beginning of the Newari New Year, and it is at the
same time a "festival of animals".

DATE : Two days before the dark moon day (New moon) in the
month of Kartik (October-November) and the following four days
PLACE : In every house, in every village and town, not only in
    Kathmandu but all over the country.

WHAT HAPPENS : 1*st Day :* This day is called "*Kag Tihar*", and
is dedicated to the crows. Homage is paid to these birds by
spreading rice grains at street crossings and corners. Crows are
supposed to be Yama's (the god of the dead) messengers. Therefore, they must be appeased. Also according to Hindu mythology
this festival is supposed to celebrate, among men, the same
"five–day rest" that Yama takes every year when he stays as
guest of his sister Yamana. Hence the name of "*Yama Panchak*"
the fives days of Yama.

2*nd day :* This day is called "*Kukur Tihar*" and is dedicated to
the dogs. Every dog, be it a watchodog or a pet is garlanded with

lowers. A "tika" mixed with grains of rice is ceremoniously put on his forehead either by his master or by the servants in the presence of the master of the house, his wife and children. Natually on "Kukur Tihar" the dog's dinner is an especially savoury one. One of the reasons for honouring the dog is that it is considered not only the most faithful companion of man and the best guardian of the house, but also the protector of the abode of the deceased.

3rd day : On the third day, it is the turn for the cows to be honoured and garlanded. Their horns are gaily painted, sometimes with gold and silver colours. This homage is paid to them in the early morning hours and, of course, it is meant to manifest, once more, the very sacred character of the cow.

There are many explanations for this essentially Hindu tradition. According to certain scholars, this consecration finds its roots many centuries back, at the time between 2,500 and 1,500 B. C. when the Aryans from Afghanistan and Persia migrated towards India and had to cross the arid desert of the northern part of the Indian subcontinent. During this migration, so it is said, it was imperative that the cows should not be slaughtered since the babies depended almost entirely on their milk for survival. Thus, the priets "deified", the cows in order to save the new generation from starvation. This procedure which consists in integrating into religion and calling *"sacred"* an imperative necessity of either hygienic, economical or social nature has often been used by many religious leaders.

These same scholars who put forward this explanation point out, as a sort of proof, the fact that buffaloes, which, after all, are close relatives to oxen and cows, are not considered sacred for the simple reason that buffalo milk is not easily digested by babies !

To come back to the Tihar festival, the afternoon of this same third day is dedicated to LAKSHMI (or Luxmi), the Goddess of Wealth. All businessmen, merchants and shopkeepers open new account-books, clean and decorate with garlands, flowers and images of Lakshmi all their safes, cash-boxes, counters, etc.

In order to invite the Goddess to pay a visit to each house, lights are placed at the doorsteps of each building, and they "lead" through various rooms and corridors, to the "puja-room", the house-sanctuary, where all private offerings and *"pujas"* are performed. In the evening, the whole town is brightly decorated with thousands of lights.

Since Lakshmi is supposed to distribute wealth to all, the eve
ning of this third day will be spent in gambling which normall;
drags on throughout the night. The most popular of thes
games involves the throwing of cowrie-shells and betting o
them according to a very complex system.

4th day : On the fourth day, oxen and bullocks are honoured
These animals, although not considered as sacred, are neverthe
less the invaluable helpers of the farmers, for it is the bulloc
or the ox that pulls the plough and performs many other heavy
tasks in the fields and on the roads.

In the Newar community, this fourth day is extremely im
portant, for it marks the beginning of the Newar New Year. I
Newari, this day is called "*Mha puja*", which means "*worshippin;
oneself*". In fact, this must be interpreted as the prayer addresse
to the gods to bring about in the suppliant"*self-realization*" i.e
his integration into the universal conscience; in other words, it i
a plea that the incessant wheel of reincarnations should stop s
that the state of Supreme Enlightenment, i.. e. the "*nirvana*", ma
be reached.

5th day : The last day of TIHAR is called "*Bhai Tihar*' o
"*Kija Puja*". It is the "*brother-sister*" day. Every man has th
duty to call on his sister–an adopted one, if necessary– It is th
sister who plays the important part of this rite, for it is she wh
pays homage to her brother, garlands him, scatters flowers on hi
head and shoulders, pronounces auspicious magic formulas t
ward off evil influences and, above all, who puts an especiall
prepared tika on his forehead. spreading the rice and the vermi
lion paste almost all over, from the brows to the hairline. The
she serves him sweet dishes, fruits, walnuts, etc. In exchange fo
all these blessings, the brother gives valuable presents to his sister

The legend that gave birth to these demonstrations of bro
therly love is told in many different versions. However, the basi
elements of the story are the following: Yama, the God of Deat
was impatient to take away the soul of a young man suffering from
a very serious illness. The boy's sister begged Yama to wait unti
she had completed the worshipping rites; according to one version
this meant for Yama to wait as long as the cut flowers she had offer
ed to her brother gave fruit or according to another, until ;
walnut got saturated with water, or a circlet of oil got dry
etc. Whatever the condition might have been, of course it neve

materialized and the boy was saved from an early death.

NOVEMBER – DECEMBER

CONSTITUTION DAY : This is not, of course, a religious but a national and patriotic day. It takes place on the first day of the month of Poush, usually on 15th or 16th of December.

It commemorates the promulgation of the 1962 Constitution which is still in force, as well as the birthday of His late Majesty Mahendra Bir Bikram Shah Dev. Many official ceremonies take place in the capital as well as in the towns and villages of the country.

H. M. THE KING'S BIRTHDAY

DATE : 28th of December.

PLACE : All over the country.

WHAT HAPPENS : Parades, processions, military and sport–shows, in particular on Tundihhel.

In the evening, all public buildings are illuminated and there is a fire–work display.

MANI RIMDU : Each year, in November-December, a three-days festival of masked dances performed by the monks of the community, the well-known "Mani Rimdu" festival takes place in the court-yard and around Thyangboche monastery, splendidly located one short day's walk from Namche Bazar, at an altitude of 12,710 ft. (3.875m) The exact date of this festival is: "On the 15th day of 10th month of the Tibetan calendar". Knowing that the Tibetan New Year (called "Losar") coincides with the New Moon of February, it is easy to figure out the date for the Mani Rindu : ten month later plus 15 days, which means that the festival usually coincides with the full-moon of either end of November or beginning of December. In the month of May, a similar festival takes place at the Thame Monastery, west of Namche.

On both occasions, Tourist Agencies in Kathmandu organize special journeys to the respective monasteries and make all necessary arrangements for lodging etc.. Tourists will have to pay a Rs. 15.– fee to be allowed to take photos or make films during the festivals.

DECEMBER – JANUARY

SETO – MATSYENDRANATH : ("Seto" means white, for there is also a red "rato", deity called Matsyendranath the festival of which takes place in April–May in Patan.)

Seto Matsyendranath festival was originally a Buddhist rite in homage to Bodhisatva AVALOKITESHVARA of whom Matsyen-

dranath (also written sometimes Machhendranath) is believed to
be a reincarnation. But nowadays this festival is celebrated by
Hindus as well, Both Hindus and Buddhists perform rites and
make offerings etc. on this occasion, either to Shiva or Vishnu, or
to Matsyendranath.

DATE : On the eighth day of the clear fortnight of the month of
Poush (mid–December to mid–January).

PLACE : First, a chariot is built and decorated with a huge mast
covered with greenery. This takes place at the corner of Durbar
Marg and a narrow lane leading eastwards, not far from Annapurna Hotel. However, the main ceremony takes place around the
magnificent gold–roofed temple called "Seto Matsyendranath"
located in old Kathmandu, on Kel Tole, half–way between Asan
and Indrachowk. This temple is built in the centre of a square
courtyard, the entrance of which is guarded by two bronze
dragon-statues.

LEGEND : White Matsyendranath is generally looked upon as
the sister of Red Matsyendranath and associated with prosperity. He looks after the welfare of everybody and, so it is believed,
should he be displeased with the behaviour of the town people,
he might send an epidemic, It is also said that, in the Buddhist
Pantheon, Matsyendranath's peculiarity was to be always late for
the worshipping rites to Lord Buddha. His excuse was that he had
first to feed all living creatures. Buddha put him on test by enclosing a tiny ant in an empty box which he warpped up in several
layers of papers, keeping the box hermetically closed. When a
few hours later, Matsyendranath finally arrived at the gathering,
Buddha opened the parcel and the box : inside he found the ant
holding a grain of rice in its mandible !

WHAT HAPPENS : The festival starts early morning in the temple's
courtyard, where the crowd gathers in large numbers to make
offerings to the god's image by sprinkling it with red powder,
petals etc. Then, the devotees light small oil–lamps, in particular
around a bronze statue of a lightly dressed feminine figure which,
obviously, is neither Hindu nor Buddhist, but in the purest turnof–the century style of fountains which, at the time, adorned squares and parks in Rome or Paris !

A very elaborate ceremony follows, led by a red-clad priest
who directs the whole rite. Matsyendranath's image is taken out
of the sanctuary and placed on a square platform with railings
decorated with hundreds of oil–lamps. The devotees touch Mats-

ON "KUKUR DAY" ALL DOGS ARE SOLEMNLY
GARLANDED

IN THE SILVERY MORNING MIST NANDI BULL

yendranath's feet with their forehead as a sign of submission and worship.

Musicians blow horns to announce the arrival of the Living Goddess Kumari who is carried from her nearby Palace to witness the climax of the festival undressing and washing of the statue.

This "*bathing*", first with water then with milk and ultimately with oil and hot water is supposed to bring about an auspicious winter season.

—It will be difficult for tourists to attend these lengthy rites unless they are prepared to get up very early in the morning and endure the cold which is frequently intense.

BASANTA SHRAWAN (also called Sri Panchami) : A spring festival and, at the same time a festival dedicated to SARASWATI, Gooddess of Wisdom, Learning and Music.

DATE : On the fifth day of the clear fortnight of the month of Magh (mid–January to mid–February).

PLACE : In the courtyard of the old Royal Palace, on Hanuman Dhoka as well as in and around all temples dedicated to Saraswati, in particular on the slopes of Swayambhu Hill, in Patan and Bhadgaon.

WHAT HAPPENS : An official ceremony takes place in the old courtyard: While the guns fire a salvo of 31 shots, the Senior priest attached to the Royal Family puts a "tika" on the King's forehead and offers him as homage and as token for good forture several slices of coconut, called "*sripal*". Musicians, singers and poets present their spring songs to H. M. the King and the other members of the Royal Family.

On the sanctuaries dedicated to Saraswati, the devotees offer flowers, prayers and rice. Some of them pick up the rice-grains and swallow them, in the belief that by doing so, they will be bestowed with talent and wisdom.

For the farmers, this is also a very special day : they sprin-kle their fields with milk to ensure a rich summer harvest, for this is the time when ploughing has to be started.

Finally, Basanta Shrawan is also the festival of teaching and learning. Schoolboys and girls stroll and sometimes form a procession, proudly carrying their slates, books and pens. All these paraphernalia have to receive Saraswati's blessings. On the following day, the younger boys and girls will attend to their first lesson in reading.

FEBRUARY–MARCH

SHIVARATRI : The great annual Shiva–festival.

DATE : On the New moon day of the month of Phalgun (February-
March).

PLACE : In and around all temples dedicated to SHIVA and, fore-
most at PASHUPATINATH. It is one of the most important of
all religious festivals in Nepal, where Shiva is the object of a special veneration particularly in his form as "Lord PASHUPATINATH".
As such, he is the guardian god of the whole country. This is why,
in his speeches, H.M. the King always invokes Lord PASHUPATI-
NATH's blessings for the welfare of the country and the people.

WHAT HAPPENS : From dawn onwards, thousands of worshippers,
many of them pilgrims having travelled for days or weeks
or even months to celebrate Shivaratri, gather on the banks of
the sacred river Bagmati. Here they immerse themselves in its
holy waters, turn their faces towards the rising sun and let water
flow slowly through their hands held together like a cup, with eyes
closed and with prayers in mind. All buildings around the
temple are filled with people and the slopes of the surrounding
hills are soon througed with tents and other encampments. There
is a never ending flow of people ascending the steps leading to the
main entrance of the temple courtyard, prohibited to non-Hindus,
where they pay homage to Shiva's most popular symbol, the
"lingam," as well as to his mount, the gigantic bull "Nandi"whose
statue stands in front of the sanctuary's door.

Along the river banks, "sadhu" (holy men) with their bodies,
faces and hair covered with ashes or besmeared with cow–dung,
are to be seen everywhere.

For the tourist, Shivarati not only offers a very colourful sight
but also helps him to realize how profound the religious feelings
of the Nepalese people are and how inextricably interlaced are
rites and daily life.

MARCH – APRIL

SAMYAK FESTIVAL : All Buddha statues of Patan are invited
to take part in a festive symbolic banquet in remembrance of the
wealth given to Patan's Sakya–clan.

DATE : On the night between the 4th and the 5th day of the clear
fortnight of the month of Phalgun (mid-February to mid-
March).

PLACE: On Nag–Bahal Square in Patan, behind the Golden Temple.

LEGEND : Once, a man from the Sakya clan was a very rich man.

But he was so devoted to Buddha that he gave all his wealth away in donations to temples, festivals and other rites.

Very soon, the found himself very poor. So he started collecting cow–dung which he piled up in one room of his house. This room, he always kept locked, keeping the key to himself, He forbade his wife to ever enter this particular room. One day, while her husband was asleep, the wife took the key and opened the door of the room : to her wild astonishment, it was full of gold coins up to the ceiling.

The wife woke up her husband and scolded him for being such a mean miser : never a good meal or a new sari, when he kept a room full of gold coins. !

The husband said it was not true at all, and his wife just had dozed off and had had a dream.

Anyway, they went together and opened the room: ther was the gold, a mountain of gold !

The husband said that this did not belong to him, but to the Gods who just used this room for storage, So the gold had to be given back to the Gods. Yes, agreed the woman, but to which God ? She was a devoted Shivaist and suggested that it should be donated to SHIVA. But her husband was a devout Buddhist. Neither of them wanted to give in, so they decided to plant two seeds : one of a camphor tree, the other of a tulsi–tree. The first was to be offered to Buddha, the second to Shiva. Whichever tree would be blooming first, that God would receive the gold.

The camphor–tree bloomed first.

So the Sakya man went around and made it known, that a great banquet would be offered to Buddha, a banquet to which all members of the Sakya clan would be invited.

WHAT HAPPENS : Huge Buddha figures are taken out from all temples and even private homes, in PATAN, during the night of the 4th to 5th. These figures are in the shape of marionette-dummies ; A man stands inside and carries the statue. They look very much alike : the face is made of shiny bronze, the hands of bronze too, but with patina, the dresses very colouful silk. The variety and richness of the ornaments, jewerly, silver chains, breast and forehead silver–engraved plates, crowns are made of silver. During the festival which took place on 5–6 March 1976 no less than 45 of these statues were carried through the streets and lanes of Patan to be finally assembled on the wide square called, "Nag-Bahal", where they were posted along two sides of the square, on the pavement. Each statue–bearer was preceeded by bands of musicians, and singers. They beat the cymbals, the drums, play a special kind of wooden flutes and some carry the 6 feet (lm. 80) long straight trumpets which are supported by a stick that the player hold in one hand. The next time this festival will take place is in 1981.

This part of merry–making lasted all through the night.

On the following morning, a huge crowd, in fact the whole population of Patan, so it seemed, assembled on the Nag-Bahal square. Each one carried a flat basket containing a heap of rice-grains. In a long queue, the women paraded in front of all the statues and spread grains of rice on the pieces of cloth that were lying at the foot of the statues. It must be added that during this festival, not only the Buddha figures are diplayed, but most of the shrines idols, statues of Gods and Goddesses (irrespective of the religion they belong to) are also carried out on this square, mostly in palanquins. Some of these statues are extremely valuable, dating back to the 13 or 14th century. Some are very well known, such as the famous image of the pink faced Matsyendranath.

This symbolic banquet, throwing rice grains and coins, takes all morning and part of the afternoon. Around 4 p. m., the statues begin their return journey to their respective temples and homes. A "SAMYAK" festival of much larger magnitude takes place every twelve years (the next time, it will be in 1992), at the foot of Swambhu Hill, where homage is paid to all Buddha "statues" existing in the whole Valley. There are more than one hundred, for certain. This festival, an exclusively Buddhist one, is nevertheless graced by the presence of H. M. the King, H. M. the Queen, their children and all high dignitaries of the state as well as the diplomatic corps.

HOLI : The most important Spring Festival, as well as the celebration of VISHNU'S victory over the demon HIRNAYA-KASHIPU.

DATE : On the Full moon day of the month of Chaitra (March-April)

PLACE : In all towns and villages of the Valley.

LEGENDS : Holi is a typical Hindu celebration. It is based on the worshipping of two of the most celebrated and popular deities: Lord Vishnu and Lord Krishna.

The first legend concerns Lord Krishna's "merrymaking" when

he was enjoying the company of the "gopis" (the cow-herd girls or milk-maids) on the slopes surrounding Pashupatinath. This explains the showy and mirthful aspect of this festival. The other source is the following Hindu epic :

Vishnu's arch–enemy was the demon-king HIRANYAKASHIPU. The latter had a young son, PRALHAD, who insisted on paying homage and offering his devotion to Vishnu, thus infuriating his father to the extreme. To punish him, the demon-king ordered his servants to attach Pralhad to a white–hot pillar. Pralhad called silently for Vishnu's help. At this instant, he saw a small ant running up and down the glowing pillar. This must be Vishnu's signal, thought the young man. So he let himself tied around the pillar. He remained unharmed. Pralhad then in a loud voice praised Vishnu for his assistance and protection. His father then ordered Pralhad to sit, together with his sister HOLIKA on an open brazier. Holika was burnt to death, but Pralhad, again, escaped unhurt. Vishnu, moved by the boys' devotion decided to put an end to Pralhad's sufferings; he took the shape of NARA-SINGHA (or NARSIMHA), i. e. a creature half–lion, half–man. It did not take him long to kill the demon by disembowelling him with his claws. Nepalese sculptors have represented this scene in form of Narasingha's statue. It can be seen everywhere in Kathmandu, Patan or Bhadgaon.

WHAT HAPPENS : Whereas Shivaratri leaves an impression of sere-nity, deep faith and silent devotion, Holi is the gayest and most carnival–like of all Nepali festivals. This is only natural, as it is essentially a spring festival. Men and boys stroll in the streets dressed in their shabbiest clothes, for one of the peculiari-ties of this festival is that coloured powder or water is sprayed on anyone within reach. There is no reprieve for Nepalis nor for fore-ign visitors: Everyone is therefore well advised to keep a wary eye open when wandering through the streets of Kathmandu, during the Holi week.

To draw the festival to a close, symbolic bamboo poles, called "chir" decorated with strips of coloured cloth are dumped in rivers and streams. These strips of cloth represent the garments of the gopis which Lord Krishna is said to have taken away while the girls were taking their bath !

PASA CHARE : (Also called Pahan Chare) : A typical Newar festival celebrating friendship and hopitality.

DATE : From the 14th day of the dark fortnight of the month of

Chaitra and the next two days.

PLACE : Essentially close to the temple of NARA DEVI, in the old part of Kathmandu, not far from Hanuman Dhoka.

LEGEND : Once upon a time, there was a man called GHANTAKARNA who lived in the street also called NARA DEVI. He was an ardent devotee of Lord Shiva to whom be paid homage by going, on foot of course, every day all the long way to Pashupatinath. However, he had a serious shortcoming : he loved to tease and "make passes" to all girls and young ladies he met on his way to and from Pashupatinath. He soon became a real nuisance in his part of the town. So, one day, the women gathered at Lord Shiva's nearby temple and implored the God to "do something" in order to protect them in future from Ghantakarna. Shiva promised them his help. The next day when Ghantakarna came to worship him, Shiva told him that he was terribly moved by his devotion, so much, in fact, that he requested him not to come any longer all the way to Pashupatinath. "Henceforth, added Shiva, it is me who will come to call on you, at the place where you live; to be certain to find you there, you will from today onwards, stay at your home and wait for me."

Hearing this, Ghantakarna felt very flattered, Only later did he realize that in fact he had become a prisoner in his own home ! Therefore he implored Shiva to let him go out in the streets at least once a year. Shiva agreed and fixed the date of Ghantakarna's free day, on the fourteenth day of the dark fortnight of Chaitra. Henceforth, on this day, Ghantakarna paraded through the streets, greeting every passer–by, man, woman or child, with a broad and warm smile as if everyone were his childhood friend This is why this festival is called the "friendly fourteenth".

WHAT HAPPENS : To commemorate the fact that Ghantakarna was reformed and now behaved courteously with everyone, PASA ÇHARE has become the "Festival of hospitality and friendship". All house–doors are left open for relatives or any other persons for that matter, to come in where they will be received with joy and be given offerings and fruits, sweets and drinks. In the evening, homage is paid to Lord Shiva, in a corner of the inner courtyard of the temple, where garbage is usually dumped; for this is where Ghantakarna lived and received Lord Shiva's daily visit for so many years.

According to another tradition an image of Shiva, mostly a simple lingam, is kept underground in the courtyard of the house.

On PASE CHARE, this image is dug out, washed and anointed with mustard oil. Then offerings are made.

At the Nara Devi temple, musicians play flutes, cymbals clash and drums are beaten very loudly to call everybody to participate in a procession that will lead Lord Shiva's image protected by a large–painted umbrella through the narrow streets and lanes of the old city.

GHODE JATRA (also called *Ghora Jatra*) : The festival of the horse.

DATE : On the 15th day of the dark fortnight of Chaitra (mid-March to mid-April) which is, at the same time, the second day of the Pasa Chare festival.

PLACE : On Tundikhel, Kathmandu's parade ground in the centre of the city. Also in Patan.

LEGEND : The origin of this festival is to be found in a legend which tells of a certain horse whose name has been lost in the passing of time and which triumphed over its arch–ememy, the demon "TUNDI". Both liked to graze on the "khel" i.e. the "lawn" now called for this reason : "Tundikhel". According to a belief which up to now prevails Tundi's spirit is still there and, once a year, it claims the life of a young boy Of course, this is not done anymore and instead, the cavalry of the Royal Army organizes a parade which is supposed to chase away this male-volent spirit.

WHAT HAPPENS : Essentially the performance of the cavalry units.

Anne–Marie SPAHR, an expert on Nepalese folklore, tells that, in the time of the Rana regime, a house was especially built on this occasion of Tundikhel, just to be set on fire and allow the fire–brigade to demonstrate speed in extinguishing a fire !

In PATAN, Ghora Jatra is a very gay festival. Here, the caval-cade is replaced by the presence of a lonely horse which, as tra-dition requires, has to be one-eyed. Should this prove impossible, any horse will do, but one of its eyes is covered with a piece of cloth. The rider, a "jyapu", demonstrates his skill in the best tradition of the "cow-boy" taming a wild horse.

On the third day of this festival, a curious rite is performed in the heart of Kathmandu's old quarters, at Asan Tole : This becomes the gathering place of the "eight sister-goddesses". In fact, they are usually only three, namely : Bhadra Kali, follo-wed by Bagmati and, finally, Kankeshwari, Each of these deities is then carried on a palanquin and the bearers manage in such a

way as to compile the three goddesses to bow to each other every time one crosses the other's way.   All this is performed in a very gay mood, but its real meaning has been lost in the mists of time.
CHAITRA DASAIN : The festival in honour of Goddess Durga.
DATE : From the eigth to the eleventh day of the cleary night of the month of Chaitra (mid-March to mid-April).
PLACE : In the old parts of Kathmandu.
WHAT HAPPENS : A procession is led through the heart of the city.

It includes an impressive huge four—wheeled chariot on which a sacred image of Goddess Durga is placed. She is the terrifying representation of Parvati, Shiva's spouse. Young men drag the chariot singing, dancing and merry—making. While the chariot is moving around, goats and cocks are sacrificed in the courtyard of Seto Matsyendranath on Indra Chowk, where Durga also was her own sanctuary. It is there that her image will be carried at the end of the procession.

ART AND HANDICRAFT

THE INFLUENCE OF RELIGION

For more than fifteen centuries, Nepalese artisans have excelled in stone sculpture, wood—carving and painting on walls and scrolls. Above all their art appears in temple architecture and decoration. It is strongly believed that the pagoda-style of architecture so typical for Nepal, was introduced by Nepalese architects and artists into Tibet and even to China.

In certain parts of the Valley, all traditional skills and handicrafts have survived to this day, for instance in wood-carvings, jewellery, scroll painting etc.

One important factor should be kept in mind : All Nepalese arts, with a few exceptions only, have their roots embedded in religion. You find it everywhere, in and on pagodas and temples, shrines and sacred fountains, palaces or funeral mounds. Whereever you look, you will see gods and goddesses in their various representations and forms, their emblems, symbols etc.

The paintings also depict religious scenes, or episodes taken from myths or legends, whether on manuscripts, scrolls or frescoes.

Of course, the two most widespread religions of the Nepalese people are Brahman Hinduism and Mahayana Buddhism (Buddhism of the great vehicle) or, better said, Vajrayana Buddhism i. e. Lamaism.

THE HINDU INFLUENCE

The multiplicity of gods and goddesses belonging to the Hindu Pantheon may be a little disturbing for the western visitor, if unfamiliar with them. Now this book is not meant to dwell on Hindu religion and its many intricacies. The identification of the apparently innumerable deities becomes relatively easy once the basic principle has been understood. This principle is the following : each deity is given not only a different name, but distinct symbols, attributes, tasks and powers, according to what it is supposed to perform. Thus, the same god or gooddess will be represented under many different "aspects" or "forms" while remaining still fundamentally the same.

Let us quote one example only : Lord Vishnu may be represented under 24 different "aspects". But his four distinctive attributes, which are the lotus, the conch-shell, the disk and the mace will always be visible, each being held by one of his four hands. Only the distribution of its attributes will be different : In his aspect as "Narasingha" for instance, his lower right hand will be holding the disk, his upper right hand the lotus, his upper left hand the mace and his lower left hand the conch-shell. In his aspect as "Vamana", the distribution will be : conch in lower right, dish in upper right, mace in upper left and lotus in lower left and so on.

Another distinctive feature is the presence of the god's "mount" or "vehicle", usually an animal on which stands, sits or rides a given god or goddess. This animal is supposed to serve the deity under all circumstances with boundless devotion.

We shall mention below, some of these characteristic features for each of the gods.

Although the expert may discover differences in the image under which Indian and Nepalese artists may represent the same divinity, in essence, they are the same, and in both countries, the three primary Hindu gods are BRAHMA, VISHNU and SHIVA.

—BRAHMA. the Creator of all the Universe and Originator of Everything. His traditional emblems are : the rosary, the receptacle of lustral water, the ladle and the book.

His mount : the goose or the swan.

His consort : SARASWATI. Here it is necessary to note that, whereas some scholars make a distinction between "MAHA-SARASWATI," as Brahma's "consort" and SARASWATI, the Goddess of knowledge, music etc. as Brahma's "daughter", others

insist that SARASWATI is both Brahma's consort and daughter.
This subtlety, again, is considered as purely academic, since
Brahma, being THE Creator, it is, in fact, his creative power which
is personified by his consort as well as by his daughter, so much
more that he has to be considered as having "created" both.

However that may be, SARASWATI is generally represented
as holding a lute, a rosary, a book and an elephant hook. Her
mount is usually the peacock. On her forehead : a radiant
crescent moon.

In Nepal, Brahma seems less venerated than he is in India.
With charming candour, Mary RUBEL writes about this fact in
her little publication "*The Gods of Nepal*." : "Brahma has declined
in power as his *job* as a Creator is largely finished. Thus, his existence is more on the philosophical level. He is no longer
concerned with the day–to–day operation in life."

On the other hand, Vishnu and Shiva are the most popular
and most venerated Gods in Nepal.

—*VISHNU* : the Preserver of Life and of the World.

His emblems : the conch–shell, the disc, the lotus-flowers,
the mace.

His mount : Garuda, the mythical being, half-man, half-bird.
His consort : Lakshmi, goddess of fortune. Her emblem is the
jewel and her mount, the tortoise.

In Nepal, Vishnu is rarely represented as Rama, or Krishna,
both very popular in India, but most frequently he appears in one
of the following aspects :

—*Narayan* (or Narain or Narayana), a word which means :
Knodledge or Universal refuge. Narayan is supposed to have
brought the world the message of universal love.

—*Narasimha* (or Narsingha), the lion-man who is worshipped by
kings and warriors. For man is the strongest of all creatures and
this is also true for the lion. Narasimha is often represented
with a lion's head and four arms, tearing apart the guts of the demon Hiranyakashipu, who, according to the legend, pretended
to be a god himself and forbade the worship of Vishnu. Hence,
the punishment.

—*Varaha,* the wild boar, a form that stems from the well-known
myth according to which Vishnu took the shape of such a wild
boar in order to plunge into the sea to kill the same demon-king
Hiranyakashipu who had hurled the whole earth to the bottom
of the boundless ocean.

—*Matsya,* the fish, which is attached to a legend unexpectedly reminding of the story of Noah and the Flood:One morning, MANU, the Creator of Human Race, so the story goes, found in the water which was brought to him for his ablutions, a tiny fish. It slipped into his hand and begged for his protection. The fish said to Manu : "I shall save you from a great flood that will sweep away all the creatures of the earth." The fish grew rapidly in size and had to be put in ever bigger receptacles until only the ocean was large enough to contain it. It was then that Manu realized that his fish must be a reincarnation of Lord VISHNU. The latter told Manu of the imminent flood and commanded him to prepare for it. He had him built a ship and when the rain started, he ordered him to embark all wise men, as well as a number of animals and plants."

—*Kurma,* the tortoise. During this flood many treasures disappeared into the oceans. VISHNU took on the form of a tortoise and recovered them all.

—*Vamana*, the dwarf. Here another legend of which VISHNU is the hero: BALI, the king of the "anti-gods" had, by his courage and ascetic life, obtained sovereignty of the three worlds. The gods who were deprived of their residences, the incense fumes of the rites and the joyous feelings provided by the sacrifices, appealed to Vishnu for his assistance. Thus, Vishnu appeared before Bali in the form of a dwarf. He simply asked him for a piece of land that he could cover in three strides. Bali agreed. In one stride, the dwarf covered the whole earth, with the second the skies and as he had nowhere else to put his third stride down, he stepped on Bali's head and pushed him into the underworld,which Vishnu left to Bali as his future kingdom and in recognition of his merits and virtues. Bali admitted defeat.

—*Buddha*, Let us simply remind that, according to Hindu mythology, the ninth reincarnation of VISHNU is BUDDHA. (One may wonder whether this could not explain, at least to a certain extend, the peaceful coexistence of both religions in Nepal).

—*SHIVA* : the Destroyer, but also the Regenerator.

His emblems : the trident, the tambourine, the tiger skin, the club, the lingam (phallus, symbol of creative energy).

His mount : NANDI, the bull.

His consort : PARVATI, who, in her beneficient aspect is also called DEVI, UMA, SHAKTI, and in Nepal, ANNAPURNA (among many other names,) i. e. the dispenser of abundance. In her terrifying aspect, she is KALI, DURGA or BHAGAVATI.

In Nepal SHIVA frequently takes the form of :

—*Pashupati*, : the master, or protector of cattle, lord of the earth, friend of life and guide of species in their development. He is also the tutelary god of Nepal who is referred to at the end of all official speeches, including in H.M. the King's proclamations or statements.

—*Mahadev* or *Maheshvar* (i.e. "Great God"), lord of knowledge and power of procreation that recreates indefinitely as and what he destroys. In this most important capacity, his symbol is the lingam, instrument of creation and source of supreme enjoyment.

—*Bhairav* (or *Kalo Bhairav* i.e. Bhairav of Death) representation of Shiva in its most terrifiying form : a malevolent god intent on destroying everything, including ignorance and evil !

In the centre of Kathmandu, there is a huge statue of Kalo Bhairav, painted in black wearing a collar of skulls round his neck.

(Bhairav is also the symbol of the Nepalese Airline where he appears with two wings in the back of his head. This choice may seem strange in the first instance, but it is easily explained since, thanks to its terrifying aspect, Bhairav is supposed to be able to ward off, chase away, eliminate all and any evil and malevolent influences which otherwise may cause unpleasant consequences.)

—*Hanuman*, the Monkey-god, venerated by many as the aspect of Lord Shiva symbolizing faithfulness and willingness to help, two qualities which Hanuman demonstrated when he assisted RAMA in his fight against the demon–king RAVANA and his recovery of his beloved wife SITA (the theme of the Hindu epic, the "RAMA-YANA"). All MALLA kings saw in Hanuman the deity who would ensure them success in their military undertakings.

Other gods much venerated in Nepal are :

—*Ganesh*, the elephant–headed god is one of the most fascinating deities of the Hinduist Pantheon. In Nepal, he is one of the most popular gods, one who is not only infallible and charitable but – even more important in the eyes of the devotees : it is He who decides over success (or failure) of all and any human enterprises : this explains why most Hindus, before addressing their prayers to any other divinity, rarely fail to begin with paying homage to Ganesh ! Thus, they implore him for granting the success in their petition they are about to prlesent to the next deity !

This almost universal "power" of Ganesh is reflected in its other popular name : "Ganapati", where pati means "master" "sovereign" or "ruler" and "gana" categories, i. e. anything that can be classified and counted. In other words, any collection of things. But Ganesh has still many other names, such as "Vignesh-vara", meaning "master of all obstacles", "Vinayaka" : le "best of guides", and, of course, 'Gajanana" where "gaja" means ele-phant, and "nana" : "face".

In certain regions of Nepal, according to C. J. Miller S.J.'s excellent book about "Faith-Healers in the Himalayas" Ganesh's name is interpreted still in another interesting sway, namely "master of the gan", since he has the power of rendering harm-less any "gan", the word used by many ethnic groups for "malevo-lent spirits" that bring sickness and death to people !

Hindu mythology tells us that Ganesh is the son of SHIVA and PARVATI. The legend says that the child had his head cut off, accidentaly, so to speak, by his own father. Indeed, one day when coming home, he found in front of his house a guard whom he did not know and who tried to prevent him from entering. (This was what his mother had asked him to do.) Parvati was struck with terror when she learnt that Shiva had inadvertently killed their son ! Shiva promised to call him back to life adding that he would chop off the head of the first living being he would meet. He went to the jungle and it so happened that the first living being was an elephant ! So he chopped off its head and grafted it on his son's body. GANESH is always dressed in red, has usually four arms and his body is covered with an ointment made of powdered red sandalwood. He has only one tusk. His mount is a shrew, often mistaken for a rat, which makes both these animals "sacred" ones.

—*Kumari,* an aspect of Durga, as a young virgin. (see more about this goddess, as she is venerated in Nepal, under "What to see", in the paragraph dedicated to the Palace of the Livinig-Goddess).

—*Manjushri,* a Bodhisattva, (i.e. a human being who reached the stage where he deserves to gain Nirvana, desists from it in order to assist others to attain the degree of detachment and serenity), symbol of wisdom–which is indicated by the Book of transcendental knowledge always resting on a lotus flower held in his left hand. In his right he brandishes a sword. With this sword he cuts all Gordian knots and strikes down ignorance. (In Nepal, he has gained another merit still, which consisted in saving the life of all the inhabitants of the Valley threatened by the floods. With his sword, he cut a passage through the Chhobar rock, west of the city, thereby releasing the waters.)

THE BUDDHIST INFLUENCE

Beginning in what is now part of Nepal (a place called Lumbini in the Terai, also named Rummindei), Buddhism, or, better said, the teachings of SIDHARATA GAUTAMA, spread over much of India and South–East Asia and penetrated into Tibet. China and Japan. Religion, philosophy, trade and art interacted throughout the whole area.

Many temples in Nepal are dedicated to BUDDHA, or to Bodhisatvas such as Padmapani, the saviour and master of re-incarnations, one of the hundred aspects of Avalokitesvara (generally represented with eleven heads and innumerable arms) or Amithaba, Matsyendranath or others.

In this field of Buddhist influences on Nepalese art a whole book would be needed. Let us merely mention the most striking features, the ones any casual visitor is bound to see while strolling through the streets. Indeed, everywhere, he will see small stone structures in a vaguely conical shape. These are called "*chaityas*" and are shrines offered by devotees in gratitude or simply, as an act of piety.

These chaityas always show four statues of Buddha, each facing one of the cardinal points. Here a brief explanation of the traditional "*attitudes*" or "*postures*", in which Buddha is represented there :

Towards North : Buddha-Amoghasiddhi, his right hand raised in *blessing.*

Towards East : Buddha-Akshobhya, his right hand with inturned palm and the tip of the fingers touching the earth. This is Buddha *Calling the earth to witness* that he resisted all temptations the demon Mara threw at him in his attempt to wrest Buddha away from his meditation and search for ultimate truth.

Towards South : Buddha-Ratnasambhava, his right hand's palm turned outward, expressing *compassion.*

Towards West : Buddha-Amithaba, his both hands folded on his lap in *meditation.*

On some of the chaityas or on painted scrolls, a fifth central figure is to be found. This will then be *Buddha-Vairocana,* always placed either above or in the centre of the four others, in any case facing the Zenith. Both his hands are folded in front of his chest, expressing *perfect sovereignty.*

Another deity is often represented, in particular as a statue

placed on the top of a stone pillar. Mostly it is either the GREEN
or the WHITE TARA, or both. The Green Tara was a Nepalese
princess and the White a Chinese one who around 640 A. D.
where both married to the King of Tibet Rong Tsang Gampo
whom they converted to the Buddhist faith. Later both Tara were
deified and are often considered as "Buddha's consort", which,
of course, they were never meant to become.

NEPALESE ART

Kathmandu Valley became, in the course of the centuries, a
real melting-pot of all these various cultural and artistic influences.
And it was mainly the Newars who were the most creative artisans.

In the course of the thirteenth century, the influence of Nepalese
art made itself particularly felt. It is said to have penetrated into
Tibet and even beyond, to China, thanks to an innovator and
architect named BALBAHU, better known as ARNIKO. Nepalese
artisans were repeatedly sent to the Emperors of China and the
Kings of Tibet, at their request, in order to work there and impart
knowledge. In Nepal itself, certain kings, in particular those of
the MALLA dynasty who reigned for 5 centuries (13th to 18th. A.D.)
over the Valley, encouraged all forms of artistic expressions.

The main characteristics of Nepalese art are delicacy, a certain
candour, a simplicity of expression, an extraordinary harmony
of form and a wealth of decorative details. From the seventeenth
century onward Tibetan influence became apparent and even, in
some aspects, preponderant. Simultaneously, Nepalese art
began to differentiate itself more and more from classical Indian
art and moved towards the Lamaistic and Tantric themes of sometimes demoniacal and terrifying expression.

ARCHITECTURE

Not long ago, a foreign visitor described Kathmandu as
"the valley where there are more religious edifices than houses".
This is only a slight exaggeration, for even today, it is difficult
to walk through the streets of Kathmandu, Patan or Bhadgaon
for more than fifty yards without coming up on a pagoda, a shrine
or a sacred water tank.

The tourist from abroad is immediately struck by the origi-
nality of the architecture of temples, palaces and private houses.
There exists nothing comparable elsewhere.

To begin with, Nepalese temples may be divided into three
categories, location–wise :
—Those that were built near, around or inside the courtyard

of a Royal palace : this is the case with several "*Durbar Square*" temples.

—Private temples, which may be built anywhere.

—Those which were built in some places of natural significance such as the top of a hill (eg. *Changu Narayan*), the bank of a river (eg. *Pashupatinath, Guyeshwari, Gokarna* etc.) or near wells or fountains (eg. *Budanilkantha, Balaju* etc.)

Besides this topographical classification, there is another one which is connected with the architectural shape of religious buildings.

Inspite of their infinite variety of details, Nepalese temples may roughly be divided into three families :

—*pagodas*
—*shikaras*
—*stupas*

However, this classification can not be used as a clue to the appurtenance, of the temple to its particular faith or creed.

Indeed, "*pagodas*" for instance as well as "*shikaras*" may be Hinduist or Buddhist; only "*stupas*" are specifically Buddhist.

However, there are two easy means of identifying which temple belongs to the Hinduist and which to the Buddhist faith :

As a rule, a Hindu temple, when it is not part of the compound of a Royal Palace, is usually built "in the open", i.e. alongside a road or a river, or, as mentioned before, on top of a hill.

A Buddhist temple, on the other hand, save a very few exceptions, is usually built inside a square courtyard to which a low gate and a very narrow passage or a lane gives access.

Furthermore, whenever the temple building is surrounded by a railing consisting of rows of prayer–wheels, it can only be a Buddhist one.

One word about these prayer–wheels which the devotee puts in motion with his hand while circumambulating–always clockwise–around the temple; the prayer–wheel fulfils its function only when spinning, for only then is the prayer or incantation radiated and diffused to the realms of the divinities; not unlike a generator that produces electricity only when rotating !

The temple prayer–wheels are usually made of a brass cylinder embossed with letters monstly of the Sanskrit script called "ranja" which was in use before the seventh century A. D.

Inside there is a long roll of rice paper wrapped in a piece of cotton; this roll bears hundreds of thousands times (of ten up to 100,000,000 !) the same "mantra" (incantation formula) as the one written on the cylinder itself, but this time in Tibetan characters of the alphabet which has been designed at the end of thes eventh century A.D. by the Tibetan scholar THONMI, surnamed SAMBOTHA, for exclusive use in Tibet, where the spoken language could not until then be written for want of an adequate script.

The literal translation of the "mantra", found in prayer–wheels is : *"OM MANI PADME HUM'*, *"OH ! THE JEWEL (mani) IN THE LOTUS (padme) !"*

There are commonly two accepted interpretations:

"Jewel", means the end of the cycle of reincarnations and "Lotus", a symbol for the deity who decides about reincarnations.

To express and repeat this formula means therefore actually to direct the prayer to PADMAPANI, the Boddhisatva "controller of re–births" whose name indicates that he is standing on a lotus-flower : The real translation could thus be formulated as follows: *"Oh ! (Padmapani, give me) the Jewel '(the benefit of non-rebirth), (which you hold in your power) in the Lotus"*. meaning the purity of the Buddhist precepts.

The second interpretation is a simpler one : *"oh (may) the Jewel (meaning Buddha or Buddha's teaching) (remain for ever) in the Lotus (meaning our own hearts, mind and soul).*

Coming back to the sanctuaries and their three most common architectural styles, namely pagodas, shikara–temples and stupas they have one thing in common :

Neither of them is conceived as a religious meeting place for devotees as it is the case with Christain churches, Jewish synago-gues or Muslim mosques.

In these Mediterranean religions, one of the most significant ex-ternal display of religious rites consists in the meeting of the devo-tees on a given day, hour and place to pray, sing, and listen to their "priest", whatever his name may be. On the contrary, although Hindus and Buddhists may assemble to celebrate certain festivals or participate in collective bathing or processions, their religion, as such, is essentially an individualistic one, where the devotee is facing his particular 'God' directly, praying and making offerings to him, without intervention of any priest, interpreter of scripts or spokesman. Their priests play an active part mainly on certain specific occasions, like wedding and funeral rites, and are called to perform these rites as they are the experts and are qualified to preside over such ceremonies.

To revert now to the stylistic families referred to above, here are some of their main characteristics :

Pagodas

They are by far the most typically Nepalese of all three types. Mostly they stand on a square or a rectangular base, and always they are of a perfect geometrical simplicity and harmony of proportions.

The base shelters the statue or image of the deity to whom the pagoda is dedicated. Above this base, there is the body of the temple itself, topped by several roofs, usually three or five rather than two or four, since it is known that odd numbers are, as rule, considered more auspicious than even ones !

Now, the higher these superimposed tiers of roofs go, the smaller they become.

The oldest of these pagodas, CHANGU NARAYAN, dates back to the beginning of the 16th century. This is rather an exception since most of the pagodas, as they are to be seen nowadays, date back to renovations which have been undertaken during the late 17th and 18th centuries.

The other peculiarities of Nepalese pagodas are :

—*The building materials* used : mostly pink bricks except for occasional square blocks of stone to reinforce the foundations. Courtyards of the temples are usually paved, also with brickwork.

—*The doors* are usually in wood, covered with carved brass or bronze plates.

—*The semi-circular decorative piece above the doors,* called "*torana*" is also made of gilded bronze plated wood. In its centre, there is usually a "*Garuda*" (Vishnu's mount : a mythical bird, half–bird, half–man), sometimes a gryphon holding between teeth and paws a winding naga. This mythical animal is called a "*kirti mukha*" and the scene symbolizes the victory of "*good over evil*", a typically Nepalese temple decoration.

—*The windows* are almost always delicately carved in wood and covered with latticed intricate decorations (glass panes were introduced in Nepal only around 150 years ago !). In the course of the renovation work started in 1974 by the Archaeological Department of H.M.G. with the cooperation of the UNESCO, on the occasion of H. M. King BIRENDRA'S coronation two unexpected things were discovered : After they were thoroughly cleaned, two sets of windows in the old Royal Palace near the entrance to the Hanuman Dhoka Square have been found to be made of ivory, instead of the traditional wood, Similarly, on the *"Shiva-Parvati-temple"* nearby, a set of three windows revealed to be of carved stone !

—*The struts,* joints that are always at an angle of 45*. They are usually very richly carved and they bear either a deity or a mythical animal.

—*The roofs* are plated with copper or gilded bronze.

—*The walls* are often covered with paintings and sometimes with turn-of-the-century multicoloured tiles, obviously imported from Europe, Whether these tiles are in harmony with the rest of the building is a topic open to debate.

—*The shape :* Whether it be a small shrine a few feet high or a temple with five stories and an ascending series of roofs, the silhouette of a Nepalese sanctuary is almost the same, with very little variety in the general outline.

—*Architectural details :* The corners of the roofs are always turned upwards and end with a human or an angel's head embossed on bronze, the face pointed downwards. As a counterbalance, the upturned corner of each roof carries a bird ready to take flight. (This was King Yoga Narendra Malla's (1684–1705) idea. Shortly before his death he made it known that "as long as the birds haven't flown away form the temple's cornices, I shall be amongst you, even if my body is no longer alive.") This curve also lightens the general appearance of the temple. Along the edges of the roofs, innumerable bell-shaped ornaments are attached, but the clapper has been replaced by a thin metal leave that tinkles in the lightest breeze, whereas the bells remain motionless. This type of decorative motif is known by the attractively onomatopoeic term *"kinkinimala"* in Nepali.

—Every temple-front is protected by two bronze or stone dragons or lions, mythical animals in any case, and is provided with one or two large bronze bells hanging from either an iron or a stone beam. Once the worshipper has made his devotions, performed his *"puja"* and, sometimes, circumambulated once or several times the temple, he shakes the clapper of the bell. The interpretation of this rite is not quite clear. It may correspond, simply to the Christian way of terminating a prayer by saying *"Amen"*.

—At the corners of the temples and prayer flags or oriflammes, and sometimes a Nepalese flag made of a sheet of bronze or gilded brass.

—Metal ribbons hang down from the roofs within a few yards of the ground ending with a flat but larger piece on which is embossed the image of a god (in Hindu temples) or of Buddha or a "*chaitya*" (in Buddhist temples). These ribbons called *dhvajas* or *patakas* are made of rectangular metal plates joined together to give the impression of suppleness like that of a flat naga (serpent). This ribbon symbolizes the "*path*" that the deity would take to descend among the faithful, or that the faithful's prayers may take to reach the divine in heaven. In general, the dhvajas are only placed on the front–side of the temple.

The ewers fastened to the roofs and walls, called "*kalashas*", symbolize the blessings that water brings to humanity; at the same time this ordinary everyday utensil is considered very auspicious.

—The ornaments at the top of the highest roof: the shape of the gables varies according to the gods to whom the temple is dedicated : three sprires symbolize the trinity of *Brahma, Vishnu* and *Shiva* in the case of a Hindu temple; of *Buddha, Dharma* (the law) and *Sangha* (the community) in the case of a Buddhist temple. The latter applies also to the three windows that are traditional on Newar Buddhist houses.

—The gable shape often reminds the shape of a bell. Sometimes there is only one, often three, and sometimes five. These "bells" are often replaced by "umbrellas" a very royal symbol in a warm country. On the temples there are anything from 2 to 13 "*umbrellas*", piled on top of each other. (Many specialists argue that these sunshades are the origin of the pagoda–style of Nepalese temples).

—*The mirrors :* They are always very ordinary ones and are of recent date. In fact, mirrors were first introduced in Nepal about 150 years ago ! Talking of these mirrors we leave the realm of religious symbols to step down to ordinary life for mirrors are only affixed to temples to enable women to put the "*tilak*", or "*tika*" mark on their forehead more elegantly and more accurately in the centre. The tika is red, orange, yellow or carmine according to the colour of the saree worn on that given day. Of course, originally the tika had a religious significance but now it is essentially ornamental, rather like the black patches that ladies of fashion used in the eighteenth century in western countries. However putting a tika mark in a temple after having said prayers and made offerings, is still a gesture of religious worship.

The general belief that the tika mark indicates that the woman

is married does not correspond to reality. The mark of a married
woman is the red streak in the hair-line. This is the case in most
of the ethnic and social groups.

The beautiful and typical of these pagoda–style temples are :
– *in Kathmandu : the Taleju Royal Temple*
– *at Patan : the Golden Temple*
– *at Bhadgon : the Nyatapola*

Shikaras

This architectural style reminds of the South Indian temples.
Their most characteristic feature is their stately dome. Certain
scholars interpret the peculiar shape of these vaulted roofs as
a folded up umbrella whereas the superimposed roofs of pagodas
would symbolize the unfolded one !

However, the base of the shikara–style temple is always a
square. The building itself is often multi–storeyed with balconies
and supporting columns or pillars. The two most famous "shikara"
temples in the Valley are the KRISHNA MANDIR temple on Durbar
Square at Patan, and, also at Patan, the MAHABUDDHA temple.

Stupas

Originally these structures were funeral mounds or reliquaries.
They usually have a semi–spheric base of earth–like the very
ancient ones located at the four cardinal points around the
city of Patan, or, of masonry, like the stupa of Bodnath. In
both cases, they are never hollow and therefore, one cannot
step inside.

The tower of stupas usually bear the all–seeing eyes of Buddha. (For more details about the smbolism of stupas see under
Bodnath.)

SCULPTURE

Wood and stone carving are the forms of art in which Nepalese
artists and artisans have especially excelled.

Stone carvings

Old pieces dating from the eighth or ninth centuries are still
to be found, even in Kathmandu itself, sometimes well preserved.
But those dating from the eleventh and twelvth centuries are
more frequent.

The style of Nepalese stone carving brings to the mind the great
periods of Indian art. The characteristics of the GUPTA (5th to
6th century A.D.) as well as the PALASENA period (10th to 12th
century A.D.) are apparent, especially as represented in Bengal

and Bihar, the two provinces closest to Nepal and having had the most active trade links with it. One of the oldest artistic centres was the University of NALANDA, near the town of Pataliputra (the present Patan), which also had a Buddhist monastery of considerable importance. Unfortunately this was destroyed and looted during the Muslim invasions in the twelvth century A.D.

However, it seems certain that some artists from Nalanda came and settled in Nepal; they might have had a considerable influence that can still be traced in works dating from the sixteenth century.

As has been mentioned earlier, the inspiration of these carvings was almost entirely religious, and the statues of gods, mythical beings, etc. were almost always carved to decorate temples or temple courtyards. In fact, *"Art for Art's sake"* was an unknown concept in Nepal. Beautiful examples of carvings are found in Changu Narayan, a temple perched on a hill beyond Bodnath, north-east of Kathmandu. This seventh century temple is the oldest in the Valley.

Wood carvings :

Most of the wood carvings now to be found in Nepal date back to the seventeenth century, or more often, to the eighteenth. These carvings were first used to decorate the retaining pillars of houses, places or temples, the window–and door–frames and the corbel tables and joists supporting the temple roofs.

The most usual patterns for pillars and window–frames are geometric in form, often incorporating flowers and leaves as well as human figures or animals, especially snakes. The joists and struts of pagodas are usually carved in such a way to serve as a support for a god or mythical beast (dragon, griffin or *"makara"*, an animal with a short, half rolled–up trunk which constitutes often the sprouts for sacred fountains). The joists usually rest on a square or rectangular wooden base where the artist carved some erortic scenes. (In India such scenes are more often carved in stone : temples of *Khajurao or Konarak,* for instance.)

EROTIC ICONOGRAPHY

The question which comes immediately to the mind, is why such carvings should appear on temples. The official explanation provided by tourist guides and guidebooks is too simple to be satisfactory, namely that the "goddess of thunder and lightning" is a young virgin. When she sees such carvings on temples, she turns away from them in horror and never strikes them. Another

explanation, which must also be taken with a pinch of salt, is
that these carvings were designed as a kind of test for the faithful,
who come in order to pray, meditate and make offerings but who
should not let themselves be distracted by such scenes.

Finally the most unfounded explanation which has lately
cropped up in speeches by tourist–guides claims that, "at a
given time in past history" (no date is spelled out and for a very
good reason too!) the "demographic statistics" showed a dis-
quientening tendancy to flatten out and thus, it was thought these
representations may have a "corrective" effect.

Needless to say that such "demographic graphs," never existed
in Nepal or elsewhere, at the time these temples–and their carvings– were completed !

All this is wrong and far too simple.

It is necessary to go back much further, to the very remote past,
and try to understand the oldest religious notions of the peoples
of the Indian subcontinent.

One must remember that in nearly all countries–and this applies particularly to India–where death lurked everywhere, in
ancient times, and every year took the shape of epidemics, drou-
ghts or floods at monsoon time, jungle dangers and other disas-
ters, it was only natural that the eternal symbol of the process of
creation should not only be represented but even divinized as a
kind of affirmation of life over the destructive death, an
invocation of fertility, or an exorcism against sterility which is
tantamount to death.

Thus, it is quite natural also that these symbols and representations should be shown on sanctuaries and temples, since they
have a holy or divine meaning.

Furthermore, since its Vedic origins, and later, under the
influence of tantrism, the symbols and vivid representations of
sexual creativity– or simply intercourse–have been part of a definite world–outlook and of certain ritual intended to invigorate the
life forces of nature.

This concept has found its strongest expression in Hindu art,
as shown among many other on the famous temples of Konarak
and Khajurao. Buddhism did not escape from these cults and
forms of art as are shown in the Tantrist iconography, doubtless
introduced into Tibet and Nepal by the Indian mystic, magician
and tantrist PADMA SAMBHAVA in the eighth century A. D.

It is worth noting that five centuries earlier, appeared the famous book "*Kama-Sutra*" composed by Vatsyayana, another Indian mystic, the first treatise on "sexology", so to speak; this book certainly inspired later the artistic expressions as found on the temples (*N. B.:* never on palaces or private houses, for the reason indicated above, namely the sacred character of these images.)

Some might still object that a certain number of these representations are far from showing the act of procreation, but are rather acrobatics, eccentricities and even copulating animals.

To this, one might answer that, once the principle of "procreation acts," as works of art had been established, nothing could prevent the artists and artisans from letting free course to their imagination, fantasy and even dissoluteness.

The famous Tibetologue and Indologue, Professor TUCCI, gives two explanations which he qualifies himself as "more or less pertinent". :

1) First of all we may suppose, that just as esoteric books were kept hidden from the non–initiated in various ways, so also the temples may have been dedicated with erotic scenes on the outside, in order to protect those performing religious rites, inside. In fact, these carvings were then designed on purpose, in order to keep the ordinary people away from what was considered truly sacred. It must also be remembered that these carvings are found only on the outside, never inside. By their presence, they indicate that inside an inviolable sacredness is preserved.

2) Especially on Nepalese temples, it will be seen that there is always a space left between the erotic carvings and the divinities carved above them on the struts supporting the roofs. This space is emphasized by a lotus blossom which acts as a hind of pedestal for the deity.

The lotus blossom in India, Nepal and Tibet signifies spiritual renewal. Therefore, under the lotus, life is represented crudely, with all its excesses, but with the innate capacity for redemption. The lotus appears as a symbol of purity and of life beyond.

Selecting the lotus as this symbol rests on its very "botanical" nature : Indeed, the lotus plant grows mostly in stagnant water, its roots embedded in mud. Its stem has to struggle through layers of dirty water, disentangle itself from the maze of submerged water–plants; the bud takes shape only after the stem has succeeded in piercing several inches above the water level, so that the beautiful flower may never be desecrated by the foulness surrounding it, but offers its open petals to the sky and the sun, i. e.

towards God. Thus, the lotus has become the symbol of the eternal aspiration of mortals toards spiritual perfection !

Finally, another explanation–and a very simple as well as credible one–has been given by L. F. STILLER, S. J. in his study "*An Introduction to Hanuman Dhoka*", published in Kathmandu in 1975, on the occasion of H. M. KING BIRENDRA'S coronation. :

"It may be better, says L. F. STILLER, to assume that the carvings have their own special religious meaning and are not so much to be taken literally as they are to be understood as a kind of coded expression of some deeper tantric mysteries, known only to initiates. The significance of the carvings is thus determined by the observer. A man of the world is satisfied with what he sees. The initiate has no eyes for the obvious meaning of the carvings but sees in them a deeper truth".

PAINTING

The earliest form of painting (during the 11th century A.D.) practiced in Nepal was that of illuminated manuscripts made either of palm leaves or rice paper. Another very characteristic form of Nepalese, as well as Tibetan, painting (it is difficult to establish which came first), are the "*thang-kas*" that have been mentioned before. They are paintings on cotton meant for temples and monasteries; usually they are hung around the abbot's place of honour, or displayed along the walls. These thang–kas are almost invariably rectangular in shape, less wide than high. Their proportions correspond often to the traditional "*golden proportions*" ($15^3/_4$ in. by $23^1/_2$ in. = 40 cm by 60 cm) or, to put it in more precise terms : 61,8 by 100).

They are commonly framed with three stripes of Chinese brocade : blue, yellow and red. The yellow one should always be in the middle, the red one nearest to the painting and the blue one, which is always much broader, outside. These three colours are supposed to represent the rainbow which "separates all sacred objects from the material world". A thin piece of silk covers the painting and protects it from sun and dust.

Usually the "tempera" technique is used together with colours of vegetable origin mixed with natural rubber. The piece of cotton is tightly fastened inside a wooden frame and covered with various layers of a special product, then rubbed with a smooth stone before the actual painting is started.

The most frequent themes painted on thang–kas, are BUDDHA and his disciples, scenes from his life, or portraits of BODHI-

SATVAS such as AVALOKITESHVARA–CHENREZI, the patron saint of Tibet, mystics such as PADMA SAMBHAVA–GURU RIMPOCHE, the teacher and magician who introduced Lamaism into Tibet, or else the founders of the various schools or sects : TSONG–KAPA, for the *Gelukpa,* MARPA and MILAREPA for the *Kargyudpa,* KONCHOG GYALPO for the *Sakyapa.* Others represent TARA, in her white or green aspect. Occasionally thang-kas have also purely decorative and abstracts designs, more frequently geometrical patterns called MANDALAS.

A mandala can be looked upon as meaning two entirely different things.

—On the one hand, it is a sort of "instrument", which assists those who want to concerntrate in meditation, a "psychocosmogram" which helps him to disintegrate from the One to the many and to reintegrate from the many to the One, to Absolute Consciousness.

—On the other hand, its purely geometrical aspect "delineates consecrated superficies (circles or imbricated squares) which protects it from invasion by disintegrating forces symbolized in demonical circles. It is also a map of the cosmos, the whole universe in its essential plan, in its process of emanation and of reabsorption... developing from an essential Principle and rotating round a central axis. "(cf. Giuseppe TUCCI : *"The Theory and Practice of the Mandala"*).

For David SNELLGROVE (cf. *"Himalayan Buddhism"*) it is a "centre of radiation and power", which he identifies also with the abode of the divinity (whom the meditant wishes to identify himself with); this would explain the four "gates" always present in any mandala of "imbricated square shape".

But let us come back to the thang-kas as works of art. The first ones seem to have appeared towards the end of the 10th and 11th centuries in Western China, during the life of TUN–HOUANG.

The oldest thang-kas which are well-preserved, (mostly in museums and private collections in the U.S.A.) date back to the end of the 14th, and the beginning of the 15th century.

In Nepal, there are hardly any thang-kas earlier than the 16th century and the ones which are on sale in the antique and souvenir shops, if "antique" at all, are hardly over 150 or, at the most 200 years old. But these are very exceptional pieces, difficult to find, and, naturally, exorbitant in price.

However, it must be said, that the canons and the thang-kas

painting technique have been preserved until to-day. Specialized artists live in Malemchi, Tharkegyang (both located in the He-ambu district, north of Kathmandu;) as well as in the Dolpo and Sherpa regions, or, near to the capital, in Bodnath even. There, in the most recent gompa (a Karmapa-monastery building) completed in 1975-1947, twelve huge thang-kas depicting the life of Buddha, are sometimes on display.

Nepalese thang-kas are very similar to Tibetan ones, at first glance. But specialists can distinguish them by means of certain details, such as microscopic inscriptions which may appear sometimes on the recto or even on the verso. The general motives and technique also may reveal their respective origin.

Besides the thang-kas and, more rarely, illustrations on palm-leaf and later paper manuscripts, a third type of pictorial art typically Nepalese are the "patas".They are series of small pictures illustrating popular epics, such as the Ramayana and the Maha-bharat. This kind of paintings or drawings are in fact, very similar to the nowadays so popular "comic strips".

Finally, the last type of paintings are the mural frescoes which are mainly to be found in Buddhist monasteries. Very beautiful examples exist in the gompas of Thyangboche, in Sherpa-land, Chame and Tharkegyang. In the Valley, they may be seen-and admired-in the lamaist gonpas of Bodnath. Nepalese artists are said to have contributed in painting the walls of the Potala Palace, in Lhassa.

Among the decorative elements frequently seen in temples-Hindu as well as Buddhist ones-is the "*svastika*", turned in either way but always straight (the design used by the Nazis in Germany was always bent at an angle of 45° and turned to the left). Of course, there is no direct link between the two symbols. Being a very simple geometric design (like a cross, a circle, a triangle or a pyramid) it is only natural that it appeared in various civilizations in an independent way. This being said, it is likely that the svastika symbolizes, in most of its shapes, either the sun, or the rotating earth, or the wheel.

HANDICRAFTS

BRONZES

The first bronze works, with alloys of copper seem to have appeared about the same time as the first stone carvings, i. e. in the eighth century A.D. However, it is very difficult to date these works of art in an accurate way.

Bronze statuary, like all other expressions of artistic creation is almost wholly religious in inspiration. : Hindu, Buddhist and Tantric deities, as well as legendary figures.

The most frequently used technique is that of the "cire perdue" (the lost wax casting). The bronzes are often gilded and in the case of later works, studded with semi-precious stones, usually turquoise and coral, both of which have been and still are extremely popular in Tibet as well as in Nepal. This method maintained itself up to the present day. It may be regretted that the semi-precious stones are now, more often than not, replaced by glass or artificial materials.

JEWELLERY

Jewellery should perhaps be considered more of a handicraft than an art. Gold and silver are used to make the very beautiful traditional jewellery peculiar to each ethnical group and region. There are the large disk-like earrings of bronze-plated copper worn by the Gurung women, the small nose-rings worn in their left nostril by many young girls, the engraved silver belts, pendant spirit-boxes, silver and turquoise earrings of the Sherpa women, the curious bullet-like necklaces of the women from Jumla, and lastly the ankle "bracelets" and heavy silver necklaces worn by the women of the Terai.

POTTERY

This is one of many handicrafts that flourishes in Patan and Thimi (which lies between Kathmandu and Bhadgaon). There you can find a hundred different kinds of terra cotta oil lamps used for the Light Festival (Diwali in Hindi, Dipawali in Nepalese) as well as the charming peacock and elephant flower-pots often used to decorate gardens and villas.

SAFEGUARDING ART TREASURES

There is more than one answer to the question often asked by tourists who wonder why, in some places, temples, palaces and private buildings seem abandoned or neglected.

First of all some figures : Kathmandu alone counts 117 main temples and about 102 viharas, i.e. religious buildings comprising sanctuaries as well as lodgings for pilgrims. Patan counts 75 temples and 136 viharas, whereas you may find 25 temples and 14 viharas in Bhadgaon. Thus, the total number of buildings which the National Department of Archaeology has to take care of, amounts to over four hundred, not having included, in these figures, other

rt treasures, such as small sanctuaries, chaityas, fountains, pala-
es, and isolated statues. The total would amount to 880 items !

Second : It should not be forgotten that during past centuries,
ery few people   had any technical or scientific knowledge as to
ow to protect carved stones, wood, murals, the structure itself of
uildings etc. Thus, little could be done in this respect. Visitors from
urope may recollect that their own cathedrals, which were built
etween the 12th and the 16th century, were taken care of in a
nore or less scientific andsystematic way as late as the beginning
f the 19th century !

Third : Many battles have been fought in the streets of the
alley's cities and villages.

Last but not least : The two latest earthquakes (in 1833 and
934) have left traces and scars.

When Nepal opened its doors and windows to the modern
utside world, there was necessarily an order of priority of all the
things to be undertaken". For lack of funds, technical means
nd know–how, archeological reseach and achievements were
ot and could not be placed on top of the priority list, when the
uthorities had to face endemic diseases, illiteracy, housing, irri-
ation, power supply, transport, communications and many
ital problems of a more pressing nature.

However, the Nepalese authorities are not only perfectly aware
f the importance of the task of art–treasure preservation, but have
tarted taking appropriate measures even at a time when technical
quipment was still very scarce.

Today, the implementation of a master–plan for the safe-
uarding of all valuable monuments in the Valley has been started
ith the assistance of UNESCO. There is not the slightest doubt
hat this plan will be completed. The best proof of this is the
nagnificant restoration work done on the Hanuman Dhoxa
quare and the old Royal Palace at Kathmandu.

One more word ought to be added. It concerns the future of
he "Smiling Valley" as a tourist centre.

It is to be hoped that those entrusted with the planning of the
ature town development programmes and problems are aware
f the treasure of exceptional value they have in hand, a treasure
robably unique in the whole world, namely the fact that, less
nan 4 miles from the capital-city, there is a second one, equally
eautiful and interesting, and, less than 12 miles away, a third
ne ! Would it be wishful thinking only to believe that these two

precious old cities of Patan and Bhadgaon could not be preser
ved as "museum-cities" where the construction of whateve
"modern" building would be radically and completely banned
Kathmandu, the political and administrative capital woul
continue its development, becoming more and more a mixe
city where the artistic-historical aspect will have to co-exis
with the modern city. This process has obviously already starte
and cannot be stopped or reversed, be it only to respond to th
increasing number of foreign visitors for whom modern hotels
restaurants, shopping centres etc. must be provided ! Thi
does not mean, of course, that the population of Patan an
Bhadgaon should be deprived from modern amenities and im
provements to make their life more pleasant, and more hygieni
for they are as much entitled to it as the Kathmanduites.

In one word, the town planners are certainly keeping in min
that PATAN still is and should remain always *LALITPUR*, th
"Town of art'., that BHADGAON should not cease to b
BHAKTAPUR, the **"Town of devotees"**, while KATHMANDU
should always be *KANTIPUR,* the **"Town of bliss".**

STRANGE THINGS SEEN WHILE STROLLING THROUGH TOWNS AND VILLAGES

Whether it be narrow streets and lanes of the old parts o
KATHMANDU, PATAN or BHADGAON, or else, on the roads and in th
villages of the Valley, the visitor's eye will more than often b
attracted and his mind be puzzled by something unfamiliar, sur
prising, eccentirc or simply strange. The following paragraph
may contribute to satisfy his curiosity and to answer his questions

ROADS COVERED WITH REAPED CEREALS

Once the harvest of rice, wheat or barley is completed, th
bundles of reaped stalks are spread all over the metallized roads i
the Valley : cars, trucks and busses passing on these roads ar
thus "invited" by the resourceful peasants, to perform task
normally entrusted to costly thrashing machinery.

PORTAGE

—*Of goods :* Undoubtedly, this is one of the first sights tha
attracts the attention of the new visitor: so many people ar
carrying so many things in so many different ways ! They ma
be carrying vegetables, fire–wood, fruit, pottery, live chicke
or else pieces of furniture, bamboo poles or pyramids of bricks
Essentially, there are two portage systems :

1) Portage of loads carried on the back, the weight being supported by a headband made of plaited strings. Mostly, the loads are contained in cone-shaped baskets called "dhoko". which are made of plaited bamboo.

2) Portage by means of something which looks like a scale i.e. one bamboo pole carried on one shoulder and two flat baskets hanging down, tied to the pole by four strings. This portage method is used exclusively by Newars. The picturesque photograph to be taken is when each of the basket contains a baby or a little child, a not unfrequent sight in Kathmandu !.

—*Of persons* : Portage of persons is often performed by means of a strange-looking cradle made of wood and cane. This palanquin is too narrow and too short to make the carried person even slightly comfortable. Mostly it is used for carrying a bride or a bride–groom on a short distance, may be to the house of her or his future in–laws. Sometimes also, sick people are carried in this manner from the surrounding hills to the cities, hours or days away. However that may be, the palanquin of this type has a curious name : "Ulin Kat", a somewhat unexpectedly distorted pronunciation of the original British designation of "William's cot", as it was called in the beginning of the East India Company's "raj". But who this William actually was, nobody seems to recollect.

FUNERALS

The body of a deceased person is carried on men's back and never in a vehicle, from his house or the hospital where he died, down to the river-bank where it will be cremated (or, if a Muslim, to the cemetery).

If the deceased was a Newar, his body will be carried on some sort of rudimentary stretcher made of two long bamboo poles linked together by 7 transversals making it look like a kind of ladder. This stretcher will be carried on the shoulders of four men, usually his closest relatives. All those who accompany the funeral walk barefooted and bare-headed. Some musicians, mainly drum-beaters, take part in the procession.

There is an interesting exception in these Newari funeral traditions: One category of deceased persons are not entitled to either the ladder–shaped stretcher or to the drum-beaters. This applies to :
—Boys who have not gone through the "*bratabandha*" ceremony–the ceremony consisting for the maternal uncle to cut the hair of a boy aged 3. 5, or 7 (always an odd, thus an auspicious

number) using a silver or gold razor leaving only on the top of the boy's head, a long but thin tuff.

—Girls who have not yet been "married" to the bel-tree (see under Chapter : "*Newars*").

If the deceased belonged to another ethnic group, his body will in most cases simply be tied to one or several thick bomboo poles which, for some unrevealed reason should have been recently cut. Two men will carry the corpse.

Now as to the colours of the shrouds: As a rule–but there are many exceptions according to local or group customs,– a white shroud will be used to wrap the body of a man or a widow, whereas a woman whose husband is still alive will be wrapped in a red one. Sometimes the shroud, whether white or red, is covered with a second piece of orange or yellow cloth. This is merely a luxury item, a costly satin called "*pitamber*".

Newars usually wrap the body–whether man or woman–in a coarse white cotton sheet. Often a red or orange cloth called "*murda*" covers it and this is traditionally a contribution made by the "*guthi*" (the meaning of which is given in the chapter dedicated to the various ethnic groups).

MENDICANTS

The mendicants whom visitors and tourists are not likely to miss while sightseeing, may be classified in three categories :

—*The professional beggars*. They are called "*gaine*" and they always carry a self–made kind of wooden violin called a "*sarangi*"; they sing local or foreign songs, and often improvise them. These "gaines" are members of a special caste of musisian-beggars who play in Nepal exactly the same role as the wandering minstrels during the Middle Ages. They are supposed– of course, this is no longer true always and everywhere–to compose their songs around some outstanding historical or social event. One of their favourites has been, for years, a song glorifying Sir Edmund Hillary and, even more so, Sherpa Norkay Tenzing's victory over Sagarmatha. Thus, they offer their songs to passers-by and, since this is their only means of livelihood, their begging is, so to speak *legitimated* and a rupee or two ought to be given to them when they have "produced" some of their songs.

—*The mendicants pressed by old-age, poverty or sickness*. These are usually to be met around the Post-Office, at Pashupatinath, etc. It is undoubtedly an act of charity to distribute some paisas or rupees to these unfortunate ones.

—*The street-urchins* who run after every tourist anywhere, in particular in Kirtipur,showing off the knowledge of the tourist's own language–which they have acquired listening to them! – They are usually as *snotty* as they are smiling–which is far from being an understatement !– They have a definite talent to touch the soft spot in the heart and mind of their prospective "victims" by singing a bit of a popular song in the language of the tourist. It is an open question whether this kind of begging based on a sort of sentimental blackmail ought to be encouraged or not. Of course, some of these youngsters may indeed have to support an ailing mother, or sisters and brothers. The answer may be : don't spoil them by giving money; rather distribute sweets, chocolate, pencils and similar useful items but even this "charity" ought to be discouraged since one kind of begging leads inevitably to more offending ones.

POTTERS WORKING

On a little square in Bhadgaon, only a few minutes walk from Golden Gate and Royal Palace, everyone will be fascinated by the way potters use their traditional wheel.

Usually, they work with a special kind of clay called "kalimati", meaning black earth that is to be found in huge quantities around the town or even on this very square of Bhadgaon. Sometimes they also select some yellow clay which turns reddish when it is baked.

Although electric power is available in Bhadgaon, potters, like most Bhadgaon artisans, prefer working with their ancestral tools and methods. Thus he casts his flat and heavy stone wheel which looks like a millstone and he makes it spin fast enough by using a wooden handle stuck in a hole of the wheel. Once it gained sufficient speed, the potter has but a short time during which he may mould his lump of earth into a pot or a jar.

Once these get their proper shape, they are decorated with the help of a wooden pen and small seals before being left in the sun to dry and to be baked, later, in a special furnace.

MEN CARRYING WHAT LOOKS LIKE A ONE-CORD HARP

These men are also a very familiar silhouette in Kathmandu's streets. They are always muslims, never Nepalis or Newaris.

They go from house to house offering their services. What services, you may ask and what about that strange looking instrument they carry on their shoulder ! It is nothing but a traditional cotton–carding tool. !

WHAT IS STRETCHED OUT TO DRY IN THE STREETS.

During springtime, it is not yet peeled rice grains which are spread on the ground to dry in the sun. The colour of these grains is yellowish, almost golden. Once the rice is dry, women will do the winnowing with the help of a bamboo tray called "*nanglo*", the chaff being blown away by the breeze, if there is any; an enchanting scene to film. (It may be noted here that, even in the middle of winter, there is hardly ever any wind blowing inside the Valley.) Coming back to the winnowing : should there be no breeze at all, the woman will slowly let the grain trickle down from the nanglo towards the ground, while another woman swings a plated bamboo tray to produce some wind.

SMALL TRAYS CARRIED BY WOMEN MOSTLY EARLY MORNINGS

From dawn onwards, all Nepalese women perform their first "puja" i.e. an offering rite to their guardian god or goddess, either at a temple, a sanctuary, or inside their home where there is always a "puja room", or, at least, a "puja–corner" in one given room. Outside sanctuaries are everywhere: i.e on the side–walks, where they often look like a wide bench; they may also be nothing more than a strangely shaped stone reminding, even remotely, of the shape of God Ganesh or some other deity. On Asan Tole, for instance, in the centre of old Kathmandu, there is a rectangular hole almost in the centre of the square; a fish–shaped stone lies on the bottom of this niche; it attracts many devotees. Certain trees too, are sacred, either their stem or their roots. Pujas are also performed at small natural or artificial holes found in given walls. These openings are considered as "doors" leading to a naga's (serpent's) nest.

In order to make these offerings, women and children carry a special "puja-tray" made mostly of brass, wood, or intertwined dried leaves. Whatever trays are used, they will always contain rice–grains, flowers, or petals (mostly red or yellow ones) red powder, called "sindur", tapers, small coins, sweets, sometimes, small pieces of red or orange ribbons, curd, clarified butter etc.

STRANGE THINGS ON SALE IN SHOPS AND IN THE STREETS

Black and red cotton plaits at the tip of which there are golden or silver tassels. They are meant to make the natural plaits of a women's hair longer and, thus, more attractive.

Flower garlands. They will be put around the neck of those
who are to be honoured or whom good wishes are extended, on
the occasion of undertaking a journey abroad, for example. Statues of gods, goddesses, kings and other venerated personalities
are also garlanded on all special occasions.

Heaps of blackish-brownish sticky-looking stuff.

There are two kinds :

When there are no flies on these heaps, it is tobacco used in
the water–pipes (called hookah).

When they are covered with flies, and more brownish than
black, it is molasses.

Both tobacco and molasses are sold by weight.

Heaps of roundish balls of grey-brown colour:

These obviously hand–kneaded balls of approx. 6 inches in
diameter are a cheap quality soap that is mixed with a special
kind of clay.

Tibetan tea:

This particular brand of tea is mainly sold in the shops on
Asan Tole, in the centre of old Kathmandu or around Bodnath stupa. It is pressed either in the shape of a brick or of a
"top" looking somewhat like the lump of earth when
a small flower pot is turned upside down. Both types of this tea
comes from Darjeeling, Kalimpong or Ilam, the tea–producing
area in eastern Nepal.

Slightly conical cigarettes:

They are thin and short; the tobacco is not wrapped in paper
but in a dried leaf more like a miniature cheerot or cigar. These
are a popular brand of cigarettes; they are called "bidi"; they do
not contain the slightest trace of any drug as it is frequently but
falsely believed.

Small bundles of greyish twisted wicks:

These are made of rice–paper and contain powders of many
different kinds of scented wood. They are called "dhup" and are
meant to be burnt in the many small oil–lamps found at all sanctuaries and temples. Burning these wicks is a part of nearly all
"pujas" offered to divinities.

Small pots made of reddish clay:

This pot shows a serrated rim and a conical tip; it constitutes
the tip part of a Nepalese water–pipe, the 'hookah". There are
also much smaller conical and funnel–shaped cups called "kakad"
which the Nepalese use as cigarette–holders, to avoid touching the

cigarette with their lips. This would be considered as unclean, not so much from the hygienic point of view, but from the "social" one, since it is never knows who handled the cigarette before.

Small round terra-cotta bowls filled with a whitish jelly:

These are simply curd containers. They are brought into town in the early hours of the morning by porters carrying dozens of these bowls cleverly put one on top of the other and piled up in the familiar looking hanging baskets.

Flat greyish triangular or roundish stones:

These are made of compressed limestone and are used to white-wash the outer walls of houses.

Greyish-beige root-like tubercules:

It is, simply, fresh ginger which is on the market most part of the year, in particular during spring and summer.

Different varieties of leaves:

There are, first, the "betel" leaves which are always kept fresh in a water-filled vessel or plate to prevent them from drying. The betel seller spreads on the leave various components, which may vary according to the personal taste of the customer, mainly lime, tobacco, spices, areca nuts, cloves. The seller then folds the leave with all its contents into a small package, called "pan" which the customer will put in his mouth whole for chewing.

Then, there are other leaves on sale everywhere : they are darker, larger and may be partly dried. These leaves–called "saal"–are often sewn together with bamboo fibres. They are used as "puja–trays" or as plates during weddings and other festivities, or on picnics. The trees from which these leaves are taken do not grow in the Kathmandu Valley itself and therefore they have to be collected where they grow (in the region of Kakani, for instance, 18 miles from Kathmandu and carried down to the Valley which takes approximately 3 hours.)

Chopped off heads of goats glaring at passers by:

On butcher's stalls, there is always a display of bright orange coloured goat meat. These slaughtered–or sacrificed–goats have been thrown in very hot water and their hair immediately scraped off. Then, the skin has been rubbed with a special mixture of mustard oil, ashes, lemon juice and turmeric. This ointment produces this orange–reddish colour. It has two advantages : it keeps the skin from wrinkling and drying out and it also repels flies.

Besides the goat meat, butchers' stalls offer only buffalo meat which often has still its black coat and fur. In Nepal, like in

India, the sale of beef is, of course, prohibited. In addition to the "open-air butchers' stalls" there are "Cold Storage" or "Fresh Food Houses", where frozen pork, poultry, fish etc. are on sale.

Black packages hanging from branches of some high trees:
They can be spotted clearly in the neighbourhood of the Western side avenue of the Royal Palace leading to Lazimpat.

They look like black packages but they are neither fruits nor bird's nests, but merely large size....bats. Bats, not vampires !

It is not quite known why they select exclusively a certain kind of tree. One sees their wings open and close, in particular after rainfall. A fine hearing may even catch their very high-pitched cry.

THINGS EXPECTED BUT NOT SEEN

First of all: DOMESTIC CATS :
The explanation of the surprisingly small number of cats in comparison to the large quantity of dogs–domestic ones and straydogs–is manifold :

1) *First,* the simplest reason : Nepalese people, as a rule, don't like cats.

2) *Second :* In the eyes of many, a cat is not of great utility, as compared, for instance, with a dog. Whereas the latter guards the house or the farm, and barks furiously when any stranger tries to trespass, the former will not budge from its warm corner near the fireplace nor even give the slightest alarm.

3) *Third :* a strong reason : In the eyes of many Nepalese, cats, in particular black ones, are nothing but "disguised bad-luck–bringing witches". This explains perhaps the first reason !

4) *Fourth.* There is rarely any reference made to the argument that *"cats eat rats"* and that rats are sacred animals, since they are the traditional mount of the elephant–god Ganesh. May be this argument is not put forward because, in fact, Ganesh's mount is neither a rat nor a mouse, but a shrew. And shrews are not so numerous as rats, at least not in the Valley.

5) *Last but not least :* it is said that in former times, there were many cats in Kathmandu but they are said to have been drastically reduced in number by dogs that killed them !

Which of all these motives is the most decisive one, is left to the reader to find out !

DRUGS AND DRUG ADDICTS :
Since a few years back, certain books, accounts, articles and films have succeeded in creating a distorted image of Kathmandu, giving to understand that this is the *"capital of drugs"*, the

"*paradise of hippies*" and so forth.

Now, the tourist will fail to see–and possibly he may even feel somewhat frustrated by not discovering–drug addicts sprawled on the pavement or opium dens full of youngsters taking a "*trip*" into the world "*beyond*".

It may therefore be necessary to put things back in their right perspective :

—There has never been in Nepal, as it is or was the case in other countries of Asia, cultivation of neither opium-yielding poppies or hashish–yielding canabis.

—The latter plant grows naturally in the hill–regions of Nepal, where tobacco is scarce. Thus since time immemorial. farmers have found to dry the canabis–leaves, roll them into cigarettes or fill a terra–cotta pipe and smoke. However this kind of smoking has never been enjoyed in order to reach ecstatic or trance states. It is plain smoking and nothing else.

—Until the end of 1973, the sale of dried canabis leaves, also called "*hemp*" or "*marijuana*" was perfectly licit and open. "*Hashish* on the contrary, which is the oil or juice extracted from the same canabis plant, was not usually on sale in the bazar but in any of the small taverns which mushroomed in the years 1969 to 1973 around Basantpur Square, Usually hashish was mixed with pastry or sweets of some kind.

Towards October 1973, the government of Nepal–as well as certain foreign governments too–felt concerned about the bad example which a certain type of youngsters gave the younger Nepalese generation : Hence the prohibition of the free and open sale of all kinds of drugs.

At the same time, the Immigration Department set up more restrictive rules as far as the extension of visas was concerned.

As a consequence of these two sets of measures, the number of so-called *hippies* or potential hippies travelling to and residing in Kathmandu reduced considerably.

—AND, OF COURSE, THE ELUSIVE YETI...

"Well, what about it ? Does he exist or not, the famous "snowman" ?

To this question, there is no clear-cut answer...yet !

However, there have been so many explorers and scientists with enough time and means at their disposal to find the answer to this enigma, one of the most fascinating of our times !

And what about all the books, studies and articles – they

totalize 1800 pages, according to the "Bibliography of Nepal" published by the Royal Academy – what conclusion do they reach?

Of course, the hurried visiting tourist has hardly time to consult any of these writings. He wants to know, once and for all, now and here.

The one fact that is undeniable and solidly established by photographs, casts and measurements made by undisputably trustworthy men, refers to the existence of the footprints, so often discovered in the snow, less frequently in mud or sand but sometimes even on layers of frozen snow or even ice.

Mountaineers who have the physical strength and the moral determination to climb on summits that are 20,000 ft. high and more, are neither of the dreamer's nor of the poets' type, and still less inclined to indulge in practical jokes.

How to explain then that between 1951 and 1974, not less than 10 expeditions took place in Nepal's Himalayas in search of the "yeti" ? If none of them actually brought back a specimen, alive or dead, all harvested numbers of foot-print "proofs".

What are they like ? Allowing for small variations, these prints normally measure about one foot in length and 4 to $4^1/_2$ inches in width. Thus, they are slightly larger than prints that would have been left by a human being – in particular by a Sherpa, whose feet are, as a rule, on the smaller side.

In 1974, a "yeti" manifested itself in a spectacular way in Sherpaland. This was the famous "Machherma incident" that triggered off many speculations and comments. The incident took place on July 11th,. at a "yarsa" (a yak pasture), located in the Everest region, at an altutiude of approx. 14,460 ft.

Let us hear what the person who was directly involved had to say : LAKPA DOMANI, a young Sherpani girl about 18 years old. :

"I was guarding my yaks at the yarsa when suddenly, behind my back, I heard a growling noise. I turned round and saw a creature that looked like a tall ape covered with dark and reddish fur. Its eyes were deeply set and cheekbones jutting out. The animal took me in its strong arms, lifted me up and carried me towards the nearby stream, where it dropped me brutally on the ground. Then, it attacked my yaks."

Five days later, the policemen's report (they had hurried up from Namche Bazar), declared : "We found the remains of three yaks ; two seemed to have been killed by heavy stones while the third had a broken neck."

Their conclusion deserves also to be quoted, be it merely as a good example of "non-commitment" ! :

"It is impossible, said the report, that this agression could have been the deed of a human being. If the yeti exists really, everything point "him" out, as the real culprit" !

But let us come back to the foot-prints : Someone must have made them, but who ?

They can not be those of a bear, for they would show the claws. A snow–leopard has also to be discarded for its paws are much smaller.

The most remarkable fact of the yeti footprints is that they generally show clearly the big toe as separated from the other four. Well, the only living creatures that possess prehensile toes are :... men and apes.

Before pursuing our inquiry, another fact of primary importance has to be reminded :

The "yeti" is in no way an "exclusivity" of Nepal, nor of the Himalayas for that matter. The presence of such or similar "ape-men" has been reported and accepted as a very casual and undenied fact in all mountainous regions of Central Asia, from Pamir to Mongolia, in Kazakstan and deep into China's Tien–Chan.

True, the description of these "ape-men" varies from one region to the other. But what is more natural than that ? Is variety not the very characteristic of everything created by Nature ! Is there only *one* kind of dogs, cats, horses, or... apes and monkeys ?

However, in all descriptions, the following common features are to be found, namely :

—upright position, walks on two legs, has an almost human silhouette

—a fur-covered body, except for the face and hands

—no language, only growls and grumbles

—frightened by human presence, lives away from any human settlement

—inability of making a fire or using tools

—lives in small family groups, not in herds or flocks.

These characteristics led specialized zoologists, such as Mr. B. HEUVELMANS, to classify the "yeti" and its Central Asian cousins among the "pongidae" species of apes. This family includes mainly orang-outangs, gorillas, gibbons and chimpanzes.

Now, it is certainly more than a mere coincidence that the first two named anthropoid apes are, undisputably, in the process of total extinction.

Therefore, it does not seem unreasonable – rather to the contrary – to assume and accept that the "yeti" and its close relatives are also "doomed" animals, exactly like the mammoths at the time when fairly developed human beings already made fire and indulged in wall-paintings in their caves in Western Europe. !

This theory would explain why there are so few left, why they are difficult to spot and why no good picture has so far been taken. That Sherpas – who are firmly convinced of the existence of the "yeti" – have a tendency to believe that they are merely spirits witch-like creatures thus becomes a secondary element.

Far more important and far more interesting is the fact that the stories told by Sherpas about the behaviour – and wickedness– of yetis are often centered around the instinct – and talent – of imitation shown by the "snowman". Well, isn't mimicry precisely one of the most remarkable attributes of the ape and monkey families and . . only of them ??

BIBLIOGRAPHY

Some recent bibliographic data concerning the yeti (in English language).

— 1949 – J.M.THORNINGTION : "*Distant cousins of the abominable snowman*"–Alpine Journal.

— 1955 – C. STONOR : "*The Sherpa and the snowman*" –London, Hellis and Carter.

— 1955 – R. IZZARD : "*The abominable snowman adventure*" – New–York–Doubleday.

— 1956 – Eric SHIPTON : "*Fact or Fantasy*"–Geogr. Journal.

— 1956 – L.W. DAVIES : "*Footsteps in the snow*"–Alpine Journal LXI.

— 1957 – B. K. ENDERS : "*The abominable snowman*"–Science-(Washington).

— 1958 – T.B. SLICK : "*Yeti Expedition*"–Explorers Journal.

— 1958 – B. HEUVELMANS : "*On the track of unknown animals*"–London–Hurt–Davis.

— 1959 – B.K. VERMA : "*Man's nearest living cousin : The yeti*"– Ill. Weekly of India (27 Sept. 1959.)

— 1959 – N.G. DYRENFURTH : "*Slick-Johnson Nepal Snowman expedition*"–American Alpine Journal.

— 1959 – C.R. BAWDEN : "*The snowman*"– "Man" 337, (Dec. 1959.)

— 1960 – W. TSCHERNITZKY : "*A reconstruction of the foot of* the "*abominable snowman*"–Nature (7 May 1960)

— 1961 – F. YAMASAKI 9: "*The Japanese yeti expedition 1959–1960*"–Japanese Alpine Club Journal.

— 1961 (?)– I. SANDERSON : "*Snowman and Woodmen*"–(Published in French translation under the title : "Hommes des Neiges et Hommes des Bois" by PLON, 1961).

— 1961 – C.O. HILL : "*Abominable snowman. The present position*" : Oryx.

— 1961 – O. TCHERINE : "*The abominable snowman*"–London–Hale.

— 1962 – : Edmund HILLARY and Desmond DOIG : "*High in the thin cold air, the story of the Himalayan Expedition*"– New–York–Doubleday.

— 1962 – M. BURTON : "*The snowman*"–Ill. London News–3 Nov. 1962.

— 1962 – E. WYSS–DUNANT : "*The yeti : biped or quadruped*"–Alpes.

— 1966 – : P. MULGREW : "*No palace for men*"–London–Nicolas Vane.

SECTION II

PRACTICAL HINTS

To

Journey and Stay

CHAPTER THREE

THE JOURNEY

BEFORE LEAVING

VISAS

Most foreigners need an entry visa for Nepal even if they intend to stay only a few days as tourists.

These visas are issued on presentation of a valid passport and two recent passport–size photographs :

– either by a Nepalese Consular Office abroad (see list and addresses below).

– or at one of the twelve authorized entry points into Nepal (see list below.)

The validity of these two kind of visas is not the same :

Visas issued by Consular Offices are valid for a stay of *one month,* against payment of a fee of approximately US $ 10 or its equivalent in local currency, for each entry.

Visas issued at one of the frontier entry–posts–including Kathmandu airport–are valid against payment of Nep. Rs. 121.– for a stay of *one week only,* but an extension of validity may be obtained without difficulties–and free of charge for the following three weeks–by merely presenting passport and two passport photos at the Central Department of Immigration located at Ram Shah Path. (Office hours : from 10 a. m. to 4 p. m., except on Saturdays and holidays.)

The fee to be paid for obtaining an extension beyond the first month, of any kind of visa amonts to Nep. Rs. 100.– per week for the second month of stay and Nep. Rs. 200.– per week for the third month of stay. The Immigration Department will extend the validity of any visa for only one month at a time.

(*) All indications concerning fares, fees, prices, rates and tariff etc. Contained in the present book are those effective during the winter 1980–81. They may have changed since and have therefore to be checked. In no case can these information be held against the author or the publisher.

Here is the list of the Nepalese Embassies and Consular Services abroad :

AUSTRALIA : Consulate General : SYDNEY, 3/87 Cowles Rd., Mosman N. SW. Tel. : 960 3565

AUSTRIA : Consulate General: VIENNAı Karpfenwaldgasse 11– Tel. : 32 11 05

BANGLA DESH : Embassy : DACCA, 248, Dhanmandi R.A. Road No 21– Tel. : 31 29 07 – 31 52 14

BELGIUM : Consulate General :BRUSSELS, 165 Bd. Lemonnier – Tel. : 11 25 15

ANTWERP, Lamoriniere Straat 143–145 – Tel. : 30 88 00

BURMA: Embassy : RANGOON, 16 Natmauk Yeiktha (Park Ave.) P. O. Tamwe Tel. : 5 06 33

DENMARK : Consulate General: COPENHAGUE, 2, Lyngbyvej – Tel. : O11 43 195

EGYPT : Embassy : CAIRO, 9, Tiba Street Dokki – Tel. ; 70 44 47 70 45 41

FED. REP. OF GERMANY : Embassy : BONN – 2, Im Hag 15 – Tel. : (02221) 34 30 97 Honorary Consulates : FRANKFURT – Flinchstrasse 63 : Tel. : (0611) 41 71 01 MUNCHEN : Neuhauser Str. 1 Tel. : (089) 26 30 09

FRANCE : Embassy : PARIS 75008 – 7, Rue Washington – Tel. 359 28 61

GREAT BRITAIN : Embassy : LONDON – 12A, Kensington Palace Gardens – Tel. : 229–1594, 229–6231,

HONG–KONG : Liaison Office : c/o H. Q. Brigade of Gurkhas – Victoria Barracks. Tel. : 523 81 11 – Ext. 3255

INDIA : Embassy : NEW DELHI, 1 Barakhamba Rd. Tel. : 38 14 84

Consulate General : CALCUTTA : Woodlands, 19 Sterndale Rd. Tel. : 45 20 24 – 45 42 93

IRAN : Embassy : TEHERAN : House No 22 Street No 4 – Pakistan Ave. Abbasabad Tel. : 62 88 22

JAPAN : Embassy : TOKYO : 16–23, Higashi-Gotanda 3 – Chome – Shinagawa-Ku– Tel. : 444 – 7303, 7305

LEBANON : Consulate General : BEIRUT. : Issa El–Khoury Bldg Tel. : 22 91 52

NETHERLANDS : Consulate General : ROTTERDAM – Sophia Kinderziegenhuis – Gordelweg 160 – Tel. : 00 31 10 –

PAKISTAN: Embassy: ISLAMABAD: No 506, 84th Street, Ramna G–6/4– Tel. : 2 36 42 2 37 54

Consulate General: KARACHI, – Block 7 and 8, Hill Park. – Tel. : 23 44 57

PEOPLE'S REPUBLIC OF CHINA : Embassy : BEIJING – No 15 San Li Tun, Tel. : 52 17 95

Consulate General : LHASSA Norbulingka Rd, 13 – Tel. : 22880

PHILIPPINES : Consulate General : MANILA – 1136–1138 – United Nations Ave. Paco (2803) – Tel. : 58 93 93

REPUBLIC OF KOREA : Consulate General : SEOUL – 286 Yang–Dong, Ingu-Gu – Tel. 22 87 66

SAUDI ARABIA : Embassy : JEDDAH, Kilo 5 – Mecca Rd. Tel. : 7 34 23.

SRI LANKA : Consulate General – COLOMBO – 92 Chatham Str. Tel. 2 63 93

THAILAND : Embassy : Bangkok., 189 Soi 71 – Sukhumvit Road – Tel. : 391 72 40

U.S.A. : Embassy : WASHINGTON. – 2131 Leroy Palace N. W. Tel. : (202) 667–4550

Consulate General : CHICAGO : 27, Sola Salle Str. Tel. : (313) 346–9090

Consulate General : SAN FRANCISCO. : 3630 – Jackson Str. Tel. (415) 751–3630

U.S.S.R. : Embassy : MOSCOW – 2nd Neopalimovsky Pereulok 14/7 Tel. : 241 69 43

AUTHORIZED ENTRY POINTS

There are twelve authorized entry–points into Nepal, by road, where short–term visas may be granted by the immigration or police officers to visiting foreigners :

One of these points is, of course KATHMANDU's "Tribhuvan airport", the only entry–point by air.

Another is the Nepal–China frontier post of KODARI, which is not yet open to tourists.

The ten remaining entry–points are located along the border with India. They are :

BIRGANJ (in the Narayani zone), opposite Raxaul in India, on the highway leading from Delhi, Varanasi (Benares), Patna or Calcutta straight to Kathmandu.

DHANGARI (in the Seti zone).

JALESWORE (near to the town of Janakpur).

KAKAR BHITTA (in the Mechi zone, on the road coming from Darjeeling, Assam or Sikkim).

KAKARHAWA (in the Lumbini zone, on a not easily jeepable road).

KOILABAS (in the Rapti zone, on a not easily jeepable road).

MAHENDRANAGAR (in the Mahakali zone on road from India).

NEPALGANJ (in the Bheri zone, near the town of Nepalganj).

RANI SIKIJAHI (in the Kosi zone, near the town of Biratnagar).

SUNAULI (in the Lumbini zone, nera the town of Bhairawa).

PASSPORT PHOTOS

Two photo–shops in town may provide passport-photos in a minimum of time :

"DAS–PHOTO", on the left-hand side of the lane branching off the main street behind Bhimsen Tower when coming from the General Post Office

"PHOTO-CONCERN", on New Road, just behind the huge "pipal"–tree.

VACCINATIONS

Although there is presently no systematic health control at Nepal's entry-points, it is advisable, for your own safety, to be in possession of the following vaccinations :

- smallpox, in all cases
- typhoid, as an extra precaution
- cholera and yellow–fever if, within five days prior to your entry in Nepal, you have stayed or transited through a country where one of these diseases is considered endemic.

Besides, such vaccinations certificates may have to be produced when proceeding from Nepal to India, Thailand or when travelling back to your home country.

FOREIGN CURRENCIES

As the import of Nepalese Rupees into the country is prohibited, it is advisable to provide oneself with such foreign currencies that are easily exchanged, be it in banknotes or traveller's checks at any authorized dealer in Nepal (banks and most hotels).

These convertible currencies are :

Austrian Shillings
Dollars (Australian, Canadian or U.S.)
Francs (French, Belgian or Swiss)
Italian Lire
Japanese Yen
Pound Sterling
Swedish Kronors
West German Marks.

MEN·WITH WINGS

ANOTHER WAY OF FLYING ABOVE THE
MOUNTAINS

LET THE WIND TAKE THE CHAFF AWAY

EVERYONE HAS TO DO HIS SHARE DURING HARVEST TIME

WHAT TO WEAR

During monsoon (approx. 15th June to 30th October): summer clothes only, and an umbrella : a mackintosh would be too warm.

In Winter (30th. October to 15th March) : summer clothes during the day and woollens for morning and evening.

In Spring (15th March to 15th. June): summer clothes only. For those who intend trekking, see special chapter dealing with trekking equipment and clothing.

HOW TO REACH NEPAL

BY AIR

REGULAR INTERNATIONAL FLIGHTS

Up to now, there is no American, European or Far-Eastern scheduled airline operating to Nepal.

The only ones to do so are the regional airlines, i.e. those from neighbouring countries (Bangladesh, Burma, India and Thailand), in addition, of course, to the National flag carrier, ROYAL NEPAL AIRLINES.

Coming from the West
From Delhi :

The non-stop services between Delhi and Kathmandu and v. v. are operated by Royal Nepal Airlines Corporation (R.N.A.C.- on the tickets : "RA") and Indian Airlines ("IC" on the tickets), under a pool agreement. However this does not mean that the passenger may use indifferently the one or the other of the two airlines. Endorsement of the issuing carrier in favour of its pool-partner is required, but seldom refused.

This flight takes and average of 1 hour and 15 minutes. ROYAL NEPAL AIRLINES operates at least daily flights (with Boeing 727) whereas INDIAN AIRLINES 5 per week (with Boeing 737). In addition, the latter operates a daily flight, without change of plane, from DELHI to KATHMANDU with intermediate stops at AGRA, KHAJURAO and VARANASI (Benares). This flight takes approximately 4 hours and 20 minutes, all stops included. All direct flights leave DELHI in the morning and have therefore good connections with most of the international carriers coming to Delhi from Europe, their hours of arrival occurring almost all in the early morning.

Traditionally, the fares of DELHI–KATHMANDU are the same on the direct non–stop as on the indirect route. The latter offers the possibility of visiting for 24 hours (or more) each of these most interesting places AGRA, KHAJURAO and BENARES.

In spring 1980, the one-way fare DELHI–KATHMANDU (or vice–versa) was US $ 111,00 and had to be paid in hard currency, except for Nepalese or Indian nationals.

Coming from the South

From Calcutta: 14 weekly flights : 3 by R.N.A.C., 4 by THAI INTERNATIONAL, 5 by INDIAN AIRLINES and 2 UNION OF BURMA AIRWAYS. The flight takes approx. 1h. 05 min. One-way fare: US $ 74.00

From Colombo: 2 weekly non-stop flights by R.N.A.C. The flight takes approx. 3h. 30 min. One-way fare: US $ 276.00

From Patna: 1 daily flight by R.N.A.C. 45 min flight. One way fare: US $ 31.00

From Varanasi (Benares) 1 daily flight by INDIAN AIRLINES 45 min flight. One-way fare : US $ 55.00

Coming from the East

From Bangkok : 9 weekly flights : 5 by R.N.A.C. and 4 by THAI INTERNATIONAL R.N.A.C. operates non-stop (approx. 3h. 50 min:) THAI INTERNATIONAL with a stop at Calcutta, but no change of aircraft. One-way fare : US $ 241.00

Furthermore, UNION OF BURMA AIRWAYS also links Bangkok with Kathmandu, changing plane at Rangoon, and an intermediary stop at Calcutta.

From Dacca : 2 weekly flights operated by BANGLADESH BIMAN : 2h.20 min. : One-way fare: US $ 79.00

From Rangoon : 2 weekly flights by UNION OF BURMA AIRWAYS 3h.25 min. : One-way fare : US $ 223.20

CHARTER FLIGHTS

Kathmandu is not linked with the outside world by tourist "charter-flights", save some exceptions, on special occasions.

Nevertheless, there are many charter flights linking European cities with either Delhi, Bangkok, or Dacca from where Kathmandu is easy to reach (see above).

BY LAND

— IMPORTANT REMARKS :

There are so many possible combinations of buses, trains, cars etc. (not to mention that on certain sectors. air–services may also be used), that it is almost impossible to spell them all out in detail here.

Only the most frequented and easy land routes will be mentioned, with, approximate indications as to the time it takes.

At this stage is should be pointed out that the time indicated for each sector can not be simply added up with the next one in order to reach an estimate for the *total* duration of the journey. For, more often than one would wish it, connections between two trains, a bus and a train etc. may take several hours, sometimes a whole day or a whole night. It is equally impossible to give even approximate time-tables or fares for trains and buses. On the one hand, they change frequently and, on the other hand, there are always different categories of trains, even of buses, which apply different fares on a same route. In general terms, it may be said transport is relatively cheap on the Indian subcontinent as well as in Nepal.

FROM DELHI

The fastest combination by train and bus is the following :
Take the special train called "Jyanti-Janta" at Delhi main station. It leaves around 6 or 7 p. m. three times a week. On the following afternoon, at approx. 5 p. m. step out at Muzzafarpur. At once, take a rickshaw to catch the bus leaving at approx. 6 p. m. for Raxaul, which is reached at 9 p. m. Spend the night in one of Raxaul's hotels or lodges. The following morning at 5.30, take another rickshaw to the border-post Raxaul-Birganj (5 Indian Rupees). Here Custom and Immigation formalities may take one hour or more depending on the volume of traffic. From Birganj, there are two possibilities: Take a "minibus" (55 Rs.) leaving at approx. 10 a.m. reaching Kathmandu around 3 p. m., or the ordinary bus (30 Rs.) leaving at the same time but arriving only at around 8 p. m. The total fare from Delhi to Kathmandu is approx. 400 Indian Rupees.

— BY TRAIN

In Indian territory, trains are fairly comfortable, in particular those called "de luxe", "express", or "trunk–line" trains; most of them have air–conditioned cars.

In Nepal, there is no railway network, with the sole exceptions of a 18 mile long line which links the Indian border at a point called Jayanagar and a 15 mile long line linking Bijulpura and Janakpur. An older railway line which linked to border town of Raxaul with a village called Amlekhganj is no longer in use.

From DELHI *to* KATHMANDU, by combining trains and buses, via the normal road through AGRA–BENARES–PATNA and RAXAUL takes approximately 2 to 3 days.

From PATNA *to* KATHMANDU, by similar combinations takes around 36 hours.

From PATNA *to* KATHMANDU, there are two possibilities :

Either take the ferry crossing the Ganges and take the train which starts from the opposite bank, as far as MUZZAFARPUR. From there, by train, to the Indian frontier post of RAXAUL. One enters NEPAL at the border–post of BIRGANJ.

Or, continue by train along the right bank of the Ganges down to MOKAMAH, where a railway–and road–bridge crosses the Ganges. From there it is also possible to reach MUZZAFARPUR.

It would take approx. 24 hours from Delhi to Patna and 1/2 hours from Patna to Muzzafarpur by the ferry. The other way would require about 4 hours.

From Muzzafarpur to Raxaul : around 12 hours.

From VARANASI *to* KATHMANDU.

It takes between 10 and 12 hours to cover the sector Varanasi-Patna. By train up to the border : 24 hours would be a fairly good average.

— BY ROAD

BY PRIVATE CAR

Customs and immigration entry-posts :

Here are the three main ones :

1) NAUTANWA (on the Indian side)-BHAIRAWA(on the Nepalese side). This leads directly to Pokhara

2) RAXAUL (on the Indian side)–BIRGANJ (on the Nepalese side). This is the most frequented crossing point, whether you come from Delhi, Varanasi, Patna or Calcutta, wishing to drive directly on to Kathmandu.

3) PANITHANKI (on the Indian side) and KAKABHITTA (on the Nepalese side). This point is used when coming from Darjeeling, Siliguri, Assam or Sikkim.

Documents required and formalities :

Crossing the border in a private car always takes some time, at best one or two hours. First there is the passport control formality to comply with (the Immigration Officers, at these frontier posts are entitled to issue visa valid for one week, prorogation may easily be obtained, but only at the Central Immigration Office in Kathmandu). Then comes the custom control of vehicle and luggage.

One document required for the car is the international *"Carnet de Passage en Douane"*, which is to be delivered by the authorities of the driver's country.

How long it takes

This is very difficult to evaluate because of the too many un-foreseeable factors : the state of the road, in particular during the monsoon season when roads are often disrupted by landslides, the changes in schedules of trains and buses, the difficulty to get advance bookings on certain sectors etc.

However, it can be said that, under fairly normal conditions, travelling by road is slightly faster on the trunk roads but slower on all others than to travel by train.

BY PUBLIC BUS SERVICES

In India, all those sectors which have been mentioned as being open to rail–traffic are also open to public bus services.

In Nepal, the following regular services are in operation :
(Nautanwa)–BHAIRAWA–BUTWAL   :
TANSEN—NUWAKOT–POKHARA–KATHMANDU
(Raxaul)–BIRGANJ–SIMRA–AMLEKHGANJ–HETAURA
DHOBANI–NAUBISE–THANKOT–KATHMANDU
(Panitanki)–KAKARBHITTA–BIRATNAGAR or   DHA-RAN–DHANKUTA (where the road ends, at present.)..
Formalities : valid passport and visa for Immigration luggage check for Customs.

The journey from

KATHMANDU TO DARJEELING

There is no direct itinerary but three indirect ones. For each of them, the first leg is easiest made by airplane :

FIRST possibility :

By plane : KATHMANDU–CALCUTTA–BAGDOGRA, then

By jeep, bus or *taxi* : BAGDOGRA–SILIGURI, then

By train : SILGURI–DARJEELING. (this last leg takes from 7 to 8 hours !)

It is therefore impossible to perform this journey in a single day, the departure times of the air services from Kathmandu to Calcutta being too late. Thus, the arrival in Darjeeling is likely to take place in the afternoon or in the evening of the second day.

SECOND possibility :

By plane : KATHMANDU–BHADRAPUR, then

By jeep, bus or *taxi* : BHADRAPUR to the Indian border post, where one has to take a car, bus or taxi to proceed to

SILIGURI.
By train : SILIGURI–DARJEELING
This itinerary will also take more than one day, for the R.N.A.C.
planes arrive at BHADRAPUR at 10 a. m. approx. and are
operated only twice a week (on Mondays and Fridays during the
winter.)

THIRD possibility :
By plane : KATHMANDU–BIRATNAGAR (daily flights)
Arrival at BIRATNAGAR at 11h.00, then, by rickshaw from the
airport to the Bus terminal at KANCHENBARI, then.
By bus : From KANCHENBARI to KAKARBHITTA,
the border post. Or, if there is no direct bus service, you have to
take the first bus leaving Kanchenbari and step out at the road-
fork of ETTARY, where other buses leave for Karkarbhitta.
This journey takes approx. 5 hours.
By taxi : KAKARBHITTA–SILIGURI, one hour approxi-
mately.
Night–stop at Siliguri is unavoidable : either in the centre of
the town, at the Hotel Ranjit–Saljany, or, a little outside the town,
at the River–View Hotel.
Next morning : by rickshaw from the Hotel to the railway -
station, then
By train : SILIGURI–DARJEELING
NOTE:- This last leg can also be made by landrover, which
takes approx. 3 to 4 hours. The fare is only approx. 10
Ind. Rs. per passenger.
A taxi will charge approx. 50 Ind. Rs. per passenger,
but, of course, this journey, if made by road, takes
much less time than by train.

WHILE ON BOARD

WHERE TO SIT ON THE AEROPLANE
WHEN COMING FROM THE WEST

On the left side of the aisle.
Ten minutes after take–off from Delhi airport, when the weather is clear, the impressive range of the Western Himalayas beings
to become visible in a distance. These are mountains located in
India (more precisely, in the areas called Khumaon and Gharwal).
It is prohibited to take pictures while overflying Indian territory. Besides, once over Nepal, the aeroplane flies much closer to
the mountains.

Approximately 25 minutes after take–off, the plane passes over the large city of LUCKNOW where the course will make a turn from due East to North–East.

The first mountain range which will be easy to identify is GURJA HIMAL (23,593ft.=7.193m.), followed closely by the bulky DHAULARIGI (26,807 ft.=8.173 m.). On the right side of this huge mountain which looks somewhat like a wide armchair, it is possible to distinguish rather dimly, a Valley which separates the Dhaulagiri Massif from the next one. This is the famous Kali Gandaki Valley leading to Tukuche, Jomosom and Mustang. The range lying on the right (eastern) side of the Valley is the long–stretched ANNAPURNA barrier which counts not less than 6 classified summits, the highest of which (ANNAPURNA 1) reaches (26,496 ft.=8.078 m.).This was the first peak above 8.000m. ever climbed by a mountaineering team, namely French Alpinists Maurice HERZOG and Louis LACHENAL, on 3rd June 1950.

A little further to the East, it is easy to identify the sharply pointed summit of Mount MANASLU (26,752ft. 8.156m.). Finally appear the three impressive and bulky summits of GANESH HIMAL (24,292 ft.=7.406 m.), the "guardians" of Kathmandu Valley.

WHEN COMING FROM THE EAST :

On the right side of the aisle.

During this flight, the traveller will enjoy a breath–taking view of the eastern Himalaya range.

The panorama begins with the impressive and huge massif of KANCHENJUNGA (also called and sometimes written Kang-chendzonga), the world's third highest mountain (28,159 ft.=8,585 m.) situated on the Nepal–Sikkim border, followed by MAKALU (27,798 ft.=8.475 m.) easy to identify for its famous ridge which ascends from its base up to the summit and which was climbed by a French expedition in 1971. Then you will see the broad shoulder of JANNU (25,289 ft.=7.710m.) another French victory, dating back to 1962.

Now the moment has come to try to locate and identify "*the third pole*", meaning World's highest peak. MOUNT EVEREST. It is not easy, for it is partly hidden behind its two "body-guards", the broad barriers of LHOTSE and NUPTSE. Nevertheless, SAGAR-MATHA'S top may be distinguished : it is not a very spectacular peak, being a pyramid of black rock sparsely covered with snow and generally wearing on its top a white cloud of blown–away snow, usually directed eastwards.

Further along our route, there lies CHO-OYU (26,742 ft. =8.153 m.) and a little later, the broad plateau–like mountain of MELUNGTSE (23,560 ft.=7.181 m.) and GAURISHANKAR (23,442 ft =7.145 m.) which is also easy to identify thanks to its triangular shaped and always snow–covered "cap" which it wears on its right side.

(At the beginning of the 19th century, it was this mountain, GAURISHANKAR, which was believed to be the highest peak in the world.)

The last mountain to be seen before descending towards Kathmandu airport are CHHOBA-BHAMARE (19,581 ft.=5.970 m.), also called sometimes "*The Almighty's finger*", and the beautifully shaped symmetric pyramid of DORJE LAKPA (22,920 ft.=6.988 m.) which, together with the peak of LANGTANG–LIRUNG (23,770 ft.—7.245 m.) dominate and protect Kathmandu Valley.

ON ARRIVAL

CUSTOMS

ON ENTRY

Tourist luggage is spot–checked. The following articles may be freely imported, on condition that they are re-exported on departure. No inventory is at present required :
- personal effects
- one pair of field glasses
- one camera and 12 rolls of film (*)
- one cine–camera and 6 rolls of film (*)
- one record–player, one radio
- one tape–recorder and 6 tapes for recording
- two watches
- one set of professional equipment (interpretation left to the customs officer)
- 15 yards of cotton material
- 10 yards of silk

(*) A special permission to import additional photographic equipment films etc... may be obtained from the Custom Authorities, on recommendation from either H.M.G.'s Foreign Offices, Ministry of Tourism or Ministry of Communications (in case professional Photo–taking or filming is planned). Such requests should however be filed with the proper authorities at least one month before the planned date of entry.

- 6 yards of woollen material
- 2 pounds of knitting wool
- 2 pair of shoes
- used clothing
- sportwear (value not exceeding Rs. 50.)
- gold ornaments not weighing more than 10 tolas (about 4 oz. or 112 gr.)
- jewellery of value not exceeding Rs. 2,000 and, provided gold or silver content does not exceed 150 tolas, about 57 oz. or 1 kg. 650 gr.

The following articles are forbidden for import :
- arms and ammunition, explosives, transmitter-radios, walkie–talkies, narcotic drugs.

As for consumer goods, the following quantities can be imported free :
- 250 cigarettes
- 20 cigars
- 4 oz. (or 115 gr.) of pipe tobacco
- 4 oz. (or 115 gr.) of chewing tobacco
- fresh fruit, value not exceeding Rs. 25:–
- sweets, chocolates, etc. value not exceeding Rs. 40.–
- tins and seasonings, value not exceeding Rs. 50.–
- medicines, value not exceeding Rs. 100.–
- beer : 12 bottles or cans
- alcoholic beverages : 3 bottles per tourist (One only for residents !)

— ON DEPARTURE

Custom Officers go through your luggage more thoroughly on departure than on arrival. in order to prevent illegal exports.

All handicraft can be freely exported without limitation (if the quantity seems reasonable to the inspector). On the other hand, all works of art, whether sculptures in wood, stone or bronze, including Nepalese as well as Tibetan "*thang-kas*" (painted scrolls) when considered antiques, i. e. estimated to be over a hundred years old, have to be individually authorized for export. The corresponding permit can be obtained from the Archaeological Department, on Thapathali Road, by presenting the objects concerned a few days before the intended departure, since the said permit may not be issued immediately.

However, this formality is not required when tourists intend to export modern souvenirs, including recently painted thang-kas, which have been purchased in a souvenir shop and which are, undisputably, not works of art over a century old.

In addition to what has just been said, it is also prohibited to export from Nepal :
— gold, silver and precious stones
— wild animals and/or trophies of any kind, skins, horns, antlers, tusks etc..
— drugs, whether in crude or in processed form.

MONEY EXCHANGE

At Kathmandu airport, as well as at other entry points, each tourist is being handed over a "Foreign Exchange Transcation Form" distributed by NEPAL RASTRA BANK. The only data to fill in are the passenger's name, home address, address in Nepal, nationality, passport number and arrival date, but *not* the amount of foreign currency that is brought into the country.

However, every time foreign currency is exchanged against Nepalese Rupees, this card has to be presented and the transaction to be noted down on it, with the rubber stamp of the bank or the hotel where the transaction has taken place.

This procedure then allows the passenger, on his departure from Nepal, to obtain hard currency (usually US $) in exchange of the *surplus* of Nepalese Rupees still in his possession. Nevertheless, this re-exchange is limited to 10% of the total amount that has been exchanged during his stay in Nepal.

The bank counters in the arrival as well as the departure lounges are open every day, from morning to evening.

The export of Nepalese Rupees is stietly prohibited.

CURRENCY VALUE

Nepalese national currency is the "Rupee". One Rupee is subdivided into 100 "paisa".

It circulates in the following denominations :
— banknotes of Rs. 1,000, 500,100,50,10, 5,2 and 1. There exist various types of these banknotes, different in size, colour and designs. On some of them, there is still the portrait of the late King Mahendra, whereas on the more recent ones appears the portrait of the presently ruling Sovereign, H. M. King BIRENDRA.
— coins of Rs. 1.00,0.50,0.25,0.10 and 0.05 paisa.The 1.00 and 0.50 coins are the largest and are made of silver alloy; so are the 0.25, although the latter are the tiniest ones. Both show on one side, a sword and on the other a trident. The

smaller coins (0.10 and 0.05) are made of aluminium alloy.
The exchange rates of all convertible foreign currencies are
published every day in the morning paper "THE RISING NEPAL".
At the beginning of 1981, the approximate average exchange
rates, as published by the Nepal Rastra Bank, were the following:

(The figures below are merely indicative and given with reservations :)

	Nep. Rs.	thus 1 Nep Rupee=	
1 English Pound Sterling	29.00	0.034	Pound Sterling
1 US Dollar	12.00	0.08	US Dollar
1 Canadian Dollar	10.10	0.10	Can. Dollar
1 Swiss Franc	7.00	0.14	Swiss Fr.
1 West German Mark	6.70	0.16	W. German Mk.
1 Dutch Guilder	5.72	0.17	Dutch Guild.
1 French Franc	2.70	0.37	French Franc
1 Swedish Krona	2.75	0.36	Sw. Krona
1 Austrian Shilling	0.87	1.15	Austr. Shill.
1 Belgian Franc	0.38	2.63	Belg. Franc
1 Japanese Yen	0.05	17.85	Jap. Yen
1 Italian Lira	0.013	77.00	Ital. Lira.

Also to be remembered : 1 Indian Rupee is equal to 1.45
Nepalese Rupee, thus 1 Nepalese Rupee equals 0.70 India. Only
Nepalese and Indian citizens are authorized to change their
respective currencies.

TIPS

The usual tip for a porter, a room–waiter etc. is one
Rupee; Therefore, it is useful, to have plenty of 1 Rupee notes
always at hand. It avoids annoyance and saves time. Taxi-dri-
vers do not normally expect tips but they accept them. 10% of
the fare marked on the meter is fine, In restaurant, the usual tip
is 10 to 15%. It is everywhere difficult to get change.

TRANSPORT FROM AIRPORT TO TOWN

The distance is approx. 5 miles (8 km). Only two arlines provide
bus services : R.N.A.C. (cost: Rs. 4.– per person) and Indian
Airlines (Rs. 5.– per person). Thai International and Union of
Burma Airways, as well as Bangladesh Biman expect their passengers to proceed on their own to town or to airport. A taxi costs
about Rs. 25.– for such a trip and each carries a maximum of
3 or 4 persons.

AIRPORT TAX

There is no airport tax on arrival. On departure each passenger is charged an airport tax of Rs. 100.– on an international flight and of Rs. 10.– on a domestic flight ("Mountain flights" included) when checking–in at the airline's counter.

NEPALESE TIME

Nepalese time is 10 minutes ahead of Indian standard time. Thus, when it is noon in India, it is 12h. 10 in Nepal. Nepalese time is 5 h 40 ahead of G.M.T. i. e. when it is 8 h. 40 p. m. in Kathmandu, it is 3 h. 00 p. m. in London.

ELECTRIC CURRENT

Voltage, all over Nepal, is 220 volts A.C. (50 cycles.)

CHAPTER FOUR

WHERE TO STAY AND WHERE TO EAT

WHERE TO STAY

NOTES :

1) Most hotels offer the following choice of ratings :
   - Bed only : this is called "European Plan" or, "E.P."
   - Bed and breakfast : "Continental Plan"
   - Bed, breakfast and one main meal : "Modified American Plan", or, "M.A.P."
   - Bed and full board : "American Plan" or "A.P."
2) Check-out time is usually 12 noon
3) All rates are quoted in US Dollars, but hotel bills may be paid in local currency. The below indicated rates are those valid in autumn and winter 1980/81. Unless otherwise indicated, they do not include the usual 10% service charge and the 12% Government Tourist tax.
   In the following list, usually only two rates are indicated : the one referring to "Continental Plan" and the "Full-board" rate. M.A.P.–rates lie somewhere in between.
4) All major hotels grant reduced rates for groups above 15 paying guests and some have special "off-season" '(June to Septermber) rates.
5) All good hotesls provide their guests with boiled and filtered water usually contained in thermos flasks to be found in each room. This water is safe for drinking. It is not advisable to drink from the taps. During meals, it is recommended to order either bottled mineral water ("Bisleri" for instance) or tea, either warm or iced.
6) During peak season (September to March-April), there may be a shortage of accomodation facilities in good hotels. Early bookings are therefore recommended.
7) Last but not least, all information contained in this chapter and referring to rates etc..should be considered as merely indicative.

HOTELS IN KATHMANDU

Hotels mentioned below are classified in alphabetical order. They have been divided into five categories according to standard. :

1. Luxury class hotels

– HOTEL DE L'ANNAPURNA: Very close to the Royal Place as well as to the centre of the old city : On Durbar Square. A very modern hotel, all 150 double-rooms are air-conditioned and provided with piped music. One bar, two restaurants (one of them serving Chinese Sze-chuan dishes), a shopping gallery, a tea-shop, snack-bar and a beauty-parlour. A swimming-pool and tennis–courts are also at the guest's disposal. Tel : 11711 – 11531 – 11552 – Telex No NP 205.

(All rates in US Dollars)

	Bed and Breakfast (Continental Plan)	Full Board (American Plan)
Single room, from :	34.00	47.00
Double " " :	50.00	76.00

– EVEREST-SHERATON HOTEL : Completed in winter 1980, this newest of all Kathmandu luxury hotels is located on the main road linking the airport with the city, from which it is distant by about 4 miles. Modern architecture and installations. 170 double rooms all air-conditioned and with piped music. Swimming pool, shopping arcade, rooftop restaurant with beautiful view on the Himalayas, large dining-room, coffee-shop, lobby lunch-bar, convention hall for 600 participants, discotheque, cultural shows, international and oriental cuisine. The hotel provides with shuffle-services by minicars to airport and to the city's centre. Telex : NP 260 – Phone : 14960 – POB 659. Two sets of rates : Low season (from May to September) and High season (from October to April incl.)

Low season rates :

	B.B.	M.A.P.	A.P.	
Single	38 to 43.–	46 to 51.–	53 to 50.–	(according to the
Double	51 to 58.–	67 to 74.–	81 to 88.–	room size and

High season rates :

	B.B.	M.A.P.	A.P.	location)
Single	43 to 50.–	51 to 58.–	58 to 65.–	
Double	54 to 58.–	70 to 74.–	84 to 88.–	"

– HOTEL MALLA : A recently completed luxury hotel. Also located very close to the Royal Palace. Its architecture, inner decoration and its beautiful garden are in traditional Nepalese style. Malla hotel counts 67 double rooms and 8 suites, all air-conditioned and with piped music. Bar, restaurant, banquet and conference rooms. Swimming-pool and tennis–courts under construction. Shopping gallery. Its address: Lekhnathmarg. Tel. : 15230– P.O.B. 787.

Single room from :	32.00	44.50
Double " " :	47.00	72.00

- HOTEL SHANGRI-LA : On Lazimpath, not far from the French Embassy, and about 2 miles (3.2 km.) from the centre of the city, 50 double rooms, 2 suites, en exceptionally beautiful garden and original artistic inner decoration. Three restaurants, bar, lounge, shopping gallery, a swimming-pool under construction. All rooms airconditioned and provided with piped music. Tel. : 12345 (easy to remember !)

Single room from :	25.50	34.00
Double " " :	38.00	45.00

- HOTEL SHANKER : Located on Lazimpath, near the Head-Office of the United Nations as well as the Embassies of France, Great Britain and India. An old Rana Palace, completely renovated and modernized. Large garden, very picturesque and quiet 142 double rooms all air-conditioned with channelled music, Bar, 2 Restaurants, conference and banquet halls. Shopping centre. Telephone 11983–11973–12973–15151–15152–P.O.B 350

	B.B.	A.P.
Single Room	20.00	42.00
Double Room	45.00	68.50

- HOTEL SOALTEE-OBEROI : Located at 4 miles (6.5 km from the city's centre. Mini-bus shuttle services are available). One of the most modern and also the largest hotel in Kathmandu : 302 double rooms, 12 suites, 6 luxury suites. All rooms are air-conditioned and provided with piped music. 2 bars, 3 restaurants, a casino, shopping galleries, open-air swimming–pool, tennis–courts, garden. Tel. : 11211–11106–11724 –11736 Telex : NP 203.

Single room from :	43,00	58,00
Double " " :	60,00	90,00

- HOTEL YAK AND YETI : The entrance lane leading to this recently completed modern luxury hotel branches off Durbar Square, opposite the Annapurna Hotel. It is located very close to the Royal Palace and the centre of the city. The Yak and Yeti counts 105 double rooms and two suites, all air-conditioned and provided with piped music. Some of its facilities :

tennis–court, swimming–pool. banquet and conference halls, and a "sauna", the only one in the whole country !

This hotel has been set up thanks to the financial assistance of the World Bank, and also to the initiative and dynamic impulsion of "BORIS", as everyone in Kathmandu's society calls Mr. LISSANEVITCH, the "man who opened Nepal to international tourism" by converting, back in 1955, an old Rana Palace into a romantic "luxury" hotel, the "ROYAL HOTEL", the only one of its kind at that time, in Nepal. (It is no longer a hotel nowadays, but the building stands, unchanged, on Kantipath).

During the late King MAHENDRA's memorable coronation festivities in 1956, Boris turned his "Royal Hotel" into the "decor" where those real or imaginary events took place, which Han Suyin described in her famous novel : *The Mountain in young*

The Royal Hotel ceased to exist in 1970. Then, Boris transformed one wing of another Rana Palace, known as the "Lal Durbar" (the "Red Palace") into the best restaurant in town, the "Yak and Yeti" a name he had previously given to his popular and picturesque Bar at the "Royal Hotel".

When the new Hotel "Yak and Yeti" was taken over by a foreign management, Boris withdrew. A few months later, he opened his own Restaurant. (see under "Where to Eat".)

Tel. : 13317 – 13318 – 15786 – Telex No NP 237 YKNYTI P.O.B. 1016.

| Single room from | : | 35.00 | 50.00 |
| Double " " | : | 51.00 | 78.00 |

2. Bungalow Hotels

There are two hotels in Kathmandu of this kind. They deserve a special mention and a separate category, for they are, each in its own style, very different indeed from what is ordinarily called "a hotel".

They are:

– DWARIKA KATHMANDU VILLAGE HOTEL located at Battisputali, not far from the city's centre, on the road leading to Bodnath and Pashupatinath. In fact, this "hotel" is a cluster of authentic and typical Nepalese houses, each with its wood-carved windows and pillars, several centuries old. All 22 rooms were renovated and clients are being provided with all modern facilities. The Swiss Manager is perfect in five languages, including Nepali ! Telephone : 12837– P.O.B. 459 – Telex NP 223 NEPCOM. Tennis and Squash courts, accross the road.

	B.B.	M.A.P.	A.P.
Single Room	20.00	25.50	30.50
Double Room	32.00	42.00	52.00

- TARAGAON HOTEL: located also on the road to Bodnath, a little further away from the city (about 5 miles approx). This hotel is a complex of red brick-and-tile very modern bungalows, surrounded on all sides by fields, open space with the mountains in the background. Bar and terraced restaurant, all modern amenities. – Telephones : 15409–15412–15634– P.O.B. 507.

	B.B.	M.A.P.	A.P.
Single Room	13.50	18.50	22.00
Double Room	23.00	29.00	34.00

3. Hotels of good standing

- HOTEL AMBASSADOR : On Lazimpat, close to British, French and Indian Embassies, at 2 miles from the city's centre. Very pleasant small garden, good meals, excellent service

	B.B.	M.A.P.	A.P.
Single room	10.00	14.00	17.00
Double room	16.00	24.00	30.00

Tel: 14232 cable address: BASS.

- HOTEL BLUE STAR : Located at one mile from the city's centre, near the bridge leading to Patan. 80 double rooms, bar, restaurant. Telephones : 13996–12376–13218–14612–14411.

	B.B.	M.A.P.	A.P.
Single Room	16.00	19.00	28.00
Double Room	25.00	31.00	37.00

Note : The above rates are those applicable to rooms without air-conditioning. Add 2 US $ to these rates for air-conditioned single and 4 $ for double rooms.

- HOTEL CRYSTAL, in the very heart of the city (at the corner of New Road and Shukra Path), only a few yards from the old Royal Palace. 31 double rooms, all air-conditioned. Bar and restaurant, panoramic-view roof-terrace. Telephones : 12638, 13811–13636–13397.

	B.B.	M.A.P.	A.P.
Single Room	20.00	23.00	25.50
Double Room	29.00	34.00	40.00

- HOTEL MAKALU, On Dharma Path, in the very centre of the city, close to the Old Royal Palace, to Nepal Bank and New

Road. 30 double rooms with attached bath. Bar and Restaurant. Telephone : 13955

	B.B.	M.A.P.	A.P.
Single Room	12.50	14.00	15.00
Double Room	15.00	17.00	22.00

- HOTEL MANASLU, On Lazimpath, close to the French Embassy, at 2 miles from the centre of the city. Located in a pleasant, picturesque old Rana Palace, 31 rooms out of which 25 double rooms, all of them with attached bath. Restaurant. bar, garden. Telephone : 13471

	B.B.	M.A.P.	A.P.
Single Room	8.00	10.50	14.00
Double Room	11.00	15.50	18.00

- HOTEL MAYALU, near Durbar Marg, very recently opened. No restaurant services, therefore the Hotel provides a lodging and breakfast only, at the rate of US $ 9,00 for a single and 13.00 for a double room. In "off-season" the rates are fixed at US $ 6,00 and 9,00 respectively–Telephone: 13596 P.O.B. 1276

- HOTEL NARAYANI, located at the top of the ascent which leads to Patan city. Very modern and spacious hotel; 68 double rooms and 4 suites. Bar and Restaurant, Swimming-pool, garden. Telephone 21442– P.O.B. 1357.

	B.B.	M.A.P.	A.P.
Single Room	21.00	25.00	30.00
Double Room	29.00	28.00	47.00

The above rates concern non air-conditioned rooms. For those which are provided with air-conditoning, add US $ 3.00 per single room and US $ 4.00 per double room, in each category.

- HOTEL SIDDHARTHA - On Kantipath (inside Jyatha lane). Near the city's centre. 16 Double rooms, all air-conditioned with attached bath, telephone and channelled music.– Roof garden, Bar and Restaurant. Telephone 15761– P.O.B. 1241–

	B.B.	M.A.P.	A.P.
Single Room	15.00	17.00	20.00
Double Room	21.00	25.00	31.00

- SUMMIT HOTEL : Located on top of the Kupandol hill in Patan, branching off to the right side (a steep stone slab covered road) of the Shanta Bhawan road. Magnificent location, overlooking the whole Valley with splendid view on the Himalayas from autumn to spring. Large garden, Restaurant, "English-type Pub", Swimming-pool and tennis-court : 28 double rooms all with attached bath.

	B.B.	M.A.P.	A.P.
Single	16.00	21.00	25.00
Double	26.00	26.00	44.00

Telephone : 21894 – Telex : N.P. 270 NATRAJ.

– HOTEL VAJRA : A newly built unconventional hotel located half-way between the old city (Chettrapatty) and Swyambhu-hill. Western and Nepali-Tibetan management. 42 double-rooms, several terraces with panoramic view on the Valley and the surrounding Himalayas. Frequent cultural events such as plays, musical and dance performances presented in a large conference-hall. An interesting "East-West library" is open to scholars.

Bar and Restaurant with Western and Chinese-Tibetan meals.

	Room only	
	Single	Double
With running water	6.00	8.00
With shower and toilet	8.00	10.00

POB 1084 – Telephone : 14545

– HOTEL WOODLANDS : On Durbar Marg, near the new Royal Palace and close to the city's centre. 60 air-conditioned double rooms, with piped music, Bar and Restaurant. Telephone: 12683– P.O.B. 760

	B.B.	M.A.P.	A.P.
Single Room	18.10	23.50	27.00
Double Room	27.80	37.00	42.50

– HOTEL YELLOW PAGODA : On Kantipath, very close to city centre, Airlines and Travel Agents Office, next to the Embassy of the Federal Republic of Germany. Bar and Restaurant, Roof Terrace, 51 air-conditioned double-rooms. Book-shop. Telephone : 15492, 15337, 15338 P.O.B. 373

	B.B.	M.A.P.	A.P.
Single Room	15.00	21.43	23.36
Double Room	23.00	34.77	37.82

4. Modest hotels

All below mentioned hotels are commendable. They offer small but clean and comfortable rooms, mostly with attached bath or shower rooms, Some have quite good restaurants. All serve breakfast. Rates are usually moderate, under US$ 10.00 for a single room on Bed and Breakfast plan, the only one which is referred to here unless otherwise mentioned. The 12% Government tax is never included in the quoted rates.

The choice depends more on their respective location and tourists preference in this respect than on the hotel's particulars. This is why they are classified according to their location.

a) *In the very heart of the city,* i.e. on or near New Road or the old part of Kathmandu

- HOTEL CAMP : on Maruhity, 16 double rooms– Telephones : 13142–13145 :

  Single Rooms :   5.00
  Double Room :   7.50

- HOTEL CONTI : On Indra Chowk, in the old city's main street 20 double rooms, Telephone 13887 :

  Single Room :   5.00
  Double Room :   7,50

- HOTEL GANESH : On Dharma Path, near Nepal Bank Head-Office. 16 double rooms most with attached bath–Telephone: 15730.

  Single Room :   4.00
  Double Room :   6.00

- HOTEL K.T. On Indra Chowk, not far from Hanuman Dhoka – 25 double rooms – Telephones 11266–14417

  Single Room :   3.50 (Room only)
  Double Room :   5.00 (id.)

- HOTEL PANORAMA – On Khichha Pokhari, close to New Road. 48 Double rooms – Telephone : 11502–13970

  Single Room :   6.00 (Room only)
  Double Room :   10.00 (id.)

- HOTEL PARAS – On Dharma Path, practically on New Road. 20 double rooms - Telephone 11233

  Single Room :   5.00
  Double Room :   7.00

b) *Around the Airlines and Travel Agencies area (Durbar Marg Kantipath – Near the new Royal Palace)*

- HOTEL BLUE DIAMOND: on Jyatha (Thamel) – POB 2134 No restaurant – Tel. 13392 – 33 double rooms

  Single Room US $ 7,50 – Double Room 10,50

- CENTRAL HOTEL : On Jamal, between Durbar Marg and Kantipath – 22 double rooms with attached bath

  Telephone 13997

Single Room :   4.00 (with Breakfast)
Double Room :   6.00 (id.)
- HOTEL GAJUR: – 16/496 – on Jyatha Thamel
  P.O.B. 1831 – Telephone 13036 – 17 double rooms
  No restaurant but serves breakfast.
  Single rooms US $ 4.20 – Double: 5.00
  Double with attached bath: 7.00
- HOTEL HARRY'S GUEST HOUSE: on Jyatha Tole 18/637
  No restaurant – Tel 11229 – 16 double rooms
  Single room common bath: US $ 2.50 - Double with
  common bath: 3.75 Double room with attached bath 4.20
- HOTEL KATHMANDU GUEST HOUSE, On Sat Ghumte, Thamel,
  beyond the New Royal Palace. A very popular hotel among
  the younger generation of tourists. Quiet, pleasant garden for
  sun-bathing and laundry drying. 62 double rooms. The
  Hotel itself does not offer meals, but, next to the Hotel is one
  of the most typical and moderate rate Tibetan Restaurants in
  town : Astha Mangal (the "Eight auspicious signs") where
  hotel guests usually take their breakfast and meals. The
  rates of Kathmandu Guest House vary according to the
  toilet and washing facilities (bath room attached or common
  toilet and shower rooms) :
  Single Room : from   1.00   to   3.60   (Lodging only) :
  Double Room : from   1.60   to   4.80
  Telephone 13628–Telegram Address : Kathhouse.
- HOTEL KOH–i–NOOR, practically on Kantipath (inside the
  lane called Jyatha) – 14 Double rooms. 8 of which with
  attached bath – Telephones 13930–11997– Restaurant
  Single Room :   4.00 (Room only)
  Double Room :   6.00 (id.)
- HOTEL NOOK, on Kantipath, opposite the Embassy of the
  Federal Republic of Germany – 30 Double rooms with atta-
  ched bath. Telephone : 13627 – Bar – Restaurant P.O.B. 594.
  Single Room :   6.00 (Room only)
  Double Room :   9.00 (id.)
  Single room :   7.00 (Room only)
  Double room :   10.00 (id)
- HOTEL SHAKTI: on Thamel Tole, Garden with Parking and
  Garden. Tel: 13087 - 16121 -
  No restaurant - 10 Single and 12 double rooms
  Single room - US $ 2.00 - Double 2.50
  Double with attached bath: 3.00

- HOTEL STAR, next to Kathmandu Guest House, on Sat Ghumte, Thamel. 44 double rooms in the older part, 12 additional in the new wing. Restaurant Telephones : 11004–12803
  Single Room :   2.00 to 5,00 (Room only)
  Double Room :   4.00 to 8,00 (id.)

c) *Miscellaneous location*
- HOTEL EVER GREEN, on Bagh Bazar, near the crossing of Ram Shah Path. 18 double rooms. Restaurant and Bar. Vegetarian, Chinese and Indian meals.
                    Room only :
  Single room   : 2.00 (no individual bath-room)
  Double   "   : 3.20 (id.)
  Double   "   : 4.00 (with individual bath room)
- HOTEL LALIGURAS, on Lazimpath, beyond Canton Restaurant. An old Rana Palace, 2 miles from city's centre Telephone 13304 – P.O.B. 291–21 Double rooms – Restaurant. Verandah.
  Single Room :   5.50 (Breakfast included)
  Double Room :   9.00   (id)
- HOTEL LHOTSE, on Kamal Pokhari, at 1 mile from the centre of the city. 15 Double Rooms – Telephone 15474
  Single Room :   8.00
  Double Rooms :   12.00
- HOTEL SAVOY, On Thapathali, near the entrance to the airport and Chinese road. at 1 mile from the centre. 10 double rooms – Telephone 12918
  Single Room :   5.50
  Double Room :   7.50
- HOTEL WHITTIES, On Teku, the road leading to Soaltee Hotel and the highway to Indian. Good parking for large cars. 15 Double Rooms. Telephone : 13839.
  Single Room :   4.50
  Double Room :   5.50

5. Other Hotels.

The following hotels are more modest still. Generally they provide only rooms, without attached baths. Neither breakfast nor meals are served. The rates vary between 1 and 3,00 US Dollars for a single room and from 2 to 4,50 for a double room (some rates are even lower).

There are mainly two parts of the city where these "hotels" or lodges are to be found : the first is near the Old Royal Palace, Basantpur and Hanuman Dhoka squares as well as, of course, in and around "Freak Street", the second is away from the city's centre and closer to Kathmandu Guest House, not far from the New Royal Palace.

It is extremely difficult to set up a complete and permanent list of all these establishments for not only they change often their name but also their management. Appreciation valid to-day may not be any longer appropriate to-morrow.

The best advice that may be given to those who attach more importance to reduced cost than to increased comfort, is to select the part of the city which suits them best, try the first lodge they find attractive and price-worthy and change quarters on the following day if they are dissatisfied or disappointed.

HOTELS AT POKHARA

Pokhara is the second largest tourist-centre of Nepal, located at 125 km. west of Kathmandu, at half an hour flight or 6 to 7 hours by car, from the capital. (Regular scheduled services by RNAC's planes and public bus services). Pokhara is magnificently situated at the foot of the very impressive Annapurna Massif. Pokhara lies at only 2,952 f., but the summits, just in front, reach 26,500 !

At Pokhara, there are three hotels of very good standing : —*Hotel Fish–Tail Lodge* (a subsidiary of Hotel de l'Annapurna in Kathmandu). Its name is the one by which is popularly called the majestic pyramid"Maccha-Pucchare", for this word, in Nepali, means "fish-tail". This name is justified by the fact that, seen from its western side, it shows clearly two summits, the highest of which reaches 22,960 ft. but to see them it needs 3 days walk. The hotel is picturesquely located, surrounded by quiet and pleasant lawns, bushes and flower-beds. The bungalows with their thatched roofs looking out towards the breathtaking panoramic view on the mountains that reflect their snow-capped summits in the mirror of the lake's waters. An ideal spot to take a couple of days rest, for instance at the end of a strenuous trek. To reach the hotel, there is a rather unexpected means of transport, seldom in use to reach a luxury hotel : a not too spacious, completely flat, wooden raft, tied to each of the lakes banks by means of a nylon rope which the visitor may have to pull himself, should there not be anybody around (there usualy is !). Once the other side is reached, there are but a few steps to the hotel itself. Fish–Tail Lodge offers only 20 double rooms, so far. Most are air conditioned.

	Rates in US Dollars
Single Room, full board	26.50
Double Room, id.	44.00

- *Hotel Mount Annapurna*. Located just in front of the airport, a little to the left, has 32 double, air-conditioned rooms. Bar and restaurant are decorated with original tibetan-style wall–paintings.

	B.B.	A.P.
Single Room	12.00	18.50
Double Room	18.00	27.00

- *Hotel New Crystal*. This hotel too, is of recent construction and also faces the airport, but towards the right hand side. It is a subsidiary of Kathmandu's Crystal Hotel. 48 double rooms.

	B.B.	A.P.
Single Room	19.00	25.50
Double Room	29.00	42.00

- *Dragon Hotel*, 10 minutes walk from the airport. Excellent location and manangement, garden, comfortable rooms with attached bathrooms, Western, Nepalese, Chinese and even japanese meals. Telephone 52, P.O.B. 15

	B.B.	A.P.
Single Room	13.50	22
Double "	21.00	34

In addition to these hotels, Pokhara offers many other accommodation possibilities, at more moderate rates :

There are several ones between Mount Annapurna and New Crystal, such as "Sun and Snow" – "Annapurna" – "Tibetan Hotel", etc..

Along the road leading to Fish–Tail Lodge and beyond, there are many modest hotels and lodges, with rates under Rs. 25.– for a double room, without breakfast or meals. One of the most pleasant one is New Green Hotel, which has a spacious parking place. Hotel Phewa Lake, near the shore, and others are more or less of the same standard.

"Comfeedera"

Pokhara invites also its visitors to a special kind of accommodation: "Self-Service Cottages". They are fully furnished, provided with running hot and cold water, linen, towels etc... kitchen facilities, and even... a caretaker who helps the tenants for purchasing food and beverages at the local market.

These bungalows are located close to the Bus Terminal and the airport, on Ramghat. COMFEEDERA, means: to live in comfort. Telephone, in Pokhara : 239

– In Kathmandu : 15812 between 10 a.m. and 1 p.m.
   Its facilities are offered at the following rates (US $) :
   A 3 persons bungalow : Nep. Rs. Per day 125.–
   (+12% government tax)
   A 4 persons bungalow :   ”   ”   ”   180.–
   A 5 persons bungalow :   ”   ”   ”   250.–

HOTELS IN THE TERAI: See under "Safari".

HOTELS IN SHERPA LAND

Under the pressure of the increasing number of trekkers the Solu–Khumbu area has become equipped with hotels, lodges etc. mostly of a a modest nature.:

—At Lukla Airport itself (9,085 ft. 2,770m.) during the peak trekking season (October–November and March–April) several planes land per day and disembark each time 15 to 17 passengers. Additional ones may have to wait one or two days before getting a seat on one of these planes.

Now, thanks to the initiative of the "Sherpa Co-operative Trekking (P) Ltd. Managing Director : Dawa Norbu SHERPA, there are 12 comfortable double rooms and 2 dormitories available. The rates for full board are :

US $ 20.–per person for a single room and US $ 30.–for a double room

This organization, which stands under the management of very experienced trekking professionals, provides also guides, porters and equipment for trekkers.

For Reservations : Sherpa Co-operative Huts (P) Ltd. On Kamalpokhari, P.O.B. 1338–Kathmandu. Phone 15887

This same organization is planning to build and manage similar Trekker's Hotels in the Everest area. (In particular at Khumjung or Kunde.)

—At Shyangboche airstrip, situated approx. 3,000 ft. (915m.) higher than Lukla and about twenty minutes walk from Namche Bazar, there are two huts built by Sherpas. The largest one stands under the management of Transhimalayan Trekking (P) Ltd. The rate is approx. US $ 15.– per person and per day for lodging only, Meals are also available.

This kind of accommodation is extremely useful, not only for those trekkers who have to wait for seats on their return planes, but also for those who may have arrived almost directly from the US, Europe or elsewhere and need to acclimatize themselves to the higher altitude.

—*At Namche Bazar* itself, the "capital–city of Sherpa–land", there are also several small hotels and lodges for tourists, at moderate rates. The same applies to similar places such as Phunki (10,660 f). Trashinga (11,150 f.) Pheriche (13,943 f.) and even Lobuche (16,174 f.)

—*Above the two twin-villages of Khumjung and Kunde,* there is the world–famous HOTEL EVEREST–VIEW, one of the highest hotels in the world, at 12,713 ft. (3.875m.) in full view of the Everest range.

It is built on a little promontory overlooking the twin villages of KHUMJUNG and KUNDE, a mere one hour's walk from the regional captial, NAMCHE BAZAR.

One of the original features of this hotel is the way it has been beautifully integrated in the surrounding landscape. Amidst the pine trees, it can hardly be seen before its monumental stone steps become visible. Another of its attractions, the major one, in fact, is the view on Mount Everest seen from the terrace, taking in the peaks of Nuptse, Lhotse and the amazingly majestic Ama Dablam.

For bookings or further information, Hotel Everest View's Office is located in Seto Durbar, on Durbar Marg, just in front of the AIR FRANCE Office. Telephone : 13845–13871. P.O.B. 283-
To reach the hotel there are four "classical" ways :

— By plane : Either from Kathmandu to Lukhla –45 minutes flight, then one and a half days easy walk
Or, directly to Shyangboche–50 minutes fllight, then half an hour walk. For air fares, see chapter: "How to get around".
— By plane and on foot : By plane to Jiri (appr. 8,000 f.) and from there in 6 – 7 days on foot or by plane to Phaplu (8,200 ft.) and from days 4–5 days walk.
— By foot from Kathmandu : Approx. 12 – 13 days walk.
Rates : (Full board per day all included)

	1st night	2 nights	3rd night and
		(US $)	thereafter
Single occupancy			
of a double room	206,00	278,00	51,00
Double occupancy	396,00	520,00	90,00

—*At Tharkegyang,* visitors and trekkers may also find a hotel which opened in 1976. Small but comfortable, these are some more Malemchi–Helambu area.

HOTELS IN THE KALI GANDAKI AREA

At Jomosom, there are three modest hotels: "Niligiri-View" near the airport, "Jomosom Hotel" close to the Police station and Foreigner's Check-Post and a third one in front of the airport.

HOTELS ON THE ANNAPURNA SANCTUARY TREK

Several lodges for tourists and trekkers are open at Landrung, Gandrung, Chomrong and beyond in the forest to Hinko.

LODGING AT LUMBINI (BUDDHA'S BIRTH PLACE)

Lumbini is a small hamlet in the Terai, which can be reached by car from Bhairawa or in a 40 minute's flight from Kathmandu. In the course of 1979, a small but commendable hotel, the "Maya Devi" (named after Lord Buddha's mother) was opened.

Under the inspiration of U THANT, the former Secretary-General of the United Nations and with the cooperation of many Buddhist communities, a vast development plan of the Lumbini Sanctuary has been set up that includes the construction of hotels and lodges.

LODGING AT NAGARKOT AND KAKANI

These are two beautiful sightseeing spots, from where the scenery is overwhelming. Both are situated approximately 24 m. (39 km.) from Kathmandu. At Nagarkot, it is the eastern part of the Himalaya range, including Mount Everest that can be seen in the distance, whereas from Kakani, it is the western part with the ranges of Ganesh Himal, Annapurna and Dhaulagiri etc that opens up to the view.

In both these places there are "guest houses" where one can spend the night at moderate rates.

In addition, at Nagarkot, there is a hotel called "Everest Cottage" The rates are : 30 Rs. for a single room with bath, 40 Rs. for a double room and 10 for a bed in a dormitory.

WHERE TO EAT
INTRODUCTION

All better Kathmandu (and Pokhara) hotels have their ow
Restaurants, serving, Western, Chinese and Nepalese meals.

There is no exclusively British or American Restaurant wit
the exception of "Aunt Jane" on Dharma Path, near New Roa

Nor is there an exclusively French Restaurant in town. Th
better restaurants are those serving good Chinese or Nepales
Indian food.

NEPALESE, INDIAN AND CHINESE

Most of the major hotels, such as Annapurna, Dwarik
Malla, Shangrila, Soaltee and Yak and Yeti serve typical Nepales
meals as well as Indian and Chinese dishes.

Besides these hotels, there are many restaurants in tow
where foreigners may enjoy the "cuisine" of these three varieties

— *Sun-Kosi*, on Durbar Marg, on the left–hand side when leavin
Annapurna Hotel. A small and cosy restaurant where Nepales
dishes are especially prepared as not to offend delicate Weste
ners by too many spices.

— *The Other Room*, the "annexe" of Crystal Hotel, on Ne
Road, near Juddha Shumsher Rana's statue.

— *Ashta Mangal*, a Chinese restaurant in a pleasant atmosphere c
Tibetan wall-paintings. Specialities : excellent chinese soup
chow-meins (with home made noodles) and "mo-mo
(called "kothay" on the menu): Tibetan raviolis stuffed wit
buffalo meat-balls; they may be ordered boiled or fried. Th
restaurant is close to Kathmandu Guest House.

— *Nanglo*, on Durbar Marg, bar, garden and restaurant, a ver
cosy and pleasant setting, which serve excellent Chinese dishe
also specializing in some "rich" Tibetan dishes. Too fe
tables for the many customers its deserved reputation attrac

— *Canton*, on Lazimpath. Authentic Chinese dishes, exceller
spring-rolls and suckling pig (to be ordered in advance). Owner
Mr. Wong, one of the best reputed Chinese cooks and restau
rant-keeper.

— *Ringmo*, also on Lazimpath. Very commendable too. Sam
Chinese specialities as Canton's.

— *Mei-Hua*, an excellent Chinese restaurant, located on the firs
floor above Air-India's Office, on Kantipath. The owners an
hosts are from Lhassa

Some other restaurants, serving primarily, but not exclusivel

hinese dishes :
  An-An, on Khichha Pokhari, not far from New Road
  Ming-Ming, on Durbar Marg, near Yeti Travels
  Nook. on Kantipath
  Om, on Dharma Path
  Siddharta, on Jyatha, near Kantipath
  Tso-Ngon, near Hotel Mayalu, on Durbar Marg, corner of
  Jamal
  Tung-Fong, on Kantipath
  U-Tse, on the road leading to Kathmandu Guest-House
  Van-Van, on Kamal Pokhari, close to Krishna Loaf Bakery.

JAPANESE

Kushi-Fuji, on Durbar Marg, near Annapurna Hotel on the
first floor.
Molisyu : on Lazimpath, on the lane leading to Hotel Manaslu.
This restaurant serves Western meals too

CONTINENTAL RESTAURANTS

In addition to the hotels, the following restaurants are to be
commended :
—*"Restaurant BORIS"*, on Battis-Putali (a particularly poetic
reetname, for this word means : "the thirty-two butterflies" !)
  BORIS' new own Restaurant is undoubtedly the most reputed
he in the whole city. The host is "Boris LISSANEVITCH",
hom we have already introduced to the reader in the previous
apter (See under "Hotel Yak and Yeti"). The biography
this fascinating personality has been written – in English – by
e French author, Michel PEISSEL under the somewhat unex-
cted title : "TIGER FOR BREAKFAST".
  At "Restaurant BORIS", Russian and local specialities, such
poultry, game, the famous "smoked bekti" fish, among many
her delicacies. A meal starts – traditionally– with a glass of
aktail" a drink whose recipe is one of Boris' secrets.
—*K.C. Restaurant,* half-way between "U–Tse" and Kathmandu
uest House. Amercian-Swiss dishes are served in a picturesque
ning place.
—*The Nest :* Hotel Ambassador's ground–floor. A very plea-
nt restaurant, located on Lazimpath.

-ABOUT NEPALESE DISHES AND DRINKS

Nepal could not qualify as a country for "gastronomy" accor-
ng to *"western"* concepts. The average Nepalese, unlike the

average European, is not on the look–out for sophisticated de
cacies. He seems satisfied with his traditional meals. In tl
respect not much has changed in the course of many decad
if not centuries.

Many Nepalese are vegetarians. (In any case, the import ai
sale of veal or beef is prohibited).

The basic food of the average Nepalese is rice and "*da*
(small lentils), or other pulses, many varieties of vegetables, gh
and fruit, Nepalese dishes are usually a little spicy and even "ho
according to western standards.

At each meal, *chilli* is always at hand, green one, in summ
eaten raw and fresh or red one, i.e. dried one, in winter).

Meat from buffaloes, goats or sheep, chicken and eggs, occ
sionally fish, are used to prepare the various Nepalese "*Curries*

The most popular drinks are fresh water and tea, usually wi
much milk and sugar added. A very refreshing drink is "*lass*
i. e. iced curd or yoghurt beaten with water and sugar.

Breakfast consists usually of a cup of tea in the early hou
of the morning. The first substantial meal is served around 9.
a.m. and since most, if not all administrations, offices and sho
remain open between noon and 2 p.m., the Nepalese do n
usually take lunch but have their main meal when they come ho
from work i.e. after 5 p. m.

Alcoholic drinks consumed in Nepal are mainly beer (loca
brewed) or, in the hills, "*chang*" a kind of light beer made of f
mented cereals) and "*rakshi*" (a stronger drink made of distill
rice or barley). Besides, Nepal produces also its own whisky, g
and rum, but no wine.

SOME DO's AND SOME DONT's

Nepalis being extremely friendly and hospitable peop
it may very well happen that a foreign visitor is invited to come
a Nepali house or to share a meal with a Nepali family.

Should this be the case a few hints might not be out of pla
in a guide–book. Of course the present paragraph will restr
itself to the most elementary rules of behaviour and not
into the very complex matter of customs, traditions, supers
tions and beliefs. These would easily yield enough material
a book in itself.

– In a Nepali house

Before entering a Nepali house, take off your shoes or sa
dals and leave them outside the door.

Be careful to put them down soles on the ground; the sight of a shoe in an upside down position would be looked upon as a bad omen.

Even if the host insists that you could keep your shoes on, it is mandatory to take them off before entering the dining or guests–room, in particular if you see the floor of these rooms covered with white linen or cotton instead of carpets. It goes without saying that shoes have to be taken off also before entering a bed-room, should you greet somebody who is sick or bed-ridden.

This custom has a twofold rationale :
- the purely hygienic one : to keep the inside of a house clean
- the religious one : not to pollute a Hindu home by taking into the room any object made of leather, which is usually a sub–product of a sacred cow.

Owing to the latter reason, no object made of leather should be worn or carried into the kitchen or near the place where food is being prepared.

- Do not express a desire to see "the kitchen" or the "storage-room" where vegetables, rice, flour and other provisions are kept. These places are the landlady's private areas and no foreigner should ordinarily intrude into them.

- It is not considered proper to ask your Nepalese hosts or friends about their caste or sub-caste, even about their religious beliefs or community. Your straight questions may often be set aside by polite but evasive replies.

- If you have to hand over some object, say a letter, a parcel or a present to somebody staying inside a house, do not pass this object over the threshold, but wait until either the recipient stepped out of the house or you stepped in. Not to do so would be considered bad manners.

- If you handed over a present to your hosts, be not surprised if they lay it aside unopened. To open a parcel in the presence of the donor is not "being done". (May be in order not to embarrass other guests who might have brought more modest gifts.)

- To whistle in the presence of other persons is, as everywhere, always a sign of bad education. To do it in a Nepali house is even worse : for an unknown reason, only a thief is supposed to whistle !

- Another unexpected "behaviourism" : Do not blow out a candle inside a Nepali house, since this would be regarded as a lack of respect for light, and any light is considered as being a part of the life-giving almighty Sun !

— **How to recognize people**

- A married woman is always easy to identify by the red line of vermilion "sindur" which runs along the parting line of her hair.
- A widow never wears bracelets or bangles except if made of copper or gold, since these two metals are looked upon as having a religious value and therefore are not regarded as purely ornamental.
- Any boy who has gone through the "brata bandha" (the sacred thread) ceremony – which is normally performed between 5 and 13 years or any adult, if dressed in white from top to bottom, indicates that he is in mourning over his deceased father or mother; usually he will wear these white garments for one full year.
- Brides and bridegrooms do not wear any distinctive ornament or sign before their actual wedding ceremonies take place.

—**Being invited in a Nepali home for a meal**

- Punctuality, in Nepal as in most countries, is showing courtesy and good manners.
- In most of Nepali households, it is still customary, for all male guests, irrespective of social status, caste or ethnic group, to gather in one part of the reception room and for all ladies and girls in another. But it will not be considered bad manners if a foreign guest moves over and talks to the ladies.
- However, you would be misbehaving if you, though a foreign guest, touched or stroked the head of a girl, even if she is still only a child, or to pat her shoulder or her back. Such marks of affection given to boys are, however, not objected to.
- Normally a dinner-party starts with a long series of drinks, soft or alcoholic ones. It is not uncommon that this part of the reception continues for over one hour or more.
- To the contrary, after the dinner, there is no prolonged get-together. Most guests will thank and take leave from the hosts a short time after coffee and liqueurs have been served.
- In some Nepali households, the lady of the house still follows the ancient custom of serving personally not only her husband and her children but also her guests. She will not attend the dinner herself and may take her meal after everybody else

has had his; sometimes she will even retire to the kitchen to take hers. The foreign guest should accept this custom without trying to "be polite" or insisting that the lady of the house should "join her guests".

— In typical and traditional Nepali houses, the dinner table will not be laid out in western fashion with plates, knives, forks and spoons. Each guest will have in front of him a large stainless-steel dish divided in compartments of different sizes. The middle one is meant to contain rice, while the smaller ones are for vegetables, pickles, meat, salad etc.. Usually a separate one will be used for "dal", a mixture of organe-yellowish lentils that is usually to be blended with rice.

— Nepalis who keep to their traditions, will mix the various components of the dish with the fingers of their right hand (even if they happen to be left-handed). Should the foreign guest not be used to this way of eating, nobody would object to his requesting for and using a fork a knive, or a spoon.

— What might be objected against him, would be to take for himself a second helping of rice, dal, vegetables, curry or even water. For he should not forget that anything he touches with his hands or even more, so, with his lips, becomes "jutho" i. e. "unclean", or "soiled", in the Hindu sense.

— This is why, among other examples, when dinner is served as a "buffet-dinner", every guest, (including foreigners,) once his plate is empty, he should put it discreetly *under* the buffet-table and never *on top* of it, where his plate, which has now become "jutho", might touch. and therefore "soil", or "pollute" a plate or a dish which has not been used yet.

— At the end of the dinner, the servants, or the lady of the house, will pass around a jar full of water, a basin and a towel, to help each guest to wash his right hand.

— It will not be considered offensive if the foreign guest requests for some more water to clean the plate he used for his dinner and take it outside to have it dried in the sun. However, this is not at all compulsory nor expected.

— But it would be out of place for the foreign guest to carry his plate to the kitchen with the intention of helping "clearing the table", for, as stated above, the kitchen is "off limits" for anybody except the lady of the house and the servants.

— The foreign guest should not manifest any surprise if he happens to see the servants cleaning pots, pans and plates with ash, for ash removes easily all greasy particles. The final washing will be done with water.

– A last observation: It is again to avoid "jutho" that induces practically all Nepalis never to touch a bottle or a jar with their lips, but to pour their content directly into their mouth, down the throat.

– Inviting a Nepali friend or acquaintance for drinks or a meal in your hotel.

This situation also may easily arise.

If the person you want to invite happens to be a very ortho-box and puritan Brahmin, he is likely to express his inability to accept your invitation, in order not to embarrass you. For his caste-consciousness could and would prevent him from taking anything that was prepared by servants belonging to a lower caste than his own. Of course, these extreme cases of total refusal become more and more seldom nowadays, in particular in Kathmandu and in circles in which a foreigner is likely to become acquainted with.

–When travelling

If you have to undertake a journey in the company of a Nepali, do your utmost not to plan your day of departure on a Saturday, which of all the days of the week is considered the most unauspicious. Should circumstances compell your leaving on a Saturday, do not show any surprise if you discover that your Nepali travel companion did not spend the previous night in his own home. He might have been in a house of friends, leaving his home and family on Friday, a more auspicious day.

– The same rule will apply if the Nepalese traveller, once he left his home, misses his train or his plane, or if the departure time, for whatsoever reason it may be, is postponed by 24 hours : he will not go back to his own home, but spend this unexpected extra-time with friends. This can only be explained by emphasizing the fact that all "rites" to make his journey auspicious having been duly performed before he left his home the first time, he is considered as "having left" and the rites can not be repeated.

– These luck-bringing ritual a would–be traveller subjects himself to will include the following: his father or mother will apply on his forehead a mixture of rice-grains and "dahi" (curd), as well as vermilion sindur paste. His relatives and friends will put garlands around his head and neck, preferably made of red or yellow flowers; he will receive some fruit to carry with him, usually bananas, oranges and coconunts, while his closest relatives will hand over to him a small satchel that contains a symbolic meal consisting of a hard-boiled egg, pieces of dried fish or meat, a small quantity of curd etc...

– Now he has left for good. But he will not forget that it is also considered very unauspicious to return home on the ninth day after the day of departure (in fact, the day of the rites of departure) Therefore, your journey has to be planned accordingly. Your companions family will be very grateful to you.

CHAPTER FIVE

USEFUL ADDRESSES AND INFORMATION

AIRLINES

Name of Airline	Office location	Phone No.
AEROFLOT	Kantipath	12397
AIR FRANCE	Durbar Marg	13339
AIR INDIA	Kantipath	12335
BANGLADESH BIMAN	Durbar Marg	11277
BRITISH AIRWAYS	Durbar Marg	12266
CATHAY PACIFIC	Kantipath	14705
INDIAN AIRLINES	Durbar Marg	11198
JAPAN AIRLINES	Durbar Marg	13854
K.L.M.	Durbar Marg	14937
KOREAN AIRLINES	Kantipath	12080
LUFTHANSA	Durbar Marg	13052
NORTHWEST AIRLINES	Durbar Marg	14387
PAKISTAN INTERNATIONAL	Durbar Marg	12100
PANAMERICAN	Durbar Marg	15824
ROYAL NEPAL AIRLINES	New Road	14511
S.A.S.	Durbar Marg	14387
SWISSAIR	Durbar Marg	12455
THAI INTERNATIONAL	Durbar Marg	14387
T.W.A.	Kantipath	14705
UNION OF BURMA AIRWAYS	Durbar Marg	14837

TOURIST AGENCIES

Name	Location	Phone No.
American Express	Jamal	13596
Annapurna Travels and Tours	Durbar Marg	12339
Continental " " " "	"	14299
Dolkha " " " "	Kantipath	15620
Everest Travel Service	New Road	11216–12217
Gorkha Travels	Durbar Marg	14895
Himalayan Travels and Tours	"	13803
International " " "	Ram Shah Path	12635

Kathmandu " " "	New Road	14446
Malla " " "	Lekhnath	15966–15968
Mercantile " " "	Durbar Marg	14839
Natraj Tours and Travels	"	12014
Nepal Express Travels	Ram Shah Path	11277
Nepal Travel Agency	"	13106
Orchid Express Travels	Kantipath	12709
Peace Travels and Tours	"	13533
Pokhara " " "	New Road	12038
President " " "	Durbar Marg	15021
Rainbow " " "	"	—
Shangri–La Tours	Kantipath	15855
Shankar Travels and Tours	Lazimpath	13494
Siddharta " " "	Kantipath	13122
Tara Tours and Travels	"	—
Third Eye Tours and Travels	"	11738
Tourist Service	Dharma Path	15251
Transhimalayan Tours	Durbar Marg	13854
Universal Tours and Travels	Kantipath	12080
Yak Travels and Tours	Durbar Marg	15611
Yeti Travels	"	11234–11329

These Travel Agencies provide guided tours and take care of all bookings (hotels, air and road travels, enter ainment etc..) Most of them are authorized money–exchange dealers.

THE GOVERNMENT TOURIST DEPARTMENT

Head - Office : In the Ministry of Tourism Building, behind the Sports Centre (Municipal Stadium – Tripureshwor)

Two Public Information Centres :
—On New Road, near Basantpur Square, on the same side as the Old Royal Palace, Phone No. : 15818
—At the Airport, in the arrival lounge. Phone No. : 15537

Both these Offices provide tourists with all necessary information concerning sightseeing in the Valley and Nepal in general, hotel accommodation, restaurants etc....A variety of publications (folders, maps, booklets etc) are available at both these Offices. All publications are in English language except a booklet about Nepal which has also been published in French and Spanish.

Every afternoon, on Tuesdays and Fridays, the Department of Tourism offers a colour film show in its auditiorium located in its New Road Offices.

The Department of Tourism New Road Office is open every day except on Saturdays from 10 a.m. to 1 p.m. and from 2 p.m. to 5 p.m. in Summer; from 10 a.m. to 4 p.m. in winter.

— FOREIGN REPRESENTATIONS

Embassies (mostly open from Monday to Friday).

BANGLA DESH : Kupondole – Patan – Tel. 21966
BURMA : Krishna Galli – Pulchowk – Patan – Tel. 21788
CHINA : Baluwatar – Kathmandu – Tel. 11289–11658
EGYPT : Pulchowk – Patan – Tel. 21844
FRANCE : Lazimpath – Kathmandu – Tel. 12332–14734
GERMAN DEMOCRATIC REPUBLIC: Tripureshwar – Kathmandu Tel. 14801
GERMAN FEDERAL REPUBLIC : Kantipath – Kathmandu– Tel. 11730–11763
INDIA : Lainchaur, Kathmandu – Tel. 11300–11954–11080
ISRAEL : Lazimpath, Kathmandu – Tel. 11251–13483
ITALY : Baluwatar, Kathmandu – Tel. 12743
JAPAN : Panipokhari, Kathmandu – Tel. 12730–13264
KOREA (North): Lekhnathmarg, Kathmandu–Tel. 21084–21120
KOREA (South) : Keshar Mahal, Thamel – Kathmandu – Tel. 11172–11584
PAKISTAN : Panipokhari, Kathmandu – Tel. 11431–11214
POLAND : 21/506– Dilli Bazar, Kathmandu – Tel. 12694
THAILAND : Jyoti Kendra Bldg, Thapatali, Kathmandu– Tel. 13910
UNITED KINGDOM : Lainchaur, Kathmandu – Tel. 11588
UNITED STATES OF AMERICA : Panipokhari, Kathmandu – Tel. 11199–12718
U.S.S.R. : Baluwatar, Kathmandu – Tel. 11255

Honorary Consulates:

. *BELGIUM* : Bishramalaya – Lazimpath–Tel. 14760.
. *SWEDEN AND DENMARK* : Khichapokhari – Meera House–Tel.: 15939-11287

International Organisations:

— *Asian Development Bank* : Babar Mahal. Tel. : 13226, 11863.
— *Centre for the Study of Communications* : c/o U.N.D.P.

Lainchaur, Tel. ; 13605.
— *Food and Agricultural Organisation* : Lainchaur; Tel. : 11939.
— *International Bank for Reconstruction and Development* : Kantipath; Tel. : 14792, 14793.
— *International Civil Aviation Organisation* : Babar Mahal; Tel. : 15947.
— *International Labour Organisation* : Pulchowk; Tel. : 21260.
— *I.L.O.'s Training Centre of Personnel for Hotels and Tourism* : Ravi Bhawan. Tel. : 15073.
— *International Monetary Fund* : c/o Nepal Rashtriya Bank.
— *National Parks and Wild Life Conservation* : Baneshwar Tel. : 15850
— *Programme for the Training of Technicians in Civil Engineering* c/o U.N.D.P.; Tel. : 21260.
— *U.N.E.S.C.O.* : c/o United Nations–Lainchaur; Tel. : 11356. 14064, 15358
— *U.N.I.C.E.F.* : Lainchaur; Tel. : 14581, 15124.,
— *United Nations* : Lainchaur–Lazimpat; Tel. : 11939, 11944, 11757, 8.30 a.m. to 12.30 p,m. and 1 p.m. to 5 p.m. (Mondays to Fridays)
— *United Nations Conference on Trade and Development* (*U.N. C.T.A.D.*) c/o U.N.D.P. Tel. : 21521.
— *United Nations Development Programme* (*U.N.D.P.*) Lainchaur–Lazimpath Tel. : 11939, 11944, 11757, 14989, 12801.
— *United Nations Industrial Development Organization* : c/o U.N.D.P. Tel. : 11939.
— *United Nations Information Centre* : c/o *U.N.D.P.* Tel. : 11939 ext. 38.
— *United Nations Office for Technical Cooperation* : Dilli Bazar, Tel. 14292.
— *U.P.U.* : Dilli Bazar. Tel. 11153.
— *World Bank* : R.N.A.C. Building, New Road; Tel. 14792, 14793.
— *World Food Programme* : c/o U.N.D.P. Lainchaur, Tel. : 11939, Ext. 27.
— *World Health Organization* : Lainchaur Tel. : 14537, 15232.
— *World Meteorological Organization* : Babar Mahal, Tel. : 12151.

Foreign Aid and Cooperation Organizations

— *Dooley Foundation* : Tel. : 13198.
— *German Volunteer Service* : Dilli Bazar; Tel. : 12405.

— *Indian Cooperation Mission* : Hari Bhawan; Tel. : 11058, 11025, 11488, 11026.
— *Japan Overseas Cooperation Volunteers:* Kawaladi Tel.: 15193.
— *Swiss Association for Technical Assistance (S.A.T.A.--HEL-VETAS)* Ekantakuna, Jawalakhel, Patan; Tel. : 21025.
— *Swiss Volunteers for Development* : c/o *S.A.T.A.-HELVETAS* Tel. : 21025.
— *U.S. Aid for Nepal* : Ravi Bhawan, Tel. : 11144, 11423, 11425 11275, 11171, 11271.
— *U.S. Peace Corps:* Lal Durbar Kamaladi; Tel.: 11692, 13875.

Foreign Cultural Associations
— *British Council* : Kantipath; Tel. : 11305, 13796.
— *French Cultural Centre* : Bagh Bazar : Tel. 14326.
— *Goethe-Institute* : Dharahara. Tel. 15528
— *Indian Cultural Centre* : c/o Indian Embassy.
— *Nepal-British Society* : c/o British Embassy.
— *U.S. Library and International Communication Agency* : New Road. Tel. : 11250
— *U.S.S.R. Cultural Centre* : New Road.

SOCIAL CLUBS

— *Junior Chamber of Commerce* : Ganga Path. Tel. : 12217. Meetings on 2nd and 4th Sundays of the month at 5.30 p,m.
— *Lions Club* : Tel. : 14612. Meetings at Blue Star Hotel, Tripureshwar, on 1st and 3rd Wednesdays of the month at 5.15 p.m.
— *Rotary Club* : Tel. : 12583. Rotary Club Building, Thapathali. Weekly meetings on Wednesdays at 5.30 p.m. except on the last Wednesday of the month : 8 p.m. (dinner).

BANKS

—Rashtriya Bank (State Bank of Nepal) : Main Office : Baluwatar on Thapathali.
   Foreign Exchange Office : New Road Gate : open to public from 8 a.m. to 8 p.m.–Phone : 12663
—Nepal Bank Main Office : New Road – Shukra Path – Foreign Exchange counter open from 10 a.m to 2 p.m. from Sunday to Thursday. On Fridays : 10 a.m. to 12.00–Phone 11185

POLICE

—Emergency Police Station : Phone   16999
—Kathmandu district Police   ”   11162

```
                    Patan            "        21005
                    Bhadgaon         "        11053
```
FIRE BRIGADES
—Emergency calls for Kathmandu :   11177
```
                    Patan                     21111
                    Bhadgaon                  11049
```
AMBULANCE SERVICES
—Emergency calls : (NEPAL RED CROSS) 15074
                24 hours per day service, free of charge

HOSPITALS AND CHEMISTS
In Kathmandu :
—Emergency cases : BIR HOSPITAL - Kantipath - Phone : 11119
```
                    SHANTA BHAWAN - Patan       "      21034
```
—BIR HOSPITAL is located in the centre of Kathmandu, on
   Kantipath facing Tundikhel. It is the best equipped
   Nepalese Hospital (X–ray service).
   There is a special ward for vaccinations and re-vaccinations,
   issuance of yellow Health Certificates etc.... Phones:
   11119– 13807– 15267– 15272– 11988
—SHANTA BHAWAN (United Mission Hospital) is a Foreign-
   staffed Hospital. (incl. a dentist). There is a Maternity
   ward, X–Ray and Operation theatre. Phone: 21553–21084
—MATERNITY Hospital (Prasuti Griha) on Thapatali, near the
   bridge leading to Patan. Phones : 11234-13216
—CHILDREN HOSPITAL (Kanti Hospital) on Maharajganj -
   Phone 11550
   —A Chest disease Hospital, at Kalimati. Telephone : 15483
   —An Eye-Clinic, Telephone : 15466
   At Patan : Hospital : Tel. 21333
   At Bhadgaon : Hospital : Tel : 12676
   At Pokhara, there is a foreign–staffed hospital, the *"Shining
Hospital"* located near the road-fork leading to Hyangcha. This
hospital is well equipped to receive the sick and the victims of
accidents. There is also a government hospital...
   At Phaplu, on the trail leading from Kathmandu to the Solu
Khumbu district, i.e. the Sherpa–land area, a 20-bed hospital
equipped with X-ray and operation unit was built with funds
collected by Sir Edmund Hillary mainly in New Zealand through
the "Nepal Himalayan Trust Fund". It was inaugurated by
Nepal's Prime Minister and Sir Edmund Hillary on 1.5.76.
   At Kunde (in Sherpa-land): a complete hospital, well equipped,

also built with funds collected by Sir Edmund Hillary
mostly in New Zealand.

At Jiri (in the way to Everest-Region) : a small hospital
installed and run by the Swiss Association for Technical Assistance – SATA

At Dharan: a complete hospital and health centre under
British supervision.

Let us also mention here, the *"Himalayan Rescue Post"*
opened in autumn 1975, at *Pheriche,* in Sherpa–land, on the trekking trail from Namche Bazar to Everest Base Camp. This
medical Aid–post is located at an altitude of 13,743 ft. (4,250 m.).

As far as *chemists* are concerned, there are a great many not
only in Kathmandu and Pokhara but also in smaller localities
as well. They have a wide choice of medicines, mainly manufactured in India under licenses from Western firms. Most of
the current products may be purchased without prescription.

WORKING DAYS AND HOLIDAYS

In Nepal, the weekly "day–off" is Saturday, not Sunday.
The current explanation is that, from time immemorial and for
motives which seem to have been forgotten, Saturday is
considered as an unauspicious day (another one is Tuesday, but
to a lesser degree.) On both these days, it is advisable, so people
think, not to undertake anything to importance.

This may be the reason why, on Saturdays, many Nepalese
offer special "pujas" and make sacrifices to various deities, in
particular to Goddess Kali, at DAKSHINKALI. It is also a tradition to anoint and massage small children, and oneself, with
mustard oil.

Under the rule of the Rana Prime Minister Chandra Shumsher
Rana, around 1918, the decision was taken to proclaim Saturday
as the official weekly holiday. (There was none before that date);
this step may have been motivated by the fact that most people
were anyhow reluctant to perform serious and weighty tasks.
Whatever the reason may have been, nowadays all Government
Offices, Banks, Post-Offices etc. remain closed on Saturdays.
However, shops stay open, in particular the small shops in the old
city as well as those specialized in selling souvenirs and other
articles for tourists. On all working days, Offices are open from
10 am. to 5 p.m., except in winter (mid-November to mid-
March), when they close at 4 p.m.

The number of official and unofficial holidays is very large.

t is impossible to give a list of dates, since the Nepalese calendar
f festivals is based on the lunar cycle and therefore the dates
ary from one year to the next.

The most important popular festival is DASAIN which usually
akes place in October. This festival lasts for 10 days during
/hich life is considerably slowed down if not quite paralysed.

Every year, the Department of Tourism issues a booklet or a
older entitled: *"Festivals of Nepal"* which tourists should get from
ither the Tourist Department Offices or Travel Agencies in order

— to avoid being confronted with closed offices on what would
ormally seem to be a working day.

— to watch the proceedings of these festivals which are always
olourful and mostly very gay; in any case they are an interesting
spect of traditional Nepalese folklore.

For more details about these events, see the special chapter
edicated to the main festivals.

POSTAL AND TELECOMMUNICATION SERVICES

Offices

The Kathmandu Central Post Office has three main offices,
ll located near Kantipath and Khichapokhari Road intersection:
— *The Foreign Post-Office,* which deals with parcels to and
om abroad only.
— *The General Post Office :* on the actual corner of the above
amed streets. Here stamps, aerograms are sold, letters registered
c. The "Poste Restante" counter is also here. Passport must
e produced.
— *The Telecommunication Office,* on Tripureshwar Marg,
hich deals with telegrams, telephone calls and telex messages.

The counters of the first two offices are open; in summer,
om 10 a.m to 5 p.m., except on Saturdays. However the Inter-
ational Telegraph Centre is open from 6 a.m. to 9 p.m., every
ay, including Saturdays. The telephone and radio message coun-
rs are open from 11 am. to 11 p.m. every day, including Satur-
ays. Telex Services remain open 24 hours a day.

ostal Airmail rates (valid from 15th July 1980)

o places inside Nepal and to India :	Nep. Rs.
Aerograms :	0.30
Post cards :	0.25
Letters up to 15 gr.	0.40
" each additional 15 gr. or part	0.25

To Afghanistan, Bangladesh, Bhutan, Burma, Pakistan, Sri Lank and Thailand :
- Aerograms 1.5
- Post cards 1.2
- Letters, per 20 gr. 2.0

To countries in the Middle-East (including Turkey), Hong-Kong Indonesia, Iran, Malaysi, Philippines, Singapore, Vietnam an some others
- Aerograms 2.5
- Post cards 1.7
- Letters per 20 gr. 3.5

To Europe, Africa, Korea and Japan
- Aerograms 2.5
- Post cards 1.7
- Letters per 20 gr. 5.2

To USA, Australia, New Zealand, Canada and all other countrie on the American Continent and the West Indies
- Aerograms 2.5
- Post cards 1.7
- Letters per 20 gr. 6.0

Telegram rates
(1) To India : Ordinary : Minimum charge : 8 words : 3.2
               Every additional word: 0.3
               Express : Minimum charge : 8 words : 6.5
               Every additional word: 0.6

(2) To any other country :
               Night Letter "L.T." (To certain countries only)
               Minimum charge: 21 words : 16.2
               Every additional word: 2.1
               Ordinary: Minimum charge : 7 words: 29.3
               Every additional word: 4.3
               Urgent: Minimum charge: 7 words: 58.8
               Every additional word: 8.4

NOTE: Words of more than ten letters (or signs) are taxed as tw

Telex rates

The Government Postal Services has opened a "telex communication centre open to the general public.

However, telex messages may also be sent either from most the First Class Hotels(such as ANNAPURNA, MALLA, SOALTEE, YA AND YETI) or from some of the larger Travel Agencies (such

Rans-Himalayan Tours, Universal Travels, Yeti Travels)
In winter 80 the rates were, approximately, the following :
For the compulsory three minutes minimum :
To India : Nep. 18.00
To Europe, America, the Far-East and Australasia: Nep.
Rs. 150.– or 200.– depending the country of destination.
For every additional minute : approx. one third of the above
indicated rates.

Philately Section

This is located on the left side of the lobby, in the building of
e General Post Office. Most of the current unused stamps are
sale there, at their face value.

CHRISTIAN RELIGIOUS SERVICES

Catholic Services (Information to be obtained by telephone :
Hotel Annapurna : 11711).
Mass, every day at 6.30 at St. Xavier's College in Jawalakhel.
On Sundays at the same college, Mass is held at 7 a.m. 8 a.m.
and 5.30 p.m. in winter, and 6.30 a.m., 7.30 a.m. and 5.30 p.m.
in summer.
At the Annapurna Hotel (2nd floor) : Mass on Sundays at
6.45 a.m. At St. Mary's School (Jawalakhel),Sundays at 7 a.m.
Protestant Services (Telephone : 13966).
On Saturdays at 10 a.m., in the "Church of Christ" on Ram
Shah Path, service held in English.
On Sundays at 9.30 am. at the Ganeshwar Temple, service
held in English and Nepali.
On Sundays at 10.30 a m.: In "Blue Room" at Ravi Bhawan.
NOTE: The above information may be found to contain inac-
curacies. Check details a little in advance, since the days and
hours of the various services may change.
Muslim Services : The most important mosque of Kathmandu
is located close to the Clock–Tower, on Durbar Marg, where
more specific information may be obtained.

SPORTS

Fishing

No licence is needed to go angling. However along certain
rts of the Narayani river that are included in one of the Wild
e reserves or that have been leased to private persons, fishing
y be prohibited. Therefore it is advisable to contact the local
thorities first.

General information regarding fishing waters and season may be obtained from H.M.G.'s Department of Fisheries.

Best season for fishing:

In many parts of Nepal, in particular in the lakes around Pokhara–Phewa Lake, for instance–all year round, best months however are February to beginning of May. But in these lake fishes are not abundant.

The two main possible catches are:

1. The "*asla*" or river–trout is to be found, but again, not in huge quantities, in the upper reaches of certain mountain stream The "asla" commonly does not weigh more than 1 or 2 lbs. I the glacial lakes such as Lake Phoksumdo, in the Dolpa distric and in Rara Lake situated in the Jumla district, some three–poun ders are reported to have been caught from time to time.

2. The "*masheer*" (*Sahar* or *Barbus Tor*), a much bigger fis is a better bet than the asla. That fish travels from the open se through India and the Terai to spawn in the headwaters of th mountain streams. The northward journey takes place in Octobe November and the southward one in March–April. These two seasons are therefore the best for fishing and the good places a the Karnali river and, to a lesser extent, the Gandaki and Ko upper parts. The mahseer likes to stay in cold water, where th river bed is strewn with boulders and pebbles. At a place calle "Chisopani" (which means "cold water"), 50 to 60–pounder (23–27 kg.) are caught every year by local or visiting angler The largest catch, with a rod line, is so far, a 95–pounder (43 kg)

Chisopani in easy reach from Kathmandu. First by a (5 times a week,) a 90 minutes regular flight by R.N.A.C. t Nepalganj, then by a jeepable road to Tanakpur.

Nearer to Kathmandu, good masheer fishing is available alon the Sun Kosi and Indrawati rivers, near the "*Chinese road* leading to Kodari. Here, the best season is October to March.

The Government, with foreign assistance, is developing th fishing possibilities in the rivers of Nepal by stocking them wit imported fry, in particular of British river–trout species, to mak fishing, especially fly-fishing, more attractive.

Golf

The Royal Golf Club (9 holes) is presently located next t Tribhuvan Airport. Visitors must be introduced and invited b a permanent member of the Club.

The extention project concerning the airport buildings ma

entail transferring the golf course elsewhere in the near futures.
A site has been selected tentatively near Bhadgaon.

Hunting

This sport is very severely regulated and special permits have
to be obtained from the Department of Forestry before any
hunting may be undertaken in any part of the country.

As already mentioned, all big game which, in the past, has
been almost annihilated, is now strictly protected. Thus, there
are no longer tiger–hunts or rhinoceros shooting. Most of the
mountain antelopes are also safeguarded. On the other hand,
permits to hunt fowl (pheasants, quail, partridges etc.), some species of the deer family (sambar, black buck), blue sheep and
wild goats, boars even leopards and bears, may be obtained.

In Kathmandu, there are three hunter outfitters who are in
a position to provide the permits and organize safari and wild
life camps. Their rates exceed one thousand US $ per person
Their names and addresses:

HIMALAYAN SAFARI, P.O.B. 1197,   Tel. : 12693.
ROYAL SHANGRI-LA HUNTING–c/o Gorkha Travels–Tel 14737

Rafting

This relatively recent sport has gained great popularity.
in a short span of time. Rafting is operated by inflatable rubber
rafts and canoes.

Near Kathmandu, the rivers best adapted for rafting are the
Trisuli, Marsyandi and Sun Kosi. Further West: the Kali Gandaki
and, in the East, the Arun. All of them offer enough "rapids"
to give these excursions an adventurous touch. Best season :
October to March. All rivers provide sandy beaches for camping.

Several tourist and trekking agencies in Kathmandu have
"all–inclusive tours" which link rafting with a trekking tour and/
or a "safari".

Sherpas have shown exceptional skill to become competent and
trust–worthy helmsmen !
The specialized "rafting-agencies", are :

- Gaida Wildlife ("Alpine Adventure Exploration" – Durbar
  Marg Tel. 11786 – POB 105)
- Great Himalayan Adventures, Kantipath, Tel 14424-POB 1033
- Tiger Tops ("Himalayan River Exploration" – Durbar Marg –
  Tel 12455 – POB 170)

Rates vary considerably, and are uneasy to spell out,
since most Agencies offer "all-inclusive multi-days rafting

tours", minimum number of participants being compulsory (four in most cases). It is safe to count on a 40 to 60 US $ rate per day and per participant. These rates include normally all services, except the air-fares to and from the departure point, if air-transport is necessary.

Safari

In the Terai, the jungle belt in southern Nepal, there are now three places where wild-life can be seen in its nautral unspoiled surroundings and where accommodation and elephant-rides are provided for tourists who are eager to take part in a "safari" not with guns or hand-grenades, of course, but with photo- and film cameras.

All three places are in or close to the Chitwan National Park :

(1) TIGER-TOPS

At about 78 miles south-west of Kathmandu lies Meghauly airstrip which R.N.A.C.'s scheduled or chartered air-services reach in approx. 30 minutes' flight. This airstrip's "terminal building" is probably the most modest in the world. No loudspeakers, no immigration or customs officers, no harassing porters and taxi drivers ! Simply a thatched roof supported by six wooden posts. There are no walls but a few rudimentary benches.

If sophisticated comfort is what tourists have been expecting at Meghauly airport, they took the wrong plane. But it is unlikely, for they have certainly come for more thrilling things than an air-conditioned lounge ! To begin with, this airfield is certainly the only one in the whole world, where the steps that enable the passengers to get off the plane are used, one minute later, to get them onto the back of one of the elephants that have been awaiting them, waving their trunks as a welcoming "Namaste"

The Tiger-Tops hotel provides all its guests, at least a two hours ride on elephant back through dense tropical jungle, where giant elephant grass grows up to 20 or 25 feet high ! There are also two rivers to ford (passengers are allowed to remain on their respective elephants !) Then they arrive at the hotel which is hidden in the lush green jungle and built on gigantic stills.

During the excursions arranged by the hotel management, you will see and chase one-horned rhinos – now only to be found in Nepal – crocodiles on the river banks, many kinds of deer, birds and monkeys.

After sunset, the guests may be invited to proceed–silently–to the "blinds" set up in the forest, to watch a leopard or a tiger

devouring the goat or the young buffalo tied to a pole as a bait in the middle of the glade below the blind.

Of course, hunting or killing any animal in the National Park is strictly prohibited but there is no objection to taking photographs or making film.

Tiger Tops rates, effective January 1981, were the following :
- Fixed tax, to be paid only once : the Natonal Park's entrance fee : US $ 4.20 per person.
- Government tax, per night and per person : US $ 2.00 at the Lodge and US $ 1.00 at the Tented Camp. Airfare, for the journey Kathmandu–Meghauly-Kathmandu: US $ 61,00 per person.
- At the Lodge : US $ 100.– per night and per person on double occupancy basis. Supplement for single occupancy : US $ 40.–
- At the Tented Camp : US $ 50.00 per night and per person on double occupancy basis. Supplement for single occupancy: US $ 25.–

For both : Two nights is the required mininum stay and full-board is also compulsory. These rates include :

At the Lodge : accommodation in twin-bed rooms with solar-heated bath-rooms and showers; all jungle tours by elephant, land-rover and canoes; all meals featuring international, Chinese and Nepalese cuisine. All sight-seeings and transfers as well as airport tax. Only extras : the bar bills.

At the Tented Camp : all same facilities and amenities, except that the accommodation is provided in comfortable twin-bed tents instead of rooms.

For further information and bookings : Tiger-Tops Head-Office, on Durbar Marg, close to "PANAM's" Office. Tel.: 12706–POB 242–Cable address : Tigtops–Telex No NP 216 Tigertop.

As a rule, Tiger Tops operates only through the winter season, i.e . from October to early May.

(2) GAIDA WILDLIFE CAMP

This camp is also located inside the Chitwan National Park, east of Tiger Tops.

For bookings and organization of an excursion with Gaida Wildlife, contact its Head-Office, located on Durbar Marg, Tel. 11786 – POB 1273.

Gaida camp can be reached comfortably by air (charters of 7–seater Pilatus Porter at the rate of Nep. Rs. 2,600 for one leg) KATHMANDU – BAGMARA, the nearest airfield to Gaida Wildlife Camp, or from Kathmandu (or Pokhara)to Bharatpur, on board of the regular daily flights on 19–seater Twin Otters; the current rate, one-way, is US $ 25.50 from Kathmandu or US $ 18.00 from Pokhara. There exists also a land-route, via Butwal and the main East-West highway.

The camp is situated near Dungla and Rapti rivers. Every day, elephant jungle rides take place for the visitors. The wild animals most often spotted are, first of all, the one-horned rhino ("gaida" is the nepali word for this impressive animal !) as well as many deer, stags, monkeys and a great variety of birds.

During the canoe-rides, the main attraction is hunting (only with cameras, of course) gavials and muggers, the two species of crocodiles that abund in the nearby rivers. Less frequently there may be river-dolphins jumping quickly out of the water.

Gaidas rates, effective January 1st., 1981, were the following :
At the Lodge : US $ 101.50 per person, for two nights
Single occupancy supplement : US $ 10.00 per night
At the tented camp : US $ 82.60 per person for two nights.

These rates include accomodation, full board, both ways transfers in Kathmandu, entrance fees, government tax, all excursions. Air-fares are not incluced.

Gaida offers an original ten-days excursion : 5 days easy mountain–trekking (up to 5,500 f.), 2 days rafting and 2 days stay at Gaida Wildlife Camp with elephant and canoe-rides. All-inclusive rate, per person : US $ 450. :

(3) HOTEL ELEPHANT-CAMP

This hotel – called "Sauraha", is located on the banks of river Rapti, near Chitwan National Park.

It is easy to reach by the regular RNAC daily flights either from Kathmandu or Pokhara to Bharatpur (for rates, see above, under Gaida Wild-Lilfe Camp) By road it takes approximately 8 hours from Kathmandu and 4 from Pokhara.

Entrance fee to Chitwan's National Park, to be paid only once : US $ 4.20 per person.

Stay at the Elephant-Camp : Double occupancy : US $ 129.00 per person for two nights. Single occupancy supplement : US $ 15,00 per night.

These rates include accommodation, all meals and excursions. For further information and booking : Elephant Camp Head Office – Durbar Marg Tel. 13976 – POB 1281– Cable : ELECAMP.

. Skating

Although Kathmandu is situated at an altitude of 4,360 ft.
(1330 m). the temperature does never reach freezing point, and,
since even in the midst of the winter, the sun is always bright and
warm throughout the day, Nepal has so far no skating ground,
whether natural or artificial.

. Skiing

For the same reason as indicted above, and although the Valley
is surrounded by hills and the country rich in high mountains,
ski-ing is not practised. Besides the climatic reasons to the physical effort required when ski-ing most of the mountain slopes
are covered either by terraces or forests, both unsuited for skiing.

Furthermore, the snowline lies approx. at 16,000 ft. (4,875m.)
during the autumn and early winter, an altitude which consitutes
an obstacle to the physical effort required by ski–ing.

Last but not least, the Himalayas are not yet equipped for
this sport : there are neither huts for overnight accomodation
nor ski-lifts, cableways etc.

Squash

Kathmandu has only one squash court. It is part of Battis-
Putali Sports Club, on the road to Bodnath.

Swimming

In Kathmandu :

Swimming-pools are open to tourists and to the public
—at the Sports Council's National Stadium
—at the Balaju Gardens (5 miles from the centre of the city–
 8 km., on the road leading to Trisuli and Kakani)
—at the Hotels Soaltee, Yak and Yeti, Annapurna and Narayani.

Elsewhere :

It is strongly recommended no to try to bathe or to swim
in mountain rivers, streams and torrents. However, once
these have reached the lowlands, they are no longer a danger
to experienced swimmers. This advice of prudence applies
equally to mountain lakes. (Remember that, even in quiet
rivers of the Terai, there may be crocodiles.

. Tennis

15 courts are open to visitors :
Hotels : 2 each at Annapuna and Soaltee, one at Yak & Yeti
Clubs : Hem's International Tennis Centre, on the road to the
airport (4 courts)

Sports Complex, behind the Municipal Stadium (3)
Battisputali Sports Centre, on Battisputali road (2)
St. Xavier's House, behind Malla Hotel (1)

ENTERTAINMENT

. **Casino :**
There is a Casino in one of the wings of the Soaltee Hotel.
It provides games of roulette, baccarat and other similar games.

. **Cinemas :**
Most of the cinemas in Kathmandu show Indian films only,
without English subtitles. Occasionally American and European
films are also shown spoken in Hindi or Nepali and mostly either
dubbed or sub-titled in English.
The main cinemas are :
In Kathmandu : Bishwa Jyoti, on Rani Pokhari
       Jai Nepal Chitra Ghar, on Naxal. Ranjana, at Phasikeba
       near New Road.
At Patan : Ashok
At Bhadgaon : Nava Durga
Usually there are three daily performances : at 12 noon, 3 p.m.
and 6 p.m. Entrance costs from Rs. 3, to Rs. 10.–

. **Discotheques**
There are two in Kathmandu (winter 77–78) :
— The *"Copper Floor"*, located at "Laliguras Hotel" on
Lazimpat. Open on Tuesdays, Fridays and Saturdays
from 8 p.m. to dawn. Telephone : 13304.
— The *"Floortapper"*, located at Tangal Durbar an old Rana
Palace at Tangal not far from Police Headquarters.
Open from 8 p.m. to dawn every night except Tuesday.
Telephone : 12910.

. **Folk–dances**
Shows take place in principle every evening from 6.30 to 7.30
in winter (October to March), at the following places :
— At the YAK AND YETI HOTEL. *Tel* 16255
— At the SOALTEE HOTEL, every evening. *Tel* 11211
— At the MANASLU HOTEL, on Lazimpath. *Tel.* 13471
— At *"Lal Durbar"* (*"The Red Palace"*), by the *"Everest
Cultural society"* Tel 15429
— On Dilli Bazar, by the *"Arniko Cultural Society ensemble"*.
The entrance rates are approx. US $ 3.30, transportation inclu-
ded if organized by a Travel Agency or the Hotel Reception desk.

These *"ensembles"* are composed of professional and amateur dancers. They perform, mainly, dances which are traditional to given ethnic groups such as the Terai people, Gurungs Tamangs from the Central Hills, or Sherpa dances of the Himalayan communities. Other dances are of a romantic character and represent *"boy-courting-girl"* scenes, while others again are of a more farmer–life inspiration such as sowing, harvest etc.

It must also be said that Nepalese folk-dances have nothing in common with the very refined and sophisticated art of classical Indian dances, where every movement of legs, feet, hands, fingers, eyes, brows and even glances has a special meaning which is not easy to decipher or interpret correctly by the non-initiated. Nepalese have no such classical dance traditions and their dances are much more spontaneous and descriptive.

. Religious choirs

Every evening, at approx. 9 p.m. in various parts of Kathmandu small groups of amateur musicians and singers gather to perform religious songs as a sort of ritual. Although tourists are always welcome to attend, these choirs are not in the least intended for them.

Some of the places where these groups may be found are :

— *In the old part of Kathmandu :*

— At the entrance passage leaving to the courtyard of the Sweta Matsyendranath temple, the one located on Kel Tole, between Asan Tole and Indra Chowk. Every evening, from 9 p.m. to approx. 10.30, a group of musicians and singers gather on a resting platform in the vestibule leading to the inner courtyard. They may be Buddhists or Hindus. Their songs are religious hymns–called bhajans-and are handwritten on beautiful yellow paper, usually in sanskrit, sometimes in newari.

— On the first floor of the Akash Bhairawa temple, located on Indra Chowk, at the end of Shukra Path. This is the temple guarded by four gigantic and fierce looking mumping dragons. The facade of this temple is almost entirely covered with European-style ceramic tiles.

A very narrow door and still narrower staircase, on the right side of the temple front, lead ta the otherroom of the sanctuary, where you will find the musicians. Do not step further inside.

— In the old Simha (or Singha) Satal temple, a two-storey building facing Kastamandap.

— *In the newer part of Kathmandu :*

— Within the compound of the new Royal Palace in its eastern wing, on the left side of a large gate there is a small entrance and a flight of stairs leading to a courtyard in the centre of which stands a shrine dedicated to "Narayan". On the 11th day following every new and every full moon, from 8 pm to 10 pm, everybody is welcome to attend a classical religious music evening.

. **Theatres**

There is no permanent theatre in Kathmandu, except in Nepali language on Kantipath, near Rani Pokhari. There are occasional amateur performances in English, which are given under the auspices of the British or American Embassy or Cultural organizations. The main acting group is the "*HAMS*" (for "*Himalayan Amateurs*").

LADIES' HAIRDRESSERS

Besides the hair–dressing saloons in all better hotels, there are :
. *Simrik,* opposite the old Royal Hotel, on Kantipath, on the right side of the street when coming from the centre of the city.
. *Eve's Beauty Parlour,* on the left side of the same street,

TO STROLL ALONE BY NIGHT

It may not be out of place to mention in this connection that it is absolutely "safe" for anybody to stroll, in groups or alone, in the evening or at night through the streets and the lanes of new or old Kathmandu, or anywhere else, for that matter. Nepalis are peace–loving and friendly people who maintain a very high standard of ethics and morals.

NEWSPAPERS AND BROADCASTING

. **Newspapers.**

Among the English language dailies published in Kathmandu, the most important are : "*THE RISING NEPAL*" (semi-official) and "*THE MOTHERLAND*", both distributed early the morning. There are no afternoon papers in English. THE RISING NEPAL covers well the news items from abroad.

* **Broadcasting**

Radio Nepal broadcasts daily news–bulletins in English at 8 a.m. and 8.30 p.m.

In addition, a cultural and tourist programme is broadcasted in English, daily from 8.15 p.m. and from 8.40 to 9.00 p.m.

WHERE TO FIND BOOKS AND MAPS

Every good hotel has its own book–stall in the lobby or nearby. In town: some of the well-stocked shops, where maps are also available :
– On Botahity Tole : Ratna Pustak Bhandar
– On Jamal Tol : Everest Book Service
– On Durbar Marg, near the main Kathmandu mosque: Himalayan Booksellers
– On Asan : International Bookshop
– On Dharma Path : Nepal Booksellers
– On the ground floor of the Mahakal Temple, facing the Military Hospital, on Kantipath : "Educational Enterprises".

MUSEUMS

The most important is the *National Museum*, located on the road to Swayambhu. Its collections include a fairly large collection of stone carvings, bronze work and paintings that give a good idea of the different epochs in Nepalese Art. Bhadgaon and Patan have their own interesting art museums.

A small one is installed, on Swayambhu hill. It contains a few sculptures of rare beauty. On Buddha's birthday in May, there is a display of magnificient old thangkas, also on Swayambhu.

"At the foot of Swayambhu hill, a "Museum of Natural History" is to be found, equally worth visiting by those who are interested in the flora and fauna of Nepal.

At POKHARA, the first zonal Museum dedicated to "Man in his environment" is an admirable introduction to the people, the culture and the environment of this region. It contains an excellent collection of costumes, tools, jewels, artefacts etc... typical of those ethnic groups that have settled since time immemorial in the Pokhara area, mainly the Gurungs.

SHOPPING AND SOUVENIR HUNTING

Kathmandu and its "satellite" cities of Patan, Bhadgaon and Bodnath are a real paradise for those visitors who are eager to take home some authentic souvenirs, be it objects or arts of handicraft, photographs, films or magnetic tapes etc.

The narrow streets crammed with people representing the many ethnic groups which form the Nepalese Nation, the rickshaws, the porters—men or women—carrying heavy loads in baskets either resting on their backs and maintained by the frontal strap or tied to both ends of a pole carried on one shoulder. These streets are the kingdom of the urchins usually clothed in rags but who are always, smiling–sometimes begging, too–and the "open-air work–shop" of the barbers, the garland–and flower sellers. A unique experience consists in strolling along these streets, looking at all these Lilliputian shops full of textile goods (imported mostly from India and from China) or of other wares such as copper–or brass–jars of all sizes, spices and candles, raw salt or heaps of tobacco or soap etc. What more does the photo - or souvenir hunter's heart desire ?

Their best hunting grounds are therefore the squares and lanes of old Kathmandu, i.e. Makhan Tole, Indira Chowk, Asan Tole and Kamalachi as well as the back–alleys of Patan and Bhadgaon or the small Tibetan shops around the Bodnath stupa.

In addition it must be mentioned that costlier articles and real antiques are to be found in western-style shops of New Road where objects of art, jewels and gems (cut or uncut ones) are on sale.

Most of these shops open at 10 am. and remain open till 7 p.m., some of them even till later. Smaller shops remain even open on Saturdays while the larger ones close.

* Nepalese objects

The *khukuri,* the Nepalese knife that is part of the Gurkha soldiers standard equipment and commonly carried by all Nepalese hillman, except Newari jyapus (peasants), is used for everything from chopping off a goat's head to sharpening a pencil.

For those interested in details : an authentic khukri shows always a small indenture or crescent–shaped notch on the blade near the handle. This is meant to guide blood in such a way as to prevent it from flowing on the handle, making it slippery.

Also : an authentic khukri carries always two tiny knives inserted in its wooden or leather sheath. Both are of the same size and aspect, but they are not identical : one is called "kardo" and is, in fact, a small knife which may be used to extract a splinter from the toe. while the other, called "chakmak" is not a sharp blade, but is used as a pocket "lighter" which is able to produce sparks and lit a fire, for inside the sheath there is always a piece of flint and some dry cottonwool.

— *Jugs, jars* and *pots* of all sizes and shapes, made of brass or copper. All these objects are sold on weight, hence the presence of a huge and heavy scale fixed on the ceiling of the shops.

—The "*sarangi*" a small fiddle on which the "*gaines*", belonging to the caste of professional mendicant–ministrels, improvise their songs. Made of one piece of wood. it has four strings (goat gut) which are played upon with a bow of horse hair.

—The "*topi*", the little cotton cap made in all kinds of colours –as well as in black–which is the traditional and typical Nepalese headgear. It is compulsory for all Nepalese to wear such a "*topi*"– and usually a black one–when entering a government office. The lopsidedness of the cap is said to recall the shape of Mount Kailash, a 22,045 ft. (6.719 m.) high mountain in Tibet, the most sacred mountain for both Hindus and Buddhists. Located near the frontiers of Nepal and India, this peak is flanked by the two Manasarovar lakes–the lake of the Sun and the lake of the Moon– whence spring the Indus, the main river of the western sub–continent, and the Brahmaputra, the main river of Tibet (where it is called "*Tsang-po*") and of the whole eastern sub–continent.

—*The cotton material usually woven in red-black-white,* used by Nepalese women, or a shawl made of very fine and extremely warm wool, called "pashmina".

—*Men's cotton shirts,* typically folding across the chest and provided with little ribbons instead of buttons.

—*The small birds* and other animals, boxes, trinkets made of brass inlaid with artificial red, blue and black stones.

Hand-made paper : which is often –wrongly– called "rice-paper", for it is actually made of the bark of a tree or bush called "bholua" or "lokhta", belonging to the "daphne" family. The paper itself is called "kagate pat". It is sold, either in crude form, at the Handicraft Center. (just near the Telegraph Office on Tripureshwor), where it is manufactured and dried in the sun, or, in many shops presented as wrapping paper, letterhead, envelopes, post-cars, block-notes etc.. usually carrying typical designs on top or in the corners. The same paper is used for manufacturing the famous "wood-block" prints (xylographs) representing a great variety of religious and other designs, mostly of Tibetan, Nepalese and even Chinese inspiration. They are available in every second shop anywhere.

Nepalese folk-music and songs, as records or cassettes are sold, among other places, in a small shop located on Dharma Path, bearing a sign-board "His Master's Voice", opposite Makalu Hotel and many other shops. There are at least four different cassettes on sale.

—*Small statues in wood, bronze or copper,* usually depicting a deity; mostly they are recent copies, for old originals are very rare and therefore very expensive. Furthermore, as already mentioned, their export is subject to a formal permit from the authorities of the Archaeological Department, on Thapathali.

—*Semi-precious stones*. The only ones that are found in Nepal are : garnet, quartz in different shades and kinds, tourmaline and aquamarine.

Specialized shops on New Road and elsewhere are also selling stones imported from other countries, in particular green and blue turquoises from Tibet and Iran, coral from the Indian Ocean, amber from the Baltic Sea etc. Turquoises and coral are the most popular ones among the Tibetan ethnic groups.

—*Papier-mâché hand-made dance masks*. They are manufactured at the village of Thimi, between Kathmandu airport and Bhadgaon. But they are also sold in the lanes of old Kathmandu. The most frequent representations are those of Ganesh, the elephant–headed god, Bhairav, the guardian–god of the Valley with its protruding canine teeth, Varahi, the wild boar god etc.

—*Tera-cotta elephants* serving as flower-pots. They too, are made at Thimi. There are other animal–shaped objects such as peacocks., horses, rhinos even etc...

A rich display of Nepalese handicraft wares (dresses, material, baskets, wooden objects, masks, hand–made paper etc... are to be found in specialized shops such as :

—"CHEEZ BEEZ BHANDAR, installed on the first floor of the house where the bookstore "Nepal Bookseller's" is located, on Dharma Path.

. "TREASURE HOUSE", on New Road, almost opposite the Tourist Information Office.

* Tibetan objects

At Bodnath

This is undoubtedly the best place to find authentic Tibetan souvenirs, items which may have been either brought directly from Tibet by refugees or manufactured in the work–shops installed in the ground–floor of the small houses surrounding the central "stupa".

Some suggestions :

—*Rustic silver-plated jewellery*, usually inlaid with fragments of turquoise. Pendants, rings, bracelets, amulets and charmboxes, earrings, plaited silver belts, horse harnesses, daggers with richly chiselled silver hilts etc.

—*Bowls for tea or tsampa* (cooked barley meal, the staple

food of Sherpas and Tibetans), made of wood and sometimes lined with silver.

—*Tinder boxes* in the shape of purses Tibetans attach to their belts.

—*Calendars, mandalas* and *magic diagrams* made of bronze or copper, decorated with typical Tibetan designs and patterns.

—*Belt buckles made of silver*, usually decorated with a two-bird motive.

—*Jackets, bags,* and multicoloured material with geometrical designs of Bhutanese type but presently manufactured in India.

—*Thang-kas* (painted scrolls) representing Buddha, Padma-Sambhava or other figures of the Lamaist Pantheon, deities, demons, also wise men or, then, "mandalas".

It is not easy to find authentic and old thang-kas in good condition and at reasonable prices.

But the art of thangka-painting has not been lost, and even new ones may be of great beauty. Some of the criteria to guide the choice of a thang-ka are the following:

—very fine, delicate design, in particular in the expression of the face, the neatness of the finger-tips and the folds of the dresses

—abundance of gold paint

—absence of bare space (in the sky, for instance or on the mountain slopes)

—the presence of "dotted" painting to depict flowers, or shadows. etc....

—*Many other objects of religious interest,* such as are used in the daily Lamaist rites: "*thunderbolts*" made of brass or bronze, shaped like two head–to–head bells, which are called "*r'Dorje*" in Tibetan and "*Vajra*" in Nepali, Hindi and Sanskrit, *human skulls* used as cups and others.

Traditional musical instruments are also on sale in these small shops, such as:

the 6 or 7 feet long telescopic brass–and–copper horns ("*ra (g) dung*" or "*dung - chen*" in Tib.)

. the human thigh-bone trumpets "*kang-ling*" in Tib.)

. copper–and–silver flageolet ("*gya - ling*" in Tib.)

. conch–shell horns often mounted with bronze or silver so as to prolong the valves of the shell ("*tung*" in Tib.) These shells are imported from the Indian Ocean.

. big–size drums resting on a wooden pivot ("*cho-nga*" in Tib.)

. small rattle hand–drums sometimes made of monkey–skulls.

("*nga-ch'ung*" in Tib. and "*damaru*" in Nepali) Between the two faces of this typical instrument, there are always two leather knobs attached, which strike the drums when they are jerked by hand.

. small brass cymbals ("*sil - nyam*" in Tib.)
. large brass cymbals ("*Bug-ch'am*" in Tib.)
. ritual bells ("*dril-bu*" in Tib.)
—*Prayer-wheels* deserve a special paragraph.

They are made of wood, ivory, silver of copper, often inlaid with precious or semi–precious stones. Make sure they contain a tightly rolled paper strip bearing a several thousand t'mes, repeated "*mantra*", i.e. a prayer formula which is, in most cases, the same as the one embossed in the copper prayer wheels fitted in the wall surrounding stupas. This prayer formula: "*Om Mani Padme Hum*" is usually translated into : "*Hail to the Jewel in the Lotus*". In fact, it is an invocation directed to Avalokita (also called Avalokiteshwara), the "Master of reincarnations", venerated throughout Tibet in the form of Chen-rezi(g), the patron–god of the country. The meaning of the prayer is a request made by the supplicant to be spared from any further re–birth and to reach the stage of "nirvana".

Coming back to the prayer–wheel itself, it may be interesting to note how the notion of *prayer* in Lamaist rituals is intimately linked with the idea of *movement*.

Thus, a prayer–wheel that is not spinning is nothing but a lifeless instrument. It only fulfils its role once it is pushed into rotation by the devotee as if this movement allowed the prayer to become active, i.e. to take off and reach the abode of the Gods somewhere in the sky. (It is tempting to compare the dynamism of a gyrating prayer–wheel with the productivity of any electric generator which also has to rotate in order to generate power !)

The same may be said about the prayer–flags which are attached to huge bamboo poles outside houses, temples and sanctuaries. They too, become active only when the wind makes the banners flutter, taking to the skies the inscribed prayers they carry. This is probably the reason why a prayer flag is never to be found *inside* a building, even a temple or a *gonpa*.

But this digression has dragged us away from our shopping tour. Therefore, let us leave Bodnath now and proceed to Patan.

At Patan.

The souvenir–hunting may continue at the Tibetan village at Jawalakhel, near Patan, where various other objects may be pur

chased such as old and new Tibetan woollen carpets (the latter
being manufactured there), jerseys, Tibetan brocade caps trimmed with fur, vests and boots, tea–bowls made of wood but lined
with silver, tea–cup stands, also of silver (they must have a match-
ing lid !) and finally, the world–famous "Lhassa-apsos",
Tibetan terriers and mastiffs. One should always make certain
of the purity of race of the puppies offered for sale by taking
advice from a Tibetan dog specialists.

In Kathmandu

There is a shop specializing in Tibetan blouses, dresses and
ornaments called the "Tibetan Boutique" – "Roof of the World"
located on Kantipath, close to the Yellow Pagoda Hotel. There,
Tibetan dresses for ladies are tailored in original materials. This
shop also sells Tibetan music in cassettes.

Another shop selling interesting Tibetan wares is "Ritual
Art Gallery" on Durbar Marg. It specializes in objects of
religions or daily use. A fascinating choice of strange things.

Now, to carry all your souvenirs, there are many shops in the
old part of the town (on Makhan Tole, for instance), selling very
practical, folding, green canvas bags which are light and very
ample. They are sold in three or four different sizes.

CHAPTER SIX

WHAT TO SEE

HOW TO GET AROUND

In the Valley

— By car

Rented cars :

"Two Travel Agencies provide rented cars. Always chauffeur-driven with no extra–charge: a driver is indispensable not only because he knows his way around, but as an interpreter, should the need arise to have to talk to a policeman, a garage owner, a station-service attendant etc..

Yeti-Travels represents AVIS : The rates in US $: (10% government tax to be added)

	TOYOTA		MERCEDE$
	Corona	Crown	
Per day	26.–	36.–	44.–
Per week	130.–	180.–	220.–
Free mileage : 50 km per day, 350 per week			
Each additional km :	0,28	0.38	0.47
Petrol is included			
Insurance : 2,40 per day			

Gorkha-Travels represents HERTZ : All taxes included :

	DATSUN	LUXURY CAR
Per day	22.–	33.–
Per week	132.–	198.–
Free mileage : 100 km. if car rented for a minimum of one week		

NOTE: The maps visitor should carry with him are:

Kathmandu map: Madhab Lal Maharajan's yellow map, 18' on 18' that carries on the recto a detailed city plan and on the verso, in red a good map of the valley, as well as detailed plan of Bhadgaon and Kirtipur

Valley map: The best is the 8 colour map published by the "Thyssen-Stiftung", scale 50.000th. printed in Munich. Size: 22' on 25'

Petrol : not included
  Insurance : 2,00 for individual insurance, 2,00 for damages
NOTE : at the beginning of 1981, the price of petrol was Rs. 9,35
        per liter (approx. US $ 0.80)

Taxis

There are many taxis in Kathmandu : easy to identify for
their number plates are white on a black background, (whereas
private cars have white figures on a red background). All
taxis are provided with meters. A taxi–ride anywhere inside the
city should not cost more than Rs. 6,00–8,00. It is also possible
to rent a taxi for half a day or a full day. The rates have to be
fixed beforehand, preferably through the hotel porter or a
reception staff. Taxis take a maximum of 4 passengers.

City-bus

For a foreigner who does not know Nepali, it is not easy to
use public bus–services, for there are neither city–maps showing the bus–network, nor time–tables given in English at the terminals. However to travel by bus is cheap.

Minibus

A certain number of minibus services run between Ratna
Park in the centre of the city. And the various towns in the
neighbourhood, such as Patan, Bhadgaon, Bodnath etc. The
fare is approx. Rs. 1,00.

Trolley-bus

The first trolley-bus line, built with the financial and technical
assistance of the People's Republic of China, was put into service
in the beginning of 1976. It links the terminal station at Tripureshwar near the Municipal Sports–Stadium with the entrance of
Bhadgaon. The one-way fare was, in winter 1980–81 Rs. 1.00

– On Motor-cycles

Several firms and shops rent Japanese–made motorcycles.
One of these shops is located at Asan Tole, on the left side of the
street. Appr. rate : Rs. 25,00 per hour, Rs. 200,00 per day or
Rs. 1.000,00 per week. A national or international driving
lincence is required.

– On Bicycles

This is the favourite way of transport for the young and the
fit: it is also the cheapest and most convenient for the distances

are not great and there are not too many "up's" and "down's."
Bicycle renting stalls are located almost in every part of the city.
For instance, at Asan Tole and Kamalachi, in the Kathmandu
Guest House area and on Lazimpath. In Autumn 1980, no
deposit was required, but the person renting a bicycle had to give
his name and address. The rental per day : approx. Rs. 5,00.

All bicycles are provided with a fixed padlock but not necessarily with a light.

– *On Rickshaws*

There are also many motor–rickshaws running between the
centre of the city and its suburbs, but since they have neither fixed
terminals nor meters, it is difficult to use them. Preference will
be given to the "muscle–driven" two–seater tricycle–rickshaws.
These are stationed near almost every hotel and on all main squares. They are provided with plastic covers to protect passengers
against sun and rain. These rickshaws have no meters. Therefore,
fares have to be fixed in advance. Inside the city, a rickshaw–ride
should not exceed Rs. 5,00.

– *On foot*

The Valley and its surrounding hills offer many pleasant walks.
Well traced tracks lead to each of the summits around Kathmandu.

Some of these tours are described in detail under the chapter:
"mini-treks in Kathmandu Valley"

. **Outside the Valley.**

—*By plane*

. *Scheduled Services*

ROYAL NEPAL AIRLINES CORPORATION (R.N.A.C.) operates
an extensive network of domestic lines which covers most parts
of the country. On this network, R.N.A.C. uses the following
types of aircraft :

— AVRO 748 (Hawker-Siddeley–Britain) : turbo-prop engines,
pressurized cabin : 44 seats.

— TWIN OTTERS (De Havilland–Canada): turbo-prop engines,
pressurized cabin : 19 seats which may have to be reduced
to 15 seats on altitude flights.

— PILATUS PORTER (Pilatus-Switzerland): turbo-prop. engines,
not pressurized but oxygen installation on board : 7 seats,
which may have to be reduced to 6 or 5 on altitude flights.

R.N.A.C.'s domestic network is centred in Kathmandu and includes the following destinations that are linked with Kathmandu either by scheduled or by charter flights depending season, weather conditions etc...

Western Nepal : Baitadi, Bhajang, Chaurjhari, Dang, Dhangadi, Dhorpatan, Dolpo, Jumla, Mahendranagar, Nepalganj, Ramechap, Rolpa Sanfe Bagar, Silgari Doti, Simikot (Humla), Surkhet and Tikapur.

Central Nepal : Baglung, Bagmara, Bhairawa, Bharatpur, Gorkha, Janakpur, Jiri, Jomosom, Langtang, Lukhla, Manang, Meghauly, Phaplu, Pokhara, Rampur, Rumjatar, Shyangboche Simara and Thangjet.

Eastern Nepal : Bhadrapur, Bhojpur, Biratnagar, Dharan, Lamidanda, Rajbiraj, Taplejung, and Tumlingtar.

Some of these flights and destinations are open only to Nepalese nationals and not to foreign tourist. Among these restricted points: Bhaganj, Dolpo, Simikot and Tikapur.

Bookings and enquires should be made at RNAC Head-Office on New Road, ground-floor. Tel : 14511 and 13772.

On its international as well as on its domestic network, RNAC grants a 25% rebate to students holding an internationally recognized student identity card.

In the beginning of 1981, the normal fares on the international direct routes out of Kathmandu were the following. These fares are expressed in US$ and have to be paid in foreign hard currency.

Changes may have been introduced since these lines were published :

From KATHMANDU ONE-WAY fare to					
"	"	"	"	BANGKOK : US $	180,00
"	"	"	"	BENARES : "	62,00
"	"	"	"	CALCUTTA : "	84,00
"	"	"	"	COLOMBO : "	180,00
"	"	"	"	DACCA : "	86,00
"	"	"	"	DELHI : "	125,00
"	"	"	"	PATNA : "	36,00
"	"	"	"	RANGOON : "	223,00

Domestic fares can be paid in Nepalese rupees.

On those domestic sectors that are mostly used by tourist, R.N.A.C. introduced, on December 1st 1979, different fares for tourists and foreign passengers one the one side, Nepalese and

Indian nationals on the other. (*)

The fares applicable to foreigners concern the following routes, expressed in Nepalese Rupees : (One–way)

Kathmandu – Pokhara	:	Nep. Rs.	360,00
Kathmandu – Jomosom	:	,, ,,	580,00
Kathmandu – Lukhla	,,	,, ,,	600,00
Kathmandu – Phaplu	,,	,, ,,	540,00
Kathmandu – Jiri	:	,, ,,	270,00
Kathmandu – Jumla	:	,, ,,	1160,00
Kathmandu – Bhairawa	:	,, ,,	540,00
Kathmandu – Meghauly	:	,, ,,	360,00
Kathmandu – Bharatpur	:	,, ,,	300,00
Kathmandu – Biratnagar	:	,, ,,	590,00
Pokhara – Jomosom	:	,, ,,	270,00
Pokhara – Bharatpur	:	,, ,,	210,00

— *"Charter" services*

Thanks to R.N.A.C.'s "STOL" (Short Take-Off and Landing) aircraft, i.e. Twin Otters and Pilatus Porter, the national carrier is in a position to provide excellent opportunities for private flights of tourist interest which may, or may not, according to the wishes of the tourist – include one or several landings or none at all. There are many small airfields in the hills and remote areas in this vast country. During the peak trekking season, these charter flights are usuallyheavily booked in advance. The most popular and most frequently used destination points of trekking parties are :

—Lukhla (35 min.) and Syangboche (40 min) the two classical starting points for trekkings into the Sherpa-land and the Everest region.

—Langtang (25 min.), a magnificent and typical Himalayan Valley just north of Kathmandu.

—Jomosom (60 min.) on the way to Dhaulagiri, Muktihnath and the Thorung Pass, the "gate" to the Manang area, which lies "behind" (i.e. in the north) of the whole Annapurna range. This region is open to tourists since 1977.

—Jumla (120 min.) on the way to Rara Lake, the Kanjiroba mountain range and the north-western corner of the country.

(*) Note: Wherever a foreign tourist goes outside the Valley, he should always be ready to produce his passport, even if he travels by plane or by bus inside the country and far from any border.

—Phaplu (25 min.) and Jiri (25 min.) which are intermediate points between the Kathmandu Valley and the Everest region.

In the beginning of 1981, the rates for RNAC charter flights were approximately the following, :

On TWIN OTTERS : US $ 720.— for a minimum of 1 hour 30 min. flight

On PILATUS : US $ 500.— for a minimum of 2 hours flight

An innovation by Royal Nepal Airlines was to set up fixed "charter fares" to over twenty-five destinations inside Nepal. The airplanes that are thus offered on a "charter" basis are :

—The 44 seater Hawker–Siddeley AVRO 749 from Kathmandu to Biratnagar for 275.00 Rupees, to Meghauly for 142.00 and a private "Mountain-Flight" towards Mount Everest and back for 164.00.

—the 19 seater De Havilland "Twin-Otter" to 23 different destination points and.

—the 7 seater Pilatus – Porter which may operate to 19 shorter airfields, in particular in the mountainous region.

Royal Nepal Airlines Helicopter Services

For commercial, tourist and rescue flights, Royal Nepal Airlines has at its disposal two 4 to 5 seater "Alouette" and one 13–seater "Puma" small–which belong to the Royal Air Flight.

The Helicopter Services Office is located on the 1st floor of R.N.A.C.'s Head–Office Building on New Road (Tel 14511– Ext. 137 and 147)

This department offers three kind of services :

—1) Pre-arranged "set-tours" for sight-seeing to a certain number of specific destinations, such as

Langtang (approx. flying–time : 1 hour)		
Helambu	" "	: 35 minutes
Lumbini and Tiger Tops	"	: 3 hours
Everest region	"	: 2 hours
Gauri-Shankar region	"	: 1 hour
Manang Area	"	: 2 hours
Gorkha Area	"	: 1 hour
Ganesh Himal Area	"	: 1 hour

—2) Charter flights on request, with or without landings, whether for sight-seeing or for filming ("Restricted areas" excluded, of course).

—3) Rescue flights to pick up tourists, trekkers or mountaineers who may have suffered an accident or been taken ill. (Details about such rescue operations, see under "Trekking").

For any such helicopter flights, the rates are calculated per hour flight : US $ 375.– for Alouette and US $ 887.– for Puma, irrespective of the number of passengers.

Mountain-flights along the Himalayan range

During the winter-season (October to March), when under normal conditions the sky is clear and the mountains well visible, Royal Nepal Airlines operates with a pressurized 44–seater Hawker-Siddeley AVRO 749, two very spectacular – in fact unique – flights.

The aircraft leaves Kathmandu airfield and proceeds to the East (i. e. towards Everest) whereas the other leaves Pokhara and proceeds to the West (i. e. towards the Annapurna range).

—Some recommendations and notes concerning both flights

It is to be recommended that passengers wishing to take part in such a "Mountain Flight" should make their booking, not only well in advance, but through a Travel Agency. Experience shows that these seem to be better placed than the individual passenger – even if he reports to the airport very early and ahead of checking-in time – to obtain the "better seats".

In principle, the seats are allotted "*when and as*" the passenger checks in, but this procedure is not always strictly adhered to, in particular when bookings concern large groups of tourists.

On both flights, the seats in the two front or the two back rows are considered "better" than those "on the wings", in particular when the passenger wants to take pictures or shoot a film sequence.

As a rule weather and flying conditions permitting, the capitain invites those passengers who are eager to take "good" pictures of the mountains, to step forward for a short while to the cockpit from where pictures and films give far better results then those taken through the cabin porthole,due to the different material the window panes are made of.

Irrespective of that, these mountain flights are assuredly a very memorable experience no tourist should miss. Another attractive point is the fact that the flight lasts just one hour, thus leaving all the rest of the morning free for other sight-seeing, shopping etc...

—Some peculiarities concerning the Mountain Flight leaving Kathmandu

1) This flight being a "domestic" one, the checking-in takes place in the "Domestic Airport "building. An airport – tax of Rs. 10.– has to be paid at the airline's counter.

2) This flight takes place every morning, and very often, RNAC operates one or two additional ones, all taking off between 7.30 and 9.00 a.m.

3) The "better" seats are those on the left had side of the aircraft as far as the outward portion of the flight is concerned. On the homebound leg, of course, the mountains will be seen from the right hand portholes.

4) Before boarding the plane, each passenger is handed over by the airline staff a folded panoramic chart of the whole Eastern part of the Himalayas that enables him to identify easily each peak as and when the aircraft is at right angle with it, that means when the passenger sees each given summit straight in front of him when looking through his porthole.

5) Here a short description of the flight :

The airplane takes off usually in a southern direction and turns towards East after a few minutes. As soon as the plane approaches the mountain range, the first mountain that is easy to identify thanks to its pyramidal shape is DORJE LAKPA (22,927 ft. – 6.998 m.). Next appears "God's finger" CHHOBA BHAMARE (19,587 ft. – 5.970 m)., which needs no description ! A huge mountain towering above all those nearby, and whose summit bears a triangular snowcap on its right side, is GAURISHANKAR (23,442 ft – 7.145 m.) A little further along and slightly in the background stand a huge "plateau", or, better said, a flat-topped mountain both sides of which are very steep icy slopes; this is MELUNGTSE (23,560 ft. – 7.181 m.). Several mountains and a few minutes later, appears, in the background the first to reach the 8.000 m. (26.750 ft.) limit: CHO–OYU, Now the plane has reached the Khumbu-Everest area, 20 minutes after take-off. This is the moment for "Top-of-the-world-photo-addicts" to proceed to the cockpit, if invited to do so. The impressive KHUMBU-GLACIER is flanked, on its northern by PUMORI (23,442 ft.– 7.145 m.) a very regular-shaped pyramid. The Glacier tumbles straight down from MOUNT EVEREST. The latter, half concealed by the horizontal wall of NUPTSE (25,850 ft. –7.879 m). to the left and LHOTSE (27,890 ft. –8.501 m.)

to the right, is not difficult to identify : it is a triangular black rock rarely covered with snow. But often from its summit a white cloud is blown off by the strong wind, towards the East.

The plane continues its flight towards MAKALU (27,805 ft.– 8.475 m.) with its famous "top-to-bottom-ridge."

While the plane is turning round in a wide circle, the huge massif of KANCHENJUNGA (28,166 ft. – 8.584 m.) which marks the border between Nepal and Sikkim, can also be seen clearly in the distance.

6) When deplaning, each passenger is given a certificate testifying that "Mount Everest has had the privilege of greeting Mr.. Mrs.. on to-day's RNAC Mountain-Flight". A precious souvenir to keep and to take home.

7) At the beginning of 1981 the rate for this Mountain-Flight from Kathmandu was fixed at US $ 45.– or Nep. Rs. 535.–

Some peculiarities concerning the Mountain Flight leaving Pokhara

1) This flight was inaugurated 1980 and was, at the start, scheduled to take place twice a week, on Tuesdays and Fridays, taking-off at 7 a. m.

2) The current rate, for this Mountain Flight alone, was Nep. Rs. 420.–

3) But it can be linked with :
. either the scheduled flight back to Kathmandu, in which case the rate is Nepalese. Rs. 690.– (instead of 420+360.–=780.– if taken separately !)
. or the scheduled flight *from* Kathmandu to Pokhara, which, added to the Mountain-Flight and the journey back to Kathmandu would be charged only Nep. Rs. 900.– instead of 1140.– which is the fare for the added–up three separate legs.

4) On the "Pokhara-Mountain-Flight" the same facilities are being offered to the passengers as on the Kathmandu–Mountain–Flight, with the obvious exception of the impossibility to make the acquaintance with Mount Everest.

Nevertheless, this flight too, is worth while, for the Annapurna range is undisputably as spectacular – if not more – than the other one. When leaving Pokhara (the best seats, on this one are those on the right hand side of the aircraft on the outbound leg, and those on the left side when returning to base) the plane is heading straight towards the magnificent, unique "Fish-Tail" Peak, the typical "landmark" of the Annapurnas. Let us remind that this mountain has so far never been scaled, and has become

the most coveted summit of the whole Himalayas ! Nepalese
mountaineers may wish to be the first to reach its peak.
Whatever the reason, it is still "off–limits" for foreign expeditions or individual mountaineers.

On the right-hand side of the Fish-Tail, not less than four very
famous mountains become visible and are very easy to identify.

Furthest away, to the East, LAMJUNG HIMAL (22,740 ft.
–6.931 m.) with its ten or eleven glaciers inexorably gliding down
its steep rocky and icy slopes.

Then, slightly to the West, appears a very characteristic one:
ANNAPURNA II (24,878 ft. 7583 m.) which all year round shows
a black "beret" on its right "ear". Its top is almost completely flat.

Close to ANNAPURNA II, a little further to the west still,
stands ANNAPURNA IV (24,688 ft–7525 m.), a lonely pointed peak.

The range slides down slightly before reaching the top of
ANNAPURNA III (26,040 ft.– 7937 m.) which leans towards the
east ridge of "Fish-Tail".

Now the plane has left "Maccha Pucchare" behind. The crucial
moment has come : where lies exactly the highest point of this
whole range : ANNAPURNA I ? When the aircraft flies as near as
possible to the mountain, it is easy to recognize its small bump
in the centre of a vast horizontal ridge. ANNAPURNA I is the
first "above 8.000 m." of this region : 8,090 m. – 26,545 ft.

All of them have been climbed several times, but there are
so many different ascent routes that "the Annapurnas", will remain an attraction for mountaineers for a long time to come.

A deep valley is now in front of you : the Kali Gandaki gorge,
which leads to the legendary "Mustang" and its former "royal"
fortified town, Lo-Manthang, and beyond, to Tibet, where the
river takes its source.

There is no mistake possible, on the eastern side of the Valley,
a short distance from Annapurna II, two very spectacular peaks are clearly visible : NILGIRI Peak and TUKUCHE Peak,
respectively 23,166 ft–7061 m. and 22,688 ft.– 6.915 m. (Nilgiri
Peak is the mountain that is depicted on the cover of the world
famous book by TONI HAGEN, the first of many photo-books
about Nepal.) On the western side of the Valley, the majestic,
impressive DHAULAGIRI, whose shape reminds of a wide armchair.
Dhaulagiri stands alone, its top towering at 26,804 ft.– 8,172 m. !

A few minutes more and the plane now circles around and
prepares for its return to Pokhara. A "technical stop" at Pokharas

airfield, and 30 minutes later, you will land at Tribhuvan Airport in Kathmandu.

—By road

In 1981 there were four main high-ways open to traffic:

KATHMANDU–RAXAUL, called *"Tribhuvan Rajpath"* leading to the Indian border (114 mi.–200km.) This is the oldest highway; it was opened in 1956. It is also Nepal's main supply line for all goods coming from or through India. This road was built with the assistance of the Indian Cooperation Mission to Nepal.

KATHMANDU–KODARI, called *"Arniko Highway"*, linking Kathmandu with the Chinese (Tibetan) border bridge at Kodari. (68 mi-110 km.) built with the assistance of the People's Republic of China. Opened in 1967.

KATHMANDU–POKHARA called *"Prithvi Rajmarg"* (127 mi.–204 km.) built with the assistance of the People's Republic of China and opened in 1973.

POKHARA–SUNAULI, called *"Siddhartha Marg"*, linking Pokhara with the Indian border (114 mi.–183 km.) opened in 1971 and built with the assistance of India.

The additional important highways are presently under completion namely :

—The *"East–West Highway"* all across the Terai, along the 600 miles (965km.)Indian border. This road will be called "Mahendra Raj Marg". It is being built, sector–wise by GREAT BRITAIN, INDIA, the U.S.A. and U.S.S.R. as well as United Nations Agencies.

—The *"Pokhara-Surkhet"* highway (250 mi.–402 km.) which will be built with the assistance of the People's Republic of China. It will link Pokhara with the town of Surkhet, the centre of the *"Western Nepal Development Area"*.

To be mentioned also, the *Lamosangu-Jiri* road which is in its final stage of construction with the financial and technical assistance of HELVETAS, a Swiss cooperation organization. This road, which will be approx. 60 mi. (96 km.) long will open up the region of Jiri that counts approx. 150.000 inhabitants, mostly farmers and cattlebreeders.

Last but not least, one word about the Kathmandu *"Ring-Road"*, which like all other highways, will contribute to the development of the country. This ring–road is approx. 20 mi. (32 km.) long and was built in 1975–1776 with the financial and technical assistance of the People's Republic of China. It includes four bridges over the various rivers of the Valley.

Regular bus services are operating along all completed highways. Here a few indications concerning these services :

—KATHMANDU–POKHARA : On this important road, transport media are available :

. *Ordinary buses* that leave the Bus Terminal located in the back of Nepal Electricity Corporation Building facing the Tundikhel Parade Ground. In autumn 1980, the fare was approx. Rs. 35.– one–way, per passenger. The journey takes between six and seven hours.

. More comfortable *mini–buses* cover the same distance in approx. five to six hours. In Kathmandu, the terminal station for these buses is located near the minaret–shaped 'Bhimsen Tower". In autumn 1980, the fare was, approx. Rs. 45.– one–way.

— KATHMANDU–RAXAUL, to the Indian border.

. By *ordinary buses* : They leave in front of the Central Post-Office and the Esso gas station In autumn 1980, the fare was approx. Rs. 36.– one-way . The journey takes about ten hours.

. By *minibus* : these services are not very regular.

On all these transport service, it is highly advisable to book seats well in advance. Bookings have to be made at the respective terminals or through Travel Agencies. Passports may be controlled at certain check posts along the route.

CAPTIVATING SITES

INTRODUCTION

The infinite variety of places to be seen in Kathmandu and its Valley does not allow to go into all the details of what has to be seen. Therefore, the present chapter will deal with the essential sites only as well as trying to provide the answers to the questions the visitor may be asking himself.

THE THREE CAPITAL CITIES AND THE MAIN SANCTUARIES

Any too condensed definition is bound to be superficial.

In order to differentiate somehow the three capital cities of the Valley, emphasis may be laid on the following points :

KATHMANDU is the "metropolis" of the country. Here is the Royal Palace, the seat of the Government and all Public Administrations, Corporations and Services. Foreign Embassies, Offices of International Organizations, Airline Offices, Travel

Agencies and well-supplied shops.

In spite of this and thanks to its architectural and art treasures, its magnificent palaces and temples, Kathmandu remained, even to–day, a "living museum". The increasing car-traffic and one–way streets will never alter this fact basically.

PATAN, which lies just across the sacred Bagmati river, has a different character. Its artistic treasures are perhaps even more valuable and more elaborate than the ones of Kathmandu. On the other hand, Patan is essentially a Newar city, not as cosmopolitan as Kathmandu.

BHADGAON, the Valley's third important city is again, very different. Although this city was, for many centuries, the capital of an independant kingdom, it has succeeded even in a more acentuated way as Patan, in maintaining its specific character as a centre of handicraft workers, artists and farmers. In many of its aspects, Bhadgaon gives the impression of being a "peasant's city". It is here that, while strolling through the narrow streets and on the old squares, the visitors feels very strikingly that he has been driven back into the 16th century, may be even into the Middle Ages, where old traditions and trades are still preserved and practiced.

* * *

. HOW TO ORGANIZE SIGHTSEEING IN THE VALLEY ?

Here is one of many possible programmes :
First half day : KATHMANDU and SWAYAMBHU
KATHMANDU (*)......

The main attraction of Kathmandu is perhaps to stroll, on
'oot, through its streets and lanes, and to discover by one-
elf the beauties of this fantastic town.

Two itineraries lead to the heart of the old city :
— one starting point is the curiously decorated White Gate that
narks the entrance to New Road.   Its construction dates back to
934, the year of the dreadful earthquake which shook and
lamaged many buildings. (at this stage let us add immediately
hat earthquakes and even tremors are extremely rare.)

From the White Gate, follow New Road towards the old Royal
'alace on the right hand side and towards Hanuman Dhoka.

— the other starting point may be the square water pond
'alled Rani Pokhari. From there, follow the narrow "diagonal
treet" which cuts across the most important part of the old city
.nd finally also reaches Hanuman Dhoka.

While strolling through these narrow streets lined with small
.nd picturesque shops where all kinds of goods are sold it is fasci-
ating to discover not only the houses ornate with masterpieces
.f woodcarved windows and balconies, but also the dozens of sanc-
uaries and temples of all shape, age and size.   Here it is real fun
o mix with the crowd that are busy selling. buying, bargaining,
arrying loads and doing their best not to be hit and hurt by the
.nconcerned cyclists and rickshaw–drivers.

Let us assume you selected the itinerary starting from the New
Road gate.

THE OLD ROYAL PALACE
Only a few hundred yards further, you pass the round-about

*) For photo–amateurs: There are so many buildings and picturesque
scenes to take in particular in the old parts of the city that it is almost
impossible to determine which is the "best moment" to take pictures.
It is advisable to go photo-hunting twice: once in the morning and
once in the afternoon.

in the centre of which stands the statue of Juddha Shumshere Ran (1932–1954), one of the last Rana-Prime Ministers. Then on your right hand side appears suddenly the dark-red brick-stone Old Royal Palace. It is an impressive nine-storey building which was erected by Prithvi Narayan Shah in the latter half of the 18th century. The Palace main building is topped by a tower called "Basantpur Tower", which was seriously damaged during the 1934 earthquake.

Restoration work of Basantpur tower began in 1974 and is by now completed.

The wooden door-pillars the windows etc. of this façade are among the most magnificent masterpieces of Nepalese wood-carving. All these sculptures were painstakingly cleaned by hand and whenever necessary, repaired during the months preceding H. M. Birendra's coronation in Febr. 1975. While admiring these doors and windows, the visitor should discover by himself, the unexpected, amusing and quaint details.

Inside this architectural ensemble of palaces, there are approximately ten inner courtyards, certain number of which are closed to the public, even to Nepalese citizens. However, three of the most beautiful ones may be visited. They are :

1) the courtyard of the "Living Goddess' – to whom a special chapter will be dedicated below.

2) the courtyard located just below Basantpur Towar, called "Laun Chowk", or "Basantpur Chowk" which includes windows decorated with hundreds of different wood-carved birds, mostly peacocks, one of the "sacred" birds of Hindu mythology.

3) the "Coronation courtyard", also called "Nasal Chowk" This courtyard may be reached

— either from Laun Chowk, by passing through the doorway which links the two courtyards.

— or through the main entrance which opens of Hanuman Dhoka Square (see below).

THE CORONATION COURTYARD

This courtyard has gone through various epochs. The oldest part dates back to the Malla era, which ruled from the 13th. century onwards.

Assuming you entered this courtyard from the main gate. i. e. coming from Hanuman Dhoka, you will notice immediately on your left hand side, a huge carved stone representing "Nar-singha", an image of Vishnu as half-man, half-lion. (more details about this deity will be found in the chapter concerning Hindu religious influence on Nepalese Art). This statue was erected in 1672 by King Pratap Malla, in order to appease this divinity whom he thought he had offended when he danced in public, disguised as Narsingha himself. On the left side of the statue, the gallery's wall is covered with the portraits of all Nepalese Sovereigns belonging to the ruling dynasty of the Shahs. In fact, this gallery was the audience chamber of the Malla Kings. The bed-like piece of furniture covered with a simple white cotton sheet is the old throne, a plain but spacious seat fitted with a long rolled cushion arm-and back-rest.

A small sanctuary comes next: it is dedicated to the "dancing Shiva" hence the name of "*Nasal Chowk*" given to this place, for, in Nepali, "nasal" means dance.

On the opposite wall, i. e. on the southern face, more magnificent wooden window-frames with the most exquisite carvings are to be admired. This façade makes a vivid contrast with the one looking west, which was built more recently, almost in a "neo-greek" style with white stucco decorative designs. That building is called Gaddi Baithak.

Almost in the exact centre of the courtyard stands the platform where since Prithvi Narayan Shah, all Kings of Nepal were crowned. Here too the present Sovereign, H. M. BIRENDRA BIR BIKRAM SHAH DEV was solemnly crowned on 24th February 1975.

Let us now go back to our starting point which was the entrance of the first courtyard, Laun Chowk, facing New Road.

BASANTPUR SQUARE

This portion of the Royal Palace's ensemble looks on the vast brick-paved square called Basantpur A narrow street leads southwards. This is the well-known (and formerly ill-famed) "Freak street", where many lodges, small hotels and taverns as well as Tibetan souvenir shops are located that sell almost anything, These are the favourite gathering places of those generally long-haired and bearded youngsters who were, and still are sometimes indiscriminately called "hippies".

THE PALACE OF THE LIVING GODDESS

At the further end of Basantpur Square, a one storey-building of exquisite proportions shows superb carved windows, among

them several "peacock windows". This is the Palace of the
"Royal Kumari", generally called "The Living Goddess". Her
Palace was built in 1757 by King Jaya Prakash MALLA.

Before going into further details about this unique building
the question that, first, deserves an answer is : "Who is this
"Living Goddess" ? " (*)

First, it should be mentioned that there is not one but eleven
"Living Goddesses" : four in Kathmandu, three in Bhadgaon
two in Patan and one each in Devapatan and Bungamati. However
the most important one is the Kumari who resides near the
Kathmandu Royal Palace, on Basantpur, This is why she is
usually referred to as the "Royal" Kumari.

Now as to the question: "Who is she and whom or what does
she represent ?" three answers are usually offered, the truth
being, possibly, a blending of the three !

1. According to the probably oldest interpretation, the
Kumari is the incarnation of the "Kumari" – also called Skan-
damata, i.e. one of the eight "Mother-Goddesses" ("Ashta Ma-
trika") of the Hindu Pantheon. (Let our Cartesian mind not be
too much disturbed by the fact that a "Kumari" -a word meaning
"*virgin*"–stands among "*Mother*-goddesses"..

2. A variant interpretation of the first one: the Kumari is the
"Virgin Goddess", also called "Kanya Kumari" among the
Hindu deities, traditionally identified with either Goddess Durga
or Taleju, in other words, one of the many forms of Shiva's
"consort", Parvati. This interpretation mainly based on two
facts:– that Durga's "classical" image is to be found on the tym-
panums of the Kumari's Palace–that Goddess Taleju has always
been favoured in Nepal by very special devotion in particular
by the Royal Family (remember that the most gorgeous of all
Kathmandu temples, the one built on the hillock of Hanuman
Dhoka, is dedicated to this Goddess and can only be visited by
members of the Royal Family !)

3. Many scholars and devout Hindu Nepalese, say that the
"Kumari" is not to be regarded as a real"reincarnation" of a given
Goddess, but merely as a living *representation* of Durga, some-
how like on a stage, an actor "is" and at the same time "is

(*) Readers particularly interested in the various aspects of the Living
    Goddess, ought to read the comprehensive study written by Michael
    Allen "The Cult of the Kumari" – published in 1975 by the Insti-
    tute of Nepal and Asian Studies, Kathmandu University.

not" a given character of a play.

Whomsoever the Kumari is really regarded as, she was first considered and venerated as the patron– goddess of the MALLA dynasty and today as the chief patron or guardian of the State in general and the Kathmandu Valley in particular. In the eyes of Buddhists she is looked upon as the "feminine principle" of knowledge and power.

To come back to the girl herself, the "Royal Kumari" is traditionally selected in a Newar Buddhist family of goldsmiths belonging to the specific clan of the "Banra" or "Sakya" living in Patan. The candidate-there may be more than one at the time of selecting a new Kumari-should be four or five years old. Her body must not have the slightest blemish and must present all thirty-two "specific signs" among which some seem rather strange:

...long, slender arms, well - rounded shoulders, brilliantly white teeth, blue or black very shining eyes, hands and feet delicately soft, a small and sensitive tongue, no gaps between the teeth, straight hair curled towards the right side, a neck like a conch-shell, a voice like that of a sparrow, a "golden shadow" etc...

In addition to all this, she must have shown unfailing courage when left alone in a dark room strewn with bleeding, freshly chopped-off heads of buffaloes. During this test, masked men, looking like demons, try their best to frighten the poor candidate.

Once she successfully passed all these tests and once the astrologers found that her horoscope is in "full harmony" with the one of the King, then only will the new Kumari be installed in her Palace. Curiously enough this important formality does not involve any special ceremony.

From that day on, the Kumari becomes, so to speak, a prisoner of her estate. She is forbidden to leave her Palace, whether alone or accompanied. She may have playmates, but they have to come to her Palace and, of course, should never quarrel with the Kumari. She may have a teacher but being considered as a goddess, there is little she is supposed to be ignorant of.

On seven occasions, in the course of one year, she is taking part in given festivals and is allowed to appear outside her Palace.

Once a year, in September, on Indra Jatra's festival, His Majesty the King, although he is himself venerated as an incarnation of the Hindu God Vishnu, pays homage to the Kumari, in spite of her having been selected among a Buddhist family : a striking example of the way both creeds are closely imbricated and also of the extreme religious liberalism and broad-mindedness of the Nepalese people and its Leader.

The bleeding loss of a milk –tooth, as well as puberty of course, or any other injury leading blood to appear, marks the end of her carrer as a "Living Goddess".

In fact, the Kumari may remain a virgin the rest of her life, as it is considered "unauspicious" to marry an ex-Kumari. This is probably less a superstition than the result of the unwillingness of anybody to marry a girl who has been brought up, not as a future housewife, but as a goddess whose wishes had always to be fulfilled at once, who was considered and treated as having unlimited power and knowledge, who, in addition to everything else, has never been reprimanded or criticized; finally, whom everybody, including the King himself, paid homage to !

However, as along as she occupies her high position she enjoys the privilege of living in a Palace which is indeed a masterpiece of artifact, a jewel of Nepalese architecture and craftmanship. In particular, the inner courtyard contains elaborate carvings of the same quality than those you have seen inside the Royal Palace itself.

The Kumari appears willingly at the middle window of the upper floor even if the court-yard is full of tourists. Each of them is supposed to pay one Rupee to be allowed to have a look at her, i.e. to receive her blessing. However, taking photographs of her is strictly forbidden. However, this prohibition deos not apply to the court-yard itself and its treasures of wood-carvings.

Leaving now the Kumari Palace, there lies a splendid square in front of you, full of pagodas, temples and sanctuaries.

KASTHAMANDAP

First, we suggest you to turn immediately on your left: there you will see a very beautiful statue of a kneeling and praying "GARUDA", the half-man, half-bird traditional "mount" of God Vishnu. This statue is in a perfect state of preservation, although it is now almost three hundred years old, having been erected in 1689 by Queen Siddhi Laxmi, the widow of King Parthibendra MALLA (1680–1687). Still further to the left–hand side, the very famous building called KASTHAMANDAP, which means"the-temple-made -of-wood". This word, slightly altered in the course of time, ultimately gave birth to the name KATHMANDU.

According to a well-established legend, this vast building is believed to have been made from the wood of a single tree, most likely a "sal" tree. The colonnades and the very unusual open platform seem to indicate that this building was not actually used as a temple but rather as a rest-house or an assembly hall. The sanctuary dedicated to Goraknath which nowadays is to be seen in the centre of the platform is a relatively recent addition. KASTHAMANDAP was renovated in 1630, the original building dating back to the 12th century.

SHIVA PARVATI TEMPLE

Now we invite you to turn back on your footsteps and proceed towards the main square. Inevitably your attention will be attracted by the somewhat unexpected "neo-greek" white-washed European style Palace. This is an eighty year old annex built along the ancient Royal Palace, on order of one of the Rana Prime-Ministers. It is called Gaddi Baithak.

On the other side, slightly to the left, SHIVA and PARVATI look out of the middle window of their temple as if they were "common people" watching the crowd moving around the square below. These two candid figures confer on their temple – for it is really one – a very "familiar" aspect. It was built in 1790 by BAHADUR SHAH, one of PRITHVI NARAYAN SHAH's sons.

HANUMAN DHOKA

A few more steps along the passage linking the two squares and you will reach the famous HANUMAN DHOKA area. Just before turning on your right, look at the corner windows of the last house : these windows are the only ones carved not in wood, but in pure ivory! This was a completely unknown fact until the army of young girls who were in charge of cleaning–with toothbrushes !–the façades of all palaces and temples in view of the Coronation festivities in February 1975, made this discovery.

Another unexpected sight, this time on your left, just in front of these two ivory windows, is a gigantic bell. It is actioned only once a year, at the festival dedicated to Degutaleju. The bell-ringing is believed to chase away evil spirits and malevolent influences. The bell was erected by RANA BAHADUR SHAH in 1786.

On the same side, a little further away, there are two drums, also of unusual shape and volume. They have remained on this very same place for no less than 180 years. It was King YUDDHA BIKRAM SHAH who had installed them in 1800. According to the tradition, one goat and one buffalo have to be sacrificed before anybody may beat these drums.

Now it is time to step on Hanuman Dhoka proper.

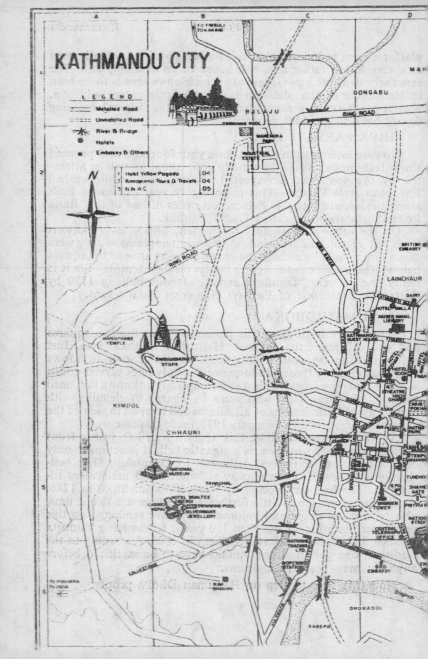

KATHMANDU CITY

L E G E N D

— Metalled Road

---- Unmetalled Road

River & Bridge

Hotels

Embassy & Others

1	Hotel Yellow Pagoda	D4
2	Annapurna Tours & Travels	D4
3	R.N.A.C.	D5

TO TRISULI
TO KAKANI

GONGABU

MAHA

BALAJU

SWIMMING POOL

MAHENDRA
PARK

INDUSTRIAL
ESTATE

RING ROAD

RING ROAD

BRITISH
EMBASSY

LAINCHAUR

DAIRY

KATHMANDU
MALLA

HOTEL
MALLA

KAISER MAHAL
LIBRARY

MANJUSHREE
TEMPLE

SWAYAMBHUNATH
STUPA

KATHMANDU
GUEST HOUSE

MAHATMA TOLE

RANI POKHARI

R.T.
THEATRE

CHETRAPATI

Vishnumati River

HOTEL
ROOM

HOTEL
MAHENDRA

HOTEL
KATHMANDU

NACHGHARH

KIMDOL

ASAN

INDRA
POKHARA

CHHAUNI

BIR HOSPITAL

RATNA PARK

NEW ROAD

TEMPLE

DARBAR
SQUARE

Bishnumati River

KHEL
TOLE

NATIONAL
MUSEUM

TAHACHAL

TUNDIKHEL

SHAHID
GATE

BAGH
DARBAR

BAGBAZAR

G.P.O.

PRITHVI PATH

NATIONAL
STADIUM

HOTEL SOALTEE
OBEROI

CASINO
NEPAL

SWIMMING POOL

SILVERMAN'S
JEWELLERY

LAZIMPAT

BHIMSEN
TOWER

CENTRAL
TELEGRAPH
OFFICE

TO POKHARA
TO INDIA

KALIMATI

NATIONAL
TRADING
LTD.

ROPEWAY
STATION

3RD
EMBASSY

Bagmati River

R.M.
BHAVAN

DHOKADOL

SANEPA

A   B   C   D

N

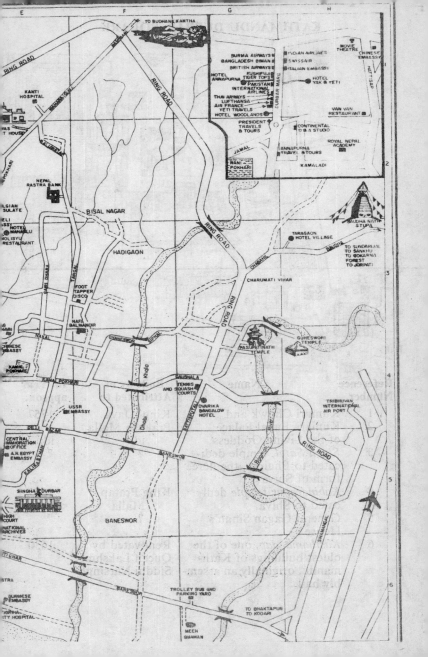

KATHMANDU DURBAR SQUARE

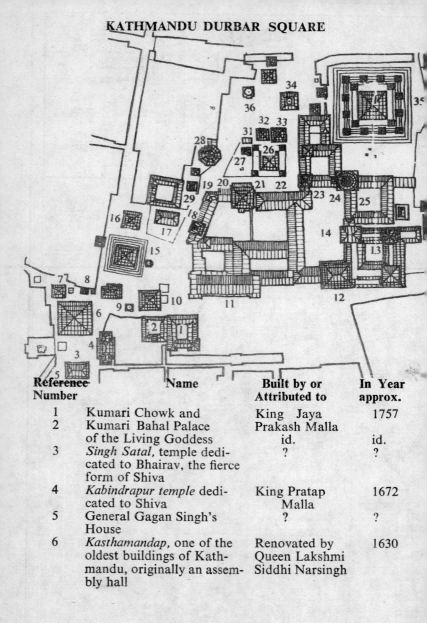

Reference Number	Name	Built by or Attributed to	In Year approx.
1	Kumari Chowk and	King Jaya	1757
2	Kumari Bahal Palace of the Living Goddess	Prakash Malla id.	id.
3	*Singh Satal,* temple dedicated to Bhairav, the fierce form of Shiva	?	?
4	*Kabindrapur temple* dedicated to Shiva	King Pratap Malla	1672
5	General Gagan Singh's House	?	?
6	*Kasthamandap,* one of the oldest buildings of Kathmandu, originally an assembly hall	Renovated by Queen Lakshmi Siddhi Narsingh	1630

7	A 2–roofed Shiva temple	?	?
8	*Lakshmi sanctuary*, also called Ashok Vinayaka	?	?
9	Statue of *Garuda*	Queen Siddhi Lakshimi, widow of King Parthibendra Malla	1689
10	*Trailokya Mohan Mandir* a temple dedicated to Narayan-Vishnu	King Parthibendra Malla	1680
11	*Gaddi Baithak Durbar* (A Rana-style Palace)	Juddha Shumsher Jung Bahadur Rana	1908
12	*Basantpur Durbar*, the main building of the ancient Royal Palace	Enlarged and renovated by King Prithvi Narayan Shah,	Oldest parts date back to 16th century
13	*Basantpur Chowk* (also called Laun Chowk), the smaller inner courtyard of the Palace		around 1770 and Spread over centuries
14	*Nasal Chowk* (the Coronation courtyard)	King Pratap Malla	1672
15	*Majudeva*, a Shiva temple	Queen Siddhi Lakshmi	1690
16	*Vishnu* temple	King Rana Bahadur Shah	?
17	*Shiva-Parvati* temple		1790
18	*Bhagavati* 3-roofed temple	King Jagat-Jaya Malla	1730
19	*Ivory* windows	?	?
20	*Shveta Bhairav Image* Protected by a latticed screen which opens only once a year during Indra Jatra festival in Sept.	Rana Bahadur Shah	1796
21	*Degu-Taleju* temple	King Shiva Singh Malla	1600
22	Statue of *Hanuman*, the "Monkey-god", in honour of whom the	King Pratap Malla	1672

	whole square has been named		
23	Statue of *Narsimha,* a form of Vishnu (inside the Coronation courtyard, on the left of the entrance gate)	id.	id.
24	*Panchmukhi Hanuman* temple (a round structure)	King Jaya Prakash Malla	1750
25	*Mul Chowk,* one of the oldest courtyards of the palace	King Mahendra Malla	1564
26	*Jagannath* temple	id.	1563
27	King *Pratap Malla* statue	Himself	1675(?)
28	*Krishna* temple	id.	1648
29	*Taleju* Bell	King Rana Bahadur Shah	1797
30	*Police* Head-quarters		20th century
31	*Kal Bhairav* image (the Bhairav of death)	Moved to this location by King Pratap Malla	1650
32	*Indrapur* temple	King Pratap Malla	id.
33	*Krishna* temple		17th century
34	*Kakeshwar-Mahadev* temple dedicated to Shiva	Queen Bhubhana Lakshmi	1681
35	*Taleju* temple, also called the King's family temple, built on a hill, has three golden doors	King Mahendra Malla	1564
36	*Kotilingeshwar* temple dedicated to Vishnu	King Mahendra Malla	1565
37	The historical "Kot" Courtyard	?	?

BHAIRAV

—Turning on your right, at the very entrance of the square, a huge latticed window hides from the eyes of the public the golden and grinning mask of "Sveta Bhairav", twelve feet high. This image was placed there in 1796, also by RANA BAHADUR SHAH with the objective of warding off evil influences.

Bhairav is one of the many (some say 64 !) terrifying representations of SHIVA. This makes him a particularly important object of devotion.

His face reveals three protruding eyes, his mouth has dog-like fangs. His neck wears a garland of human skulls while others are placed on his headgear. As most of Hindu deities, Bhairav is endowed with many arms and hands. One may mention the trident (one of the traditional SHIVA symbols) and the sword that enable him to destroy evil spirits, evil people and ignorance; one of his other hands is holding a severed hand–a reminder of the punishment inflicted on thieves. Elsewhere, there are three decapitated heads which, according to certain scholars symbolize the fate of men who are nursing with bad thoughts or intentions.

The devotees who prostrate themselves before this sacred image, whether in the morning, in the course of the day or late in the evening, rarely fail to offer flowers, fruits, incense or coins placing them in the bowl Bhairav holds in his lower right hand.

It may seem strange that it is this fierce image which was selected, many years back, by ROYAL NEPAL AIRLINES as its symbol and insignia, The most likely explanation is precisely, to ward off all malevolent influences. There is still a better ground, according to some, namely the fact that Bhairav (when he is called Akash Bhairav) also represents the "God of the Sky."

AROUND HANUMAN's STATUE

Pursuing your way, still along the same wall which is actually a more recently added part of the Palace, the main entrance door to the Coronation court–yard is now just in front of you. It is a curious narrow door decorated with a series of naively coloured statues of gods, goddesses and mythical animals that leads to it. More interesting however is the huge statue of Hanuman, the "Monkey–God" which stands on a pedestal next to the entrance. This statue was erected by King Pratap MALLA. Like

all other members of his dynasty, he was particularly devoted
to Hanuman who led them to victory in all military undertakings, as the legendary monkey-god HANUMAN had helped Rama
to rescue his wife SITA when she was a prisoner of the demon-
god RAVANA, according to the Hindu epic RAMAYANA.

The statue you are looking at is wrapped in red cloth and the
face of the God is covered with thick layers of red vermilion and
mustard-oil. It may be safely assumed that these layers date
back to the year when the statue was set up in the year 1672,
over three hundred years ago!

On the left side of the statue, there is a low wooden fence.
which protects a slab of engraved stone inserted in the palace's
wall. This has been put there, also by King PRATAP MALLA,
who had the ambition of being recorded, in future history, as a
linguist and a poet. Thus, he ordered a poem to be engraved–on Friday 14th. January 1664–in devotion to goddess
KALIKA. He used not less than 15 differerent languages and
among them, one part of the text is written in *firingi*" which the
King thought to be the common language of all *"foreigners"*,
i. e. all Europeans ! In these two lines, it is easy to decipher
the French words "hiver", written "l'hivert", and "automne",
written "avtomne", and the English or German word "Winter".

TALEJU TEMPLE

—A little further still, the visitor will discover and contemplate, standing on a hillock, the magnificent Royal *"Taleju
Temple"*, dedicated to the Goddess Taleju Bhawani who is very
warmly venerated in Nepal, as another form of Durga. This temple
opens once a year and then only for the Royal Family, on the
Durga-puja Festival which takes place in November–December.

Goddess Taleju was the guardian Goddess of the first Malla
Kings, (14th and 15th centuries). The three golden doors are
oriented towards the West; thus they are brilliantly shining in the
setting sun, a magnificent photo to be taken in the late afternoon.

OTHER SITES

—Returning on your steps, there are three more temples
to look at,

First, the *Kakeshwar-Mahadev*-temple dedicated to Shiva and
erected in 1681, then the twin temples of *Indrapur* and *Krishna*.
On their left side, the well-known image of "Kala Bhairav"
("the Bhairav of Death") a stone-sculpture rather crudely hewn

in a slab of rock, always covered with layers of very bright colours. Bhairav, as already mentioned, is the "terrifying aspect" of SHIVA, when representing the power of destruction; hence the symbols of death which are his main ornaments. This image dates back to the second half of the 17th century. According to the legend, this stone, fully sculptured, was found one day, in a field in the north of the city, by workers who were building a water-pipe from Budanilkantha to the centre of the city.

Just behind Kala Bhairav's statue and slightly to the left, there stands another temple: *Jagannath Mandir,* built in 1563 by King MAHENDRA MALLA. This temple rests on a three-tier platform. A trident and three eyes decorate each of its three doors. These are traditional symbols of MAHADEV, another name of SHIVA. This pagoda is renowned for the erotic sculptures on the wooden struts that sustain the lower roof.

—Opposite Kala Bhairav's image there is another sanctuary still, built in an entirely different architectural style : it is the octogonal *Krishna Temple* built in 1648 by King PRATAP MALLA, to regain some of the prestige he lost in an unsuccessful attempt to conquer Patan. Officially, however, he is supposed to have ordered the construction of this temple in memory of his two queens Rupamati and Rayamati, who both died very young.

—Now the time has come to take another turn upwards the end part of HANUMAN DHOKA Square, walking to the point where the narrow diagonal street starts. Its first segment is called MAKHAN TOLE, the second INDRA CHOWK, the third and last, KAMALACHI. The square separating the first and the second segment is KEL TOLE, the one separating the second and the third, ASAN TOLE.

Before leaving HANUMAN DHOKA, you will note a very original temple : it is the one bult in "gumbhaj" style which dates back to the 16th century : a square building surmounted by a bulbous dome. This is *Kotilingeshwar Mahadev* temple. (Kathmandu possesses another temple of the same style, built by the Rana Prime Minister JUNG BAHADUR RANA, close to the bridge leading to Patan. But that temple is of a much more recent date.)

THE DIAGONAL STREET.

Now we are on Makhan Tole. On the left side, a half-buried statue of GARUDA which in former times, must have stood in front of a now demolished temple.

Once in this narrow street, the visitor can not help feeling that he has suddenly been carried back by 5 or 6 centuries and that he finds himself in some strange Middle-Age town. Here he has to make his discoveries by himself.

However, three buildings may be pointed out for him. They are:

1) On the first square and on its left side stands a temple which does not look like one for it is hardly customary to see a sacred building almost entirely covered with flowery, colourful ceramic tiles. They reveal all too clearly their European origin and peculiar turn-of-the-century style. Another unusual detail is the sanctuary itself : a statue made of plain silver that is located not on the ground-floor as usual, but on the first storey of this strange building. Four fierce looking, jumping dragons guard this temple from all evil influences. This is Akash Bhairav.

2) On the second square, (called "Kel Tole") when coming from Hanuman Dhoka, also on the left side of the street, stand two other dragons. They protect entrance to one of Kathmandu's finest Buddhist Temples : MATSYENDRANATH-THE-WHITE (Seto Matsyendranath). It is built in the typically Nepalese golden-roof pagoda style. All around the main building, prayer-wheels reveal its Buddhist character.

Originally it is said to have been dedicated to LOKESHWAR, the Bodhisattva more often called AVALOKITESHWARA. Its image is kept inside the small sanctuary, behind a gilded door which seals off the inner shrine. On Seto Matsyendranath festival-in December-January-this statue is taken out, bathed and carried around the city in a colourful procession.

In the courtyard's entrance, musicians and singers gather every evening to sing religious Hindu songs for many hours without intermission. Visitors are always welcome there,-or better said, the team does not take the slightest notice, nor interest, in those who come to listen to their performance. They sing for their own enjoyment and by doing so gain religious merit.

3) Between the second and the third square, on the left side again, stands one of the oldest and most beautiful private houses of Kathmandu. On the ground floor, two small doorless shops offer their wares : one is selling onions, chilli, vegetables and spices, while the next sells tobacco-pipes, whole ones or in parts. All along the façade, in particular around the first floor, a series of exquisite woodcarvings depict many small figures and scenes of daily life. They contrast in a very interesting way the erotic and esoteric representations usually found on temples.

ASAN TOLE

The last square, ASAN TOLE is really what may be called a "Nepal in miniature". There are many small shops all around (among others, candle shops), platforms where rice, salt and other commodities of an essential nature are offered for sale. On one side of this square, there is a fruit and vegetable market every morning. In one of the corners, a shop sells nothing but tobacco while another concentrates on molasses or puja articles. On the far end of the square stands one of the finest and most interesting small temples, a two-tiered golden-roofed one, dedicated to God GANESH. This temple attracts not only the devotees but hundreds of pigeons as well which seem to resent the presence of a small gilded bird perched on each tilted roof–edge of the pagoda, looking as it would soon be taking off... but never does !

Another small temple is placed almost in the centre of the square. That one is dedicated to Goddess ANNAPURNA.

Around the temple, men of all age, usually every scantily dressed, are sitting, idle. They are porters waiting for anybody who needs hiring their services. Hence the name of "porter's market", sometimes given to ASAN TOLE.

On this same square, there is still something else, very typically Nepalese, to be mentioned: one of the smallest, albeit most popular shrines to which one of the most complicated but how very characteristic popular legends is attached. It would be difficult not to tell it briefly (if possible !)

First let us show it : This "sanctuary" is to be found on the ground, in the midst of refuse, rotting fruit, small heaps of old paper etc. But your eye will soon focus on a rectangle, usually filled with water. In the centre of this rectangle there is an oblong stone. This is the holy place, for this stone has to be looked at as representation of a fish. Some imagination is needed.

Now to the story behind it :

Once upon a time, the wife of a well–known astrologer named BARAMI was expecting a baby. Of course, the father hoped and prayed for a son. Also was he most eager to be able to calculate immediately the most accurate and complete horoscope of his child. To this effect, he had a bell attached to the bed of his wife and the sound of this bell would tell him the exact minute and second of the birth. The instructions hereto had been given accordingly to the midwife. All his tables and instruments were ready when suddenly he heard the bell ring. It rang once, thus indicating that the baby was a son. His dearest wish and most fervent prayers had been fulfilled ! At once, Barami started to concentrate on his calculations. They took him many hours, for it was essential for him to learn what the stars could tell about his first-born son's future, of course.

Alas, to his great dismay, the computations revealed that this baby, this son, was not his own ! He checked again his figures and diagrams, but the result remained always the same.

Unable to overcome his grief and sorrow, BARAMI abandoned his wife, the child and his home and took refuge at Benares.

The baby grew up (he was given the name of DAK) and, like his father, studied astrology and soon became very famous.

One day, a very important king–some say it was Emperor Ashoka of India in person–called on all renowned astrologers to ask them to calculate the most auspicious day for beginning a pilgrimage. Barami, as well as Dak were present but, of course, they did not know each other. Dak was the first to find the answer and all others had to agree that his conclusions were correct. Barami, among others, was so impressed by the skill of this young man, that he implored him to accept him as his pupil. Dak agreed.

Several months later, in the course of one of their common journeys, they reached Kathmandu, Here, Dak decided to put Barami on a test. He asked him to reply, as fast as possible, to the following three questions :

— Which is the next auspicious day
— What would fall from the sky
— Where would that celestial object touch ground.

Barami gave a correct answer to the first queston, mentioned that a fish would fall from the sky and foretold that this fish would drop on the place where Asan Tole stands to-day. Barami even calculated that the place the fish would fall would be twelve arms length from the corner of the Annapurna temple.

Dak pointed out that there was an error in his calculations and added that he was certain that the fish would drop on the ground much closer to the temple.

On the specified day, both Barami and Dak met at Asan and, of course it was Dak's prediction that proved right.

He ventured to suggest Barami that his error may have been due to the fact that he had not taken into account the strength and direction of the prevailing wind.

Barami had to agree But Dak's remark gave him more food for thought : "What if a similar minor error, so he said to himself, crept in my former computations, for instance the ones which I had made to learn about my son's personality and future ?"

After some hesitation, Barami opened his mind to Dak about this. Immediately Dak asked him, whether, on that previous occasion, he had not failed to take into consideration the time which had elapsed between the ringing of the bell by the midwife and the moment the sound of the bell reached his ears. ?

Startled and confused Barami decided to make his calculations all over again. As was to be guessed, the result was now a completely different one. He rushed to the house where he used to live years back and whom did he find there ? His good wife chatting gaily with Dak ! One may well imagine the pride of Barami when he found out that the most brilliant of all astrologers of the country was his own son, his first-born son whom he had so foolishly refused to recognize !

There is a typically Asian appendix to this legend : Who had now to pay homage to whom ? Barami, the father, to his year–long "Guru" whom he now had found out to be his son, or Dak to his father as every son is supposed to do ?

Priests and pandits were consulted on this tricky issue and they found a Salomonic solution : "Since the ties which linked Barami and Dak were as strong as they were strange, only a common action could commemorate the extraordinary fact of a father having become his son's pupil !"Thus, it was decided that they should start carving a stone so as to give it the shape of a fish and place it exactly on the spot where it had fallen from the skies. This was done and it explains the importance of that apparently so insignificant "sanctuary" located in the middle of busy Asan Tole !

Whatever streets and lanes you choose, it would be most surprising if, at a certain corner, you would not find yourself facing an extraordinary lump of wood sticking out of the wall and literally covered with thousands of iron-nails of all sizes and shapes. About this item, see next chapter.

OTHER MONUMENTS OF INTEREST

Many more spectacular buildings have to be mentioned :
The new ROYAL PLACE for instance. It is called Narayanhity Durbar and is located at the northern end of Durbar Marg. It was built on a piece of land where an older Palace was standing before. The new one was inaugurated on the occasion of the then Crown Prince, now King BIRENDRA's wedding, in February 1970.

The SINGHA DURBAR, the former residence of Chandra Shumsher and subsequent Rana Prime Ministers, was used from 1750 as the Central Secretariat where all Government departments and services were installed. It was almost completely destroyed by a fire which broke out during the night of 3rd July 1973. Only the main façade could be saved. But it is being restored and rebuilt.

The BHIMSEN TOWER, also called "Dharahara" which is located near the Central Post Office. It looks like a minaret but this resemblance is purely casual for it is not a religious Muslim building at all : The Dharahara was built by Prime Minister BHIMSEN THAPA in 1830 to serve as a watch-tower.

A TREASURE HUNT THROUGH KATHMANDU'S HIDDEN LANES (See map on page 270)

For visitors who have a few hours to spare (two are enough), or who would like to break away from programmed sightseeing tours, here is an itinerary for a walk which will take them to some of the best among the innumerable art treasures scattered on the streets, squares and backyards of this amazing city.

We shall assume that you are already familiar with the Durbar Square where you may have admired the Old Royal Palace, the Coronation Courtyard, the red-faced monkey-god Hanuman Statue and the two-storied "SHIVA-PARVATI TEMPLE with the divine couple cosily leaning out of one of its upper, central windows.

Let this temple be the starting point of your walk. You will easily find it on the enclosed map. Follow the arrows.

1. Turn right into a street called Yetakha (or Yatka) Tole. After a while you will see on your left a signboard reading HIMAL HIKER'S Home, (A) and an old carved wooden balcony on your right, Turn left and enter the courtyard of YATKA BAHAL (B). Behind the stupa in its centre, you will spot four magnificent "salabhanjika" wood-carved struts with lovely figures of tree-nymphs gracing an ancient house. They are among the very few fourteenth century struts preserved in the Valley. One of the four is the only one in Kathmandu showing such a fairy holding a baby in her arms ! The only other struts in Kathmandu dating from before the sixteenth century, very beautiful ones too, though smaller and less well preserved, are those inside the Yitum Bhal, nearby.

2. To reach YITUM BAHAL (C), turn right from Yatka Tole and soon, after the street swings a little to the left, a sharp turn to the left leads to a huge rectangular courtyard filled with

many votive "chaityas", pipal trees and children. On the left side, guarded by two lions, you will find the doorway to Yitum Bahal proper. Before entering, have a look at the remarkable sixteenth century "torana" (tympanum), illustrating a famous episode in the life of Gautama Buddha, when, while seeking enlightenment under a pipal tree in the gardens of Bodh Gaya, he was tempted by the demon Mara (later called the "god of desire."), and his alluring daughters. On this torana, Buddha is seen quietly touching the earth with his right hand-palm inside-calling it to witness that he had not let himself be distracted from his purpose.

Step inside and on your left you will see a graceful chaitya decorated with figures of four standing Buddhas (they are usually in a sitting position!) displaying a traditional hand posture ("mudra") on each of its four sides. On the right hand side of this fourteenth century monastic compound, you will notice on the second floor two metal plates and, in the far corner, a strange and huge wooden mask with protruding eyeballs. These tablets record a popular old legend about an ogre called Guru Mapa, who used to feed on bad (later also on good) children, but who was persuaded to change his "diet" when offered a generous buffalo-meat feast once a year. Nepali parents still use Guru Mapa as bogeyman when ordinary disciplinary measures fail.

Before leaving Yitum Bahal, look up at the struts over the entrance. The one on the far left and the two on the right date from the same period as those you saw at Yatka Bahal. Note the hunched dwarfs supporting the graceful, slender nymphs.

3. Leaving Yitum Bahal, turn left and continue along the left side of the huge courtyard until you reach a little passage leading out into the street. Here you turn right and you are in Kilagal Tole (D), a quaint, picturesque little square. Explore it for a while and you will be rewarded by discovering some informal aspects of Kathmandu's daily life. Past Kilagal, continue straight and when you come to a crossroad, turn left and follow the small street leading to Bhangemuda square. While coming onto this busy spot notice on your right, at shoulder level, a mass of nails driven directly or through a coin into a big lump of dark wood. In the centre of this strange looking object there is a tiny, three-inch high golden image of a deity, embedded in the wood. This is VAISHYA DEO, the "toothache god" (E). Indeed, according to an ancient belief, pounding a nail into this wood is sure

to cure one's toothache. A more refined interpretation is that, whenever a close relative passed away, a nail driven in here will clinch any evil spirit barring it from following the deceased's soul.

4. The small Narayan Temple standing in this square, dates from the sixteenth century. The main attraction here is on the northern side of the square : the sixth century two-feet high BUDDHA(F) carved in a slab of black stone and executed in the classical Gupta style. This is indeed one of the most beautiful and oldest statues in the whole country. It is also iconographically important since Gupta-period works of art are not many in Nepal. It stands awkwardly in the ground right in front of – almost leaning against – the wooden door of a private house, Except for a slight wear caused by worshipping hands it has been preserved intact for over fourteen hundred years.

5. Following the same streeet, always in a northern direction, you will soon see on your right, in a brick-lined inset in the wall, a lovely ninth-century stone relief of SHIVA AND PARVATI (G) in the classical UMA–MAHESHVARA posture, enthroned on Mount Kailash with Nandi the bull and deities in the background.

6. A few steps past Uma-Maheshvara, turn left into a small alley guarded by a pair of mythical lions seated on high stone pillars with yellow jars placed in two niches, This alley leads to KATHESIMBHU (also called Shigha Bahal or Ghata Vihara), easy to identify by the impressive, sixteenth century stupa in the centre. This stupa is supposed to be a replica of the one built on Swayambhu hill outside the city. According to general belief, this stupa was erected for those for whom the road and the steep steps and slopes leading to Swayambhu were too strenuous. Performing their devotional rite and acts at Kathesimbhu would bring them the same merits. Thus the name *Kathesimbu,* a contraction of *Kathmandu* and *Swayambhu.* Located approximately at the place marked (H) on the map, there stands a maginificent, large, eighth century AVALOKITESHVARA PADMAPANI statue. According to the iconographic tradition, a Bodhisattva who, though enlightened, refuses to enter nirvana in order to help others to acquire Supreme Knowledge too – usually lowers his eyes gazing down to earth in compassion. He holds a lotus flower in his left hand, while his right is extended down, palm outward in a boon-giving gesture. The centre of his crown bears the image of his spiritual parent, Buddha Amitabha.

7. Step out back into the street, turn left and continue north

until you reach Thaity Tole, a square with a smallish fifteenth century stupa near its centre. Turn right and enter the first street to your right, called Teudha Tole. There is a short - cut that by-passes Thaity Tole as marked on the map. Both join on a small square decorated by a sort of canopy, guarded at each of its four corners, by a bronze monkey. Just opposite this curious structure, don't miss a narrow passage on your left. It leads into a courtyard called Chha Bahal, which is picturesque and typical. The temple on its right side is worth looking at. It is called Ratna Ketha Mahavira by some, Cigal Mandir by others. Note the wall-paintings on the upper part. They represent two of the four fierce-looking temple guardians that are to be found on all lamaist temples and gompas. The Buddha statues and figures, as well as the prayer wheels reveal its appurtenance.

The narrow passage at the far end of Chha Bahal leads to two other, very similar courtyards. There is nothing very spectacular to see there. We would rather recommend to come back to the same street (Teudha Tole) and then turn right. A short distance from here you will see, on your left side, a recess. There stand three chaityas, a very old stone trough and a very modern water tap. At this point turn left into another narrow passage. It will lead you into a courtyard called DVAKA BAHAL (I), a name familiar to anyone in these parts. There you will find a chaitya. Its pedestal has four niches. Two of them shelter seventh-century Bodhisattva statues: a Padmapani and a Vajrapani. Although small, these sculptures are also among the most precious extant examples of Licchavi-period Nepali art (5th. to 8th. century A.D.)

Now your "treasure hunt" is nearing its end. Cross this courtyard. Its exit leads to a street called Jyatha Tole which you follow in a northern direction again, i. e. you turn left. A few hundred yards further on you will come to a road crossing where you have to turn right. Soon you will see, on your right hand side, the very richly decorated, though not so well preserved doorway of CHUSYA BAHAL (J), one of the oldest "viharas" (celibate Buddhist monasteries) in Kathmandu. Its entrance is guarded, as usual, by two big white mythical lions.

After another three minutes' walk along the street, passing Koh-i-Noor and Siddharta Hotels you will reach Kantipath, one of Kathmandu's main arteries with which you may have become familiar by now. On your left there is Hotel Nook, on your right, Third-Eye Tours and Air India, and, in front, across the street,

Hotel Yellow Pagoda.

Let us hope that you will have found this walk along the lanes and into the courtyards of Kathmandu rewarding, and the city's reputation as a living museum of art well deserved.

SWAYAMBHU (*)   (See map on page 272)

At approximately 4 miles (6.5 km.) west of the centre of Kathmandu, on top of a hill which can be seen from any point of the Valley, lies the famous SWAYAMBHU sanctuary, the oldest "*stupa*" of the country and one of the oldest in the world. Its foundation is said to have been laid over 2,000 years ago, i. e. shortly after BUDDHA'S birth. SWAYAMBHU is a very holy pilgrimage for Buddhists and Hindus alike.

There are various roads leading to this temple : it can be reached on foot, which implies ascending no less then 365 steep steps or by a winding road which ends half-way up the hill. Of course, climbing up the steps means gaining valuable merits for the devout. Besides, while taking this arduous way, you will see many interesting statues, mostly of animals which are the traditional "vehicles" or "mounts" of the "Dhyani Buddhas" the statues that are placed in niches all around the main stupa. (See their location as well other details about them, on the map.)

On the platform that tops the hill, a recently built monastery can be visited. It belongs to the "nyingma-pa", i. e. the non-reformed Lamaist order, also called the "red-hat" school or sect. Usually its monks perform their rituals in the early morning and again, in mid-afternoon. Visitors are welcome and may even use tape-recorders and flashlights, but should leave their shoes outside.

On the east side of Swayambhu hill, above the flight of steps on which monkeys love frolicking stands a gigantic gilded and somewhat damaged "*r'dorje*" ("*vcjra*", in sanskrit, an object that is commonly called '*,thunderbolt*", although its shape reminds more of a double crown) This object rests on a pedestal which bears, on its base, the twelve animals of the Tibetan calendar.

(More about this ritual object will be found in the chapter "The five lamaist gompas of Bodnath".)

(*) For photo—amateurs : To take good pictures of Swayambhunath, it is advisable to visit this place in the afternoon. Not only the monument itself is in a good light but the view over the whole Valley and the mountains in the background is extremely beautiful, especially in winter.

Swayambhu's stupa is surrounded by many sanctuaries and "chaityas", conical shaped stone structures which always show on each of its four sides, a "dhyani"-Buddha in his traditional posture.

Shelters for pilgrims and small shops add to the picturesque aspect of this sacred place. Monkeys of the rhesus family roam and gambol around freely. Occasionally they snatch things away from careless visitors or pick up and eat grains from the offering places.

On each side of the vajra stands a small temple : they are dedicated to Anantapura (on the left side) and to Pratapura (on the right side) respectively.

It is compulsory to circumambulate always clockwise around any Buddhist shrine, sanctuary, stupa or temple. Thus starting from the top of the staircase and turning to the left, the visitor discovers, just behind the Anantapura temple, a small construction which symbolizes one of the five elements, namely "earth". In the next corner, the second sanctuary symbolizes "air". Turning the right, there is a large veranda-like building which serves as a rest-house for pilgrims. This is on the left hand side whereas on the right, two pillars support magnificent "Tara" statues in bronze and, in between, another pillar carries a peacock, a sacred bird.

From this point, the attention is attracted by the crowd that gathers in front of a small temple in front of which a priest usually performs complicated rituals. This temple is one of the most popular sanctuaries of the Valley : it is dedicated to AJIMA, the "goddess-protecting-against-small-pox". She is a deity of the Newar Pantheon but is equally venerated by non-Newars. In AJI-MA, Buddhists see a representation of Gautama's mother, Maya.

Before leaving Swayambhu the visitor should spend a few minutes to contemplate the few but beautiful samples of Nepalese stone sculpture which are to be seen in the Museum located on top of the flight of steps leading to the car parking place.

At the bottom of the hill, there is a small cluster of modest houses which are favourite hippie's gathering and dwelling places in the years 1966–1973. No wonder, these youngsters liked this place where everybody, even without resorting to drugs, feels carried "out of time and out of space".

Second Half Day : PASHUPATINATH and BODNATH

PASHUPATINATH (*)

This "golden roofed temple" is located on the right bank of the holy river Bagmati, a tributary of the Ganges, which explains why cremations of Hindus take place here. The ashes are scattered in the river and will eventually reach the "Mother of all rivers".

This explains why PASHUPATINATH is one of the most venerated places of pilgrimage for all Hindus. King Bhupalsingh MALLA who had it built in 1694 dedicated the temple to Lord SHIVA in his capacity as "Pashupati", i. e. the "Lord protector of animals".

Non-Hindus are not allowed inside the temple's courtyard but, having crossed the narrow bridge, may climb up the steps leading to a terrace from where the view is superb.

PASHUPATINATH is also a real museum of art :

At the far end of the cremation bank, on the right side before reaching the entrance door of the next temple, a magnificent bust of Buddha hewn in a stone slab dating back to the 7th century A. D., sticks out of the ground.

On the terrace too, there are some master-pieces of Nepalese stone sculpture, in particular an admirable Shiva head carved on a "lingam" that stands on a cylindric masonry This head is one of the purest works of art of the whole valley and it is perfectly preserved although it must be at least 13 centuries old.

Across the river, there are several small doors fixed to the rock; they lead to cabins where hermits live in meditation.

BODNATH (or Boudha) (*)   (see map page)

About 5 miles (8 km.) from the centre of Kathmandu stands one of the most extraordinary monuments, the famous "stupa"

Note for photo amateurs: The best time for taking pictures of Pashupatinath temple and its golden roof glittering in the sun is in the eaely hours of the morning Besides, it is also the time when most devotees take their ritual baths. As far as cremations are concerned, there is on fixed nor even a customary hour of the day.

(*) *NOTE for photo-amateurs:* Since the four sides of the Bodnath stupa are absolutely identical, any time of the day *is* "auspicious" for taking good pictures of this fascinating monument. But refrain from taking your first poto while you are still standing in the passage coming from the main road, for you would inevitabiy have several electric wires accross your snapshot, and across Buddha's face. Therefore, turn to the left once you have stepped out of the narrow passage: at a distance of about

of Bodnath, a landmark for the whole valley, one of the oldest Lamaist shrines around which an authentic Tibetan Village has sprung up in the course of past centuries.

A few hundred yards before reaching BODNATH, the road passes by another, possibly still older stupa of similar style, called the *"Chabahil"*; there are many "chaityas" of the Licchavi period as well as a magnificent Buddha Statue. At the Bodnath stupa, visitors will seldom fail to be truly fascinated by the cold but penetrating glance that the "everlasting, all-embracing" Buddha casts in all four directions. The sign painted between and slightly above the two eyes is, of course the "Third Eye", which is able to *"see beyond and inside"*. Just below, the question-mark-like design is not meant to represent a nose, but the number "one" in the Devanagari script, thus symbolizing the *"oneness"* of BUDDHA, or according to another interpretation a remainder that here is but *ONE* way to bliss and salvation, i.e. to follow the rules of conduct laid down by Siddhartha Gautam twenty–five hundred years ago.

Also note that there are neither lips nor mouth since the divine Buddha is content to see everything but has not to speak to his followers for all he had to say is included in his teachings. There are no ears either, for Buddha is not supposed–originally, at least–to be a God to whom prayers should be addressed.

The base of the shrine is in the shape of a *"mandala"*, a geometrical and cosmogonic representation of the universe, at the same time as it is a tool for meditation. In a Stupa, the cubic base symbolizes the earth. The white-washed mound of the stupa symbolizes another element, namely water (does not a drop of water on a smooth surface take the shape of a half-sphere ?) The central tower represents fire, the crescent above: air and finally, the flame on top : ether.

As for the thirteen steps between the mound and the pinacle, they represent the thirteen stages one has to go through before attaining perfect knowledge, i.e. enlightenment which is called *"bodhi"*, hence the name Bodnath. (The Swayambhu stupa is slightly different : instead of thirteen steps, there are thirteen concentric crircles around the spire.)

As already mentioned briefly elsewhere, any Buddhist shrine,

---

12 yards, there is a doorway on your left from where a picture cf the spire may be taken free from electric wires in between. There are not many of such privileged spots in Bodnath.

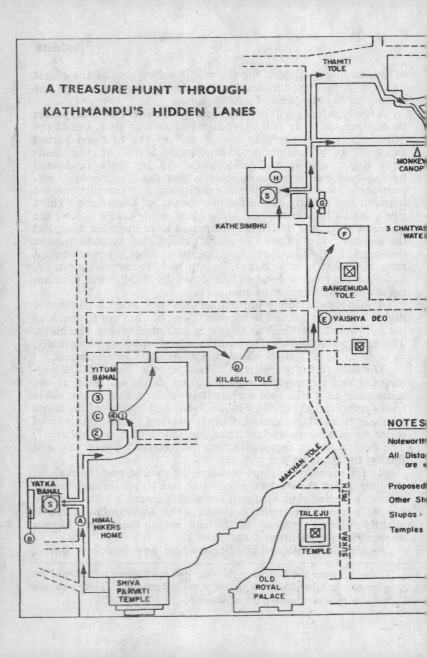

A TREASURE HUNT THROUGH
KATHMANDU'S HIDDEN LANES

THAHITI
TOLE

MONKEY
CANOPY

H

S

KATHESIMBHU

G

F

3 CHAITYAS
WATER

BANGEMUDA
TOLE

E VAISHYA DEO

D

KILAGAL TOLE

YITUM
BAHAL

3

C 4 1

2

NOTES

Noteworth

All Dista
are

Proposed

Other St

Stupas :

Temples

MAKHAN TOLE

YATKA
BAHAL

S

A HIMAL
HIKERS
HOME

B

SUKRA
PATH

TALEJU
TEMPLE

SHIVA
PARVATI
TEMPLE

OLD
ROYAL
PALACE

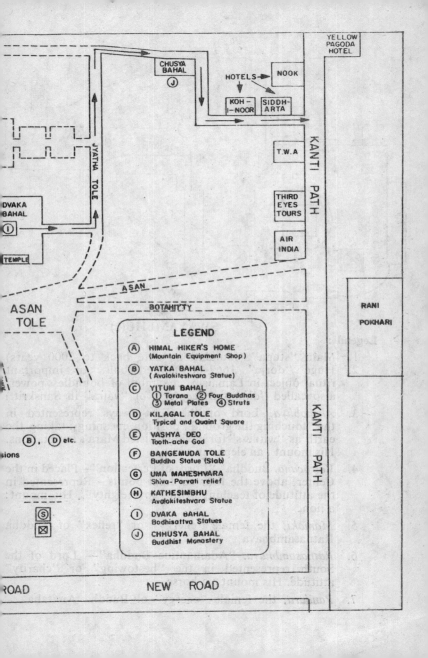

YELLOW PAGODA HOTEL

CHUSYA BAHAL ⓙ

HOTELS → NOOK

KOH-I-NOOR   SIDDH-ARTA

T.W.A

JYATHA TOLE

KANTI PATH

THIRD EYES TOURS

DVAKA BAHAL ⓘ

AIR INDIA

TEMPLE

ASAN

ASAN TOLE

BOTAHITTY

RANI POKHARI

ⓑ, ⓓ etc.

sions

KANTI PATH

ⓢ
⊠

LEGEND

- Ⓐ **HIMAL HIKER'S HOME**
  (Mountain Equipment Shop)
- Ⓑ **YATKA BAHAL**
  (Avalokiteshvara Statue)
- Ⓒ **YITUM BAHAL**
  ① Torana ② Four Buddhas
  ③ Metal Plates ④ Struts
- Ⓓ **KILAGAL TOLE**
  Typical and Quaint Square
- Ⓔ **VASHYA DEO**
  Tooth-ache God
- Ⓕ **BANGEMUDA TOLE**
  Buddha Statue (Slab)
- Ⓖ **UMA MAHESHVARA**
  Shiva-Parvati relief
- Ⓗ **KATHESIMBHU**
  Avalokiteshvara Statue
- Ⓘ **DVAKA BAHAL**
  Bodhisattva Statues
- Ⓙ **CHHUSYA BAHAL**
  Buddhist Monastery

NEW ROAD

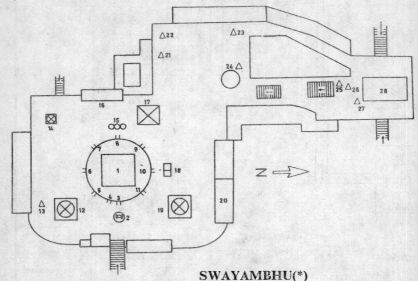

SWAYAMBHU(*)

Legend :

1. Main "stupa" (foundations date back to 2000 years)
2. Huge "dorje" 1667–68 (thunderbolt, an important ritual object in Lamaism, a symbol of boundless power, also called "diamond scepter", or "vajra" in Sanskrit.)
3. *Akshobhya,* Lord of the East-always represented in the "touching the ground" position, meaning : taking the earth as "witness" for having resisted Mara's temptations. His mount : an elephant.
4. *Vairocana.* Buddha "Lord of Perfection"—Placed in the Center, above the four cardinal points - Represented in the attitude of teaching or of "sovereignty". His mount: a lion.
5. *Mamaki,* the female "energy" or "reflex" of Buddha Ratnasambhava
6. *Ratnasambhava.* "Adamantine Buddha"— Lord of the South represented in the "bestowing" or "charity" attitude. His mount : a horse
7. *Pandara,* the female "energy" of Buddha Amitaba.

8. *Amitaba,* Buddha "Boundless Light", Lord of the West, represented in the meditative attitude. His mount : a peacock.

9. *Tara,* the female "energy", of Buddha Amoghasiddhi.

10. *Amoghasiddhi,* the Buddha "Boundless triumph," Lord of the North, represented in the "blessing" or "protecting" attitude. His mount : a garuda.

11. *Locana,* the female "energy", of Buddha Akshobhya.

12. *Anantapura Sanctuary,* built around 1646.

13. *Vasupura,* symbolizing the first "element": earth

14. *Vayupura,* symbolizing the second "element" : air

15. Two pillars supporting a white and a green *"Tara"* as well as a third pillar with the sacred peacock on top.

16. A Buddhist-Lamaist temple (*'Gompa'*) serving also as a shelter for pilgrims.

17. A two-tier temple dedicated to *Hariti,* the she-devil who is said to have been feeding on children, but later reformed and became the "protector" of children. This deity, under the Newar name of AJIMA, is venerated as preventing (or curing) small-pox.

18. *Nagapura,* symbolizing the third "element": water

19. *Pratapura* temple,— erected in 1646

20. Another Lamaist *"gompa"* temple-monastery, called Mahayana Bhikhu Sanggha Karmaraj Mahavir

21 and 22: Statues of *"Buddha the Luminous",* also called Dipamkara Buddha, consideredas the ninth predecessor of Sakya Muni, the historical Buddha.

23. *Agnipura,* symbolizing the fourth "element" : fire

24. Stone slab bearing the oldest inscriptions found so far at Swayambhunath (dated 1372 A.D.).

25. Statue of *Sadaksheri,* a representation of Avalokiteshwara with four arms.

26. Statue of *Akshobya* (see under No. 3)

27. Statues of Buddha *"Dipamkara"* (dating from around 1000 A.D.).

28. *Shantipura,* symbolizing the fifth "element": the sky, or ether

(*) "The self born"

temple or sanctuary has to be circumambulated "clock-wise"; walking the other way round would be considered as most disrespectful. According to certain scholars – or to a legend – this rule finds its origin in the fact that, even during Gautama's lifetime, his disciples always wore robes that left their right arm and shoulder bare. Now, when they gathered to listen to Buddha's lectures and sermons, they first went around their Teacher, presenting Him–as a gesture of respect and subservience–their *bare* right arm, a gesture which is not dissimilar in its deeper and symbolic meaning with the present-day custom of lifting one's hat, thus, exposing a most vulnerable part of the body to the person to whom submission is to be manifested. Finally, still another explanation refers to the gyratory movement of the planets around the sun.

In ancient times, stupas were built as cenotaphs to contain and preserve holy relics, be it a tooth or even a hair of Lord Buddha himself or of some venerated lama or mystic. Therefore a stupa is never a hollow building and the question whether it is possible – or permitted – to step inside does not arise.

Once you have walked half-way around, you will find a sort of sanctuary and a door giving access to the flight of steps leading to the upper platforms. These are open to the public.

All around the stupa, there are numerous souvenir shops where, from time to time, some rare, even ancient and valuable objects are to be found. All these houses and nearly all the shops are owned by Tibetans. Some have installed their workshops in the ground-floor, mainly silversmiths who manufacture copies of ritual and decorative typical objects. It goes without saying that the ever growing number of tourists is driving prices up each year by a considerable percentage !

THE FIVE LAMAIST GONPAS

These is much more to see in Bodnath than the stupa in the centre and the shops around !

Now that Tibet is closed to pilgrims as well as to the practice of Lamaism–or any other form of Buddhism for that matter–Bodnath has become a pilgrimage centre almost as important as BODH GAYA (in India, where Buddha reached Enlightenment), SARNATH (near Benaras, where Buddha delivered his first sermon), or DHARAMSALA, (northwest of Delhi where the Dalai Lama retired and which is now the spiritual centre of all Tibetans in exile).

In Bodnath, various religious communities have settled down,

long before the Chinese occupation of Tibet, They seem to be
thriving well and no obstacle prevents their religious activities.
Thus, these communities offer the visitor an authentic image of
monastic life and rites, performed by Tibetan "lamas" (there are
only a few Nepalese monks among them). They are clad in dark
red and should not be called "bonzes", for these belong to another Buddhist school, the "Hinayana", and are usually clad in
yellow robes. They live in Sri Lanka, Burma, Thailand and Japan.

Bodnath's "lamas" live in or near their respective "gonpas"
(tib. for monastery). Each of the main "Mahayana" (also called
here "Vajrayana ") school has built its own, (see below.)

Some information and notes common to all gonpas:
Ritual objets :

Once a monk reaches a given rank in the hierarchy of his
community, he is given the privilege of holding in his hands
two most sacred instruments, namely: in his right, the
"r-dorje" ("vajra" in sanskrit) and, in his left, the "bell"
("ril-bu" in tib. and" gantha" in sanskr.) Both instruments
are made of bronze. The "r-dorje" looks like two opposed crowns.
Its usual name is "thunderbolt "but, in fact, it means" diamond".
Indeed, the r-dorje is above all a symbol of "power". Thus calling "adamantine" was appropriate, since diamonds were regarded as made of an indestructible matter and therefore, able to destroy any other substance. In the Tantric interpretation, it represents the male symbol, whereas the bell represents the female.

Another ritual object always present in gonpas is the holy
silver water jug. Its tap is usually decorated with two or three
peacock feathers sticking out., (In Buddhism as well as in Hinduism, the peacock is considered as a very sacred animal: it is believed that its feathers, when crushed into powder and smoked
in a pipe, renders innocuous the effect of any snake poison! Also,
to swing peacock feathers over the body of of a sick person,
chases away those evil spirits that have caused illness etc...)

In all gonpas, a certain number of other objects are also
usually to be found :

– large and small-size *"oil–lamp,"* which are used for
burning wicks dipped in clarified butter ("ghee")

– *heaps of rice* maintained in conical shape by three
concentric rings. Usually, a jewel ornates the top. Devotees
leave coins or stick incense in the rice-mound.

– *round "mirrors"* which are used by monks to help them

concentrate in meditation. Their decoration-often nothing but tiny circles–on the mirrors represent symbolically the main points and lines traditionally found on "mandalas".

 – *cups and chalices* of various shapes, sometimes kept in showcases together with

 – *elaborate "tormas"*, i.e. pointed conical "cakes" made of dough and coloured butter. They are supposed to be "food" offered to deities, in certain rites symbolizing the latter themselves.

Musical instruments.

As a rule, religious rites celebrated in a "gonpa" always include the use of some or all of eight traditional Tibetan musical instruments. They are not used with the view of an "artistic" performance, like an orchestra (or a church-organ, for that matter) of the Western World, but to underline and accentuate given passages of prayers, or the reading of sacred books.

The instrument are listed hereunder in the "hierarchical" order. (It has to be noted indeed that not *any* monk is entitled to play *any* given instrument. There is a definite correlation between the monk's rank and the instrument he will be allotted.)

On top of the ladder, we find the
 – *large cymbals* ("bugcham", in tib.)- they are the most difficult to handle and to play correctly. Indeed, the variety of sounds they can produce in the hands of an expert cymbalist is surprisingly wide: from the most acute, strident and metallic clashes down to the most subtle, quavering trill. Next comes the
 – *oboe or flageolet* ("gye-ling" in tib.) a very beautiful instrument, for it is mostly made of silver with inlaid precious stones or golden decorative motives. The oboe too, can be played in manifold ways.
 – *the long telescopic trumpets,* ("ra-dung" in tib.) do not yield much modulating possibilities. Normally they produce either a very bass or then a shrill note. It is difficult to play correctly and it requires powerful lungs !

 – *the small a two-faced "damaru"drums* ("nga-chung" in tib.)
 – *the trumpets made of a human thigh-bone* "(kang-ling" in tib.)
 – *the conch*
 – *the small cymbals* "sil-nyam" in tib.)
 – and, at last, *the big standing or hanging "gong"* ("cho-nga" in tib.) which is usually standing on a wood-carved "leg" or hanging on a "U-shaped" This instrument is normally entrusted to low-rank monks or even young novices.

Wall paintings that are to be seen at the entrance of any "gonpa".

1) First of all, *the four temple "guardians"*. They are tall, sometimes gigantic figures, usually two on each side of the main door leading inside the "lha-kang", the main assembly-hall.

Two are smiling, the other two fierce-looking. The former are supposed to invite with kindness all those who want to offer prayers, "ka-ta"s (white honorific scarves) or oblations, the latter ones to ward off any malevolent spirit or person.
– The smiling ones :

Towards the North, the yellow faced Kuvera ("Namtosa" in tib.), often called "god of wealth". In his right hand he holds a banner while his left rests on his lap. nestling a mangoose-like animal that ejects coloured "marbles" out of its mouth : these are supposed to be jewels.
Towards the East, normally white-faced, we have Dhritara-shtra ("Yulkor-rung" in tib.) His more popular name is "King of the Gandharvas". the name of beings that feed themselves on incense exclusively! He always holds a guitar-like musical instrument.
– The fierce-looking ones :

Towards the South, the green-faced Virudhaka ("Pha-kyepo" in tib.), also called "King of the Khumbandas" the giant-demons. He is always represented pulling his sword out ot its sheath.

Towards the West, Virupaksha ("Jami-zang " in tib.) is easy to identify by his red face. He is sometimes called "King of the Nagas". On his knee rests either a small "chorten" or a basketful of "jewels".

2) The "Wheel of Life".

This is one of the most complex, albeit popular images of Tibetan gonpa-decorations. In short, here its description and most common interpretation. :
In Tibetan, this "wheel" is called "Kor-lo". Above all, it symbolizes the endless cycle of reincarnations. It is held in the claws and the fangs of a three-eyed demon. By this, the artist intends to illustrate and remind how repulsive it is to stick to... life ! It is well known that in the Buddhist concept, life is merely illusory, something one should be eager to leave behind once and for all, without delay nor regrets.

Somewhere in a corner of the painting, be it on the right or on the left, there is Buddha, always standing erect, *outside* the wheel, for *he* succeeded in "freeing" himself from the circle of re-births, since he reached Enlightenment and since, some years later, he "dissolved himself" in the All, reaching Nirvana.

In the centre of the image, there is a circle which contains three animals holding one another by "mouth-and-tail", symbolizing that the three "fundamental vices" they represent, are tied one to the other and can not be separated. The three animals are : the red rooster, symbol of lust, the green snake representing hatred and the black boar that stands for ignorance.

Around this central circle, there is a ring divided in two halves : one has a white background and shows human beings led upwards by a celestial guide; the other half has a dark background and another chain of human beings, the "doomed" ones; to resisting being dragged downwards by a hellish conductor.

Now come the six main divisions of the wheel : they represent the six worlds in which a human being may be reincarnated.

But before describing them one by one, attention has to be drawn on the central part of the lowest compartment:

Here, you will easily spot the "judge". A peculiar judge however, since he does not decide upon rewards or punishments. He merely holds a mirror– usually in his left hand. This mirror is the real and only "judge".   For it will reflect all the deceased's "thoughts, words and deeds" of his whole life on earth ! In front of the "judge" (who is, in fact, "YAMA", the "god of the realm of the dead") there stands a curious being, half bird, half man. He holds a scale. White balls – symbols of the "good" thoughts–words–deeds –and black ones, symbols of the "bad" ones, accumulate on the two scale-pans. The algebric result of the deceased's "karma" – the name given to the relationship between cause and effect –will raise or drop either the "good" or the "bad" scale-pan and, thus, decide in which of the six worlds, the deceased will be reincarnated.

Now which are these six worlds ?:

– At the bottom: *hell :* or, better said, "hells" in plural, for, in fact, there are at least two : the "hot" one, where the docmed are plunged in cauldrons filled to the rim with boiling oil and the "icy" one, were naked sinners are shivering in oceans of ice or impaled on ice–pinnacles.

– A little above these hells, there is the world of the *"pretas"* a typical Tibetan creation: "pretas" are the "eternal greedy ones," those who, during their earthly existence, have always been the slaves of their desires and ambitions. Now they are doomed to

suffer from hunger and thurst without being able to quench either.
Their belly is monstruously swollen, thus preventing them from
standing upright : they have to crawl on the ground.   Their belly
craves for food and drink but their throat is so narrow that it does
not let anything pass through it. And if by accident, some food or
drink penetrates into their stomach, it will at once trigger-off
spears of steel or flames !
   – The last of the inferior worlds is the that of *animals*.
It is represented in a rather pleasant, idyllic, pastoral way :
All animals, whether tame, wild or mythical seem to live in
peace and harmony.
   – Now comes the *"world of men"* the one everybody has
lived in. Here are familiar scenes of everyday life in towns or
villages, the labourer and cattleherd, the weaver and the black-
smith. Somewhere in a corner stands Buddha to remind all hu-
mans of the "path" his teaching shows them to reach eternal bliss.
   – Above the world of the human beings, there is the *"World
of the Titans"*– also called the *semi-gods* and, in Tibetan, the non-
gods ("lha-mayin"). Originally, "titan" was the word used for
those "gods" who, like Satan, had to be expelled from heaven.
Now, they are shown as warriors waging a war against the gods,
trying, in vain, to conquer the "tree of knowledge" which
separates the World of the Titans from the next one:
   – The *"World of the gods"*, where everything looks beautiful,
and serene. Now, it should be kept in mind that as Lamaists see it,
there is merely a difference of degree and not of kind between
human beings and "gods" for gods lead a life very similar to the
one of men and they too, have to be watchful not to "spend" the
merits which led them to the world of the gods, for, they too,
may be "downgraded" !

   A last word about this concept of worlds of reincarnation :
In the concept of Tibetan and Lamaist philosophy, neither the
rewards nor the punishments are meant to be for "eternity". As
long as the "beings " find themselves inside the Wheel of Life,
there is always a way by which they may ultimately be delivered
and reach enlightenment and nirvana, although they may have
to go through many re-births.

   Now remain to be explained the series of the small images
on the wheel's outer ring : at first glance, they may be looked upon
as simple scenes of "daily life" : birth, happy encounters, a couple
sipping a cup of tea, travelling by boat, ultimate death. But

here too, there is one or several hidden meanings as is the case with almost all expressions of Tibetan iconography. Many subtle and complex interpretations have been given by scholars.

Taken clockwise, one of the simple and most commonly adopted interpretation is the following :

– On top : *an old blind woman* walking with the help of a stick : she represents primordial ignorance. Ignorance creates elementary impulsions.

– *the potter* illustrates them, for his hands are the most important means of getting to "feel" the outside world. (Another interpretation is that, like the potter who decides what shape his jar will take, so any human being is the "sole master of his own fate").

– *the monkey picking up a fruit :* to taste good and bad, another "elementary impulsion" that creates consciousness.

– *two men in a rowing boat* (sometimes the artists add one or two more !) they symbolize the fact that "consciousness creates sense of individuality," also that of separation, difference, etc... Thus, it is tempting to see in this image the illustration of a world-widely known saying : "two men in one boat can only proceed in one direction", meaning that everything which, in a human being is "differentiated" and in opposition, such as will-power and laziness, ambition and modesty, love and hate etc... have, somehow, to "get along".

– *the empty house showing an open door and five open windows.* Sense of individuality allows" sensorial perceptions". Thus the house represents our mind, its five windows are our five senses through which we perceive the outside world. Once they have penetrated inside the house, they are consciously or unconsciously "analysed" by our intellect. The result of this analysis will then materialize in either speech or action, both being "let out", by the open door.

– *the couple in embrace...:* sensorial perception creates the desire to be "in contact".

– *the man whose eye is hit by an arrow:* contact creates excitement of the senses. The man is obviously "aware" of pain – as he could also be aware of pleasure.

– *the husband holding the cup of tea his wife is going to fill :* feeling of the senses enhance "thirst" for more and more sensorial perceptions.

– *the monkey grasping a fruit from a tree:* desire leads to eagerness for gain.

– *the expecting mother* : eagerness to gain, to "grasp" is conditioned by the continuity of existence.

– *the delivery of the child* : birth is the necessary conditon of this continuity of existence.

– *the man carrying on his back the body of a deceased person*. wrapped in "foetus position" in a bag. The necessary condition for birth is death, and vice versa.

The eternal cycle of birth, death and re-birth is symbolized by the wheel in itself.

3) *The eight auspicious signs,* also called "eight glorious emblems" (In sanskrit: "Ashta mangal", in tib. "Tashi-Takgay".)

These signs are to be found not only in temples but also in private houses, on banners, pictures, thang-kas, silverware, jewels etc... since they are considered as unfailing "luck-bringers". :

– *the wheel,* representing the wheel of knowledge, of the moral and religious code of conduct ("dharma" in sanskr.)

– *the royal umbrella,* symbol of the power that protects against any evil influence

– *the banner of victory,* representing the victory of Buddha's doctrine, but also victory over ignorance, vain desires and death

– *the two golden fishes,* symbolizing those who have been "saved" from the "ocean of the successive lives", also "wealth" because of their golden coating

– *the endless knot,* which is the illustration of the eternal re-beginning of everything, also the solidity of bliss

– *the flower-vase,* which is supposed to contain jewels, sacred water, even ambrosia, the magic long-life drink

– *the conch-shell,* which proclaims the glorious achievements of all those who have reached enlightenment

– *the lotus flower,* symbol of purity and of the spiritual forces that have been released from their terrestrial roots.

4) Last but not least, *the fable of the "four unanimous brothers"*, a picture that is to be seen in gonpas and elsewhere too. It represents always a huge tree bearing red fruits and/or flowers. In the shade of this magnificent tree stands an elephant. On his back there is a monkey who, in turn, carries a rabbit on his shoulders. On top, a bird, perches on the rabbit's head.

Each of these four animals holds either a fruit or a flower in his trunk, paw or beak. The fable recalls the statements made by each of them :

– the bird is the first to talk : "if we are all here, it says, in the cool shade of this tree and enjoy its fruit and flowers, all this we owe it to me, for it was me who planted the seed and covered it with earth."

-- the rabbit replies that this seed would never have sprouted if he, the rabbit, had not managed, every day, to sprinkle it with his "water".

-- the monkey brushes away both previous statements and boasts that the real vital part, it was he who played it, by putting his "dung" on the spot where the seed had been dug in the earth. And this he did for days and weeks on end.

-- The last to talk is the elephant: admitting that in the very first stages, his three companions may have given some "insignificant contribution", it was he--and he al onefor he is strongest of all animals -- who, for years and years, protected the young plant which later became a small tree and now has grown so tall. He chased away, day and night, all those wicked animals that wanted to eat the plant, nibble at the leaves, and thus, he, the elephant, made it possible for the tree to develop in such a splendid way.

The moral of the story is, of course, that only by mutual cooperation and coordinated efforts can anything fruitful be achieved. Also that no one should think nor boast that his own merits are greater than the next one's.

Thang-kas

Almost all "lha-kangs" are decorated with large-size thang-kas that hang either from the ceiling above the two rows of the monk's seats, or along the walls.

On special occasions, the most precious ones will be displayed in the main hall. All represent religious figures, symbols or also mandalas.

The peculiarities of each of the five gonpas.

1) The "Chinya Lama's" gonpa.

It is very easy to locate for it is the pink two-storey building that stands just on the opposite side of the lane leading from the the main motorroad to the stupa. The building faces the only gate through which there is an access to the stupa's upper galleries. Also, this gonpa is the only house that has two sets of steps of steps joining up at a balcony on the first floor.

The "abbot" of this gonpa is the "Chinya Lama", so called because he allegedly lived some years in China. Many consider

him as an unofficial representative in Nepal of the Dalai Lama.
However true that may be, he is undoubtedly a very picturesque
elderly man who is always happy to receive foreign visitors in
his private rooms on the first floor of the builiding next to the
gonpa. He also likes to display his art treasures, thang-kas and
other objects. He may even be willing to sell some of them.

There are but a few monks in his gonpa which is not of
major interest.

2) The "nying-ma–pa" gonpa.

On the same side as the former, it stands at a right angle
to the circular road. It is a yellow building with a roof decorated
by two deers, one of each side of a "dharma – wheel".
(These deers are to remined those which lived in
Bodh Gaya park). The religious community using this
gonpa belongs to the non-reformed nying-ma-pa school,
often called the "red-hat sect". It was introduced into
Tibet around the middle of the VIIIth century A.D. by the mystic
magician and wise Padma Sambhava (also called "Guru Rimpoche" -the precious teacher), born in Urgyen, a village located
nowadays in Northern Pakistan. Padma Sambhava was called to
Tibet by King Thi-Srong De Tsen. It was mainly under the influence of Guru Rimpoche that Buddhism in Tibet and later in
Nepal, is so strongly tainted by tantric concepts, rules and rites.

Padma Sambhava is always easy to recognize, for he is
usually represented in a cross-legged position sitting on a lotus
decorated cushion. He wears a cap, the orners of whch are turned
upwards. The top of his cap bears a jewel or some other ornament.
Against his left shoulder leans a long scepter terminated by
trident and three impaled human heads—His left hand holds a
cap containing "ambrosia", the life-giving elixir, while his right
hand holds the "r-dorje" Around his lips, a fine moustache and
a light thread of a curled beard always adorn his face.

3) The "gelug-pa" gonpa.

Turning around the left side of the nying-ma-pa gonpa and
following for a few yards a narrow lane, you join up with a
wider one where you turn to the right. Another 30 yards from
here, on the left-hand side, there is an open gate leading to a
courtyard where a few meagre trees grow. At the far end of this
courtyard : the "gelug-pa" gonpa, surrounded by other lower
buildings, the monk's cells.

Between the courtyard and the main building itself, a sort

of vestibule whose walls are covered with old frescoes. To the left, the fable of the four animals, to the right, a wheel of life, in front the four guardians etc. Here shoes have to be taken off. Inside is the "lha-kang" where the offices take place.

This gelug-pa gonpa counts many young monks who have still years to learning in front of them before they will eventually be able to bind themselves to the community by permanent vows.

To be noted : the statue at the back of the "lha-kang" does not represent Buddha or any of the venerated Bodhisatvas, but simply, the founder of the gelug-pa order, TSONG-KAPA, who inspired and led one of the most important reforms of lamaist buddhism at the turn of the XVth century, about one hundred years before Calvin and Luther started their own reform against the Roman Catholic Church.

The name "gelug-pa means :" those who belong to the virtuous order". Let us recall also that the Dalai Lama is the supreme Head of the "gelug-pa" at the same time he is the spiritual leader of all Lamaist Buddhists. (Presently, the Dalai Lama lives at Dharamsala in North-Western India).

To visit the last two gonpas, the village of Bodnath has to be left behind you.

4) The "sakya-pa" gonpa

This building is also painted in yellow, but was completed much later than the gelug-pa. It is surrounded by smaller buildings and fields. The order it belongs to was founded in 1071 by a Tibetan mystic called Kon-Kong-Cho-Gyalpo who took his inspiration from the Indian philosopher Nagarjuna (2nd. century A.D.) and the Bodhisatva Manjusri.

Here the fresks of the vestibule are particularly worth studying. They are of much better quality than the ones at the gelug-pa gonpa. On the left of the main entrance door, a very elaborate "Wheel of Life" and, on the right, the "universe" as usually depicted in Tibetan iconography, centered around "Mount Meru" (on maps, it is called Mount Kailash and is located north of Lake Manasarovar, in Tibet. It is the source of both the Indus and the Brahmaputra, hence its great importance).

5) The "ka-gyupa gonpa"

This is the tallest and most recently built of all Bodnath monasteries. Its impressive white building was inaugurated in 1975. Its contruction was partly financed by donations from the United States, Scandinavia and some other non-buddhist countries.

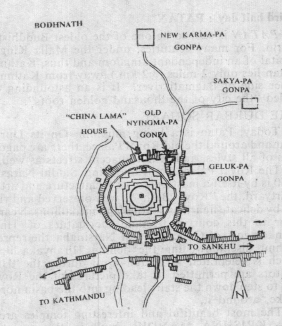

BODHNATH

NEW KARMA-PA GONPA

SAKYA-PA GONPA

"CHINA LAMA" HOUSE

OLD NYINGMA-PA GONPA

GELUK-PA GONPA

TO SANKHU →

TO KATHMANDU

N

The "order" of the "ka-gyu-pa" was founded in the 11th-12th. century, mainly under the influence of the famous mystic Marpa and his disciple Mila-Repa (whom he treated in a very hard way, according to the legend and his biography).

The main hall is very elaborately decorated. The wall facing the entrance is dedicated to three main deities. Their statues are enclosed in huge "show-cases". In the centre, Buddha, of course, with his third eye and his dark blue curled hair, as prescribed by tradition. On his right, "Dorje Semba" a classical representation of the Adi-Buddha called Akshobhya. On his left, Padma Sambhava.

This gonpa owns a series of 12 exquisite large-size thang-kas, painted in 1974–1975, depicting Buddha's life. Unfortunately these thang-kas are only displayed on special ceremonies.

Third half day : PATAN*

PATAN is said to be one of the oldest Buddhist cities in the world. For many centuries, under the Malla Kings, it was the capital of an independant kingdom and thus, Kathmandu's rival. Patan lies only 2 miles (3.2 km.) away from Kathmandu, on the other side of Bagmati river. It is an astounding town, rightly called "the city of the thousand golden roofs".

THE DURBAR SQUARE

Today, Patan is a living museum. On its Durbar Square, near and around the old Royal Palace, there are pagodas and temples of all styles, and in all adjacent streets as well.

The Royal Palace, built by King Siddhi Narasimha around 1650 is by itself a masterpiece of architecture and art. In the inner courtyard, the "Royal Bath" is well preserved and richly decorated by delicate figurines, statues and medallions. Near the entrance door to this courtyard, stand the statues of Hanuman, the monkey-god, of Ganesh and of Narsingha, the representation of Vishnu disembowelling the demon Hiranyakashipu, a legend which is celebrated in March-April during the "Holi" festival. Visitors are permitted to take pictures of the Royal Bath but not to step down the stairs leading into the basin nor to touch the snake, around it.

The most beautiful and interesting temples are :

– KRISHNA MANDIR, built in the purest "shikhara" style, popular all over India. Its friezes around the balconies are covered with some of the finest stone sculptures to be found in Nepal : they represent scenes of the Hindu epic "RAMAYANA".

– THE "GOLDEN TEMPLE" ("Hiranya Varna Mandir") at a 5 minutes' walk from Durbar Square. This temple stands in the centre of a square courtyard, as most of the Buddhist sanctuaries in the Valley. Its three-tire golden roofs are of unique splendour. The whole temple is one of the finest examples of Nepalese architecture. Visitors should not step into the lower courtyard but may visit the old Lamaist temple on the first floor.

— The "TEMPLE OF THE THOUSAND BUDDHAS" ("Mahabuddha Temple") is located at a fifteen minutes' walk

(*) Note for photo-amateurs: One visit of Patan is not enough. It is advisable to proceed to Patan once in the morning and once in the afternoon in order to take advantage of the lighting on Durbar Square and the other spectacular sites.

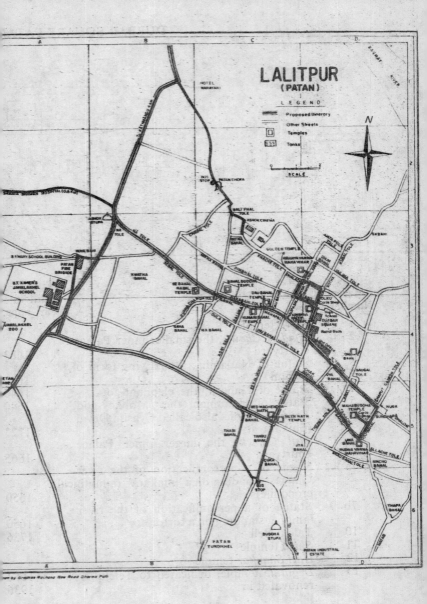

LALITPUR
(PATAN)

LEGEND

Proposed Itinerary
Other Streets
Temples
Tanks

SCALE

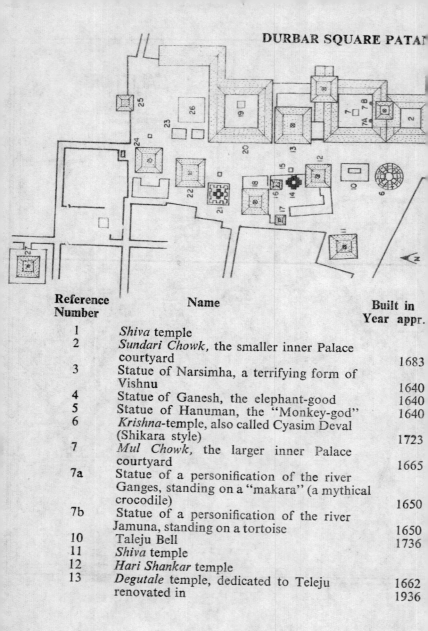

DURBAR SQUARE PATAN

Reference Number	Name	Built in Year appr.
1	*Shiva* temple	
2	*Sundari Chowk,* the smaller inner Palace courtyard	1683
3	Statue of Narsimha, a terrifying form of Vishnu	1640
4	Statue of Ganesh, the elephant-good	1640
5	Statue of Hanuman, the "Monkey-god"	1640
6	*Krishna*-temple, also called Cyasim Deval (Shikara style)	1723
7	*Mul Chowk,* the larger inner Palace courtyard	1665
7a	Statue of a personification of the river Ganges, standing on a "makara" (a mythical crocodile)	1650
7b	Statue of a personification of the river Jamuna, standing on a tortoise	1650
10	Taleju Bell	1736
11	*Shiva* temple	
12	*Hari Shankar* temple	
13	*Degutale* temple, dedicated to Teleju renovated in	1662 1936

14	Statue of Narasimha	1589
15	Statue, on a stone pillar, of King Yoga Narendra Malla	1700
16	Small *Narayan* (Vishnu) Temple, two tiers	
17	Another *Vishnu* temple	
18	*Jagannarayan* temple	1565
19	*Mani Keshar* Chowk, inner Palace courtyard	1734
20	Golden door and "torana" above. Figures of Shiva and Parvati	
21	*Krishna* Mandir (temple) Shikara style. In front, a Garuda on a pillar	1636
22	*Vishvanata* temple	1676
23	*Mani Mandap*	1700
24	*Bhimsen* temple	1680
25	*Ganesh* temple	
26	Square pond for ritual ablutions	
27	Golden Temple (Kva Bahal) 19th century A.D	

from Durbar Square in one of the side streets. This temple has two unique features :

1) It is built in the purest "shikara"—style although it is, of course, a Buddhist and not a Hindu sanctuary.

2) it is literally covered, on all four sides as well as from top to botton by thousands of small figurines of Buddha, all moulded in bricks.

Since this courtyard is very narrow, it is difficult to take a good photograph of this monument. Visitors are therefore welcome to go up to the first floor of the house standing opposite the entrance: from there it is easy to take a good picture.

— "MATSYENDRANATH TEMPLE". It lies in the western direction from Durbar Square at about 8 to 10 minutes on foot. It is undoubtedly one of the most beautifully located temples of Patan, in the centre of a quiet grass covered square lawn or courtyard. Matsyendranath is one of the incarnations of Avalokiteshvara who is venerated in Nepal (sometimes under the name of Lokeshwar) by Hindus as well as by Buddhists. Some scholars point out that the mythical animals which adorn the four cornerstones of this temple may be representations of the "yeti". The question remains open.

Let us mention also that Patan has a small museum, located in the left wing of the Royal Palace. It deserves a short visit.

"The Khumbeshwar temple".

A little outside the "centre" of Patan, this temple is worth visiting. Besides the fact that it is the only one, apart from Bhadgaon's famous "Nyatapola" which has also 5 tiers, it is one of the oldest (first built at the end of the 14th century). As many other Nepalese temples, this one is dedicated to Shiva, and for this reason, the architects left a small plot of grassland behind the main building, to enable Shiva's mount, the "Nandi-bull" to go grazing (!) Another curious feature of this temple is the water pond. This is the place where the famous "Janai Purnima" festival takes place in July-August.

The most precious silver "lingam" is kept inside the temple and is offered to the devotees veneration only on that occasion.

"The Jawalakhel Tibetan village".

Beyond the famous St-Xavier college lies the Tibetan village of Jawalakhel, formerly called the "Tibetan refugee camp", that it was, in the beginnings.

The entrance to the "village" is marked by a huge heap of "mani"–engraved stones, dominated by a huge pole of prayer flags. On the left, the village proper. On the right the older halls where carpets are being woven by women and girls. These installations have originally been donated by the Swiss Association for Technical Assistance. Today this carpet industry is entirely managed by the Tibetans themselves and constitutes one of the most prosperous enterprises of their community.

Fourth half day : BHADGAON (*)

The third of the Valley's ancient cities is another century-long rival of Kathmandu. It is situated at about 8 miles (13 km.) from the capital. Like Patan, it has an impressive number of artistic treasures: it is rightly called "a living museum" as well as "the most medieval city of the Valley". The historical centre of the town is the Durbar Square with its Royal Palace, called "The Palace of the 55 windows", a magnificent example of eighteenth century Nepalese architecture. It was built by King Bhupatindra Malla whose kneeling statue was erected just in front of the Golden Gate, another masterpiece of Nepalese handicraft. Both the Palace and the Gate were completed in 1853–1854.

(*) Best time of the day for good pictures of Bhadgaon's main temples and palaces is in the afternoon.

Durbar Square Bhadgaon

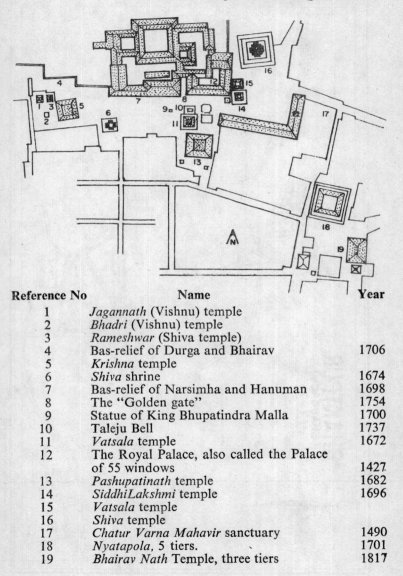

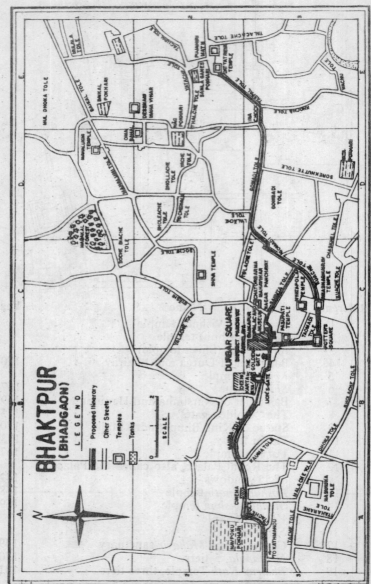

BHAKTPUR
(BHADGAON)

LEGEND

Proposed Itinerary
Other Streets
Temples
Tombs

SCALE

0   1   2

N

DURBAR SQUARE

Drawn by Graphles Rachana New Road Dharma Path

Other monuments deserving to be visited in Bhadgaon:

— The temple of TALEJU, which houses in the wing looking over Durbar Square, a magnificent collection of Nepalese wood and stone–carvings, as well as many beautiful thang–kas. This collection, which is exclusively Nepalese, makes it possible to study the differences in style and design between Nepalese and Tibetan painted scrolls. The latter are on sale in far larger quantities in antique and curio shops.

— The small temple of BATSALA and its gigantic bell. Both date back to King RANJIT MALLA (1737). Nepalese bell-founders were reputed in old times for many centuries : even the Kings of Tibet used to order bells from Nepal.

In front of this temple, as already mentioned, stands Bhupatindra's column. It is of harmonious proportions, topped by a "naga" (a sacred cobra) wound around the column with the traditional little bird standing on its head; according to the legend, introduced by Bhupatindra Malla himself ; *"as long as this little bird has not flown away, I shall still be in your midst, even after my death"*, the King used to say.

The capital of the column represent the petals of a gigantic lotus flower. The King's head is protected by a triple umbrella, a symbol of royalty and divinity all over Asia that inspired Nepalese architects to provide their temples with three or more superimposed roofs which were meant to *"protect"* the deity placed inside the sanctuary.

— The *"Potter's Square"*. Instead of proceeding directly from Durbar Square to the Nyatapola temple, as most of the tourist groups do, it is more picturesque and interesting to go across the Durbar Square and, turning the back to the Royal Palace, to take the small lane going down. Within five minutes, there is the "Potter's Square" an authentic village-place of the Middle-Ages, where not only potters but weavers and other artisans are found working with their traditional tools.

— The NYATAPOLA temple is to be reached in another five minutes' walk from the "Potter's Square". This temple too, was built by King Bhupatindra Malla, in the year 1708 and was dedicated to a Tantric deity, Siddhi Laxmi. With its splendidly harmonious proportions and its five roofs, this temple is not only the most beautiful in the whole Valley but also the tallest. It is a glorious example of Nepalese religious architecture. The steps are guarded by five pairs of strange statues: each of them is supposed to be ten times stronger than the one below ! On top, the deity itself, then, at a lower stage, two pairs of mythical animals, then two elephants and, lastly two traditional armed temple–guards, who, thus, are supposed to be the "weakest ones".

— The BHAIRAVANATH Temple (also called Akashabhairava) one of the few temples with a rectangular, instead of a square base. The first construction of this temple dates back to the seventeenth century but has been renovated since. One interesting detail is the size, tiny indeed, of the divinity's statue to which this huge temple is dedicated : the statue is hardly ten inches high and is located in a niche in the middle of the façade. What a surprising disproportion with the height of the building itself !

— The DATTATREYA Square, ten minutes' walk from Nyatapola Square. The temple standing in the centre of this place is one of the oldest in the Valley : it was built in 1427 during the reign of King YAKSHA MALLA; the two monumenatal guardians at the entrance are the wrestlers Patta and Jai Mal (whence the name MALLA of this dynasty that reigned over the Valley for 5 centuries !). Behind this temple stands the "PUJARI MATH", an old typically Newar building, sometimes called "monastery", which was completely restored by a West German team of specialists. The building was offered as a wedding present to the then Crown Prince Birendra, now the King of Nepal. The narrow street which runs along the left–hand side wall of the "monastery" has two magnificent "peacock" windows.

Panoramic View–Points

Sunrise and sunset over the Himalayas :

— *DHULIKHEL* (4,921 ft., 1500 m.)

One of the most spectacular scenic views which may be contemplated while staying in the Kathmandu area is to watch the sunrise or the sunset over the snow-capped mountain ranges. Undoubtedly one of the best spots to do this and in easy reach, for it only takes approx. one hour by car, is the village called DHULIKHEL. The car will take you across the Valley along the Chinese highway, by-passing Bhadgaon, then you will pass through the historical village of BANEPA. From there onwards, the road climbs and winds up in the midst of paddy-fields up to a low pass from where Dhulikhel is reached shortly afterwards. The two rivers at your feet are the Indrawaty and the Sun Kosi. Five minutes after having left behind you the village of Dhulikhel, the car reaches a platform from where the whole range of central and eastern Himalayas (i.e. from Ganesh Himal to Mount Everest) can be seen in clear weather. The spectacle of the rising sun is the most beautiful for the fairy–like display of coulours evolves more gradually then is the case at sunset which lasts only a few minutes. From this platform, the braver tourists may climb up in twenty–five minutes to the near–by hill-top which is topped by a small Shiva sanctuary. However, the view in itself is almost the same from this higher spot than from the car parking place below.

— *DAMAN* (7,874 ft. — 2.400 m.), *NAGARKOT* (7,000 ft. —2.134 m.) and *KAKANI* (6,398 ft. — 1.740 m.) are three more view-points where tourists may spend a few hours (there are modest tourist bungalows at Nagarkot and Kakani, but no night accommodation at Daman) to contemplate the sunrise and the panorama. These three points are located, respectively : *DAMAN*, on the road leading to the Indian border, at 50 mi. (80 km.) south of Kathmandu.

NAGARKOT, east of the city, at approx. 15 mi. (24 km.) beyond Bhadgaon, and

KAKANI, north-west of Kathmandu, at approx. 18 mi. (29 km.) on the road to Trisuli.

Whereas the view from Nagarkot is similar to the one from Dhulikhel, the ranges which are to be seen from Daman and Kakani are different, for they point towards central and western Nepal, i.e. from Ganesh Himal to Annapurna and Dhaulagiri.

At Daman, The Government Tourist Department built a panoramic tower for the visiting tourists.

Other interesting places

There are so many picturesque spots in and around the Valley that it is almost impossible to give a complete list of all of them. Wherever one goes, villages, temples, sanctuaries etc. offer an ample harvest of souvenirs of all kinds. Here are only a few names and details concerning the most popular and easily accessible of these places.

INSIDE THE VALLEY

— **Budanilkantha** : five miles (8 km.) to the north of the centre of Kathmandu is a place for worshippers of Vishnu. In the square pool, the statue of the god reclines on a bed of nagas (cobras) 15 feet long. This stone statue dates back to the seventh century

A. D. It is one of the holiest places in the Valley. The devotees put red powder on Vishnu's forehead and splash themselves with the stagnant water of the pool; some of them even take a sip of it. The pond is surrounded by a "vihara" i. e. monastery and pilgrim resthouse buildings. The King of Nepal is not supposed to enter this sanctuary for it is believed that he would be struck if he casted a glance on the god whose reincarnation He is. The name Budanilkantha is in no way related to Buddha. Some scholars think that Budanilkantha refers to the legend of farmer who, while ploughing his field, hit what he thought to be a stone or a boulder. Having dug it out carefully, he found himself looking at this huge statue buried in the ground.

This interpretation is said to be based on the fact that in a given old language, the word "buda" meant "buried in mud".

But of course, as usual, there are many other legends, one which records simply that a hermit whose name was "Nilkantha" and who was very old lived at this place and discovered the strange statue of Narayan.

— **Changu Narayan :** Located at approx. 15 mi. (24 km.) from Kathmandu, this is the oldest temple of the whole Valley and one of the most interesting ensembles. Its foundations date back to the 7th. century A.D. To visit Changu Narayan is a must!

It can be reached by car via Bodnath. Beyond, the road follows the brickwall that surrounds the King's forest sanctuary, called *"Gokarna",* where deer, peacocks, monkeys and other animals are plentiful and protected. Then, the road turns to the north–east towards SANKHU. Before reaching this village, the car has to be left on the side of the road. A footpath leads across the paddy-fields and the river Manohara where, sometimes, the bridge is swept away by the monsoon rains. The last stage consists in climbing up the hill on which stands the temple of Changu Narayan. This ascent takes roughly 40 minutes. The temple is dedicated to Vishnu (often called Narayan, in Nepal). In the courtyard, there are many masterworks in stone sculpture. The oldest piece is a Garuda, the mythical half-bird, half-man, the mount of Narayan, which dates back to the 5th. century A.D. (*Changu* is another name for Garuda).

Further, Changu Narayan is renowned for the fact that here is to be seen the oldest stone inscription so far found in Nepal: it dates back to the 6th century and refers to the victories harvested by King Man Deva (496–524 A.D.)

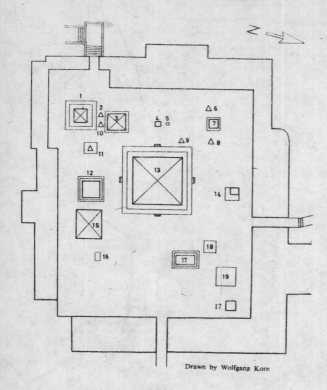

Drawn by Wolfgang Korn

CHANGU NARAYAN

Legend :

1. Lakshmi/Narayan temple
2. Statue of Narsimha (13th century)
3. Shiva pagoda
4. Statues of King Bhupatindra Malla of Bhadgaon (1687-1729) and of Queen Bhuvana Lakshmi
5. Kneeling Garuda Statue (464 A.D. one of the oldest works of art in Nepal.
6. Vishnu mounted on Garuda (around 6th century A.D.)
7. Krishna temple
8. Statue of Vishnu (9th century A.D.).
9. The oldest inscription so far found in Nepal (464 A.D.) dating back to the Licchavi era
10. Vishnu "Vikrantamurti" (6th century A.D.).
11. Statue of Vishnu Vishvarupa (6th century A.D.).
12. Temple of Shiva (18th century).
13. Main temple of Changu Narayan, dedicated to Vishnu
14. Natyeshwar sanctuary
15. Bhagavati (Vishnu's name in the Hindu "Purana" poems) temple
16. Statue of Ganesh, the elephant-god, son of Shiva
17. Small Shiva temple.

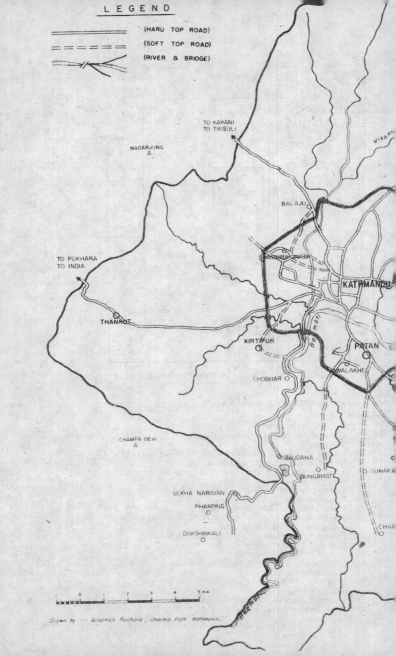

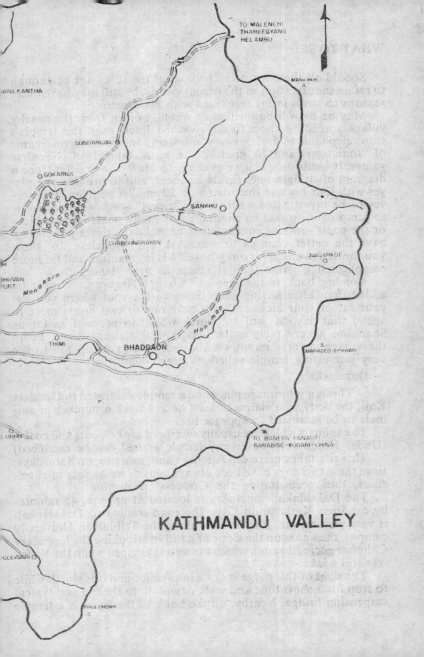

KATHMANDU VALLEY

Should all these art or archeological treasures not be enough to retain the attention of the casual visitor, he still may have other reasons to stroll in his courtyard with his camera.

May be he will be thrilled to watch women from the nearby village spreading their freshly washed linen over the temple's stone elephants to dry, or two youngsters concentrating on a game of "four tigers and 20 goats", the most typical of Nepalese games. It needs only a piece of chalk to draw on some flat stone a diagram of straight lines inside a square, and to provide one player with four big and the other with 20 smaller pebbles. It deserves to be investigated whether the "tigers" – whose objective is to jump over, in fact to eliminate, as many goats as possible – or the goats – whose endeavour is to make the tigers prisoners – have the better chances to win. Ask any Nepalese to show you the design and try it out yourself ! It is great fun, and far more complicated a game than it seems at first glance.

Coming back to the temple of Changu Narayan, it must be added that, after having gone down to the spot where you left your car or your bicycle, if you have one or two hours more to spend that day, it will be worth while to proceed as far as Shanohu, a very picturesque and typical Newar village. From the village, a forty minutes walk will take you up hill to the very interesting temple called "Vajra Yogini"

— Dakshinkali

This is a pilgrimage place and a temple dedicated to Goddess Kali, the deity who claims at least once a week a number of animals to be sacrificed to appease her.

The animals which are usually sacrificed are he-goats and cocks. (Under Hindu rule, never any female animal can be sacrificed)

This rite takes place on Tuesdays and, more so, on Saturdays, since these two days have been always considered as very unauspicious, thus necessitating the Goddess' protection.

The Dakshinkali sanctuary is located at approx. 45 minutes by car from Kathmandu-City. The road leading to Dakshinkali is very picturesque. First it runs along the Tribhuvan University campus, then goes up the slope of a hill overlooking the legendary Chhobar gorge, through which the waters escaped when the Valley was still a lake.

The sight of this gorge is quite impressive and it is worth while to stop for a short time and walk downhill to the old and typical suspension bridge. Nearby, on the bank of the river, is a temple

dedicated to Ganesh. The visitor may regret that the scenery has
been spoiled by the construction of a cement factory right there.

Further along, the road winds into a hilly region. Before
passing through the small village of Pharping, it reaches the very
peaceful old sanctuary called SHEKARA NARAYAN, dedicated to
Vishnu. This is a beautiful and interesting place : there are ponds
filled with crystal-clear water and sacred fishes; stone statues,
some of which date back to the Licchavi era (7th century A.D.)
contribute to the beauty of this spot. There is also a representation
of Vishnu as the dwarf Vamana (see the legend in the chapter
dealing with Hindu deities), as well as shrines, hermitages for
Hindus and Buddhists, rock-carvings and caves in the cliffs, etc.
A few hundred yards further along the same road lies DAKSHIN-
KALI, hidden in a shadowy grove. The place of the sacrifices in
itself is uninspiring and the whole atmosphere is somewhat grue-
some for Westerners.

— **Gokarna** : Located at approximately 3 miles north-east of
Bodnath on a fairly good motorable road, lies the small village of
Gokarna, a very popular pilgrimage place marked by "Gokarna
Mahadev", a magnificent Shiva temple built on the banks of the
sacred Bagmati river. This place owes its holy character mainly
to the fact that it is at the confluence of three rivers ("Tribeni"),
which justifies the building of an important sanctuary. In its present
aspect, it dates from the latter half of the 16th century, but its
foundations are said to date back to the Licchavi dynasty. Stone
carved images of various deities line the path leading from the main
road down to the temple as well as surround the main building
itself, a unique feature in the whole Valley. Among these deities
there are two representations of a bearded BRAHMA (also an
unusual feature !), three of DURGA in various aspects, one of
AJIMA, the goddess that is believed to cure smallpox (or to prevent it !) and also, a curious and rare representation of a three
headed, three-armed and three-legged "God of Air", to whom
devotees appeal to get healed of fevers.

Since this temple is built on the banks of the Bagmati, cremations take place – almost every day –. On "Father's day" ("Aun-
chi"), i. e. on the New Moon day of the month of Bhadra – mid-
September, thousands of pilgrims, devout Hindus, bathe in the
sacred river's waters to pay homage to their progenitor when he is
still alive, or to his memory, the year after his death. This ceremony takes place in the first fortnight of September.)

This temple is the first important one to be renovated in 1980 within the framework of the "Master-plan for the conservation of the cultural heritage in the Kathmandu Valley", drawn up by HMG in cooperation with UNESCO.

GOKARNA is also the name of the "Royal Wild-life Natural Park" the entrance of which lies one mile outside Bodnath. The most spectacular way to watch the various animals living inside the Park is to take part in a "Gokarna Safari" on elephant's back. (For further information : Telephone 13333 in Kathmandu or write to POB 2063)

— Kirtipur, this small medieval Newar town is located on top of a hill some 6 miles (10 km.) south–west of Kathmandu, It is an old fortress which used to be the strategic key to the Valley; King Prithvi Narayan Shah the Great, the unifier of modern Nepal had to assault Kirtipur three times in the course of 6 years before he could conquer it, and subsequently subdue Kathmandu, Bhadgaon and Patan, in 1768–1769. A cruel episode is attached to the conquest of Kirtipur which, although historically true, has never been completely clarified as to its real motives: What happened was that when the defenders of Kirtipur surrendered at last to Prithvi Narayan Shah, the latter ordered that the nose and lips of all male inhabitants–with the sole exception of those who could play a wind instrument–should be chopped off. It was said that this was an act of revenge for the loss of the eye of Prithvi Narayan's brother. In fact, another explanation may be that this decision was taken in order to frighten the inhabitants of the Valley when seeing so many mutilated faces of Kirtipur-people strolling in the streets of Kathmandu, Patan or Bhadgaon. The sight of these disfigured men must indeed have reminded the population of a human skull, symbol of death. This deterrent effect did not fail to work out well, as far as Prithvi Narayan Shah was concerned, since the conquest of the three "capitals" of the Valley took him finally less time than the occupation of Kirtipur.

This historically important little city is worth visiting : it kept intact its buildings, temples as well as its traditions and artefacts.

MINI–TREKS IN KATHMANDU VALLEY

Since practically all the hills surrounding Kathmandu Valley are linked with each other by trails and tracks, an infinity of "mini-treks" can be undertaken without need for detailed maps, special equipment, guides or loads of food. And none of these treks is strenuous or even difficult.

Among the most interesting ones, the following deserve to be mentioned :

—**To Shivpuri (8,980 f. = 2,713 m.)**

From Kathmandu, by car to Budanilkantha.

Leave the sanctuary itself on your left hand side as well as the main road leading to the British Budanikantha School Campus, a complex of red brick houses visible from far away. Proceed along the narrow village street straight on and pass over the first small saddle-back bridge. Immediately after having crossed, descent on your right-hand side the few stone steps and follow the lane along the farmer's houses and the fields, always keeping on to your left. After approx. half an hour, start ascending and try to reach the trail which climbs up, partly steep and zig-zaging, along a barren ridge. A motorable road and a high brickwall cut across the footpath. Local people may show you how to reach the two isolated houses which you will have spotted from far below. They are the old and the new buildings of the Buddhist–Lamaist convent of NAGE-GYANG that lies about mid-way between Budanilkantha and the top of Shivpuri. Only a few elderly nuns are permanently living this "gonpa".

Now, behind the higher of the two buildings, follow the trail that climbs up, lined with prayer flag poles. It is advisable, whenever there is a passer-by, to make certain that you are on the 'Shivpuri jane ma mulbaato" (the main-track to Shivpuri).

The trail leads through a magnificent forest that has but few clearances, but many forks. Since there are no signboards, the best guess is to follow the steepest track. From the convent to the summit it should not take more than one and a half hour.

On top of Shivpuri stand several sanctuaries and man-made stone platforms. If you are lucky, you may meet the "sadhu" whose abode he chose up there. This "holy man" lives in seclusion, praying, meditating, reciting mantras and performing 'pujas" (offerings). But he does not stay there all year round.

During the winter months (October to April), the panorama of the Himalaya range, as seen from the top of Shivpuri, is breath-taking. In front of you, the massive four summits of Ganesh Himal, followed, towards your left, by the peaks of Manasu, Himal-Chuli and Lamjung, Clear weather is needed to spot the Annapurnas in a far distance.

There are two itineraries to walk back to Kathmandu. The shorter consists in following roughly the same track as the one you took to go up. Budanilkantha is to be seen clearly from everywhere and shortcuts are many.

The longer road leads more to the East – South-East, first along the ridge, then down towards Bodnath Stupa which is also to be seen from the top. This would take a little over 2 hours.

—To Pulchowk

This is the highest of all the hills surrounding Kathmandu: (7,188 f. = 2.800 m.)

A motor-road leads right to the top, but it is far more sportive to follow the footpath which branches off the main road, near Godavari College, south of Patan and cuts across the winding motor-road at many places.

It takes approx. 2 to 3 hours to reach the top, through a beautiful forest where rhododendrons are plenty. They are in full bloom in April-May. About half-way up, there is a now abandoned iron-ore mine.

On the top itself, the buildings, antennae and other sophisticated equipment are part of the modern radio-communication system of Nepal which has been set up to the greatest part thanks to Australian assistance.

While the view from Shivpuri is oriented towards Central and Western Nepal, it is the Eastern Himalayas that are visible from Pulchowk, including, in very clear weather, Mount Everest in the far distance, to the right. Gaurishankar, with it white triangular cap, is easy to identify.

—To Banepa, Panauti and Namo Buddha
—Banepa

This "mini-trek" may take more than one day, depending on whether some stages are to be made by car or all of them on foot. From Kathmandu to reach the first target, the town of Banepa, (some 17 miles-27 km.) in the eastern direction, the easiest way is to take a public bus or a car. For a short while, in the 15th century, Banepa was ruled by Rana MALLA as an independent kingdom. In this typical Newar town, two relatively old pagodas built in the two-storey Nepalese style are worth visiting. They date back to 1752 and are both dedicated to NARAYAN. An intresting nearby village in NALA, located a few miles north of Banepa.

Nala shelters two interesting pagodas; One of the only two four-tier pagodas which still subsist in the Valley (the other one is located in Harisiddhi, a village south of Patan) and a very old Buddhist temple dedicated to Avalokiteshvara. This temple is not built in the traditional architectural Nepalese style but looks rather like a little more elaborated rich man's residence. But there is the shrine which protects the image of the deity, a three-foot high statue dressed in silk clothes and crowned with a silver head-gear and feather-like ornaments.

Both the Banepa Narayani and the Lokeshwar temples at Nala are decorated with quantities of kitchen utensils and vessels made of copper, brass or wood. They are offerings made to the divinities, mostly by young married couples, to propitiate their new homes. Or they symbolize the utensils deceased may need once they will have reached "the other side".

— **Panauti.** Once in Banepa, the visitor should not fail to continue hiking (either by car or on bicycle) down to Panauti which is another Newar town rightly proud of its treasures of decorated houses, beautiful wood-carved windows and many temples. One of them is particularly remarkable for it shelters two huge statues of Bhairav inside and–like the Shiva Parvati temple on Durbar Square in Kathmandu–human figure looking out of the first floor windows. One of the temples dates back to to the 15th. century.

A good occasion to visit Panauti is the time of the *"Makar Sankranti"* festival which takes place on the 1st day of the month of Magh. (around mid-January)

The festival consists mainly in collective bathing at the confluence of the three rivers. Here lies the religious importance of Panauti for such geographical points are always considered as especially auspicious. Therefore many festivals are performed at Panauti, the most spectacular being this collective bathing which is supposed to wash away all sins.

Every 12 years, a famous *,"mela"* (fair) takes place at Panauti which lasts for the *whole* month of Magh. The next one is scheduled in January 1986.

–Namo-Buddha

The final stage of the mini-trek is the ascent of NAMO BUDDHA hill. The best is to start very early in the morning from Banepa and visit first the very picturesque town of Panauti.

A 45 min. walk will then lead you on top of the hill overlooking Panauti. The small temple there is dedicated to Goraknath.

It should not take more than 4 hours from Panauti to the top of NAMO BUDDHA hill. The trail climbs through shrubs and a forest up to the final staircase. A magnificent, albeit small stupa, decorated, as to be expected, with the "all seeing-eyes of Lord Buddha" stands near the top. This stupa is visited by thousands of devotees on a yearly pilgrimage that takes place in early spring.

Above the stupa, on the topmost point of the hill, in the shadow of a century-old tree, you will spot the massive and very ancient stone-slab which illustrates the legend of this place.

First the name : "Namo-Buddha" means "Hail to Buddha", where the world "Namo" – related to "namaste" or "namaskar"- is a salute of respectful deference.

Then the legend. This place of worship dating back many centuries (nobody knows exactly the date of its creation,) it is not surprising to find several versions. The two most frequently told are the following :

–"Once upon a time" says the story-teller, Buddha happened to walk in this part of the country and heard that a tigress had been killed by a hunter on top of a nearby hill. So Buddha went in search of the beast and found it at the very place where today the engraved stone slab stands. Here lay the tigress, surrounded by its four or five hungry whining cubs. Buddha felt such compassion for these innocent animals that he tore his own body to pieces and gave his entrails to the cubs to devour. The cubs went on feeding themselves greedily. They grew up and became strong animals which, ultimately, took revenge on the hunter who had killed their mother.

– The other version is slightly different : Here, it was no Buddha, but one Prince of the then ruling family who found the tigress. But she was very much alive, surrounded by her cubs. She told the Prince that she was unable to provide enough milk for all her small ones and implored his help. The Prince took his sword (a modern version would certainly refer to his "khukri" !) and cut slices of his own body, thus giving the tiger cubs fresh meat for food. Wanting her share too, the tigress assaulted the Prince and was about to maul him to pieces

The Prince had just the time and the strength to ask the tigress why she was attacking him so viciously, although he had shown so much compassion for her cubs. The tigress replied that he should neither be sad nor angry but, to the contrary, he should rejoice about his fate : thanks to his good deed, he would die as a martyr and be reborn as a Buddha, reaching straight the ultimate blissful goal of all human beings : Nirvana.

Coming back to NAMO BUDDHA: once you have enjoyed being on this peaceful and historical place, with the glittering Himalayas in the background, it may be time to think of going back.

Instead of returning to Panauti, a more interesting trail would be to follow the one leading to Dhulikhel and the "Chinese Road", where it is always easy to find regular bus services or other means of transport to drive you back either to Banepa or even all the way to Kathmandu.

It will be remembered that Dhulikhel is one of the spots from where the mountain range of the Himalayas is best to be seen, either at sunrise or at sunset.

—To Nargarjun (7.600 f. = 2.316 m.)

This is another worth-while walk, which can hardly be called "mini-trek". Not more than three hours are needed to reach the top of this hill and go down again.

Nagarjun lies roughly half-way between Budanilkantha and Swayambhunath. It can easily be reached the road to TRISULI, entering the main gate on the left side of the road.

Nagarjun is completely surrounded by a brickwall, for, in the course of 1976, it has become a "wild-life sanctuary". In the thick pine forest covering the hill, there are indeed various species of deer, many varieties of birds, fowl, wild cats, marters and even leopards, but not many !

On top of the hill, a modest Buddhist stupa is quite interesting, be it only as a foreground for a picture of the surrounding landscape. The panoramic view is best on a winter morning, when the Valley is still covered with a layer of silvery mist.

OUTSIDE THE VALLEY

The "Chinese Road"

This road was built with the financial and technical assistance of the People's Republic of China by Chinese and Nepalese engineers. It links Kathmandu with the Chinese border and, beyond that, it continues up to LHASSA, the capital of the *Autonomous Region of Tibet*. The road starts near Kathmandu airport, where a fork permits by-passing Bhadgaon before reaching Banepa. Beyond, the road starts climbing towards a pass, from where one road branches off towards Dhulikhel, before going down-hill with bends and turns until reaching the bridge across the river Indrawaty. This part is probably the most spectacular of the whole excursion. A few miles after the bridge there is the picturesque small village of Lamosangu (the starting point of the trek to the Everest region) soon followed by a larger village, Barabise, located on the other side of a second bridge. It is in the vicinity of Barabise that the hydro-electric power station, built with Chinese assistance is visible on the right hand side. From here on, the road follows the narrowing valley of the Sun Kosi. It is difficult to get even a glimpse of the mountains towering on both sides, for the valley is deep and its slopes are covered with forests. The border is defined by a wide bridge, where taking photographs is strictly prohibited. On the Chinese end of the bridge stands a Chinese–style sentrybox while on the Nepalese side there is a Nepalese–style one. Much more noteworthy than the bridge or the sentry–boxes is the fact that this border point is located at a mere 5,900 ft. (1.798 m.) ! Decidely, the Himalayas are not an "impassable barrier")

— Pokhara and its Valley

125 miles (200 km.) west of Kathmandu, i. e. 35 minutes by plane or 6 to 7 hours by bus along a very picturesque road, lies the magnificent Valley of Pokhara. (When travelling there, be it by air or by land, foreigners are requested to carry their passports with them.)

The plane lands on a somewhat rough strip and stops near an impressive tree whose heart–shaped leaves flutter in the air stirred up by the plane's engines. When you deplane, you are stunned by a stupendous view : The whole range of the Annapurnas (there are 5 summits bearing the same name !) with

Machha Puchhare's steep pyramid right in their centre.

Pokhara, rightly called the "gate to Annapurna" is a place which is not only a beautiful spot where a few days rest are most rewarding but also the starting point for many unforgettable treks : towards the North–West (Dhaulagiri range), to the North (Annapurna and Machha Puchhare areas), to the North-East (Lamjung massif) or to follow the traditional "highway" in the direction of Tibet, i. e. along the Kali Gandaki Valley through those places with the romantic names as *Tatopani* (hot water), *Sikha, Dana, Tukuche, Jomosom, Muktinath* and *Lo Manthang*. With the exception of the last one mentioned, all these points have been reopened for tourists in June 1976. (They had been "off–limits" for two years).

Coming back to the view one enjoys from the airport : Machha Puchare means *"fish-tail"*; for this mountain, when seen from the West–after two or three days' walk from Pokhara towards the North–West, presents two slightly separated ends.

Of its two summits the highest reaches 22.960 ft. (6.997 m.) Neither of them has ever been scaled. The only attempt ever made was in the spring of 1957 by a British Expedition led by Col. J. O. M. Roberts. The Sherpas who accompanied the team are said to have refused to climb any higher, once they had reached a point just approximately 165 ft below the summit, in order "not to disturb the goddess whose abode is this very peak". (From the rationalist's point of view, this story is difficult to accept : if really this mountain was supposed to be the "abode of a divinity", isn't it surprising that a more religious name has not been given to the mountain, calling it instead, so prosaically : "fishtail", while so many other Himalayan peaks are actually named after gods and goddesses, such as Annapurna to begin with, Ganesh Himal, Gauri-Shankar and many others.)

Coming back to the panorama as seen from Pokhara, it must be pointed out that the range that looks so close, is, in fact, much further away. In the Himalayas, distances have this disconcerting propensity of "expanding into space" much more than in other countries, so it seems !

Pokhara airfield lies approx 17 mi (27 km.) – as the crow flies – from the foot of Machhe Puchhare and approx. 24 mi. (38 km.) from its summit !

Visitors would, of course, like to identify the peak of Annapurna I, the first summit "above 8.000 m." (26,247 f.) ever climbed by mountaineers (Maurice Herzog and Louis Lachenal, in June 1950). Now, the only – and easiest – way to spot the peak is to get up in the early morning and to watch carefully which one of the many humps will receive the very first pink touch by the rising sun.

Pokhara owes its reputation as a tourist resort more to its exceptional situation than to its attractions in itself, for its bazar, though colourful, has few monuments to offer for sight–seeing. The town lies about 3 miles north–west from the airport but its main hotels : Fish–Tail Lodge, New Crystal and Mount Annapurna are all three at a very short distance from the air strip.

Where does this strange but melodious bell-ringing come from ? It gets louder and louder. One mule, two mules, a whole caravan of mules moves slowly down the road from the village. Each mule wears on its head a huge red yak tail fly–whisk, and an embroidered triangular piece of cloth on its forehead.

The caravan–driver, who is usually a Thak or a Tibetan, is wrapped in his typical "*chuba*", the long–sleeved red–brown garment of all those who live in the upper valleys and the high plateaux. The caravan is likely to come from Jomosom or Tukuche and part of its load certainly consists of salt from the Tibetan dry lakes and another part of raw yak–wool.

In one or two days' time, the caravan will start its return journey northward, carrying this time, to be delivered in Tibet, manufactured goods of all kind and, may be, some bags of rice or barley if the local harvest has left a surplus.

There are two sites that deserve to be visited as "a must", in Pokhara : the surprisingly deep canon of the Seti river, just across the airfield (watch out for possible planes landing or taking–off !) The bridge across this canon is hardly any longer than 30 feet (9m.) whereas the water level is at least 100 feet (30 m.) below !

The other sightseeing spot is "Fadke", also called "Devin's Fall" : a facinating geological curiosity. It is named after a "European girl" who is said to have been swept away by the rushing torrent and plunged in the 100 feet deep vortex while" taking a romantic bath "with her boy-friend. Nothing more reveals this legend ! The gorge ends up in what is likely to be a subterranean chasm where the stream disappears. So far, it has never been completely explored.

In addition to these two natural sites, it is recommended to visit the large compound, close to both airport and the city's heart, where the ethnographic museum is located. This area will gradually be developed into a cultural centre, where examples of local architecture, folklore programmes etc... will be presented. It also serves as a public recreation park, with typical indigenous trees shrubs, flower-beds etc...

Many pleasant walks may be undertaken in the Pokhara immediate surroundings :

About one and a half hour walk towards the North-West will lead the tourist to the interesting Tibetan village of Tashi-Palkhel located on the top of a low cliff. Originally this used to be a "refugee camp" for those Tibetans who had followed their spiritual leader, the Dalai Lama into exile through Sikkim to India. Some of them preferred to settle down in Nepal, whereas others came straight from Tibet to Pokhara, crossing the border between Kyirung and Rasua Ghari.

It can no longer be considered as a "camp" for everyone is free to leave it if he so wishes, and, furthermore, it has developed into an almost prosperous community, thanks to the carpet industry for which almost all the inhabitants contribute somewhow. Tashi Palkhel has also its own school and even a "gonpa".

At one day's walking distance, a pleasant excursion consists in climbing up-hill to the old fortress of Sarangkot, following the trail that leads up from Pokhara's the main temple called the Bindu Basini temple.

Still further along lies another magnificent scenic point, a village called Naudanda from where a beautiful panoramic view covers the whole range of the Annapurna and Lamjung massifs. By car, the most picturesque excursion is the one that leads to the two twin lakes, Begnas and Rupa, on the left side of the main Pokhara – Kathmandu road, about 5 miles away to the North.

—Chitwan National Cark

This Wild-Life Preservation Park lies in the Terai, very near to the Nepali-Indian border.

The best season to visit this beautiful spot that offers so many exciting features to the tourist, extends from October through to the end of April, beginning of May. There is no rain then and the mornings and evenings are pleasantly cool, though never cold, while during the day it is never too warm. Only between December and February is warm clothing to be recommended.

Monsoon begins to make itself felt in May-June by occasional downpours and plenty humidity.

The two kinds of animals for whose preservation this National Sanctuary was mainly created are:

(a) the tiger, of which around 30 have been spotted and which are said to be increasing progressively in numbers, now that hunting and poaching have been eradicated.

(b) the one-horned rhinoceros that exists no longer anywhere else in the world. In addition, the Park is the protected homeland of many species of deer and antelopes, monkeys, leopards, wild boars on the ground, hundreds of varieties of birds in the air and crocodiles (gharials and muggars) as well as river-dolphins in the waters.

As far as the details about the journey, accommodation, lodging facilities, rates etc... are concerned, please refer to the chapter "Safari".

– **Lumbini** (Buddha's birthplace)

This sleepy small village in the Terai, which was known by the name of Rummindei, at the time of Gautama Siddhartha's birth (around 560 B.C.), where his father was the sovereign of the principality of Kapilavastu,

Lumbini is located about 75 miles south-west of Kathmandu and is to be reached by air via Bhairawa, whence the East-West highway leads to Lumbini itself in about half an hour.

In fact, there is presently little to be seen in this revered place, save a stone pillar bearing an inscription commemorating the visit Emperor Ashoka made there in 250 B.C., a temple and a somewhat modern Buddha statue.

Thanks to the initiative of U THANT, the former Secretary General of the United Nations and a fervent Buddhist, a broad plan for developing the whole Lumbini site has been drawn up. It will provide hostels for tourists and pilgrims, vast gardens, library, a museum and a huge temple. At present there is only a modest hotel, "MAYA DEVI" to accomodate visitors.

– **Phaplu**

Roughly half-way between Kathmandu and the range of Mount Everest lies the picturesque Sherpa village of Phaplu.

Little known yet, the Phaplu area deserves a visit. Here begins the Himalaya, with its dense pine forests, the slopes covered with giant rhdodendrons which are in full bloom in March and April, nature, beauty and warm hospitality everywhere.

Sir Edmund Hillary, the conqueror of "the third Pole", was

one of the first to fall in love with this region.   He set up simultaneously a hospital, a school, an airfield and built the bridges in
the upper Khumbu area of Lukhla. At Khumjung and Kunde,
he started taking care of the Sherpas A hospital was erected
there, manned by doctors from his native New Zealand. Later
he set up a hospital at Phaplu as well.

In the immediate neighbourhood of Phaplu, there are some
very interesting spots to visit :
   – Chiwong Gonpa, an authentic Buddhist–Lamaist monastery,
located at an altitude of 9,400 feet, only a half-day walk from
Phaplu. It is one of the largest monasteries in Eastern
Nepal.   It contains many precious manuscripts, painted
scrolls ("thang-kas"). Visitors are welcome to attend the
always fascinating daily rites and ceremonies. Should you reach
CHIWONG during October and November, which are the best
months to visit this area, you may witness the "Mani Rimdu"
festival, a Sherpa religious event in which all monks dressed
in their silk robes and wearing their ritual masks, perform dances
for two days.
   – Chialsa, two hours walk from Phaplu : a Tibetan village
built and inhabited by refugees. There you will find carpets,
handicrafts and many old and new souvenirs to take home.
   – Ratnage Danda, at 10,000 feet, is a hill nearby. From
there , at sunrise or sunset, you will enjoy a magnificent view of
the whole Everest range. It is an easy three hours walk from
Phaplu, through a dense pine forest.
   – Dudh Kund, in other words, the "Milky Lake" lies a little
higher up, at around 15,000 feet. A more peaceful spot is hard
to find anywhere in the world. It is worth while to trek there
although is takes about 4 to 5 days back and forth.

– Provincial Towns

BIRATNAGAR (50.000 inhabitants), NEPALGANJ (25,000
inhab.), DHARAN (23.000 inhab.), BHAIRAWA (20.000 inhab.) and others offer but very little attraction to the visiting
tourist. For that reason, there are only very modest hotels and
restaurants available.
One exception may be mentioned : JANAKPUR (15.000
inhab.) for this small town is–according to the legend–the birthplace of Sita, the devoted wife of Lord Rama, the hero of the
Indian epic "The Ramayana". What gives some weight to the
legend is that Sita's father's name was Janak, and he is said to

have been the sovereign of the "Kingdom of Mithila". There is a beautiful Hindu temple erected in Janakpur that attracts many thousands of Hindu pilgrims every year, not only from Nepal but also from India.

Let us mention here that it is in the region of Janakpur that the local women are producing those very picturesque and original hand-paintings usually on white, rough cardboard, which are called, precisely : "Mithila paintings". They are on sale everywhere in Kathmandu.

Another provincial town which is worth visiting is GORKHA, roughly half-way between Kathmandu and Pokhara (but not on the main road). Gorkha is the cradle of the presently ruling Shah dynasty. It is really worth climbing up the hill (it takes abou tone hour from the village itself to the top) and visiting the beautiful Palace from where Prithvi Narayan Shah set up to unify the whole country. (Unfortunately, it is prohibited to take photographs, even of the magnificent wood-carved windows. To reach Gorkha, it is recommended to take a plane to the nearby airfield of Palingtar (one short day walk from Gorhha.)

SECTION III
TREKKING

INTRODUCTION

WHAT IS TREKKING ?

To trek means to start off from a given town, village or airfield and to wander through fields and hills, through forests and along valleys or mountain slopes up to any altitude, usually not much higher than 18,000 or 18,500 ft. (5.500 to 5.650 m.).

Mostly this wandering will be done along paths and tracks (the latter word being cognate with the expression "trek") without having to use specialized equipment for rock and ice climbing, nor oxygen.

Another definition of trekking is a negative one : "While trekking one has never to use one's hands", which makes it something quite different from mountain climbing or "alpinism" as it is generally understood.

Some more has to be added, in general terms :

As the distances are fairly considerable–a real trek takes not less than 8 days and more than often 15 or 20 days–and as there are few hostels or rest–houses, in certain areas few villages even, trekking parties have to hire porters to carry all the food they will need on their way, in addition to clothing, tents and sleeping equipment, as well as medicines, since supplies are sparse and difficult to come by.

So far the material side of trekking. But even more important is the psychological aspect : trekking means to live intensely every minute of each long day, and to enjoy the calm beauty of the mountain valleys, ridges, passes and summits. It also means to create and maintain a deep, solid and sincere spirit of confidence and solidarity not only with your trekking companions, but also your sherpas, guides, cooks, kitchen–boys and porters.

Last but not least, trekking means to get to know more about the heart of the Nepalese people, the farmers, the cattle–breeders, their customs and traditions, to appreciate their smiling welcome and their unconditional hospitality. Needless to say that, on the reverse side, trekkers should avoid behaving in such a manner as to make these friendly people of the plains, the hills and the mountains change their attitude towards foreigners.

The following additional considerations must also be emphasized :

As the Himalayan Rescue Association very aptly expressed it in a pamphlet that every trekker should read before leaving Kathmandu :

"The Himalayas begin where other mountain ranges leave off. Kala Patthar or Everest Base Camp, favourite destination points for trekkers, are located over 3,000 ft. (914 m.) higher than the Mont Blanc, the highest summit in Western Europe !

Now the higher one goes, the less oxygen is available to breathe.

The body is capable of adapting to the thin cold air, but you have to give it time to do so, this is what is meant by "acclimatization." If you go up too fast, you are asking for trouble in the form of mountain sickness, however physically fit you may be... or feel".

To put it in other words :

"To go trekking certainly does not mean breaking a record or rushing to gain a day or even an hour. Beware of the "do or die" attitude in the Himalayas, for all too often, it has meant more "die's" than "do's". (A special chapter will deal more in detail with Health Precautions.)

CHAPTER SEVEN

PREPARATIONS

USEFUL ASSISTANCE

Unless you have undertaken a series of treks yourself, and have a solid personal knowledge of the itineraries, the distances, the quantities of food needed, etc. and unless you may count on some absolutely reliable guides, cooks and porters, it is not an easy matter to prepare a real trek, i. e. a journey that will take you along valleys, over passes and along moraines, on mountain tops away from roads and cities for a fortnight or more.

Although it is not mandatory to undertake a trek through a specialized agency, it is warmly recommended to call upon one of them for it is in a position to provide you with all you need, and above all, on whose experience and knowledge of the trails and all trekking conditions you may rely.

A further paragraph will deal with the legal provisions ruling the organization of treks.

Below, in alphabetic order, a list of trekking agencies which were operating during the winter 1980/1981 :

–In Kathmandu

ALPINE ADVENTURE EXPLORATION– Maharajganj – Tel. 11786

ANNAPURNA MOUNTAINEERING AND TREKKING – – Durbar Marg, near Yeti Travels – Tel. 12736 – POB 775 – Cable : *Amtrek*

DOLKHA TREKKING, Kanti Path – Tel. 15620

EXPLORING NEPAL, Ram Shah Path

EXPRESS TREKKING, Naxal – Tel. 13017 – POB 339

GAURISANKAR TREKKING SERVICE – Lazimpath – Tel. 12112 – POB 881.

GREAT HIMALAYAN ADVENTURE – Netra Bentawa – Kantipath – Tel. 14424 – POB 1033 – Cable : *Himtrek*

HIKING SERVICE – Ang Kami Sherpa – Dharma Path/Paku – POB 1566.

HIMALAYAN EXPLORER – Thamel

HIMALAYAN JOURNEYS – Stan Armington – Kantipath – Tel. 14626–POB 989.

HIMALAYAN ROVER TREK – Dawa Sherpa and Dinesh Gurung – Naxal Tel. 12691 – POB 1081 – Cable : *Rovtrek*

HIMALAYAN SHANGRI-LA TREK – Ram Shah Path – Tel. 13303 – Cable : *Wildlife*

HIMALAYAN TRAVELS AND TOURS – B. K. Shrestha – Durbar Marg – 11682, 13045 – POB 234.

HIMALAYAN TREKKING – Lakpa Tensing – Ram Shah Path– Tel. 11808 – POB 391.

INTERNATIONAL TREKKERS – Col. P. Ongdi and Rindzen Lama – Maharajganj-Sallaghari Tel. 11786 – POB 1293 – Cable : *Intrek*

INTERTREK NEPAL – On new Road, opposite Tourist Information Centre, Manager : Ang KUSANG Sherpa. POB 223 – Telephones 11216 – 12217 – 12251 – Telex : NP 279 ETS.

KANCHENJUNGA TREKKING – Gana Shyam Paudel – Ram Shah Path – Tel. 14139 – POB 1296 – Cable : *Hit*

MALLA TRAVELS & TOURS. Dr. Harka GURUNG. On Leknathmarg, in the front wing of MALLA HOTEL. POB 787 – Telephone : 15966 – 15968 – 16637 – Telex NP 266 MTT

MANASLU TREKKING – Mohan Lal Rai – Durbar Marg – Tel. 12959 – POB 1519 – Cable : *Manastrek*

MOUNTAIN TRAVEL : Col. Roberts and Al Reed – Durbar Marg – Tel. 12808 – POB 242 – Cable : *Trekker*

NATRAJ TREKKING . – P. P. Prasai – Durbar Marg – Tel. 12014

NEPAL TREKKING – Kusang Norbu Dawa – Sath Gumte (Thamel) – Tel. 14681 – POB 368 – Cable : *Netrekking*

NEPAL TREKS AND NATURAL HISTORY EXPEDITIONS– D. D. Shrestha and Bob Fleming Jr. – New Road – Tel. 12985 – POB 459 – Cable : *Neptrek*

SHERPA COOPERATIVE TREKKING – Michael Cheyney – Kamal Pokhari. Tel. 15887 – POB 1338 – Cable: *Sherpahut*

SHERPA SOCIETY – P. P. Pant – Ramshah Path – Tel. 14775 – POB 1566 –

SHERPA TREKKING SERVICE – Khalden Sherpa – Kamaladi Tel. 12489 – POB 500 – Cable : *Sherpatrek*

SUMMIT EXPEDITIONS – Mr. John LINDEMAN – c/o SUMMIT HOTEL - Kupandole – Patan Telephone : 21810

Specialized in expeditions and rafting, with rubber rafts and canoes. Telex : N. P. 270 NATRAJ - KATHMANDU.
TRANSHIMALAYAN TREKKING – Moti Dhar – Durbar Marg – Tel. 15271 – POB 283 – Cable : *Transeview*
YETI MOUNTAINEERING AND TREKKING – Ram Shah Path. Tel. 14619.

During the season 1980/1981, these organizations charged between 25 and 40 US S per day and per trekker – depending on the number of participants and the duration of the intended trek (the more participants and the longer the trek, the lower the rates).

The rates also depended on the quality of the services provided, both in terms of more or less experienced guides and porters on the one hand, equipment and food on the other.

Normally, these rates include tents, mattresses, sleeping bags, all kitchen equipment as well as, of course, all guides, cooks, kitchen–boys, porters, food and drinks. Some organizations may grant a rebate if the trekkers bring with them their own sleeping equipment.

– **At Pokhara.**

The management of all main hotels : Fish–Tail Lodge, Mount–Annapurna, New Crystal, as well as the smaller hotels in front of the airport, are in a position to provide equipment and trekking staff.

Mountain Travels has also his permanent representive in Pokhara. For all necessary details hereto, it is recommended to contact Mountain Travel's Head Office, in Kathmandu.

Recently, two shops specializing in selling and renting trekking equipment and gear, as well as in providing guides, and porters opened in Pokhara, a few hundred yards from the airport.

Both are located right after the bend of the road leading to Phewa Lake and Fish–Tail Lodge : On the right side of the road, you will find "Annapurna Mountaineering and Trek", while on the left side, there is : "Pokhara Tours and Travels".

—**Elsewhere.**

Anywhere in the hill villages, it is fairly easy to recruit porters in particular when they are needed for two or three days only. But Sherpas are to be found exclusively in the Sherpa regions (Solu, Khumbu, and Helambu). Even this statement is not absolutely correct, for the increase of high altitude expeditions and trekkers in general entail sometimes–in particular during the peak-season, October to December, a real shortage of "Mountain man–power."

On the airstrips of Lukla, Syangboche, Langtang, even Pokhara etc. it is not too difficult to contract guides and porters who have just accompanied a party about to embark on an airplane back to Valley. Mostly these guides and porters are only too happy to start another trek with a new group of trekkers "going up".

HEALTH PRECAUTIONS

Medical hints

Trekking implies a constant physical effort and you feel the stress. Over a longer period this is very beneficial but over a shorter one it can be dangerous. This stress is caused by change in environment, harsher climate, great variations of temperature within twenty–four hours, and thinner air, i.e. less oxygen.

Even the change of your way of life from the almost completely "automated", air-conditioned, comfortable and sterilized life to a primitive one, close to nature, a life totally different where the most elementary things become primordial again: all this may contribute in producing stress. For those who are not accustomed to open–air life, who are unfamiliar with mountains and perhaps physically not very fit, it will be still more important to take all necessary precautions. First of all, it is imperative to undergo a thorough medical check-up prior to setting off on a trek, irrespective of age ! Statistics seem even to indicate that young men between 20 and 30 are more likely to get into mountain–trouble than older people! Of course the generally admitted fact is that the younger tend to be more daring and sometimes over–confident in their own strength than older people.

Here again, the Himalayan Rescue Association gives the following simple and practical advice :

"Plan your trek with utmost care".

"The idea of snatching a quick holiday may be all right for the seaside but it does not give the respect due to the Himalayas".

"Always allow one or two extra days in your programme".

"In no case and on no account try to beat a record".

"If you start your trek by using an aeroplane to land on an altitude airstrip, do not go much higher that first day".

"Once you are above 12,000 ft. (3.600 m.) spend two consecutive nights at the same altitude, for mountain sickness may appear even below 11,000 ft. (3.350 m.). It is imperative to allow another two consecutive nights when above 14,000 ft. (4.250 m.)".

"During the "rest–day" between these two nights, climb about 1,500 ft. (450m.) or more, above the campsite and go down again".

"If you have allowed yourself one extra night or day of rest and acclimatization, in no case try to make up for what you (wrongly) consider as having been "lost time".

"Last but not least, be always on the alert for any symptom of altitude sickness" (for further details about them, see next paragraph.)

. Mountain sickness

This is the most excruciating and serious danger that threatens the careless trekker. Mountain sickness claims every year far too many victims in the Himalayas, mostly among young men and women who, disregarding all warnings, want at all costs to go *"Too Fast, Too High"*.

Unfortunately there are no reliable means of detecting in advance who is more vulnerable to this mysterious disease. To treat it with contempt is, no doubt, disastrous. Here are some facts which might prove useful :

One important point to keep in mind is that there is no preventive medical treatment. Some studies indicate minor benefits to be obtained from furosemide '("*Lasix*") or Actazolamide ("*Diamox*"), which are both diuretics. But taking these medicaments need a compensation by absorbing potassium in certain proportions which should be determined exclusively by a doctor, Besides, the efficiency of this prophylaxis is currently controversial for the side effects incurred by taking these drugs indiscriminately and without constant medical supervision can be as incapacitating as mountain sickness itself.

The first symptoms of the sickness are :
— reduced excretion of urine
— bad headaches and even worse migraines
— loss of appetite
— insomnia

At this stage, a good night's sleep, induced by a tranquilizer or an aspirin, help to ensure that you can set off next morning.

However, these first danger signs must be taken seriously and from now on your climb will have to be slower and more gradual than up to now.

The symptoms of the next stage are:
— nausea and vomiting

— more and more breathlessness
— a feeling of heaviness in the chest
— severe fatigue
— apathy
— blurred vision, loss of balance, mental confusion.

Even the slightest touch of these symptoms must be taken very seriously indeed and necessitates the one and only remedy : *To descend immediately at least* 3,000 *ft.* If the case is not serious, twenty–four or forty–eight hours spent at this lower altitude should enable the trekker to continue his way, on condition, however, (and this is essential) that he does not hurry in order to make up for the lost time.   If the symptoms persist, *he must come down for good.*

It may not be out of place to remind you that, unlike in Europe or in the U. S., there are neither mountain clubs nor huts offering accommodation for the night, nor permanent telecommunication enabling those who need urgent assistance to get it.

A special chapter dedicated to emergency cases follows below.

. Medical Kit

Since there are neither hospitals (except in the villages of Phaplu and Khumjung,) nor medical posts (except the "Trekkers Aid–Post" at Pheriche, see hereunder) nor chemists in the villages, it is highly recommended that each trekking party should have its own medical kit. In Kathmandu, most medicines made in India can be obtained in any of the many medical stores.

The composition and the size of the medical kit depends of course on the number of persons in the party, their medical knowledge and habits, as well as the planned duration of the trek.

Here, very briefly, are some of the medicaments which are recommended.*

. Pro-forma are to be mentioned here some basic items such as cotton–gauze, adhesive bandages, scissors, needles and safety-pins, a thermometer, tweezers, "mercurochrome" and iodine, cotton wool, sticking plaster, band-aids, forceps, etc.
. More specific items now :
— *To protect the skin against sunburns* : the most effective preparation is a 5% solution of para-aminobenzoic acid in

---

* There is an excellent scientific work for those who would be interested in a more comprehensive study of this question J A. Wilkerons:"*Medicine for Mountaineering"*—Seattle published by "The Mountaineers" 1975

WHEN MOTHER AND CHILD TRAVEL TOGETHER

IN WHITE: A GOAL FOR AN EXPEDITION
IN DARK: A GOAL FOR TREKKING

NEARER TO THE GODS

WHO WALKED HERE?
THE "YETI"?...

55% ethyl alcohol. The pharmacist will compound this mixture which will be carried in a plastic dropper bottle.To be applied on half an hour before exposure. Attention: it may stain clothing. Another good product is zinc oxyde cream.

— *To protect eyes* : well-fitted sun-glasses or goggles. Collyrium or opthalmic liquid such as a 10% sodium sulfacetamide of 15 ml. made by "Royal Drug" or any other ointment containing bacitracin, choliramphenical, neomycin, whereas those containing hydrocortisone, predinisone or cortisone are to be avoided.

— *Against sore or infected throat* (frequent !) : codeine (15 mg. tablets), or Listerine. Also gargling with a warm salt-water solution.

— *Against coughing* : 2 tablets of codeine (30 mg.) every 6 hours for a day, when coughing does not produce sputum.

— *Against common cold* : First of all, Vitamin C (tablets) as a preventive. Then aspirin containing Vitamin C and, a course, abstain from smoking.

— *Against diarrhoea* (the most common plague of trekkers !) the simplest medicine is tincture of opium, of which ten drops in a small amount of water up to five times a day should be absorbed. Or "paregoric" (camphoreated tincture of opium) can be used. Good substitutes would be 2–3 Lomotil tablets.

Should the disease degenerate in dysentery, a treatment of antibiotics with an initial dose of 2 pills followed by 1 pill every 6 hours, preferably before eating, is indicated, while drinking plenty of water is recommended.

To sterilize water. This is such a "must" that to mention it may seem superfluous. All water that will be used for cooking or drinking has to be purified (sterilized) or boiled, or better both. The easiest way of purifying water is to add 8 drops of iodine to 1 litre (1 US quart) of water and wait 15 minutes before drinking. There exist also (but not necessarily in Kathmandu) other sterilizing tablets such as "Water Purification Tablets of Iodine", Halazone or Clonazone which become active one hour after they are dissolved in water. Of course, these precautions may be relaxed whenever the trekker finds himself above the vegetation line, where the danger of finding polluted water, by villages or pastureland up-hill, is non-existent. This is the case above 15,000 or 16,000 ft. (4.600 – 4.900 m.)

— *Against headache* : Aspirin or similar tablets.
— *Against infections* : Antibiotics, such as tetracycline, 250 mg. tablets. Penicillin G, 400,000 unit tablets or Ampicillin, 250 mg. tablets.
— *Against sleeplessness* : Meprobamate or other sedatives. These can help to have a good, sound sleep. However, sedatives should be used with caution at high altitudes for in the presence of some forms of mountain sickness, they may be dangerous, even fatal.
— *To prevent blisters on the feet* (another "classic" which makes trekkers suffer all too often!) moleskin, band-aid has to be used as soon as a tender or hot spot is felt or better still before! There exist some creams and powders ("Burrow's solution" for instance) which are believed to be efficient preventive products.
— *Energy–giving tablets* containing glucose, vitamin C and coramine have sometimes fatigue-killing and stimulating effects when high altitude trekking exerts special strain on heart and lungs. Some doctors consider their efficiency more on the psychological than on the physiological level.
— *Against muscular pain and spasms* : these are innumerable creams and ointments with analgesic properties.
— *Against stuffed noses and sinuses* : Phenylephrine HCL (1/2 %) nose spray or drops. In Kathmandu such as preparation is available under the name of Fenox.
— *Last but not least* : a few words must be added on two items: leeches and frostbites.
. Leeches: When trekking during the monsoon or in early autumn, September and beginning of October, these ugly creatures can turn in a real plague. They are so thin that they creep easily through the lace holes of the trekker's shoes ! Since they are provided with some anaesthetic substance, their bite is not felt at all when they start sucking blood. Once they are gorged, their anticoagulant substance provokes prolonged bleeding. Trekkers should resist the urge to tear them off the skin while they are sucking, for part of the creature (their "gob") may remain inside and produce infection.
It is wiser to use some of the efficient repellents, such as Dibutyl Phthalate with which clothes and socks should be sprayed. A simpler way consists in soaking socks and stockings in a concentrated salt-water solution. Ankles should be protected by bandages or "puttee".

. Frostbites : *Preventive measures :* Plenty of warm clothing, solid and high mountain boots, where feet are completely at ease. Several layers of gloves. All connecting points between the different parts of clothing should be well protected to prevent cold air infiltrating. Further: acclimatization to altitude, abundant food and in particular very abundant drinking are also a "must".

. *Symptoms :* finger and toe-tips getting cold, skin changes its normal colouring. More serious : loss of sensitivity, pain in hands or feet.

. *Some do's :* Increase the quantity of liquid absorbed, keep moving fingers, hands and toes, take constantly glucose tablets (glucose should always be in easy reach) Descend when the loss of sensitivity does not lessen.

. *Some don'ts:* Don't "beat" fingers or toes to activate blood circulation. Don't take off gloves or shoes, unless you are under a tent or in a warm room or place. In open air, once removed, shoes could no longer be put on !

Wind is relatively more dangerous than cold alone. This is why, usually, fingers are more often exposed to frostbites since they are less protected than feet.

ORGANIZING THE TREK

Logistics and number of participants

The most important problem consists in correctly evaluating the needs, in men, food and equipment, to perform the intended trek under the best possible conditions.

— *Manpower*

The Sherpas (For simplicity's sake, we shall use the word Sherpa, although very competent and experienced guides (Sirdars) may be recruited in other ethnic groups too, such as Tamangs, for instance.)

The Sherpa Sirdar is the man responsible for the logistic organization as well as the interpreter, the "band-leader" of the porters, while his assistant, usually a man from the same ethnic group, is in charge of the food, the supplies, and the cooking.

NOTE: Some of the medical information contained in the above chapter have been taken with the kind permission of the author from Dr. Stephen Bezruchka's excellent book : "A guide to Trekking in Nepal" third Edition – Kathmandu 1976.

It will therefore be necessary to have as many Sherpas and cooks as there are, or might be, separate groups within the same trek. Thus enough Sherpas and cooks have to be hired accordingly. It also must be remembered that Sherpas are not porters (except in very high altitude) and will not carry loads in addition to their personal effects, while cooks will only carry those and kitchen gear.

The Porters

They have no other major tasks to perform than to carry the loads and, occasionally, to help picking firewood, fetch water from wells or streams etc. On larger treks, there is usually one kitchen–boy who is in charge of such duties.

It should not be necessary to emphasize the crucial importance of taking into account the physical possibilities of the porters. When planning the following day's route, the gradient of the track, the altitude, the possible presence of snow or ice, the number of hours needed to reach the next campsite, all this has to be taken into consideration.

In short, no effort should be spared to build up, right from the start, and to maintain throughout the duration of the whole trek, a harmonious and solid "team spirit".

One should never forget that even the most energetic and experienced "sirdar" will never be able to force porters to carry their loads if they are too tired or if, for some other reason, they refuse to proceed beyond a given village, pass or rock-house. It is no fun to carry a "dhoko" on the back all day long, up and down the tracks, across ice-cold streams and, if need be barefooted, on snow-covered slopes. Thus, the success of a trek rests largely on these sturdy men–and women-porters.

To come back to logistics, two yardsticks, albeit very approximate ones, may be mentioned here :

a) Each trekker may be considered using about 4 lbs. (1 kg. 8) of food per day (wrappings, tins etc. included, of course). This yardstick is somewhat on the liberal side. Calculations should not omit the weight of the permanent personal effects such as tents, sleeping bags, extra clothing and footwears etc.

b) Under average conditions and in medium difficult terrain, a porter can carry packs weighing 60 to 65 lbs (27 to 30 kg.) If male porters are scarce, women porters may be contracted. They are sturdy strong and gay. They carry up to 55 lbs (25 kg.) while knitting or singing (or both) on their way. Two porters per trekker and per week have to be considered a reasonable average. Of course some porters may be dismissed as and when the food supplies diminish.

As far as the *ideal number of participants* is concerned, it is impossible to spell out an absolute rule. One should always keep in mind that the larger the party, the slower the progress and the greater the risks that one or several members may not be able to follow. Experiene shows that four well-acquainted friends, constitue a fairly good trekking team.

. **Rates**

Beginning 1981, the rates were approximately the following :
Sirdar : Rs. 30–45 per day (or more if the trek is considered a strenuous one).
Sherpa-cook : Rs. 25–30.–
Kitchen–boy : Rs. 20.–
Porters : Ordinary porter (low altitude) Rs. 25.–
Altitude porter : Rs. 25.–30.–

At the end of the trek, when the services of these various companions has been satisfying and also when some additional efforts have been requested (such as passing a difficult stretch of road, walking over seven hours in one day, trekking through snow and wind, carrying additional loads because one porter may have become sick or has abandoned the party etc...) it is customary to distribute some "extras" either in kind, in money or both. Psychologically, it is obviously important not to wait until such rewards are claimed !

Sirdars, guides and porters earnestly hope to be allowed to keep, at the end of the trek whatever equipment, clothes, shoes, socks, goggles etc. they have been given. It is, of course, imperative that all sirdars and guides, as well as the cooks and kitchen-boys have to be provided with adequate clothing and sleeping equipment, either by the trekking agency or by the members of the party. This would apply to porters as well, if their services are needed in areas where they can not find any shelter againt cold and wind. This has become compulsory by government decision taken in 1980, but the equipment may be claimed back from the porters at the end of the trek.

Trekking Permit

Since 1963, the Government of Nepal closed certain areaa to foreigners and trekkers and established the "Trekking-Permit" system.

The restricted area runs roughly some 15 – 20 miles along the Northern border of the country. Excepted are some of the Himalayan peaks, which although located on the frontier itself or near it, may nevertheless be climbed if special permission is granted by the Nepalese Mountaineering Division of the Ministry of Tourism. But such "expeditions" are ruled by separate legal regulations than "trekkings".

Trekkers must obtain their "trekking permit" before leaving Kathmandu.

Here are the main rules governing these trekking permits :

1) The Department of Immigration is the sole authority to issue these permits. This Department is located on Ram Shah Path in Kathmandu; its offices are open every working day from 10 a. m. to 4 p. m. It takes normally 24 hours to get the Trekking Permit. (Beware of Saturdays when the Department remains closed). Two passport-photos are required.

2) Trekking permits will be issued for trekking in one area only at one time.

3) Trekkers will be permitted to trek along the itinerary specified on the Trekking Permit.

4) : Fees : For the issuance of a Trekking Permit : Rs. 60.– for the first week of the first month of planned trekking. Additional Rs. 60.– will be charged for each subsequent week falling within the first month of trekking.   This fee is raised to Rs 75.– for each week during the second month of the planned trekking. (In this latter case, the extension fee for the visa will not have to be paid – see under Visa regulations)

5) The validity of a trekking Permit can not exceed the validity of the Nepalese visa.

6) The trekking permit has to be produced at each "checkpost" *en route.*

7) Trekkers who intend to by-pass Kathmandu and start trekking directly from some other place, Pokhara for example, will also have to obtain their trekking permit prior to departure. They must therefore apply to a branch office of a recognized trekking agency located at Pokhara which will process the application through the Immigration Department in Kathmandu. In other words, a trekking permit can not be obtained directly at a frontier post, as it is the case for an entry visa, nor elsewhere in the country with the exception of Kathmandu itself. However, it is planned to open a Branch Office in Pokhara who would also be

empowered to deliver Trekking Permits. It is advisable to get confirmation on this point beforehand.

To get to know the sirdar, sherpas and cook, and make last hour arrangements.

The waiting period for the trekking permit is best employed to get to know your trekking companions.

There are many topics to discuss : the itinerary, the number of porters needed, how to get them to the trek's starting point.

Other problems have to be settled too : checking all out-going and return bookings, and re-confirm them, organize the dispatch and transport of some equipment, if necessary.

Last but not least, to buy such supplies and equipment which have not been brought from abroad.

There are now many shops in Kathmandu selling or renting all kinds of trekking equipment (tents, mattresses, sleeping-bags, down clothes, shoes, crampons etc.) at reasonable rates. These shops are to be found mainly in the neighbourhood of Kathmandu Guest House or on "Freak Street" near Basantpur Square.

SUPPLIES AND EQUIPMENT
. Food

More and more provisions can now be bought on the spot, i.e. in Kathmandu. But it is wise to do the shopping with the sirdar who knows the quantities needed and the quality of the items probably better than you. And the current prices too!

Certain specialized shops will deliver the purchased goods to your hotel.

The main items to be purchased locally are all basic food such as rice, sugar, tea, flour, butter, noodles, dal, (lentils), salt, spices, biscuits, cheese, oatmeal, sweets, jam, bacon powder and condensed milk etc...

A specialized firm, "Trekkers Food"– located on Lazimpath– POB 304 – Tel. 14860 produces excellent dehydrated food which is highly recommendable :

Some of their products :

5 varieties of soups packed in 50 gr. plastic bags, (Rs. 5.– a package).

3 varieties of porridges, cereals etc... (200 gr. packages at Rs. 10.–)

3 varieties of powdered vegetables: onions, cabbage and carrots (100 gr. packages at Rs. 8.–)

3 varieties of dried fruit slices: apples, pineapples and "naspati" (pears) in 100 gr. packages for 8 – 12 Rs. each)

For those who like to have at hand a provision of bread, *Krishna Loaf Bakery* (on Naxal) may put aside, when ordered one day in advance, either long-shaped "French" or brown "German" bread that will last 5 to 6 days.

As far as cooking, utensils, cutlery "dhokos" (carrying baskets) strings for tying up the porter's loads, torches, paraffin lamps, reserve cells and batteries, plates, mugs, water bottles, cigarettes, kerosene cooking stoves, candles and matches etc. all these items have also to be purchased in Kathmandu (or Pokhara).

Now, here are a few items which are to be brought from abroad: special soup-powders (reckon one per day and per person) bovril, liquid and in cubes, tins of pâté and fish, sausages, corned beef and cheese, chocolates, soft drinks in powder form etc...

. Camping Equipment

— *Tents*. For certain treks, if you are not going above 15,000 ft. and stay in more or less inhabited regions, you may not require a tent. A small group of 4 or 5 trekkers at most, accompanied by, let us say, 2 guides and a few porters will always find accommodation in villages.

However, the real Himalayan trekker will usually prefer spending every night in his tent, not only to get away from the noise and the dirt of some farmer's houses (but above all, in order to enjoy the sunrise from the spot he will have carefully selected the previous evening for this purpose.)

Of course, the tent has to be waterproof, as light as possible, and have a fly-sheet.

— *Sleeping equipment* : A mattress (don't forget the pump !) or a foam rubber pad, which is lighter but bulkier, are the main requisites, together with a down sleeping bag provided with a hood and side zipper. Some trekkers like to cover themselves up with a completely insulating "space-suit" of extremely light metallized plastic material. It is very compact and protects efficiently against humidity.

— *Clothing* : Two pairs of shoes, one of them a pair of lightweight convas boots or tennis shoes with gripping rubber soles and one pair of leather waterproof mountain boots. Leggings to keep out the snow and down bootees for the night. An extra pair of light slippers can add to your comfort.

Several pairs of woollen socks of different thickness, as well as thin socks, but nylon is to be avoided. Thermo underwear, long-johns and vests; a thin vest and at least two woollen shirts.

Two pairs of pants : a pair of shorts for the first stages of the trek, and warm pants of corduroy or wool. Two sweaters, a thin one to be kept in the rucksack if not worn, and a very warm one for nights and high altitudes (those sold at the Tibetan camp in Jawalakhel are of good quality). A wind breaker, light but strong and waterproof, a down jacket and, if you are going high up or trekking in winter, down pants.

— *Miscellaneous :* Ice-axe and crampons if the terrain makes them necessary, as well as ropes. Also leggings to keep the snow out, as you often cross snow drifts even below 18,000 ft. (5.500 m.)

Thermometer and altimeter, plastic mapholder, pen-knife, a rucksack made of nylon which is as light as possible.

A little shoulder bag to carry the small things you want to keep by you : a note-book, pencil, compass, filter and lenses for your camera, extra rolls of film, some sweets.

The rucksack will contain your picnic lunch or sandwiches. a pullover, sunglasses, gloves, a cap, a woollen shirt, a small medical kit.

CHAPTER EIGHT

WHEN TO TREK AND WHERE TO GO

MOUNTAIN BIBLIOGRAPHY

BOOKS

The three best books on trekking in Nepal, both extremely well documented, easy to read and covering all relevant aspects,

1) *"A guide to trekking in Nepal"* by Dr. Stephen BEZRUCHKA, a Canadian practitioner who has spent many years in Nepal. His book (in its third edition) is published in Kathmandu by "Sahayogi Prakashan" at Tripureshwar (Tel. 11489).

This book not only describes in detail all that must be known before undertaking a trek, but also gives a very comprehensive description of the most popular and spectacular treks, accompanied by very clear and up-to-date maps.

In addition, there are chapters on Health, Hill and Mountain Peoples, National History, the Nepali language and a section on trekking ethics.

2) *"Exploring Nepal"* by Mr. Stan ARMINGTON. an American engineer who is also residing in Nepal since several years and has been intensively trekking for at least five or six years. Presently he is Managing Director of Himalayan Journeys in Kathmandu. His book is "designed to help prepare a trek in Nepal" and is full of excellent advice based on a wealth of experience. It is published by "La Siesta Press" in Glendale – California– 1975.

3) The most recent book describing minutely almost every "nook and corner" of Nepal is *"Vignettes of Nepal"* by Dr. Harka GURUNG, former Minister of Tourism, Geographer and expert in many fields of Nature. This book is published by Sajha Prakashan, Kathmandu.

Besides these books three sets of concise trekking publications with maps, photographs, diagrams and other useful information are available :

a) In English : Mr. John HAYES series called *"Nepal Trekking*

Guide Books" – Published in Kathmandu by Avalok Publishers in 1976.

) In German : Dr. Christian KLEINERT'S : *"Nepal Trekking B. C. Tourenblatter"* which describe 15 different trekking itineraries. Published by "Bergverlag Rudolf Rother", Munich. An English translation is planned.

) In Japanese : Tomoya LOZAWA's *"Trekking in the Himalayas"* Published by "Yama-To-Kekioku-Sha cy." at 1–1–33, Shiva Daimon – Minata-ku-Tokyo 1976. An English translation is planned.

On the life, customs and origins of the Sherpa ethnic group, here is a famous book by Professor C. von Furer-Haimendorf ntitled *"The Sherpas of Nepal"* published by John Murray, London 1964.

Four well-known specialists, i.e. Toni Hagen, G.O. Dyrenurth, Erwin Schneider and C.von Furer-Haimendorf wrote n Everest itself : *"Mount Everest, Formation, Population and Exploration of the Everest Region"* published by Oxford University Press, London 1963. Another classic is David Snellgroves" *'Himalayan Pilgrimage"*. It is a sequel to his *"Buddhist Himalaya* now unfortunately out of print. Snellgrove describes all the Tibetan parts of Northern Nepal (Dolpo, Mustang, Thakkhola, Nye-Shang, Nup-ri and Tsam regions).

Sir Edmund Hillary, the conqueror of Everest, describes his recollections of the invaluable assistance given to him by the Sherpas, in a book entitles *"School-House in the Clouds."*

Very useful to take with you on your trek is the small, very well composed *"Trekker's Pocket-Pal"*.

Area maps for trekkers

There are several "series" of maps available in all major book shops.

For the two most popular areas, namely the Everest on the one hand and the Annapurna region on the other, two excellent and up-to-date maps are especially to be recommended :

They are multicoloured and include not only detailed written description of the main routes but also a useful glossary of Nepalese words and sentences.

The publisher : Madhab Lal Maharjan. Their name :..

1) KATHMANDU to Mt. EVEREST – ROLWALING HIMAL – Mt. MAKALU & ARUN VALLEY (scale 1 cm= 2 km. 5)

2) POKHARA TO JOMSOM & MANANG (scale 3.5 cm=
10 km.)

Other "series" are the less elaborate: "MANDALA" Trekkin
maps, on bluish paper, "GRAPHIC ARTS MAPS" etc...

Covering the Eastern part of Nepal, there are the 8–coloure
series of magnificent and most accurate "Erwin Schneider" map
published by "Freytag – Berndt und Artaria" in Vienna – Kor
markt 9. But they are also available in Kathmandu.

This series includes now :
– "Khumbu-Himal" in a 1: 50.000 as well as a 1: 25.00
scale (the latter inserted in the book written by MM.Toni HAGE
G. O. DYRENFURTH, Chr. v. FURER–HAIMENDORF
and Erwin SCHNEIDER, "Mount Everest").
– "Rolwaling Himal"
– "Lapchi Kang"
– "Tamba Kosi"
– "Shorung-Hinku and Dudh Kosi"

In the same series, the best of all maps covering "Kathmand
Valley", and Kathmandu–City.

CHOICE OF SEASON

There are two good trekking seasons:
1) Autumn : from mid-October to the end of December.

During day-time, you will enjoy the sunshine, a clear sk
and a magnificent view of the mountains. This is (almos
guaranteed. January and February have also excellent weathe
but the nights, in altitude, are of course much colder : In th
evening and during the night : –4° F. against +8° in October
November. These temperatures are likely to be found abov
15,000 ft. (4.570 m.). Of course, treks planned to remain below th
altitude may be undertaken all through the winter season.

The autumn season is the most popular because of thes
favourable weather conditions. Also the water supply does no
raise difficulties, all streams and rivulets being well provided.

The only inconvenience of trekking in the early autumn sea
son, as long as monsoon has not completely vanished (i. e
until mid-October, sometimes), is the risk of leeches up to 9,00
feet (2.740 m.), in particular on tracks used by cattle, on mois
and grassy land. Mostly they aim at feet and ankles.

Some of them hang on twigs and the rim of leaves. They ar
on the outlook for their victims and let themself drop o
shoulders or necks. The trekker should be on his guard in orde

to flip them away before they have fastened themselves with their suctorial organ. Once they have, it is better to let them gorge themselves with blood. They will then drop off by themselves.

Of course, a radical method to get rid of leeches at any stage is to burn them with a match or the tip of a cigarette. To pour a drop of iodine on the creature is also usually fatal.

2) Spring : March–April. Usually the weather is fine, in particular in the morning hours. Below 8,200 ft (2.500 m.) it is pleasantly warm approx 80° F 27° C.) However, in the afternoon, there is a tendency for cloud formations over the mountains that may lead to rain and thunderstorm.

However, there is one strong attraction for spring-trekking, namely the fact that rhododendrons are then in full bloom. This is Nepal's "national flower" The rhododendron plant is no longer a bush like in Europe, but it grows to gigantic trees upto 60 ft. (18 m.) high. They bloom at 5,000 ft. (1.500 m.) up to 8,200 ft. (2.500 m.) or 9,000 ft. (2.750 m.) and are covered with white, pink or red flowers. (The higher the altitude, the paler the colour!).

Two inconveniences of spring-trekking: there may be scarcity of water at low altitudes, and, above 11.500 ft (3.500m.) snow may still cover grassy slopes and pastures.

A FEW SUGGESTIONS FOR TREKS

For Less Than A Week

Starting from Kathmandu.

To Langtang

This beautiful Valley, just north of Kathmandu can be reached in 20 min. (by charter flights only) up to the airstrip of Langtang (11,500 ft. = 3.500 m) a unique airstrip indeed for, during most part of the year, it is covered with "edelweiss" flowers !

A pleasant short walk leads from the airstrip to Kyangshin where the Swiss Association for Technical Assistance set up, as far back as 1956, one of their many cheese factories.

From there, various treks can be undertaken, either northwards to reach after three to four hours the top of Yala Peak (16,000 ft. 4.877)m. or along the Langtang Valley itself towards Langshisa, at the foot of the Trupaiku glacier and the imposing pyramid of Dorje Lakpa. A more strenuous trek leads to and over Ganja-La Pass (16,800 ft. 5.120 m.) from which one reaches

Kathmandu, via Tharkegyang and the Indrawaty Valley.

The more classical trail back consists in following Langtang Khola Valley to Syabrubensi where it meets the other river the Bhote Kosi which comes from Tibet. It takes approx. three days from Langtang village to Betrawati and Trisuli, where it is easy to find transport (buses, trucks or jeeps) to drive you back to Kathmandu.

There is a short-cut along this trail by-passing Syabrubensi leaving the main road and taking the track between Ghora Tabela and Syarpa. This leads to Chedang and the picturesque Gosainkunda lakes.

To the Monastery of Thyangboche (12,710 ft. − 3.875 m.)

This is the spiritual centre of the whole Sherpaland and one of the most frequented places of worship and pilgrimage.

To reach this place, you may fly to either of two airstrips Lukla (9,085 ft. − 2.770 m.) or Syangboche (12,300 ft. − 3.750 m.).

In the first case, you will need two more days of walk. The first day you will reach easily (6 hours approx). the village of Jorsale (also called Thumbug) or, with a little additional effort NAMCHE BAZAR itself, the capital-city of the Sherpaland.

In the second case, one day is enough to reach, via the magnificently located Everest-View Hotel, the village of PHUNKI at the bottom of the Valley (10,650 ft. − 3.246 m.) and then climb up the partially steep track up to the monastery. This "gonpa" is located on a promontory looking straight towards Mount Everest and its guardian-mountain Nuptse (25,850 ft. − 7.879 m.) with, on its right side, the magnificent pyramid called Ama Dablam (22,493 ft. − 6.856 m.). Two other splendid peaks are the flattened "snow-saddle" called Kangteiga (21,932 ft. − 6.685 m.) and the sharp-edged Thamserku (22,336 ft. − 6.808 m.) to the south-east and the massif of Khumbu − Yul-lha (18,900 ft. − 5.760 m.) to the West. All these beautifully shaped, snow-covered mountain peaks add to the whole area's atmosphere of serenity peace and harmony.

In the course of this trek it is also a "must" to visit the two twin-villages of Khumjung-Kunde, where Sir Edmund Hillary built a school and a hospital, the first to be constructed in the whole area. The practitioner in charge is, traditionally, a New Zealander (like Sir Edmund himself) who is assigned there for two years. while his wife teaches English. Kunde is located at 12,400 ft. (3.780 m.)

The Thyangboche Monastery is not a very old one : it was built approx. 60 years ago. There are – depending on the part of the year – between 10 and 20 monks living permanently near the Monastery. They welcome visitors to their cermonies and rites. They perform, in November, the famous and very colourful masked dances of the "Mani-Rimdu" festival. Thyangboche monastery belongs to the non-reformed Nyingma-pa, or "red hat" sect.

At about 3 mi. (4.6 km.) beyond Thyangboche towards the northeast, in fact towards Everest Base Camp and Kala Patthar, lies Deboche with its well-known Lamaist convent and, after Milingbo, you reach the village of Pangboche (12,146 ft.– 3.985 m.) where the "gonpa" shelters the precious two "relics" the "yeti's scalp" and its (or his ?) mummified paw (or hand ?)

To Malenchi and Tharkegyang

Take the Chinese road as far as Panchkal (3,000 ft – 914 m.) From there you reach the picturesque Sherpa village of Tharkegyang (8,400 ft. – 2.560 m.) after a two-and-a-half day's trek along the Malenchi river. One more day will enable you to reach Malenchi Village on the other slope of the Valley, situated at 8,300 ft. – 2.530 m.), just opposite Tharkegyang. This is also a Sherpa village, where the visit of the gonpa is worth-while as well as of some of the thang-ka painters who are producing these typically Tibetan-style scrolls, even to-day.

Starting from Pokhara

To Chandrakott

After crossing Pokhara village (2 1/2 miles long-5 km.), which can be done by bus of jeep, turn left toward the Anglo-American "Shining Hospital" to reach the Seti Khola Valley which you follow to the Tibetan village (formerly a Refugee camp, This authentic village is worth a visit, in particular to have a look at the carpet-weaving halls. After having passed the village of Hyangja, well-known for its *"gaine"* (beggar minstrels), you have to walk for two hours through the paddy-fields, which are often somewhat muddy !

Having left Pokhara in the early morning, you can reach the few houses of Suikhet (3,600 ft. 1.100 m.) in the afternoon. With a little extra effort you can get to Naudanda at the top of moderately steep ascent, a two hours' climb, before nightfall. The advantage is that you are then above the hot area, as Naudanda

is at 4,782 ft. (1.457 m.) roughly the same height as Kathmandu (Remember that Pokhara is at only 2,952 ft.– 900 m.)

On the second day, you walk for three hours along the beautiful ridge over stubble fields, passing through the village of Khare
(5,400 ft. – 1.546 m.) and Lumle (5,100 ft. – 1.554 m.) The
same evening you can easily reach the end of the spur at Chand-
rakott (5,130 ft. – 1.563 m.). All along the way, you will see the
impressive massif of the Annapurnas and in front of you the
splendid pyramid of Macche Puchhare (22,960 ft– 6.997 m.)

You have to return by the same ridge, but just after Naudanda,
you can take a right fork and come straight down to Lake
Phewa, cutting out the long walk across the paddy-fields and
Pokhara town.

Starting from Kathmandu

FOR ONE OR TWO WEEKS
   To Gosainkund lakes

There are two tracks leading to this beautiful group of mountain lakes, where an important pilgrimage of Hindu devotees
takes place every year in July, in honor of Lord Shiva, who is
supposed to be present in the middle of one of the lakes in the
shape of an emerging rock.

The two itineraries are the folliwong :
– Either by bus or truck to Trisuli and Betrawati, then, on
foot past Ramche, Dhunche, Chin-Gompa – Monastery up to
the ridge overlooking the lakes.
– Or proceed directly on foot from Kathmandu via Sundarijal
and Malenchi in a westerly direction up to the Suryakund pass
(approx. 14,700 ft. 4.480 m.) which dominates the whole "necklace'
of lakes. The trail downwards, through the rocks and rubble,
is not diffcult to find. On the shore of the lowest lake, there are
some stone houses which may offer some protection if the trekkers
have no tent. This place is located at an altitude of approx.
13,700 ft. – 4.175 m.
   To Malenchi, Tharkegyang and Langtang.

Usually the trekking parties leave Kathmandu by the Kodari
road as far as Panchkal, from where an easy track follows the
Indrawaty river and slowly climbs up towards Tharkegyang.
From this picturesque Sherpa-village onwards, the real mountain
trekking part starts. Three days of partially difficult climbing,
the track ultimately leads to the narrow passage of the GANJA-

LA pass (16,805 ft. – 5.122 m.) which is overlooking the magnificent Langtang Valley. It takes only one day to reach it, although the way down is not always comfortable. Once you have reached Langtang Valley, there are many side-treks which may be undertaken from Kyangshin, a small settlement near the airstrip, where two buildings have to be visited : the Buddhist gonpa and the cheese-factory. The two most popular, and most spectacular walks starting from Kyangshin are :
– to follow the upper Valley of Langtang towards Langshisa glacier and the Massif of Dorje Lakpa.
– To go slightly to the north-east climb up towards the Yala Peak and Yala–glacier.

The road down from the Langtang Valley to Betrawati and Trisuli is almost a "high-way" which does not need to be described in detail. Busses run regularly between Trisuli and Kathmandu, taking between 6 and 7 hours.

To Solu-Khumbu (Sherpa-land)

Without the slightest doubt, the most beautiful–of all trekking areas in Nepal. Here you find the mountains – including the highest of world, – the Sherpa people and a series of authentic Tibetan Lamaist monasteries. What else is there to be desired ?

Whether you fly from Kathmandu to Lukla or to Syangboche, the approach into the Sherpa-land will be the same.

In this region there are three main valleys to explore; In fact there is a fourth, the one leading from Thame-Village in North-western direction towards the famous Nangpa-La, but this route is still within the "restricted area for foreigners".

It is one of the traditional trade routes between Nepal and Tibet, over which caravans of yaks use to carry medicinal herbs, barley, rice, manufactured wares to Tibet where these goods are exchanged against salt from the dried-out lakes of the Tibetan high plateuaux, and raw yak-wool. (This trade still goes on nowadays although in a more reduced way as in former times.)

But let us go back to the three "open" valleys. They offer more than enough beauty and variety to satisfy even the most insatiable trekker :

They are:
The Gokyo Valley, which leads from Kunde-Khumjung straight north towards the string of lakes and the Ngojumba glacier at the foot of Cho-Oyu.
The Imja Khola Valley which you can follow from Namche

Bazar via Thyangboche up to one mile before reaching Dingboche, where it forks :
— One of the two branches, the one on the left hand side, ascends in a north-westerly direction towards Pheriche, Dusa, Lobuche and finally to Gorak Shep lake, from where you may climb the Kala Patthar hill (18,192 ft. 4.445 m.) Here you have the most extraordinary panorama of the whole Everest range, at a few miles as the crow flies.
— The other branch, a little less frequented, goes off in an easterly direction to Bibre and further to Chukkhung, which is the starting point for the ascent of Island Peak (20,013 ft. 6.100 m.) This summit requires special training and equipment, for there are several very steep rocks and ice slopes to "negociate".

To Kala Patthar and Mt. Everest Base Camp:
This being the most popular trek it deserves to be dealt with in a little more detailed way.
First rule : Do not undertake this trek unless you have at least 15 full days at your disposal :
Second rule : Allow enough time for gradual acclimatization if you want to enjoy this trek, and not to leave your weaker companions behind.
There are two main ways to undertaking this trek :
1) If you have enough time, you may want to start trekking right from Kathmandu (or, better said, from either Lamosangu or Barabise on the Chinese road and from there proceed eastward) which will take you between 12 and 14 days to reach Namche Bazar. You may then either come back the same way, still on foot, or fly back.
2) If you have only about 15 days, you must plan using one of the STOL airplanes, to take you to the Khumbu area.
The recommended itinerary given below deals only with the second of these possibilities.
To start this trek, there are two landing fields.

Let us consider both routes :

a) You have decided to fly **from Kathmandu to Lukla** (9.085 ft.=2.770 m.)
First day : proceed to the village of Jorsale/Thumbug (9.000 ft.=2.743 m.) located at the foot of the ascent to Namche Bazar, but not beyond.
First night : Stay at Jorsale Thumbug
Second day : Proceed from Jorsale (Thumbug) to Namche

Bazar (11.286 ft.   3.440 m.)

Note : The most colourful and picturesque day to visit Namche
Bazar is on Saturday, which is the weekly market day.

Second night: Stay overnight at Namche Bazar or in its immediate
neighbourhood, such as the Syangboche airstrip (12,300
ft. = 3.750 m.) Khumjung-Kunde (12,400 ft. 3.780 m.) or Hotel
Everest View (12,713 ft. 3.875 m.)

   b) You have decided to fly **from Kathmandu to Syangboche**
airfield. Then, here is what a careful trekker ought to do;

First day : No walking on this first day, except, possibly, to one
of the neighbouring places such as Namche Bazar, Khumjung-Kunde or Hotel Everest View.

First night: There is accommodation to spend a night at the Sherpa
Lodge (managed by Transhimalayan Trekking) at Syangboche airfield itself, or, then, proceed to one of the three
above mentioned places.

Second day : Stay the whole day in the same area strolling leisurly
around.

Second night : Same as for the first night. Your companions
who chose the first alternative will join up with you and the
programme, henceforth, will be the same for both, i. e. :

Third day : Start early in the morning from wherever you spent
the night and proceed first to Phunki (10,650 ft. 3.246 m.)
then up to Thyangboche Monastery (12,710 ft. 3.875 m.)

Third night : Stay overnight at this magnificent place : Thyangboche.

Fourth day : Take a day-walk up and along the ridge east of the
Monastery and return to your camp.

Fourth night : Stay at the same place as the previous night.

Fifth day : Proceed from Thyangboche straight to Pheriche
(13, 943 ft. 4.250 m.)

Fifth night : Stay at Pheriche where there are four small inns
and also the Himalayan Rescue Association's AID POST,
manned during trekking season by a qualified doctor.

Sixth day : Undertake a day-walk over the eastern ridge down to
Dingboche village (14,270 ft. 4.350 m.) which is located at the
entrance of the beautiful Chukkhung Valley leading to Island
Peak (20,01 ft. 6.100 m.) Return to Pheriche.

Sixth night : Stay at Pheriche.

Seventh day : Proceed from Pheriche to Lobuche (16,174 ft.
4.930 m.) There is some accommodation in Lobuche. Most

advisable to have one's own tent.

Seventh night : Stay at Lobuche.

Ninth day : Proceed from Lobuche to Gorak Shep Lake (16, 860 ft. 5.170 m.).

Eight night : Stay at Gorak Shep.

Ninth day : Ascent to Kala Patthar (18,192 ft. 5.545 m.). It will take you between one hour and one and a half. The most magnificent view of the whole Everest-Nuptse-Lhotse range. Mt. Everest's top is exactly in front of you, at a distance of a mere 6 miles (9.6 km.) as the crow flies, but 10.837 ft. (3.303 m. above your eyes Everest Base Camp lies about 3 hours away from Gorak Shep Lake. It is located at approx. 17,388 ft. 5.300 m. The view on the surrounding massif may be less spectacular from the Base Camp as from Kala Patthar, but you are much nearer to the ill-famed Khumbu Glacier Icefall.

The descent from Gorak Shep to the Monastery of Thyangboche takes not more than two days and another two (or one and half) are needed to reach Syangboche airstrip, Khumjung-Kunde, Hotel Everest View or Namche Bazar. You must count between six and seven hours walk from to return to Lukla airstrip.

No special precautions have to be taken in regards to altitude sickness while ascending, of course.

Starting from Pokhara

Up the Kali Gandaki

There are two roads : On the way up, once you have passed through Syangja and along the paddy-field, it is better, instead of proceeding to Suikhet, to turn right and climb up to Dhampus, Landrung and Gandrung. The latter two are typically Gurung villages. From Gandrung over the Deorali Pass (9,000 ft. – 2.743 m.) it is also a very pleasant track, for it by-passes the steep "staircase" leading to Ulleri. From Deorali you reach easily Ghorepani pass.

Once you have crossed the latter, you are approaching the "thak" country. The Thakali villages are very pituresque with their fire-wood piled on the flat roofs of their houses, their streets often paved and lined with numerous shrines of "mani"–walls. All these villages, Sikha, Tatopani (hot springs !) Dana, Ghasa, Lete and Larjung offer accommodation facilities in thak-hostels. The most spectacular stretch of this track is the Kali Gandaki gorge, one of the deepest in the world : the torrent runs at a little over 8,500 ft. (2.590. m.) whereas the Annapurna flanking in in the East and the Dhaulagiri in the West, are both over 26,250 ft. (8.000 m.) high ! The wall of this gorge, perfectly vertical at some places stretches up more than 5,200 ft. (1.585m.)!

Having passed Dana (there is a check-post in this village), it is most advisable to cross the Kali Gandaki (there is a well-built bridge) and follow the trail on the left (Eastern) bank until you reach a second bridge which brings you again on the right (Western) bank that you follow now up to Ghaza. This deviation from the "straight" road that remains all the time on the Western bank avoids several very dangerous stretches.

After Larjung, you reach Tukuche, the "capital-city" of the Thakland.

Nowadays, treks may again be organized not only up to Jo-MOSOM (which was the "limit" of the forbidden area from 1963 to 1974) but to two more extremely interesting points further north resp. north-east, namely the village of KAGBENI, 7 miles north of Jomosom and the famous Hindu sanctuary of MUKTINATH, some 13 miles north-east of JOMSOM, where an "eternal divine flame springs forth from the earth", in fact an escape of natural gas.

Between TUKUCHA and JOMOSOM-KAGBENI-MUKTINATH has the distinct impression of having entered progressively into a region which has undoubtedly Tibetan features : the mountain slopes are barren, the country side is arid, a few dejected weeping willows remind of photographs taken in Lhassa, Shigatse or other Tibetan towns. This impression is strongest in the area around MUSTANG, – locally LO-MANTHANG – but the latter remains still inside the restricted zone, whereas another interesting locality much further to the east : MANANG has been "opened" in APRIL 1977. On the way back from JOMOSOM towards POKHARA, you can visit, just outside TUKUCHA, the picturesque monastery of "Gyuper Gonpa". on the right-hand side of the road, about ten minutes' walk from Tukuche.

One noteworthy peculiarity of the upper Kali Gandaki Valley is the extremely strong wind which sweeps the valley : roughly from 10 a. m. onwards, the winds blow from south to north and, in the afternoon, it continues till dark! It is better to take this into account when planning this trek, unless you like to have sand blowing in face, and pebbles machine-gunning your legs !

As indicated above, the return road, from Gorapani southwards should deviate from the one taken on the way "up". Instead of crossing again Deorali pass towards Gandrung, it is easier to follow the main track and pass through Ulleri, for from the village to the river down below, there are not less than 1.630, steps hewn in the path. It is certainly less tiring to take them downwards than upwards ! And it takes less time (1 h. 30 min. to go down, and at least one hour more to go up) not to count the additional 1000 steps that lead from Ulleri Village up to the pass, when going up !

To the Annapurna "Sanctuary"

This is undoubtedly one of the most rewarding treks.

You start off the same way as for the Kali Gandaki : After the paddy-fields up to Dhampus, Landrung, and Gandrung. But from there, instead of turning west towards Deorali, you follow in a northern direction from Kyumni Khola towards Chomrong (many orchids are to be found here, blooming in October-November). Here you spend the night, as the whole next day is needed to cross the dense wet bamboo forest which takes six to seven hours of hard and sometimes unpleasant walking when the path mingles with a rivulet. The forest leads to "Hinko" marked on all maps as if it were a village, whereas it is nothing but a huge overhanging rock where twenty to thirty people can find comfortable (!) shelter. (Hinko is located exactly at 10,000 ft.–3.048 m.)

Next day, after a rather steep two hour's climb, you "emerge' out of the forest and reach "Machha Puchhare Base-Camp", where one small hut was built in 1974. Now, you have attained an altitude of 11,800 ft (3.597 m.). To reach the real "entrance" of the Sanctuary, there is still one hour, or a little more, to go. But now, it is an easy walk, on grass-covered slopes; one by one the peaks become visible and when you arrive finally at the Annapurna's glacier's moraine (13,270 ft.– 4.045 m.) you find yourself in an incredibly beautiful, almost completely closed amphitheatre surrounded by 12 peaks ranging between 23,000 and 26,000 feet. (7.000 m.– 8.000m.). Certainly a unique panorama the world over. It becomes even more impressive if you succeed, after having crossed the glacier, (which does not present the slightest difficulty nor danger for it is entirely covered with boulders, to climb up to either Raski Peak (17,388 ft. 5.300 m.) or Tent Peak (18,700 ft. 5.700 m.), the latter however requiring technical skill and equipment, as well as knowledge of ice and rock climbing.

But even those who will stay one or two well-deserved rest

days at the Sanctuary itself will never forget the atmosphere of purity and beauty radiating from these summits, ice-walls and slowly tumbling glaciers.

Those who have gone there will no longer have to ask why this famous mountain (Machha Puchhare) is called "Fish-tail"!

An excellent book by Gunter Hauser, with remarkable photographs, entitled "Eisgipfel und Goldpagoden" (Icepeaks and Golden Pagodas) published by Bruckmann in Munich tells about an expedition in this area.

Other treks in Central Nepal

There are many more attractive trekking possibilities in this area, some of which are described in the specialized literature which has been mentioned at the beginning of the present chapter:

Let us simply mention briefly some of them :

The LAMJUNG and the NAMUN PASS that can be reached either from Pokhara via Siklis, by starting from the Palungtar-Gorkha airstrip or leaving the Kathmandu-Pokhara road at a place called Dumre. This trek would take between 12 and 17 days NAMUN PASS is a little difficult to find and is very steep.

– The "NORTH WEST ANNAPURNA SANCTURY" which could be called the "mirror-image" of the better known "Annapurna Sanctuary", described in the previous paragraph.

This "north-western" one is limited in the north–west by the Nilgiri Massif, in the north, by the "Grand Barrier" and in the south by Annapurna I.

It can be reached by branching off from the Gandaki main trail at the village of Choya and from there, the track–which is said to be steep, difficult to find and very strenuous–proceeds in a south-eastern direction. To be on the safe side, 18 to 20 days are indispensable.

– In the area at the northern tip of the Kali Gandaki also, there are many "side-treks" worth undertaking. Climbing towards the North-West from Tukuche for example, there are magnificent areas on the slopes of the Dhaulagiri Massif (up to the Dhaulagiri eastern ice-fall offers a breath-taking panorama) or towards **Dhampus Pass.** On the eastern side, the Tilicho and Nilgiri ranges provide many treks in the immaculate landscape of glaciers and rocks.

Pokhara-Kathmandu

This is, of course not a mountain-trek; nevertheless it is undoubtedly a very interesting walk which allows you to get in touch with many different ethnic groups, different types of villages etc. On the way, the visit of the city of Gurkha and of its magnicent historical castle, from where Prithvi Nayayan Shah the Great started off in 1744 to unify Nepal, are what tourist-literature usually calls "a must".

Furthermore, this road passes the picturesque villages of Arughat and Nuwakot, where another old fortified palace may be visited.

Starting from Jumla
To Rara Lake

Along easy paths and through a series of poor but picturesque villages, you reach within four or five days the magnificent shores of glittering Rara Lake. From Rara Lake it should be possible to continue due north in the direction of Mugut, the gate to the western and north-western regions of Nepal which are still untouched and where customs and religious traditions have remained unchanged through the ages, such as the Dolpo, Phoksumdo, Tcharbung areas. But all these are still closed to foreigners.

FOR MORE THAN TWO WEEKS.

First of all, it is always possible and even recommended to extend any of the above mentioned treks by exploring adjacent valleys or mountain passes, a forlorn village here or a yak pasture, there i. e. a cluster of houses which, in Sherpaland, are called "yarsa".

There are also an infinite number of treks which would take more than a fortnight, for instance to walk from Namche Bazar to Darjeeling, via Taplejung and Phidim, or to proceed along the whole ARUN Valley (in the eastern part of Nepal) up to the foothill of the Kanchenjunga Massif or towards Makalu Base Camp. Still others are to be undertaken in the Central and western part of the country.

The three pre-conditions for such a trek are :
    a) to be in excellent physical condition and have some training
    b) to have enough days at your disposal to avoid becoming the victim of the "time-complex" which affects nowadays too many Westerners.
    c) to be ready to make do with a simple diet and only elementary comfort.

One of these treks deserves a special paragraph :

AROUND THE ANNAPURNA RANGE, AND MANANG

This trek takes between 18 and 22 days. After having remained in the "restricted area" for over 15 years, the Manang region has been declared "open" for tourists and trekkers in the spring 1977, thus, enabling now to undertake the famous "Round the Annapurna Range" trek.

It can be contemplated clock-wise or anti-clock-wise, i. e.: Either starting from Jomsom and after Muktinath, crossing the Thorung Pass (17,770 ft.)and proceeding then to Manang along the Marsyangdi Valley down to the Kathmandu-Pokhara road.

Or from DUMRE, a point on this Kathmandu-Pokhara road, following the Marsyangdi upstreams, reaching Manang and proceeding over the pass down to Muktinath and Jomsom.

It is the latter route which is positively to be recommended, the other to be rejected, for various reasons:

a) Dumre being located at 1350ft. the acclimatization to altitude is much more progressive than by starting from Jomsom (3,700 ft.)

b) There are no proper camp-sites, water or firewood on the whole long (7 hours) ascent from Muktinath to Thorunh Pass whereas coming from Manang there are two good campsites with shelters for porters and water, at 14,100 ft.-4.300 m. and at 14,800 ft-4.500 m. respectively.

c) There is an airstrip in Jomsom. It is always safer to head *towards* an airfield, when having had a strenous trek than to fly back to the starting point and having to face nothing but days and days of walking before reaching a road, should some emergency occur.

Of course, trekkers who have 25 or 26 days at their disposal would want to walk down from Jomosom to Pokhara, which takes approx. 5 days.

From all points of view, this trek is certainly one of the most fascinating, for it offers all types of scenery, flora, various types of ethnic groups; it also includes several magnificent Tibetan gompas (monasteries) that can be visited : Pisang, Gyaru, Braga Bo-Dzo and, last but not the least, the really breath-taking sights of the mountains stretching from Manaslu to Lamjung, the whole Annapurna Range, and further, the Grand Barrier, Nilgiri, Tukuche Peak and Dhaulagiri.

For those who have some more days at their disposal, it is recommended to spend two days climbing up, from Manang in a north-eastern direction, to reach the ridge looking over the famous "Great Frozen Lake" (16,400 ft.) one of the highest lakes of such considerable size in the world (4 miles long, 1 mile wide) which is frozen almost all year round.

Normally, trekkers used to proceed to the "Frozen Lake" when they intended to reach Jomosom via the "Tilicho Pass".

(Also called "Meso Kanto" on certain maps.) This pass (17,380 ft.: 5.300 m.) is declared "restricted area" for foreigners. However it is still allowed to trek up to the shore of the lake. Then it is mandatory to turn back to Manang and follow the "classic trail" via the Thorung-Pass (17.700 ft. : 5.400 m.) and down to Muktinath and Jomsom.

NOTE : Since the short stretch between Larkya-Pass and Thonje is also "restricted", the equally interesting trek" "Around Mt. Manaslu" can not yet be undertaken.

List of authorized summits for trekkers

CATEGORY "A" (*)

Name	Altitude in Meters	Feet	Location
1. Tent Peak	5.500	18,040	Annapurna Region
2. Mardi Himal	5.555	18,220	id.
3. Pokhalde Himal	5.802	17,030	Everest Region
4. Ganjala Chuli	5.806	17,043	Langtang Region
5. Mera Peak II	5.820	17,087	Everest Region
6. Paldor	5.874	19,332	Ganesh Himal Area
7. Rumdung Peak	6.021	17,748	Rolwaling Area
8. Pisang Peak	6.071	17,778	Manang Region

CATEGORY "B" (*)

Name	Altitude in Meters	Feet	Location
1. Lobuche Peak	6.119	20,070	Everest Region
2. Island Peak	6.187	20,181	id.
3. Kwangde Peak	6.194	20.316	id.
4. Chulu East	6.200	20,336	Manang Region
5. Parchamo Peak	6.282	20,605	Rolwaling Area
6. Hiunchuli Peak	6.333	20,772	Annapurna Region
7. Kusum Kangri	6.367	20,870	Everest Region
8. Fluted Peak	6.370	20,759	Annapurna Region
9. Mera Peak I	6.431	21,073	Everest Region
10. Chulu West	6.630	21,746	Manang Region

Number of Trekkers and tourists

A safe guess is that approximately 15% of all tourists visiting Nepal undertake some kind of trekking. This estimation may however vary from one country to the other.

So far, there is no precise statistics about trekkers, but here are the official figures of foreign tourists who came to Nepal in the course of 1979.

Country of Origin	Number
India	37523
U.S.A.	18555
France	17671
Fed. Rep. of Germany	12679
Japan	11680
U.K.	11231
Australia	7500
Italy	5975
Spain	5252
Canada	3172
Netherlands	3139
Switzerland	3056
Sri Lanka	2514
Belgium	2345
Austria	2199
Latin America	1867
New Zealand	1850
Denmark	1827
Thailand	1720
Sweden	1600
Israel	1184
Miscellaneous	7737
TOTAL with India	162276
TOTAL Without India	124753

(*) *NOTE:* The climbing fee for summits of Category "A" is Rs. 315.–per trekker (Sherpas and porters excluded) with a minimum of Rs. 630.– while for summits of Category "B" the minimun to be paid is Rs. 1.260.– The permit, to be issued by Nepal Mountaineering Association, Ram Shah path, is valid for 2 weeks. An additional fee of 25% is levid for each additional week. The regulations specify also a certain number of conditions to be respected, in regards to equipment, insurance etc... for guides and porters.

CHAPTER NINE

WHILE ON TREK

THE PART PLAYED BY THE "SIRDAR"...

The title of "Sirdar" is given to the Chief-Sherpa (he may also be of another ethnic origin, a Tamang, for example).

It is the "Sirdar" who has to fix, with the members of the group on one side, the porters on the other, the exact itinerary planned for each day.

It is most important that the stage planned should not be too strenuous, neither for the members of the group or for the porters. The Sirdar must ascertain that the latter know as exactly as possible what is expected from them.

Another very important task of the "sirdar" is to act as a "guide". Perhaps this not like a professional alpine climbing guide, for he may not have the necessary technical experience but the group must be able to rely on the sirdar's knowledge of the route, or, at least of the region in general and thus prevent one's getting on a wrong. The Sirdar will use his excellent sense of orientation as well as his ability to talk to the local people, to find a short-cut, a well of fresh water, a camp-site etc.

Thus, the "Sirdar" acts also as an interpreter. If the weather is too unfavourable for pitching the tents somewhere in the open, it is he who will negociate the access to a suitable farmer's house as sleeping quarters.

Moreover, it is the "Sirdar" who will be sent by the trekking group leader to go shopping in the village for firewood, fresh vegetables, fruits, eggs, etc. He will always be in a better position to bargain over a chicken or a mutton-leg.

In the morning he will supervise the fair distribution of the porter's loads and suggest the reduction of the number of porters as and when the provisions carried have been consumed underway to the extent that one or more porters have become redundant. (When recruiting them, this point has also to be taken into account by the Sirdar : he can not promise all porters to go along with the party from beginning to end).

If the party is a numerous one and the trek is planned for more than a fortnight, it is always advisable to hire an assistant to the Sirdar. One of the two will have to remain near the group-leader while the other is walking at the end of the long line of porters to make sure that none of them stays behind or gets lost.

Still another duty of the Sirdar is to act as a treasurer : He is responsible to the group-leader for the amounts the latter has handed over to him to cover all minor expenses and to pay advance salaries to porters.

This is a practice which can hardly be avoided, for the porters, before joining the party, have to give some money to their family and a so, they have to buy their food. It may be necessary to remind here that until now, it is a accepted custom that porters have to provide their own food. The trekking party has to supply meals, as well as equipment only to the "sirdar", his assistant (s) and other guides, cooks and kitchen-boys as well as "altitude porters", if any. Another important fact has to be added here, namely that neither the "sirdar" nor his assistants are to be asked to carry anything else but their personal belongings, at least not until the party has reached the snow-line or starts climbing in areas where ordinary porters would not be able to follow.

One of the many remarkable qualities of the Sherpas, the quality which makes them usually the best high-altitude guides is what is commonly called their "third lung" which enables them to be perfectly at ease at 18,500 ft. (5.600 m.) and higher up. At these altitudes, they are really invaluable since they can easily add another knapsack on top of their own while climbing. Many of them– if not all – have enough technical experience on rocky terrain and glaciers, and know how to handle ice-picks, crampons and ropes. If the trek is planned to reach such areas, the choice of at least one such competent sirdar is of course a necessity.

It also goes without saying that in high altitude, the sirdar, as well as all other guides, cooks, porters etc.. are to be provided with the same type and quality of equipment as the trekkers use for themselves.

Last but not least, the Sirdar, whether a Sherpa or not, is for the trekker the best of companions under all and any circumstance. His loyalty, endurance and resourcefulness have no limits.

A TYPICAL DAY ON TREK.

When on a trek, it is customary to get up at dawn. No real trekker would like to miss the magnificent sight of the rising sun that gives life to the snow-capped peaks by tinting them first in pale pink, then in red and finally in glowing white. Furthermore, dawn is the moment when all birds start singing, whistling and chirping; Don't forget that Nepal is a birds' paradise where about 800 varieties have been recorded.

John BUCHAN was right when he wrote. *"One of the misfortunes of advancing age is that you get out of touch with the sunrise. You take it for granted and it is over and done with before you settle yourself for the daily routine".*

Now since there is no "daily routine" while trekking, it is much more exalting to be awake and aware of the sunrise ! Generally, it is the cook who, before anybody else, leaves his tent in order to prepare the "early morning tea" which he will bring to each of the trekkers while they are still in their tents.

Unless precise orders to the contrary have been given the previous evening, (or once and for all), this cup of tea is likely to be served mixed with a lot of sugar and milk.

The next step is to get all things together, sleeping bags, mattresses etc. in their respective plastic or canvas bags, dismantling the tents and preparing dhokos and other loads while breakfast is being served outside.

The day may follow two different patterns, either the "Sherpa-style day" or the "western" one.

In the first case, breakfast will consist of one or more cups of tea (or hot chocolate, or coffee, whichever is available) and a few biscuits. There may be a piece of cheese and/or chocolate, if within reach, but nothing which needs cooking or lengthy preparations. Then, the trekkers start simultaneously with the porters (who will also restrict their first breakfast to a cup of tea). Later, between 10.00 and 10.30, sometimes even at 11 a.m. there will be a long halt at a convenient place where there is plenty of water and firewood. There, the porters will start cooking their morning meal, i.e. huge amounts of rice with dal (small yellow lentils) or tsampa (a kind of porridge made of grilled, then boiled barley flour, the Sherpas staple food), mixed with vegetables, spices, etc. The trekkers will take advantage of this halt to have their real breakfast with porridge, eggs, some tinned food (e.g. paté or tinned fish) cheese, bread (or chapatis : a kind of pancake made of wheat flour) butter, marmalade, etc.

This "brunch" seldom takes less than one and a half hour's, more often nearer to two hours.

The party then goes on, makes another short halt at around 1 p.m. but not always, for a quick cold lunch "out of the knapsack", the main meal being served in the evening at the camp-site. It will consist of soup, meat, rice, spaghettis or potatoes, vegetables, tinned food, cheese, fruit-salad, etc. Around 6 p.m. or earlier everybody retires to his tent.

In the second case, the "western style" day will be slightly different : A full breakfast will be served in the morning and will include porridge, coffee, eggs, etc. which need preparation and therefore will not allow the party to leave the camp before 7.30 or even 8 a.m.

The porters will insist on having their "brunch" in the course of the morning which means they will be way behind the main party during the whole afternoon. Since they walk at a much slower pace, they may reach the camp-site much later than the rest, which entails serious in inconvenience (in particular when it's raining). The trekkers would then halt for one hour around mid-day and have their quick lunch then.

If the road does not pass through too difficult terrain, trekkers usually walk four hours in the morning and three in the afternoon. In more difficult areas or at higher altitudes, 4 or 5 hours in one day is a reasonable average. To count the number of "miles covered" in one day makes little sense, as it all depends on the "ups" and "downs". The only factual yardstick is to count the number of hours spent on walking. In reasonably difficult terrain one may count on climbing an average of 1,100 or 1,300 feet in one hour of trekking when the track goes smoothly uphill.

THE TREKKER AT SANCTUARIES AND "GONPAS".

In the district called "Solu-Khumbu, the Sherpa-land", as well as in the Thakhhola region (the valley of the Kali Gandaki) trekkers will very often see stone-walls covered with engraved slabs, mostly bearing repetitions of the sacred "mantra" (prayer formula): *"om mani padme hum"* (Oh, jewel in the lotus) which covers the slab completely. Now it is important to note that one is always expected to go around these walls (as well as around chortens, the many small sanctuaries also in these regions), by following the path "clockwise". This explains why there are always two paths around such monuments, to enable all passers-by to walk the "right way". To do otherwise would be considered, not only by the local inhabitants but also by your own Sherpas, as a lack of respect.

"Gonpas", also pronounced "gumpas" "gompas", etc. are the names given to temples, monasteries and convents. They are always sacred places. It is recommended to take shoes off before entering such a place. Lamas, monks and nuns are, as a rule, very hospitable and glad to welcome and foreigners. They do not object to their visiting their "gonpa", taking pictures (even with flashlight) or recording on magnetic tape, rites, ceremonies, prayers, songs and music. Handing over to the abbot a "kata", a ceremonial white scarf which your sirdar will always know where to buy, as a sign of respect is an elementary courtesy. One offers the kata spread over both extended forearms. Should hospitality have been given to the trekking party (it is not customary to ask permission to spend the night inside a gonpa, except if there is a terrific rain or snowstorm outside and no other shelter available) it is a tradition to give a donation, in banknotes, to the Abbot (On the basis of 5 or 10 Rs. per trekkers).

Sometimes also, one comes across small hermitages. It is not recommended to disturb the lama or layman who has decided to retire for years (or even for the rest of his earthly life) in prayer and mediation.

There may be no better way to end this chapter than to quote a text which the author found, some ten years ago, affixed to the door of the "guest-house" near the Thyangboche monastery:

"I am happy to welcome you at Thyangboche.

"This is the religious centre of the whole "Sherpa-land". in fact, the entire Solu-Khumbu area.

"A very modest rest-house has been built on the far end of the meadow, facing Chomo-Longma (Mount Everest).

"It has been erected with the funds collected from friends and visitors who have come to this sacred and beautiful place. If you wish, you may contribute to our meagre funds to enable us to make it more comfortable when you come again, for we hope you will. Anything you may wish to give will be gratefully accepted.

"While you are a guest at Thyangboche, whether you stay at the rest-house or in your own tents, I wish to request you to abide by the few rules in observance of the Divine Dharma.

DEVOTION IN ITS PUREST FORM

SLOWLY BUT SAFELY TOWARD

...ONE OF THE MOST MAGNIFICENT SPOTS ON EARTH

SYMPHONY

"Please do not kill or cause to kill any living creature in the area of this holy place. This includes domestic fowls and animals, as also wild game.

"Please remember that this holy place is devoted to the worship of the Perfect One, and that nothing should be done within these sacred precincts which will offend or cause to hurt those who live here in humility and serenity. May your journey in peace and walk in delight, and may the blessings of the Perfect One be always with you."

Ngawang Tenzing Zang-Po
The reincarnate of Thyangboche.

– DEALING WITH AN EMERGENCY

As it has been indicated above, the Himalayas are not "organized" as the Alps are in Europe or the Rocky Mountains in the U.S.A., where mountan climbing, ski–ing etc. have been practiced for many decades. Here there are neither chalets nor rescue posts, telephone, emergency squads, etc.

This state of things justifies to give hereunder some information about the existing facilities and same hints as to what should be done in case of a real emergency.

1) List of wireless stations

—Postal Stations (open to the public in general)

It may be of interest to give hereunder the complete list of all telecommunication wireless stations operation in Nepal. These are open to the public from 10 a.m. to 5 p.m.; however the hours during which messages may be sent change from one stating to the other and enquires should be made at each point.

These stations operate like ordinary telegraph offices : as soon as the message has been received at the Telecommunication Central Office in Kathmandu, it will be delivered by cyclist to the addressee as indicated by the sender or the latter will be advised by telephone.

The following list is classified zonewise :

Name of Zone	Locations of wireless stations
Bagmati	Chautara, Dhading, Kathmandu, Rasua Garhi.
Bheri	Bardia, Kailakha, Jajarkot, Nepalganj, Rajpur Surkhet
Dhaulagiri	Jomosom, Beni, Dolpo.
Gandaki	Bandipur, Gorkha, Kunchha, Kusma, Manang, Pokhara, Syangja.

Janakpur   Charikot, Jaleshwar, Janakpur, Malangawa, Rame-
             chhap, Sindhuligarhi.
Karnali   Humla, Jumla, Mugu,
Kosi   Biratnagar, Chainpur, Dhankuta, Dharan, Inerwa,
             Terhathum.
Lumbini   Arghakhanchi, Bhairawa, Butwal, Gulmi, Krishnana-
             gar, Palpa, Parasi, Taulihawa, Tribeni,
Mahakali   Baitadi, Dadeldhura, Darchula, Mahendranagar.
Mechi   Bhadrapur, Ilam, Phidim, Taplejung,
Nanayani   Bharatpur, Bhimpedi, Birganj, Gaur, Hetauda.
Rapti   Ghorahi, Koilabas, Pyuthan, Rolpa, Rukum, Salyan,
             Tulsipur.
Sagarmatha Bhojpur, Diktel, Okhaldhunga, Rajbiraj, Siraha,
             Udaipurgarhi.
Seti   Achham, Bajhang, Bajura, Dhangari, Silgarhi Doti.
—*Other wireless stations* (exclusively for cases of extreme emer-
gency):

In addition to the above mentioned Postal Stations, there
are, in certain localities, wireless stations, operated by Police,
Army or other authorities such as
* Police Wireless station at Namche Bazar,
* Meteorological Office at Syangboche Airport
* Control-tower of certain airfields such as Jiri, Dhorpatan,
Lukhla.
In case of extreme urgency and emergency, the authorities
in charge of such stations may accept to forward messages, but
these would, normally, reach the respective Head-Offices in
Kathmandu of the authorities concerned from where they would
be forwarded by telephone or by messenger.
But, we repeat, these stations are not open to the public in
general and are not to be used for pirivate meassages.

2) **To whom emergency messages must be addressed :**
Since most of such messages aim at requesting a rescue operation, they must be simultaneously addressed (when sent through
Postal Services) or forwarded (when sent through other stations),
to
– R.N.A.C.'s Head-Office (Telephone 14511 – Ext. 136–137)–
Helicopter Division. They will endeavour to carry out the flight.
– the Trekking (or Travel) Agency that organized the trek
of the party of which the casualty is a member
– and, in any case, the Embassy or Consulate of the casualty
concerned.

It is self-understood that before calling for a helicopter, the party should always try to carry the injured or sick person to the nearest airstrip on which a R.N.A.C. STOL aircraft could land, or to the nearest town or hospital.

3) What information an emergency message must contain

The following information must be included in any "emergency message" calling for an airplane or a helicopter rescue operation.

– The degree of urgency, by specifiyng either 'Most Immediate' or 'A.S.P,' meaning As Soon as Possible..

(Note : "Most Immediate" messages must be restricted to cases when possibility of death has to be considered within 24 hours).

–The following medical information :

* What kind of sickness or injury
* Specify whether the case is one of "mountain sickness"..
* If a stretcher has to be provided
* If oxygen is required

–The following personal data :

* Name and nationality of casualty
* Age and Sex of casualty
* Number of people to be evacuated (whether sick, injured or to accompany the casualty).
* Sender's name and/or organization
* How and by whom rescue operations cost will be paid

–Whether or not, an airplane or a helicopter is to be sent and where to exactly.

This last question may seem superfluous. In fact it is not, since experience proves that on many occasions, a trekking party refrained from spelling out distinctly its wishes, limiting themselves to give all details about the physical condition of the person concerned and leaving it to the doctor in Kathmandu to take the decision whether an immediate rescue operation should be launched and by what means. Of course, this procedure is not practicable.

4) Cost of a rescue operation :

At the time when R.N.A.C still had its own helicopters (4 seater-Bell), the rates were fixed at US $ 700.– (or Rs. 8186.)– per hour.

Normally, it takes an average of two hours and twenty minutes to complete a rescue operation by helicopter or by Pilatus Porter, at a place located near to Syangboche airfield or, if a helicopter is available, half-way between Thyangboche Monastery and Kala Patthar, at an altitude of approx. 14,000 ft. (4.267 m.)

Thus the cost of such a rescue operation including the flight from Kathmandu to the rescue place, the pick-up time and the flight back would amount approx. to nearly US $ 1750.– (Or Rs. 20,415.–)..

These rates (in force end 1980 apply to the Alouette helicopter. The rate for the larger Puma helicopter is approx. US $ 1725.– or Rs 20,000.– per hour)

It is but natural that R.N.A.C. in the case of rescue operation, insists that ability to pay for the operation is well and clearly established in writing beforehand.

Important suggestion.

It is highly advised that all trekkers who intend to proceed above 13.000 ft. (3.960 m.) should, before they leave, subscribe, either in their home country or on arrival in Kathmandu, to an insurance policy covering the cost of any rescue operation, be it by ambulance, airplane helicopter or a combination of these means of transport. (Too often, so-called "rapatriation by airplane insurance policies" which holiday-makers contract customarily, exclude a certain number or sports – such as "mountain-climbing" which the insurance companies consider as involving too great a risk. They also exclude very often air-transport "other than regular scheduled flights".) Greatest care is to be observed when contracting such a "holiday-insurance.."

5) The "Trekkers Aid Post" at Pheriche.

Thanks to the generosity of the Department of Surgery of the Tokyo Medical College (Professor Yoshihiro Hayata's Foundation), a "Trekker's Aid Post" was built and installed at Pheriche, a *yarsa* ground and hamlet located at an altitude of 13,943 ft. (4.250 m.) It was inaugurated on 29th October 1975.

This post is neither a hotel nor a hospital, but it is sufficiently provided with equipment and medicines to be able to assist those who need medical help. The post is placed under the supervision of Japanese or Western practitioners. The initiative of this "Aid-Post" is to be put on the credit of Kumar Khadga Bikram Shah, Chairman of the Nepal Mountain

Association.

The selection of Pheriche as the place for this first well-equipped Himalayan Aid-Post was motivated by its altitude. It is placed at precisely the "critical height" of roughly 14,000 ft. (4.260 m.) where most of the cases of mountain sickness start.

On the other hand, Pheriche (which is not a permanently inhabited village but just a summer grazing spot for yaks) is situated on the most frequented of all trekking "roads", the one leading from Lukla, Syangboche, "Everest-View Hotel" or Namche Bazar to the world famous "Kala Patthar" view point and to the Everest Base Camp. Approximately, it is estimated that over 3500 trekkers stroll along this track during the two trekking seasons (autumn and spring, in total 4 to 5 months).

During 1977, thanks to the preventive action of this AID-POST, no casualty was recorded in the Khumbu–area.

It may be hoped that similar initiatives will be taken by other organisations, in order to equip other Himalayan trails with several of such much needed, not to say "vital", Aid-Posts.

SECTION IV

HIMALAYAN

EXPEDITIONS

CHAPTER TEN

THE ODYSSEY OF MOUNT EVEREST

(29,028 ft. 8848 m.)

INTRODUCTION

This chapter, like any of the preceding ones, does not claim to be without omissions. It is not intended to be a detailed record of all Himalayan expeditions undertaken in the course of the past decades. Its purpose is simply to refresh the memory of those who are professionally interested in the fascinating adventures which the French mountaineer Lionel Terray so aptly called; "The conquest of the useless". The purpose of this chapter is also to pay homage to the memory of those valiant conquerors, who did not reach their goal.

Honour to whom honour is due : Mount Everest deserves a special section !

The highest point of our earth has been baptized "The Third Pole" by Mr. Gunter. O. DYRENRURTH, the well-known Swiss-American Himalayist.

But Mount Everest has many other names :

First of all, its present name goes back to Sir George EVEREST, the Head of the Cartographic Survey of India team who was in charge of mapping this part of the Himalayas. In fact, it was one of his Indian assistants, Radhanath Sikhadar who actually discovered, in an undisputable way that a certain summit which was then merely called "Peak No 15" was, really, the highest mountain ever measured. This discovery was made in 1852.

In Sanskrit, Hindi and Nepali, this mountain has been called, since time immemorial,; "SAGARMATHA". which can be translated, in an appoximate way, as "The summit of the sky". In Tibetan and Sherpa languages, it is always referred to as "CHOMO-LUNGMA"– sometimes spelled JOMOLUNGMA or KANG CHAMOJUNG – which means "Goddess-Mother of the Earth".

The conquest of this "highest point on earth" has a long history. Here is a brief account of its most important milestones.

ATTEMPTS MADE FROM THE NORTHERN (Tibetan) SIDE

Since Nepal remained closed to foreigners until 1950, the first attempts to conquer Mount Sagarmatha were made from the Tibetan side, above Rumbuk Glacier. Here are the main stages of this fascinating story :

1873 : First attempt, by Gen. C. G. Bruce, a British mountaineer. Unsuccessful.

1921 : Another British trial : C. K. Howard-Bury led the first expedition, accompanied by H. T. Morshead, E.O. Wheeler, G. H. Mallory and C.H. Bullock. An advance party reached the North Col (27,315 ft. – 6.985m.) but had to turn back. Dr. A.M. Kellas died when trying to reach Base.

1922 : Second expedition, this time with provisions of oxygen containers for the first time. General G.C. Bruce was the leader. His companions, G. H. Mallory, E. F. Norton, T. H. Somervell. The latter reached 26.803 ft (8.170 m.) and, in a second attempt, thanks to the use of oxygen, G. I. Finch and his Sherpa Tedjbir Bura reached the highest point ever climbed so far : 27,315 ft. i. e. 8.325 m. Again a tragedy marked this attempt : an avalanche below the North Col swept away and buried seven Sherpas. Their bodies were never found.

1924 : G. C. Bruce also led the third and so far most important expedition (350 porters !). The leader had to abandon, due to sickness, two porters died of frostbite. On June 4th, without oxygen, E. F. Norton reached a still higher point as hitherto : 28,122 ft. (8.572 m.). Three days later, G. L. Mallory and A. Irvine attempted the final assault to the summit. They may have reached it, but they never came back and their fate will never be known.

1933 : Human effort having failed, man introduced their flying machines to help them in the conquest of the worlds highest point. On 3rd and 19th April, Sagarmatha was overflown and many photographs were taken.

1933 : H. Ruttledge, leading another British expedition did not score much better than his predecessors, nine years ago. The highest point reached by two members of the team, W. Harris and F. Smythe was 28,125 ft. (8.573 m.) The last 900 feet (275 m.) still resisted stubbornly.

1934 : First solo attempt : Towards the end of March, M. Wilson, a British mountaineer set out from Darjeeling, crossed Sikkim and reached the Rombuk glacier. He met his death before gaining the North Col, at an assumed altitude of 22,000 ft. (6.705 m.)

1935 : Eric Shipton leads yet another British expedition, whose principal aim was to conduct a thorough reconnaissance of the whole area around and above North Col. Bad weather conditions forced the team back. Eric Shipton and W. Harris almost lost their life in an avalanche.

1936 : H. Ruttledge came back and tried again. Bad weather compelled him again to withdraw near the North Col.

1938 : Another unsuccessful attempt, this time by a team led by H. W. Tilman. Highest point reached : 27,200 ft. (8.291 m.)

1942 : For the first time, a North-American undertook a reconnaissance, with the help of a small airplane. He successfully flew over the mountain. He was Col. Robert Scott.

1947 : The second "solo" attempt met with the same fate as the first one : Earl Denman, a Canadian, almost reached the North Col but could not proceed much beyond. He claimed to have reached a point located at 23.490 ft. (7.160 m.)

ATTEMPTS MADE FROM THE SOUTHERN (Nepalese) SIDE

Autumn 1950 : First expedition "via the south route", by Charles Houston, his son and W. Tilman. After having successfully crossed the frightening and dangerous "icefall" of the Khumbu Glacier, they proceeded into the "Western cwm", but could not go beyond.

Autumn 1951 : Third "solo" – attempt. This time by a Danish mountaineer, K. Becker-Larsen, accompanied by four Sherpas. He first tried the southern approach, turned back, managed to get across Nang-Pa La – a pass above Thame, located at 18,745 ft. (5.715 m.) He went all around the Massif, finally reached Rombuk Glacier and succeeded in setting foot on the North Col, but there, he had to turn back. He arrived safely in Darjeeling a few days later.

Autumn 1951 : An important *reconnaissance* expedition led by Eric Shipton, undertook a systematic study of the Southern Route without intention of reaching the summit. Among the members, a newcomer from far-away New Zealand : Edmund Hillary.

Spring 1952 : The first Swiss expedition led by E. Whyss-Dunant. They left Kathmandu on March 29th with 165 porters and 20 Sherpas under the leadership of Norkay Tenzing. After having reached the South Col, Raymond Lambert and Norkay Tenzing undertook to ascent to the summit on May 28th. They reached the highest point ever : 27,886 ft. (8.500 m.) Then they had to turn back.

Autumn 1952 : Encouraged by the "near-success" of the previous expedition, another Siwss team set out in autumn under the leadership of Dr. Gabriel Chevalley. This team also established its "assault camp" on South Col but was driven back by bad condition while attempting to climb above 26,300 ft. (8.016 m.) One Sherpa died, struck by an ice boulder.

FIRST SUCCESSFUL EXPEDITION AND SUBSEQUENT ATTEMPTS AND CONQUESTS

Spring 1953 : Finally Sagarmatha gave in : A British expedition led by Col. John Hunt set out to take revenge on all the previous failures of the past 32 years : The team included B Band, T. Bourdillon, Dr. Charles Evans, A. Gregory and two New-Zealanders : Edmund Hillary and G. Lowe. The ascent was undertaken via the Khumbu icefall and the South Col. In the morning of 29th May, for the first time in history, Mount Everest was conquered : EDMUND HILLARY, in company of SHERPA NORKAY TENZING, reached the top of world's highest peak This historic event coincided with the coronation festivities of H. M. Queen Elizabeth II. (Norkay Tenzing is generally counted among the Indian Sherpas)

Spring 1956 : The second successful expedition was Swiss, under the leadership of Albert Eggler. They followed the same route as the British three years before : Two ropes reached the summit : On 23rd May : J. MARMENT and E. SCHMIED and on the following day, 24th May : R. REIST and H. V. GUNTEN (all four summitteers were Swiss nationals).

Spring 1960 : First Indian attempt, via the South Col as well. This expedition led by Brig. Gyan Singh brought three members Kumar, Gombu and Gyatso up to 28,300 ft. (8.626 m.), missing a mere 728 ft (222 m.) which the bad weather did not allow them to ascend.

Spring 1960 : First successful Chinese climb of the northern side of Mount Everest: The three summiteers were all Chinese nationals : WANG FU CHOU, CHOU YING HUA and GOMPA No further details were given at the time.

Spring 1962 : John Dias, the leader of the second Indian expedition was not more successful than his predecessor. However team members Kholi, Dang and Gyatso progressed up to 28.600 ft. (8.717 m.) still nearer to the summit than their colleagues two years before. But they too, had to retreat.

Spring 1962 : First combined venture of American and Swiss climbers under the leadership of W. Sayrs. The attempt had to be abandoned.

Spring 1963 : First full-fledged, magnificently equipped expedition, led by Norman G. Dyrenfurth. This was, so far, the largest expedition : 19 American climbers and scientist, 1 British Transport Officer (Col. J. O. M. Roberts), 1 Nepalese Liaison Officier, 47 Sherpas and approximately 900 porters. For the first time, Everest was climbed via the West Ridge as well as via the now "classical" South Col route.

Via the South Route : On May 1st : J. WHITTAKER and
          NGAWANG GOMBU
               On May 22nd : B. BISHOP and L. JARSTAD
Via the West Ridge: On May 22nd too, three hours after the two just mentioned climbers, T. HORNBEIN and W. UNSOELD also reached the roof of the world." All summitteers were U. S. citizens, with the exception of Nagwang GOMBU, who was of Indian citizenship.

Spring 1965 : This was the year when a strong Indian expedition, under the leadership of Lt. Col. Mohan Kohli found its reward for all the previous attempt that ended in failure. This time, four teams suceeded in reaching the summit : the dates and the names :

    On 20th May : Capt A. S. CHEEMA and NGAWANG GOMBU (the first to have climbed Everest twice !)
    On 22nd May : Two other Indian Sherpas : SONAM GYASTO and SONAM WANGYAL
    On 24th May : C. P. VOHRA and ANG KAMI
    On 29th May: Capt. H.S. AHLUWAHLIA H.C.S. RAWA and SHERPA PHU DORJE, the first Nepalese Sherpa to be "on the top". It was also the first time that 9 members of the same expedition were able to reach the summit within the wide span of nine days. Weather conditons had been exceptionally favourable. The route followed was the "classical" South Col ascent.

Autumn 1969 : The first Japanese expedition, led by Yashiro Sujita. The ten Japanese members of the team tried climbing up the Western cwm to find a route along the South face, but they did not succeed. Phu Dorje, the Nepalese summiteer of

1965, met with a fatal accident during this unsuccessful attemp
Spring 1970: Again along the South route, another, much stronge
Japanese expedition (Leader: Saburo Matsukata) comprisin
thirty-eight Japanese climbers, succeeded this time brillantly
On May 11th two members reached the top : Terno MATSUR
and Naomu UEMURA. On the following day, May 12th a thir
Japanese, Katsutoshi HIRABAYASHI, accompanied by Nepales
sherpa CHOTARE, did the same. It was during this same expedi
tion that Yuichira Miura put on his skis somewhere near South C
and skied down the slopes of the highest mountain in the world
After having descended a short distance with incredible speed
in spite of the parachute attached on his back – he tumbled an
fell, but remained practically unhurt. Another "first" was establi
shed during this expedition : a new altitude record by a woman
Miss Setsenko Watanabe reached the South Col (26,194 ft. 7984m
Spring 1971: An unsuccessful attempt to ascend Everest entirel
by the West Ridge route. This was an "international"
expedition in its fullest sense : Not less than members of 1
different nationalities took part. The co-leaders were Norma
Dyrenfurth, a U. S. citizen, and James Robert (U.K.). Th
strongest team ever to attempt the summit consisted of 32 member
which included 18 climbers ! Earlier efforts on the South Wes
face claimed the life of H. Bahugana, an Indian member of th
group. Later appeared a rift among the members with the resu
that those of all "Latin" countries abandoned, while all "Anglo
Saxon" and Japanese pursued their attempt and finally reache
27,400 ft. (8.351 m.) the highest point ever reached along thi
terrifyingly steep West face. But at that stage, they too had t
abandon and to go down to Base Camp. The "Internationa
Expedition" was called off.

Autumn 1971 : First Argentine Expedition, led by Hector Cativ
Tolosa. It was the sixth attempt of a post-monsoon climb
Bad weather forced the team down after having reached 26,240 m
(8.000 m.), on South Col.

Spring 1972 : Dr. Karl Herrligkoffer, a West-German mountai
neer, tried his luck via the West face, but had to give up afte
the assault team had reached 27,390 ft. (8.348 m.)

Autumn 1972 : Again the South-West face tempted a valiant and
experienced team: Under the leadership of Chris. Bonning
ton, a group of British climbers spared no effort but they could
not go beyond 27,000 ft (8.230 m.) and had to retreat.

Spring 1973 : After two and a half years of failures, this was the time for a new spectacular success : The first Italian Expedition ever, realized its aim : Led by Guido Monzino, a very strong and exceptionally well equipped Italian team put no less than seven of its memers on the top of the world :

On 5th May : Rinaldo CARREL and Miko MINUZZO, accompanied by Nepalese Sherpa LHAKPA TENSING and Nepalese climber SYAMBU (the first Tamang to reach world's highest point, thus breaking, so to speak, the "monopoly" of the hitherto "Sherpa" Himalayists.

On 7th May, another assault took place : Fabrizio INNAMO-RATI, Virginio EPIS and Claudio BENEDETTI, together with Nepalese Sherpa SONAM GYALTSEN, also stepped on Sagar-matha's proud head.

Autumn 1973 : Micheo Yuasa was the leader of the second Japa-nese successful team. To start, the team attacked the South-West face, reached a point slightly higher (27,490 ft.   8.379 m.) than Chris. Boningnton's companions one year back,but the Japa-nese, instead of giving up, "switched" over to the classical South Col route, which allowed Yasuo KATO and Hisashi ISHIKURO to get to the summit on Oct. 26th.

Spring 1974 : First Spanish attempt: Unsuccessful. Under the leadership of Juan Ignazio Lorento Zugaza, the spearhead of his team had to withdraw although it had reached a point only 1148 ft. (350 m.) below the summit.

Autumn : 1974 : The first French attempt to climb Everest ended in a tragedy. The Expedition leader, Gérard Devouassoux was buried under an avlanche, together with 5 Sherpas, just below Lho-La, at an altitude of 22,635 ft. (6.900 m.). Devouassoux's plan was to try an entirely new route, i. e. over the "West shoulder" up the whole West Ridge. After the catastrophy, the Expedition abandoned.

Spring 1975 : May 16th : For the first time in history, a women succeeded and won the decade-long challenge. She was Junko TABEI, a 26–year old Japanese teacher, the assistant-leader of the "All-women" Japanese Everest expedition (The leader was Mrs Eiko Hisano). But they had Sherpas to accompany them. Junko Tabei reached the top assisted by Nepalese Sherpa ANG TSERING. The road was the "normal" one, via the South Col.

Spring 1975 : A few days later, on May 26th, another woman also succeeded : PHANTONG, a Tibetan girl, assistant-leader of the Chinese team that had climbed Rombuk Glacier and the North side.

This same expedition scored eight more laurels for the other Chinese or Tibetans who were successful : Sonam NORBU, LHOTSE, SANDRUP, Kunga PASANG, Tsering TOBGYAL, Ngapo KHYEN, DARPHUNTSO and HOU-SHENGFU.

Autumn 1975 : Also a "first" : British Expedition, once more led by Chris Bonnington, this tieme succeded in conquering the difficult and so far unclimbed South-West face. On September 24th. (never had an attempt been made at such an early date !) two members reached the summit: Doug SCOTT and Dougal HASTON Two days later, Peter BORDMAN and Nepalese Sherpa Sirdar PER TEMBA followed.

Spring 1976 : The first joint British/Nepalese Army Expedition did not accomplish their original plan. Under extremely difficult circumstances, it succeeded nevertheless to put on top of the world two of its British members : On May 19th, Sgt. Brummie STOKES and Corporal Bronco LANE. It took them not less than 9 hours to climb from Camp VI, pitched at 27,486 ft (8.378 m.) to the summit, a mere 1542 ft (470 m.) higher !!

Autumn 1976 : To celebrate the 200th anniversary of the United States of America, Phil Tremble headed a strong a l American team. Six weeks after having established Base Camp, two climbers, Dr. Chris CHANDLER and Capt. Robert CORMACK reached the summit, on October 8th.

Spring 1977 : A light New Zealand Expedition led by Keith Woodford had to abandon due to extreme unfavourable conditions.

Autumn 1977 : Since a long time, South Koreans were anxious to challenge Sagarmatha. One of the team, SANG DON KO accompanied by Nepalese Sherpa PEMBA NORBU, made port on the summit, on 15th September, They stayed there for one hour, This, is so far, the earliest post monsoon climb and also one of the fastest, since the Koreans had established their Base Camp on August 9th and pitched their assault camp on South Col 30 days later.

Spring 1978 : Twenty-five years after the first success, the "Third Pole" was climbed by a mountaineer without using oxygen. The Austrian expedition was led by Wolfgang NAIRZ who reached the top on May 3rd, together with two other Austrians,

Horst BERGMANN and Robert SCHAUER. Their Sherpa, who reached the top as well was ANG PHU, who thus marked his second ascent of Everest. Five days later, on May 8th, Italian climber Reinhold MESSNER and his companion Peter HABELER (Austrian) were the two who succeeded the undertaking without oxygen masks.

A third team went up on May 11th., Austrian Oswald OEITZ and W. German Karl REINHARD, Finally, on 14th of May, a solitary member of the same group, Austrian Franz OPPURG, also reached the top. All of them via the South Col.

Autumn 1978 : This was to be another "big" successful Expedition: A German-French undertaking, the co-leaders being Dr. Karl Herrligkoffer for the German members and Pierre Mazeaud for the French, went up separately, but by the same South Col route. First on top were the three W. Germans Josef MACK, Herbert HILLMAIER and Hans ENGL, on 14th October. Second were the French : Pierre MAZEAUD, Jean AFANASSIEFF and Nicolas JAEGER, on 15th October. They were accompanied by their Austrian cameraman and climber kurt DIEMBERGER. Another team reached the top on 16th October: L. HUPHAUER, W. KLIMEK, both W. Germans, and Robert ALLENBACH (Swiss) and Mrs Wanda RUTKIEWICZ, (Polish) the third women to conquer Everest.

In additon, on the same 16th October, three Nepalese Sherpas followed. They were : MINGMA, ANG DORJE and ANG KAZI.

Weather conditions having stayed on the favourable side, two additional West German climbers "made it" on October 17th : Georg RITTER and Bernd KULLMANN.

Spring 1979 : Now it was the turn of the Yougoslavs. They succeeded in climbing the steep West face. Two ropes reached the summit: On 12th of May Jernej ZAPLOTNIK and Andrej STREMFELJ. Theree days later : Stane BOZIC Stipe BELAK as well as Nepalese Sherpa ANG PHU. The Expedition leader was Ales Kunaver who, later, organized the Sherpa Training Center at Manang.

Autumn 1979 : Under the leadership of Dr. Gerhard Schmatz, yet another strong West German ("Swabian") attacked Mount Everest via the South Col. A team of six climbed on top on October 1st : Gerhard SCHMATZ himself, thus breaking the previous record of 'Everestian-veterancy" held hitherto by Pierre Mazeaud who was 49 years old when his dream materialized, whereas Dr. Schmatz counted 51 when he stepped on the top of the World. His companions were Hermann WARTH, Tilman FISCHBACH and Gunther KAEMPF, all W. Germans, Hans v. KAMEL, a Swiss national and Nick BANKS from New Zealand. Four Nepalese Sherpas accompanied them: PAR TEMUA, SUNDARA, LHAKPA GYALBOV and ANG GYALBU On the following day, 2nd October, a second team succeeded also : Reached the top Mrs Hannelore SCHMATZ, the Expedition leader's wife, RAYMOND GENET, from the U.S.A. and ANG PHURBA, a Nepalese Sherpa. While stepping down from the summit, these three mountaineers realized that they could not reach the nearest camp. Thus they had to bivouac, at the frightening altitude of almost 27,700 ft. (8.442 m.). Mrs Schmatz and R. Genet died of exhaustion and cold. Their Sherpa however succeeded getting down but suffered severe frostbites.

Winter 1979–1980 : Another memorable "first" indeed : Never before had Sagarmatha been temped, thus, conquered in the midst of the winter. Well, on 17th of February, two Polish climber succeeded : Lesek CICHY and Krzysztof WIELICKI. They were members of a small but excellent team led by Andrzej Zavada. They too followed the "normal" South Col route.

Spring 1980 : Here came the Japanese again, but this time from the "other", i. e. the Chinese -Tibetan side. On 2nd May, Yasuo KATO reached the summit after having climbed along the North-East face. Thus this famous mountaineer is the first non-Sherpa too have reached the "ceiling" twice and the very first human being ever, to have ascended first from the Nepalese side (in Autumn 1973 !) and later from the Tibetan.

Not satisfied with this double record, two other members of the same Japanese team accomplished also something that had never been done before namely to climb the straight North face up to the top. Their names : Ozaki TAKASHI and Shigehiro TSUNEO. The historical date : 10th of May.

Spring 1980 : Two more successes marked this first half-year of 1980 : The Spanish (Basque) Expedition led by Dr. Juan Ignazio Lorento brought two of its members without oxygen to the top : The Spanish climber Martin JAWALETA and his Nepalese Sherpa PASANG TEMBA. The route : the South Col. The date : 14th May.

Spring 1980: As an exceptional case, the Nepalese authorities had granted permission to a second team to climb the same face, albeit a little later : It was again a Polish team led by the same leader Andrzej Zavada. Two of the members reached the summit : on 19th May : Andrzej CZOK and Jerzy KUKUCZIK, without using Oxygen.

Summer 1980 : A new first: On 20th August Solo-climber Reinhold MESSNER succeeded reaching the top, from the Chinese (North) side, from the Base Camp to the summit without any companion.

Having now noted all these names, dates and details, may be some of the readers might be interested in having this long "odyssey" cut short in a few figures, easier to remember :

Counting only those expeditions undertaken after 1950 when Nepal opened up to foreign visitors, but including those attempts made from the Chinese (northern) side, there have been 38 attempts (one of which was a reconnaissance expedition, not meant to bring any one of its members to the top)

Thus out of these 37 attempts :
- 6 were made from the Chinese side and 31 from the Nepalese
- 23 were undertaken in Spring (out of which 15 were successful
  12 " " in Autumn (out of which 6 were successful
  1 in Winter and 1 in Summer, both successful.

The number of victorious summiters amounts to 107 who were able to leave their footprints on the top of the world. In fact, the latter has been conquered 112 times : Indeed : two mountaineers, the Japanese Kato Yasuo and Reinhold Messner have both climbed Mount Everest from the Nepalese side first and from the Chinese side later. Besides those two foreigners, three Sherpas have been on the summit twice. Their names deserve to be mentioned : First there was Ngawang GOMBU who went twice up the classic route via the South Col, on 1st May 1963 as a member of the North-American expedition and on 20th May 1965 with the Indian one. Then came Ang PHU, the first to climb on top via two different ascent routes : on 3rd May 1978 with the Austrians and on 14th May 1979 via the West face as sirdar of the Yougoslav expedition. Last: Par TEMBA who succeeded the extremely difficult ascent via the South-West face with the British expedition in autumn 1975 and on 1st October 1976, via the South Col, with the "Swabian" team.

Among the 107 victorious "Everesters", there were 4 women :

Janko TABEI, a Japanese, on 16th May 1975, followed, ten days later, by the Tibetan PHANTONG (on the North face). Then there was Wanda RUTKIEWICZ, a Polish mountaineer, who succeeded her attempt on 16th October 1978 as a member of the German expedition and, finally, on 2nd October 1979, Hanne-Lore SCHMATZ, from the Federal Republic of Germany, who, unfortunately met her tragic death while spending the night in a bivouac at 8.400 m. (Her husband had succeeded reaching the summit the day before.

Analysing the dates on which these attempts were made, it is a striking fact that the month of May seems to be the most auspicious, and, during the month of May, the last week :
Indeed : 15 mountaineers reached the summit between 1st and 10th May; 22 between the 11th and the 20th and not less than 29 between the 21st and the 29th (no attempt has ever been made neither on 30th nor on 31st. !)

Last statistic, per nationality (This time, we shall include even those who have been there twice, making the total of 112 :
19 Nepalese (18 Sherpas and 1 Tamang)

13 West-Germans	5 British
12 Chinese-Tibetans	5 Poles
10 Indians	4 Yougoslaves
9 Japanese	3 French
8 North-Americans	2 New Zealanders (among
7 Austrians	whom, the "pioneer")
7 Italians	1 Spaniard and
6 Swiss	1 South-Koreans.

MOUNTAINS ABOVE 24,248 ft. (8.000 m.) THAT HAVE BEEN CLIMBED

A chronological sequence of all "above (26,248 ft.) 8000 m." summits conquered.

Date	Name of Summit	Altitude in m.	in ft.	Name of summiters	Expedition's Leader	Nationality
3 June 50	Annapurna I	8.091	26,538	Maurice Herzog Louis Lachenal	M.Herzog	French
29 May 53	Mt. Everest	8.848	29,028	Edmund Hillary Norkay Tensing	J. Hunt	British
19 Oct. 54	Cho-Oyu	8.153	26,741	Herbert Tichy Sepp Joechler Pasang D. Lama	H. Tichy	Austrian
15 May 55	Makalu	8.475	27,800	Lionel Terrary Jean Couzy	J. Franco	French
25 May 55	Kanchenjun-ga I	8.585	28,159	Joe Brown George Band	C. Evans	British
9 May 55	Manaslu	8.156	26,752	Toshio Imanishi Gyaltsen Norbu	Y. Maki	Japanese
18 May 56	Lhotse	8.501	27,883	Fritz Luchsunger Ernst Reiss	A. Eggler	Swiss
13 May 60	Dhaulagiri I	8.167	26,794	Peter Diener Kurt Diemberger Albin Schelbert Ernst-Forrer Nima Dorje Ngawang Dorje	M. Eiselin	Swiss
11 May 70	Makalu S-E Summit	8.010	26,272	Hajima Tanaka Yuichi Ozaki	Y. Itoh	Japanese
12 May 70	Lhotse Shar	8.383	27,497	Josef Mayerl	S. Aeberli	Austrian

14 May 73	Kanchenjunga West Summit (Yalungkang)	8.420	27,619	Takao Matsuda H. Higuchi	Japanes
				Rolf Water	
29 Apr. 74	Annapurna South	8.026	26,325	Yutaka Ageta J.M. Anglada J.P. Sangines E. C. Abad	J. Anglade Spanish

SOME SUMMITS ABOVE 22,966 ft. (7.000 m.) STILL TO BE CONQUERED.

Note: It is not certain that permission to attempt their conquest will be granted by the Nepalese authorities in all cases.

Some peaks may be considered as "abode of gods" and, therefore, should not be desecrated. while others may be "reserved" for purely Nepalese mountaineering teams. It is indeed interesting to observe that the Himalayas attract more and more the local and younger generation of mountaineers, although, until recent years, almost all high altitude expeditions have been foreign ones.

"Virgin" Peaks above 26,248 ft (8.000 m.)

Name of Massif:	Located in	Altitude		Attempts made by
Kanchenjunga Middle peak	East Nepal	8.496 m.	27,875 ft.	Nobody
Kanchenjunga South Peak	-id-	8.474 m.	27,803 ft.	Nobody
Lhotse Central Peak	-id-	8.410 m.	27,592 ft.	Nobody

"Virgin" Peaks between 26,248 ft. (8000 m.) and 24,607 ft. (7,500 m.)

Nuptse-Middle Peak	East Nepal	7.815 m.	25,640 ft.	Nobody
Ngojumba I	-id-	7.806 m.	25,611 ft.	Claimed but not confirmed
Nuptse-West Peak	-id-	7.795 m.	25,574 ft.	Nobody
Nuptse-East Peak	-id-	7.703 m.	25,273 ft.	Nobody
Dhaulagiri IV	West Nepal	7.661 m.	25,133 ft.	2 Austrian

Peak	Location			Climbed by
Fang Peak	-id-	7.647 m.	25,089 ft.	2 British 5 Japanese
Dhaulagiri V	-id-	7.617 m.	24,972 ft.	Nobody 2 Japanese
Ngojumba III	East Nepal	7.601 m.	24,968 ft.	Nobody
Peak "38"				
East of Lhotse Shar	-id-	7.589 m.	24,900 ft.	Nobody
"Virgin" Peaks Between 24,607 ft. (7.500 m.) and 22,964 ft. (7000 m.)				
Nagpai Goom West Peak	-id-	7.352 m.	24,120 ft.	Nobody
Twin Peaks on Kanchenjunga	-id-	7.250 m.	24,114 ft.	1 British 1 German 1 Swiss-German
Nangpai Goom Middle Peak	-id-	7.296 m.	23,938 ft.	Nobody
Dome Kang (Sikkim border)	-id-	7.260 m.	23,820 ft.	Nobody
Gamma Peak (Dhaulagiri Massif)	West Nepal	7.149 m.	23,453 ft.	1 Japanese
Peri Himling	Central Nepal	7.127 m.	23,380 ft.	Nobody
Himlung Himal	-id-	7.126 m.	23,377 ft.	1 Dutch 1 Japanese
Pabil (Ganesh Himal)	-id-	7.120 m.	23,360 ft.	Nobody
Nangpai East Peak	East Nepal	7.110 m.	23,327 ft.	Nobody
Drohmo (Kanchenjunga)	-id-	7.009 m.	22,991 ft.	1 Japanese 1 Swiss
Dorje Lhakpa	Central Nepal	7.00 m.	22,966 ft.	1 British 1 Swiss

PRESENT RULES TO OBTAIN A CLIMBING LICENCE

Before undertaking any climbing expedition in the Nepalese Himalays, it is imperative to obtain prior permission from His Majesty's Government, Ministry of Tourism.

The rules to be followed have been laid down in the "Mountain Expedition Regulation", 1976, published in the Official Gazette of January 26th, 1976.

The main points of these rules are the following :

(1) The request to obtain the licence must be made at least six mounths in advance

(2) The request must be made in the form prescribed by His Majesty's Government of NEPAL and be recommended by a renowned or recognized mountaineering association of the home country or the Embassy of the concerned country.

(3) The expedition must comply among others with the following obligations :

a) Payment of a "royalty", fixed at 15,000 Rupees for Mount Everest, 14,000 Rupees for other peaks above 8,000 meters, 12,000 Rupees for peaks between 7,501 meters and 8,000 m., 10,000 Rupees for peaks between 6,000 meters and 7,000 m.

b) Admit up to Base - Camp, a Government appointed Liaison Officer for whom a daily allowance of 36 Rs. has to be paid and who has to be provided, by the expedition, with full equipment, food etc.

c) Personal accident insurance has to be covered by the expedition in favour of the following personnel (in case of death)
   - Liaison Officer for an insured amount of 200,000 Rs.
   - Headman, Guides and high altitude porters above 6,000 meters : 150,000 Rs.
   - Guides and high altitude porters between base-camp and 6,600 m. : 75,000 Rs.
   - Base camp porters and workers : 50,000 Rs.

d) Pay the following allowances :
   - To Headman and high altitude guides and porters : 30 Rs. per day
   - To Base camp porters and workers : 25 Rs. per day.

e) To give to all persons who accompany the expedition up to the last camp, equal opportunity to reach the summit.

f) To follow the authorized itinerary and not change the objective of the expedition nor the access route without prior permission from the government.

g) Accept, at any time, the inspection of the expedition's equipment by the liaison officer.

h) To burn and bury all containers, boxes etc. used by the expedition at Base Camp and elsewhere.

i) To forward information concerning the progress, success failure or accidents exclusively through the Liaison Officer.

LIST OF SUMMITS FOR WHICH A LICENCE MAY BE APPLIED

NAME	Feet	Meters
1. Everest	29,028	8.848
2. Lhotse	27,890	8.501
3. Makalu I	27,805	8.475
4. Yalung-Kang	27,625	8.420
5. Dhaulagiri I	26,795	8.167
6. Manaslu	26,759	8.156
7. Annapurna I	26,545	8.091
8. Annapurna II	26,040	7.937
9. Kangbachen	25,925	7.902
10. Nuptse	25,850	7.879
11. Himalchuli	25,801	7.864
12. Peak 29 (Dakura)	25,705	7.835
13. Dhaulagiri II	25,430	7.751
14. Dhaulagiri III	25,312	7.715
15. Jannu	25,293	7.710
16. Dhaulagiri IV	25,135	7.661
17. Fang	25,088	7.647
18. Makalu II	25,065	7.640
19. Dhaulagiri V	24,990	7.617
20. Annapurna III	24,764	7.548
21. Annapurna IV	24,688	7.525
22. Gangapurna	24,459	7.455
23. Churen Himal	24,183	7.371
24. Dhaulagiri VI	23,845	7.268
25. Putha Hiunchuli	23,773	7.246
26. Baruntse	23,688	7.220
27. Annapurna South	23,684	7.219
28. Manaslu II	23,468	7.154
29. Pumori	23,442	7.145
30. Tilicho Peak	23,399	7.132
31. Mount Api	23,392	7.120

32.	Glacier Dome	23,182	7.069
33.	Nilgiri North	23,168	7.061
34.	Kang-Guru	22,988	7.010
35.	Lamjung Himal	22,920	6.986
36.	Numbur	22,815	6.954
37.	Nilgiri Centre	22,769	6.940
38.	Tukuche Peak	22,703	6.920
39.	Kanjiroba	22,579	6.882
40.	Patras	22,507	6.860
41.	Ama Dablam	22,493	6.856
42.	Nilgiri South	22,437	6.839
43.	Kang-Teiga	22,339	6.809
44.	Nampa	22,159	6.754
45.	Baudha	21,890	6.672
46.	Thamserku	21,729	6.023
47.	Dhampus	19,724	6.012
48.	Kagmara I	19,554	5.960
49.	Jagdula	19,000	5.791

CONCLUSION

Here ends this survey of some of the aspects of NEPAL.

Initially, the objective of this book was simply to provide answers to some of the questions visitors might ask themselves.

If I have, at times, been more elaborate, it is because this fascinating country deserves really much more than a mere list of facts and figures.

Even the most casual visitor cannot help being struck and moved by

. the smile that lightens the face of even the most humble,

. the warmth with which the foreigner is welcomed and received,

. the simplicity and sincerity of the Nepalese who live in a perfect harmony with all their gods, their goddesses and their fellow countrymen.

Not to mention the beauty of the scenery :

. the sunrise on winter mornings when a silvery veil of mist covering the Valley gradually fades to reveal the snowcapped Himalayas glittering even more gloriously

. the paddy-fields which, just before the monsoon breaks, drape themselves in shining soft green velvet

. the terraces climbing up the slopes of the hills, testifying every year afresh, to the tenacity of those who till their meagre fields

. the barren and boundless highlands where caravans of yaks
carry their heavy loads of salt along the immutable tracks
and...beyond time and space, from the top of the golden spires
of the stupas, the eyes of the Perfect One looking upon this
blessed land with serenity and all-embracing compassion.

BIBLIOGRAPHY

Here are some of the many boohs of interest dealing with
various aspects of Nepal and which are availa le in English :

ANDERSON, Mary M. : *"Festivals of Nepal"* – London – George
Allen and Unwin Ltd 1971

ARAN, Lydia : *"The Ant of Nepal"* – Sahayogi Press, Kathmandu
1978

BAJRACHARYA, Manih Lal : *"A Catalogue on Nepal"* –
Eastern Trading and Investment Co. – Kathmandu, 1973

BERNBAUM, Edwin : *"The Way to Shambala"* – Anchor Press/
Doubleday Garden City, New York 1980

BERNIER, Ronald M. : *"The Temples of Nepal'"* Voice of
Nepal – Kathmandu 1970

BERNSTEIN, Jeremy : *"The Wildest Dreams of Kew"*, Simon &
Schuster, New–Yorh 1970

BEZRUCHKA, Stephen Dr. : *"A Guide to Trekking in Nepal* –
Sahayogi Prahashan – Kathmandu – 1976

BISTA, Dor Bahadur : *"People of Nepal"* – Department of Publicity, Ministry of Information and Broadcasting– Kathmandu
1967

COLLECTIVE WORK : *"Cultural Heritage of Nepal"* – Kitab
Mahal – Allahabad 1772

COLLECTIVE WORK : *"NEPAL – An Introduction to Nepalese
Culture"*
Sahayagi Prakashan – Kathmandu 1975

DEO Shantaram Bhalchandra : *"Glimpses of Nepal Woodwork"* –
Indian Society of Oriental Art Calcutta 1968–1969

DHAKWA D. R. : *"Encyclopaedia of Nepal"* : Sahayogi Prakashan – Kathmandu 1974

DHUNGYAL T. P. and ARYAL I. R. *"A New History of Nepal"* ;
Voice of Nepal; Kathmandu 1970

DURST A and WOLGENSINGER M. L. : *"Nepal"* – Ed. Silva–
Zurich 1966

FLEMING Robert L. Sr., FLEMING Robert L. Jr. and BANG-
DEL L. S. *"Birds of Nepal"* Published by Robert Fleming Sr.
and Jr. Box. 229, Kathmandu 1976

Dr. GURUNG, Harka : *"Vignettes of Nepal"* – Sahayogi Press 1980

HAGEN Toni : *"Nepal, The Kingdom of the Himalayas"* : Kummerly and Frey – Bern, 1961 and 1971

HOAG Katharine: *"Exploring Mysterious Kathmandu"* – Avalok-Kathmandu 1976

HORNBEIN Thomas F. : *"Everest, the West Ridge"* : Sierra Club – San Francisco, 1965

HUMPHREYS Chr. : *"Buddhism,"* Harmondsworth – England 1952

HUNT, Sir John : *"The Conquest of Everest"* Hodder and Stoughton – London 1753 and E.P. Dutton – New-York 1964.

FURER-HAIMENDORF, Chr. von : *"The Sherpas of Nepal"* – John Murray London 1964.

FURER-HAIMENDORF, Chr. von : *"Himalayan Traders"* – John Murray London 1975

KARAN, Pradyumna Prasad : *"The Himalayan Kingdoms"* – Nepal, Bhutan and Sikkim – Princeton – New Jersey 1963

KAZAMI Takehide : *"The Himalayas – A Journey to Nepal"* – Kodansha International Ltd. Tokyo - 1968

KESAR LALL : *"Nepalese Customs and Manners"* – Ratna Pustak Bhandar – 1976

LOCKE, John K. (S.J.) : *"Karunamaya"* – Sahayogi Press 1980

MAJUPURIA, Indra and Trilok Chandra : *"Marriage Customs in Nepal"* – Raj Rattan Press – Jullunder – 1978

MAJUPURIA, Indra and Trilok Chandra : *"Sacred and Useful Plants & Tress of Nepal"* – Sahayogi Prakashan, Kathmandu 1978

MIEROW D. and MISHRA H. *"Wild Animals of Nepal"* – Kathmandu, Ratna Pustak Bhandar

MILLER, Casper J. (S.J.) : *"Faith-Healers in the Himalayas"* Centre for Nepal and Asian Studies University Press 1979

MINISTRY OF COMMUNICATIONS: Department of Information : *"Facts about Nepal"* – H.M.G. Government Press February 1975

PEISSEL, Michel: *"Tiger for Breakfast"* – The story of Boris Lissanevitch of Kathmandu – Hodder and Staughton – London 1966

RAJ, Prakash : *"Kathmandu & the Kingdom of Nepal"* – Lonely, Planet Publications – Victoria, Australia 1978

RANA, Pashupati S.J.B. and MALLA, Kamal P. : *"Nepal in*

Perspective" C.E.D.A. – Kathmandu 1973

RANA, Pramode Shumshere : *"Rana Nepal – An Insider's View"* Sahayogi Press – 1978

RANA, Pudma Jing Bahadur – *"Life of Maharaja Sir Jung Bahadur of Nepal"* – Ratna Pustak Bhandar Kathmandu – 1974

ROSE. Leo E. : *"Nepal – Strategy for Survival"* – Oxford University Press – Bombay 1971

RUBEL, Mary : *"The Gods of Nepal"* – Bhimatan Harsharath – Kathmandu 1971

SAKYA, Karna and GRIFFITH, Linda : "Tales of Kathmandu"– House of Kathmandu – Kathmandu 1980

SEN, K. M. *"Hinduism"* – Harmondsworth – England 1961

SHARMA, Nagendra, : *"Nepal A to Z"* Sahayogi Press 1978

SHRESTHA D. B., SINGH C. B. and PRADHAN N. M. : *"Ethnic groups of Nepal and their ways of living"*. H.M.G. Press– Kathmandu 1972

SIMPSON, Colin : *"Kathmandu"* – Angus and Robertson Ltd. 1967 – London, Melbourne and Sydney

SINGH, Madanjeet : *"Himalayan Art"* – UNESCO - London 1968

SLUSSER, Mary : *"Kathmandu"* – A collection of articles" University Press – Kathmandu 1966

SNELLGROVE D. *Buddhist Himalaya* – Oxford, England 1957

SNELLGROVE D. : *Himalayan Pilgrimage"* – Bruno Cassirer – Oxford – London 1961

STANTON, J.D.A.: *"Forests of Nepal"*–Murray – London 1972

STILLER, L.F. (S.J.) : *"The Rise of the House of Gorkha"* – Manjusri – New Delhi 1973

STILLER, L. F. (S.J.) : *"An Introduction to Hanuman Dhoka"* Institute of Nepal and Asian Studies – Kathmandu – February 1975

STILLER L. F. (S.J.) : *"The Silent Cry"* – Kathmandu 1976 Sahayogi Prakashan

STILLER, L. F. (S.J.) : *"Planning for People"* Sahayogi Press Kathmandu, 1980

SUYIN, Han : *"The Mountain is Young".* – Jonathan Cape London 1958

THAPA, Netra Bahadur; *"A Short History of Nepal"* – Solomon and Bros. – Kathmandu 1951

THAPA, N.B. and THAPA D. P. : *"Geography of Nepal"* – Orient Longmans – Bombay, Calcutta, New Delhi 1969

THAPA R.J. and BANNERJEE N. R. : *"Nepalese Art"* –
Kathmandu 1966

TUCCI G. : *"Nepal – The Discovery of the Mallas"* – George
Allen and Unwin" – London 1962

TUCCI G. : *"Rati Lila"* – An Interpretation of the Tantric
Imagery of the Temples of Nepal" – Ed. Nagel – Paris –
Geneva – Munich 1969

ULLMAN J.R. : *"Man of Everest : Tenzing"* – George Harrap –
London 1956

VAIDYA, Karun Kar : *"Folk - Tales of Nepal"* – Pioneer Publications Kathmandu 1961

WADDELL L. A. : *"The Buddhism Lamaism of Tibet"* –
Cambridge 1967

WALDSCHMIDT E. and R. : *"Nepal : Art Treasures from the
Himalayas"* Oxford and I.B.H. Publishing Co. – Bombay –
Calcutta – New Delhi 1967

WRIGHT, D.: *"History of Nepal"* – Susil Gupta – Calcutta 1958

BIBLIOGRAPHIES OF NEPAL

The two most important bibliographic works are :

–*"BIBLIOGRAPHY OF NEPAL"* – Published by the Royal
Nepal Academy – Printed at Sahayogi Press, KATHMANDU-
1975

This impressive volume contains 8327 references of books,
reviews, studies, etc... covering all fields and aspects of Nepalese
topics.

–*"BIBLIOGRAPHIE DU NEPAL"* – Published by the National
Centre for Scientific Research in PARIS 1969. It comprises
only works on Nepal written in European languages totalling,
4,515 titles ! A supplement covering the publications printed
between 1967 and 1973 has come out under the title : "Supplement Vol. I".

Pronunciation of Nepali words.

In this book, the reader will have found many names and words unfamiliar to him. It may therfore not be devoid of interest to give hereunder a few indications as to their more or less correct pronunciation.

Vocals : "A" and "O" are pronounced as in English and may be long or short as in many other languages too.

"E" is pronounced as in "Cafe" or/in "end"

"I" is pronounced as in "ring or "field" but never as in "time"

"U" is pronounced as in "put" or"rule", but never as in "tube"

"Y" is pronounced as in "yeast" but never as in "my"

Consonants :

The only few peculiarities are the following :

"ch is pronounced "tch" as in "trench or "churn".

"chh" is pronounced "tchh", as in "catch him"

"kh" is pronounced "k h", as in "York-ham"

"ph" is pronounced "p h", as in "top-hat" and not "pheasant"

"th" is pronounced "t h", as in "hot-head" and not "then"

"j" is pronounced "dj" as in "jail

Accentuation : The accent is laid on the first or second syllable, never on the third, even if the word counts more than three syllables.

The Nepalese Numbers

1.	ek	11	eghaara
2	dui	12	baara
3	tin	13	terha
4	chaar	14	chaudha
5	panch	15	pandhra
6	chha	16	sora
7	saat	17	satra
8	aath	18	athaara
9	nau	19	unnais
10	das	20	bis

ABOUT THE AUTHOR

Mr. Robert RIEFFEL has been living in the India-Nepal area since 1961.

Born at Strasbourg (Eastern France), he graduated in law at the University of his native town before becoming a professional journalist.

For ten years, he was a special correspondent and Bureau Chief for the French News Agency in Poland, Rumania, Finland and Sweden where he worked actively as the Free French Legation's Press Attache from 1942 to 1945.,

After the war, he spent 16 years in South America, first as the Director of the French Government Information and Press Services (Latin American Division) and later as Commercial Manager, AIR FRANCE.

In 1961, he was assigned to NEW DELHI as General Manager, AIR FRANCE, for South-East Asia. It is from that date on he became acquainted with NEPAL where he was appointed, in 1970, as General Manager ROYAL NEPAL AIRLINES, on an assignment which he held for over two years.

Then, he became AIR FRANCE Manager for Nepal; during 1972, and 1973 he undertook extensive lecture tours mainly intended for Travel Agents and Pressmen, in over 30 cities of Asia and Europe with the objective of presenting and promoting Nepal as an ideal Tourist country. Presently he is the Honorary Consul for Belgium in Nepal.

Mr. RIEFFEL is very much keen on mountain sports.

Since 1964, he has undertaken not less than 18 trekkings, totalling 330 days of walking and climbing in the Himalayas of Nepal.

The present book is a completely revised edition of "NEPAL NAMASTE", published in Kathmandu by SAHAYOGI PRAKASHAN. Its first edition was published in English and French by AIR FRANCE in Paris (1974). The present new version has also been published in French by one of the major Travel organizations in France, "DELTA".

Mr. RIEFFEL is married and has one son and two grandsons who live in South America.